VOCATIONAL AND ADULT EDUCATION IN EUROPE

VOCATIONAL AND ADULT EDUCATION IN EUROPE

Edited by

Fons van Wieringen
University of Amsterdam

and

Graham Attwell
University of Bremen

KLUWER ACADEMIC PUBLISHERS
DORDRECHT / BOSTON / LONDON

A C.I.P. Catalogue record for this book is available from the Library of Congress.

ISBN 0-7923-5975-5

Published by Kluwer Academic Publishers,
P.O. Box 17, 3300 AA Dordrecht, The Netherlands.

Sold and distributed in North, Central and South America
by Kluwer Academic Publishers,
101 Philip Drive, Norwell, MA 02061, U.S.A.

In all other countries, sold and distributed
by Kluwer Academic Publishers,
P.O. Box 322, 3300 AH Dordrecht, The Netherlands.

Printed on acid-free paper

Printed in the Netherlands.

Contents

Acknowledgements   ix

Vocational and Adult Education in Europe   1
     FONS VAN WIERINGEN, AND GRAHAM ATTWELL (EDS)

Introduction to Section 1   21
     FONS VAN WIERINGEN

Skills-based full employment: the latest philosopher's stone   29
     COLIN CROUCH

Enhancing the Operation of Markets for Vocational Education and
     Training   49
     HARM VAN LIESHOUT

Market and Institutional Patterns in the Development and Activities
     of the French Vocational Training System   87
     ELSA PERZONNAZ AND PHILLIPE MÉHAUT

Reasons and policies to stimulate lifelong learning   107
     HESSEL OOSTERBEEK

The Future of Vocational Education and Training   131
     FONS VAN WIERINGEN

Introduction to Section 2   155
   GRAHAM ATTWELL

Cross Cutting Themes in the Education of VET Professionals in
   Europe   161
   GRAHAM ATTWELL, AND ALAN BROWN

Learning in Work Teams as a Tool for Innovation   175
   JEROEN OSTENK

How the Learning Organisation Evolves   193
   MASSIMO TOMASSINI

VET systems and criteria for effectiveness   215
   FONS VAN WIERINGEN

Searching For Educational Quality   239
   JAN AX

Introduction to Section 3   263
   GRAHAM ATTWELL

Sectoral Strategies of Labour Market Reform   269
   LAURA DRESSER, AND JOEL ROGERS

Evaluation and Decision Making in Swedish Adult Education   289
   ÅSA SOHLMAN

The Role of Distance Learning in Achieving Lifelong Learning
   for Community Pharmacists   303
   LINDSEY BAGLEY

Bridging the gap between education and work   317
   KENNETH ABRAHAMSSON

Forming an Educational Policy that meets Practical Needs   343
   NIKITAS PATINIOTIS, AND DIMITRIS STAVROULAKIS

Introduction to Section 4   353
   FONS VAN WIERINGEN

Enterprise Related Training: A Survey   357
   WIM GROOT

Participation of SMEs' employees in Continuing Training in the
    Alentejo Region   375
    EDUARDO FIGUEIRA

Returns of Labour Market Training under Conditions of Recession   393
    IIRIS MIKKONEN

Outcomes of Vocational Education/Training versus General
    Education   409
    RAINER H. LEHMANN, AND RAINER PEEK

Functional Literacy Skills of School Leavers in Flanders   423
    D. VAN DAMME, L. VAN DE POELE, AND E. VERHASSELT

Index   431

Acknowledgements

The authors would like to acknowledge the help of Renata Jungeblut, Dirk Stieglitz, Emma Roso and Alyson Waters in the editing and production of this book.

Chapter 1

Vocational and Adult Education in Europe
Introduction to the volume

Fons van Wieringen, and Graham Attwell (eds)
University of Amsterdam : University of Bremen

1. THE SYSTEM OF VOCATIONAL & ADULT EDUCATION AND TRAINING IN EUROPE

The system of vocational and adult education and training in Europe offers young people and adults the opportunity to learn to play an effective part in the workplace and elsewhere in society.

Vocational and adult education and training is regarded in the different European Union (EU) countries as crucial to the maintenance of employment, economic growth and the social integration of disadvantaged groups. In an economy and a society which are increasingly based on knowledge and information, these tasks can only increase in importance.

Despite differences in the organisational patterns and funding mechanisms of the systems of vocational education and training in the various countries, there are also clear parallels, in particular at the level of policy plans or established policy trends. Examples of such parallel trends include the emerging realisation that knowledge and expertise are factors essential to the maintenance and growth of the European economies, the need for education systems to respond effectively and flexibly to new skills requirements, the major role of education in the effort to combat marginalisation and social exclusion, and the growing awareness that learning must in future become far more of a lifelong and career-long process. It is not possible to judge immediately whether the present systems of vocational education and training can meet these requirements, but various publications have pointed to weaknesses in the systems which demand swift remedial action.

In the course of discussion on vocational education and training in the various EU countries, the definition of the system has been expanded. Initially, it was confined to initial and further vocational education for young people. However, there has been a growing realisation that the further development of the vocational education and training system depends on a broader viewpoint, including the systems of general (academic) education and the provision of opportunities for continuing vocational education and training.

Opportunities for learning are not limited to the education systems themselves. Outside the education system, but within the public sector, many regional and local authorities provide their own training programmes, whilst in most countries there are special training schemes for the unemployed. Outside the public sector, private institutions, Chambers of Industry and Commerce, enterprises, suppliers and other organisations offer high quality training for many participants. Heavy expenditure is required on industrial training to maintain and update the skills of the workforce. Continuing vocational education and training is being developed mainly in the private sector, privately run training courses and on the job learning.

Last of all, there is the extensive (but virtually undefined and un-quantified) informal sector of education. Learning may take place on-the-job, on individuals' own initiative, or from the media. This sector is expected to increase considerably in importance, if only because of the rapid advances in information and communication technologies. The interaction between formal and informal learning situations will be high on the future agenda of policy-makers and planners.

Given the general concern to guarantee the economic competitiveness of Europe, to promote innovation, and to safeguard our standard of living, it is very important to strengthen the European knowledge infrastructure. In this context it is extremely important that vocational education and training should be integrated in the national knowledge infrastructure and that the curriculum should be updated. Vocational education and training institutions will need to be able to respond quickly and effectively to rapid changes and new needs within society. On the other hand, the sector will also need to assume a greater responsibility for instigating necessary changes within society. Vocational education and training should not only respond to changing educational needs, but can itself also become a driving force for change. In this respect, special attention needs to be paid to the relationship with small and medium-sized enterprises and to the potential role of vocational education and training in promoting innovation and entrepreneurship. The questions which arise in this context include how innovation and knowledge transfer can be achieved within vocational education and training and the role of vocational education and training with regard to innovation in the knowledge infrastructure. Is it possible on the basis of national and international empirical evidence to reach any conclusions about the factors that may impede or promote this process of mutual interaction?

2.   THE FUNCTIONS OF VOCATIONAL AND ADULT EDUCATION

The systems of vocational and adult education perform social-economic and social-cultural functions.

2.1   Social-economic

The recent upsurge of interest in vocational and adult education is, to some extent, inspired by recent theories of macro-economic growth. An important new idea in this field is that 'knowledge' has the characteristics of a public good. This means that once knowledge is available, it can be made available to many users at relatively little extra cost. Recent literature in this field has focused interest on how exactly knowledge features as a factor in the macro-economic production function. Varying specifications can lead to differing conclusions about the knowledge policies that should be pursued within Europe.

Economic growth is a necessary precondition for a rising standard of living in any country, and, in a situation of an increasing population, economic growth is required just to maintain existing levels of prosperity. Education and training are major determinants of economic growth. Studies show that more than a third of all economic growth between 1973 and 1984 could be ascribed to the rising level of education in the working population. However only a sixth of that percentage could be ascribed to the growth in participation in higher education. Other sectors - and we would refer in this respect particularly to vocational education and training - prove to be at least equally important determinants of growth. In addition, there are signs that a relatively high level of participation in continuing (vocational) education tends to promote a more equitable distribution of income.

The idea of VET and other forms of education as a personal and collective investment is now gaining ground.

Regarding the relationship between the labour market and the vocational education and training curriculum, there is an ongoing debate as to whether students should be trained for initial employment or whether VET should focus on knowledge and skills for future career development. Initial training to enter an occupation calls for basic knowledge specifically related to that occupation, while education for life calls for the inculcation of more general skills which will enable the individual easily to absorb new knowledge at a later stage. The first type of training will generally be associated with a smooth transition from education to work but may lead to problems if unforeseen developments occur in the future. The second type of training is likely to be associated with a more difficult transition from education to work, but will equip the individual better to cope with unexpected events in future. At present there is a fairly broad consensus of opinion that knowledge is being superseded at an increasingly rapid rate, and a shift in favour of the second type of training would therefore be an obvious development. The question then is what the basic package of general skills should include.

The increasingly rapid obsolescence of knowledge has implications for the division of responsibilities for training the workforce. Adults will have to be increasingly self-reliant in ensuring that they are equipped with marketable knowledge. Employers will make a limited contribution where they see that it is directly in their own interests to do so. And because workers will quickly encounter financial constraints or will be discouraged by lack of information and feelings of uncertainty, there will be a task for government in ensuring that lifelong learning is open to everyone.

There will be a special problem in this respect at the lower end of the labour market. The reduction in opportunities for unskilled and low skilled jobs means that many people in this position possess insufficient productive skills to earn their own living. To make them attractive to an employer they need either wage subsidies or intensive training to increase their productive potential. This involves a wide range of labour market institutions. The difference between gross labour costs to employers and net wages received by workers is an important factor, and the way the social security system is organised is crucial.

2.2   Social-cultural

The recognition that investment in human capital is essential to the maintenance and improvement of European economic competitiveness has led to greatly increased interest in education and training within labour organisations. Although, in principle, staff training may be seen as the responsibility of the employer, governments are often involved in efforts to improve the quantity and quality of training activities. The way in which this is done will vary from one EU Member State to another. Examples of government intervention include tax relief, specific measures to improve the position of the less well-educated and/or older workers, and specific schemes for small and medium-sized businesses - a sector in which the level of formal training is clearly inferior to that in larger companies.

Vocational education and training is expected to contribute to the social and cultural development of participants, so as to enable them to exercise the rights and duties of democratic citizenship. Participation in the labour market (or preparation for it) is an important precondition for this, but not an exclusive one. Even outside the world of work, individuals need skills to enable them to participate in the life of society. In both cases, this includes such basic skills as literacy and numeracy.

Education and training systems in Europe are seen as having a special responsibility towards groups at risk of marginalisation and social exclusion and towards those with limited existing prospects on the labour market. The combination of increasing labour productivity and the gradual erosion of the basic standard of living of those who have become barred from the labour market, now threatens to produce a group who are semi-permanently excluded. Young people and new immigrants are particularly at risk. Here too, efforts must be focused on preparation for the world of work, for example through practice-oriented vocational education. But the definition of paid work, and therefore the scope of vocational education and training, must also be expanded. This will probably only be possible within the context of a coherent local and regional policy of integration focusing on housing, education, culture and work, of the kind now being put into place in a number of countries. For adults with no prospect of employment, the vocational education and training system will have to seek a different approach.

Vocational education and training is part of the overall education system and, as such, also contributes to the cultural and personal development of the individual. In initial education and training, it is important to ensure that the culture of the educational institution and of young people do not become too far divorced. By responding to youth culture (or rather youth cultures) the education system can provide important motivation for young people to learn. In adult education on the other hand, it is more a question of offering access to creative and leisure pursuits. For some people this will be first-chance education, but a growing category of better educated older people will participate as a conscious enrichment of an existing way of life. Response to this growing demand may come from self organisation, as well as from public and private organisations.

3.   THE CONTENTS OF THE BOOK

The book consist of five sections. The first section looks at the social distribution of vocational and adult education. This is followed by sections focusing on vocational and adult education at the sectoral and institutional level. The fourth part of the book looks at changing forms of learning and pedagogy. The final section of the book looks at the returns, or economic aspect, of vocational and adult education

3.1   Social distribution of vocational and adult education

The first section of the book focuses on two aspects of the social distribution of vocational education and training. An initial examination of the more traditional approaches from the field of adult education is followed by a discussion of the more modern and integrated approaches originating from the concept of life long learning.

3.1.1   Adult education

There are several countries in Europe in which adult education is well developed and has long traditions. Sweden provides a prime example of this approach. In Sweden it has recently been decided to expand adult education through a new state sponsored programme. The programme is targeted towards the unemployed and towards those employees who failed to complete upper secondary school education.

The programme is designed as a governmental response to the challenge of life long learning. At the same time it represents a shift from short-term policies towards a long-term strategy to combat unemployment. In his contribution Asa Sohlman discusses the impact of the new programme and looks at ways to improve the knowledge base and decision making processes through   monitoring and evaluation .

3.1.2   Life long learning

A lifelong learning model not only demands continuous vocational education and training, but also has implications for the way in which initial training is organised. Initial training courses need to establish a foundation for processes of lifelong learning. Initial education also provides the occupational knowledge base on which can be built new skills and knowledge. Those who have failed in their initial education are frequently deterred from later participation, both because of a negative perception towards institutionalised learning and because of the personal expense of such activity.

With regard to the feasibility and possible form of a lifelong learning model, a number of questions make themselves urgently felt. First of all, there is the question of the exact nature of the knowledge to be included in foundation programmes. Many empirical analyses show that the probability of workers participating in industrial training increases in proportion to their level of formal education. This suggests that if workers are sufficiently highly educated, they have a better chance to update their knowledge through industrial training schemes. That conclusion may be over-simplistic. Company policies are also a major factor. For example, innovative companies, adopting learning organisation models, may provide training for the whole work-force, including those with a low level of formal education. Lack of formal education is not therefore in itself an obstacle to participation in industrial training. Accordingly, the question is what conditions would increase equal opportunities for different groups of workers to gain more equality in access to on-going industrial training.

An alternative approach to the establishment of the knowledge foundation is to place a greater emphasis on a combination of learning and work experience during initial training. One argument is that people who have learned to combine learning and work during their initial training will have less difficulty in doing so later in their careers.

The concept of lifelong learning and its increasing importance is one of the prevailing educational themes of the 1990s. The need to re-skill and extend the knowledge base of the professional workforce has escalated in response to economic and social developments throughout the European Union. However the growing urgency to provide more and better education and training is not always met with the necessary funding and resources.

The question is not only whether lifelong learning and continuing education works but also how governments can put such a model in place. It can be argued that the current method of funding education strongly encourages a heavy concentration on initial education and training and strongly favours the publicly run institutions. Various alternative funding models have been proposed with the aim of supporting alternative training modes and providers. One proposal in this respect is the training credits model. One problem with these proposals is our ignorance of many behavioural parameters. The aim of providing training credits is to ensure that individuals undertake training when they need it, rather than entering the labour market with an 'overdose' of knowledge. The idea is that people should save a number of credits for a rainy day (when unemployment looms and they need further training or retraining). As yet, however, little is known about how people respond to decision-making problems of this kind in conditions of uncertainty. There is further doubt as to the efficiency and effectiveness of a market based initiative based on individual responses in responding to the future need of society. Apart from this, the proposals display a general failure to resolve a number of important practical questions. For example who should get credits and how many? At what point (age/level of education) should the credits be issued? How much would trainees themselves have to pay? Who would decide whether a training credit should being used for company training: the employer or the worker?

3.2   Vocational and adult education at the sectoral level

3.2.1   Sectoral characteristics

The vocational education and training sector can be viewed as an industry. The particular characteristics of an industrial sector have an influence on the way individual companies operate within it. Economists are particularly interested in those conditions that determine competition within an industry. Such factors include the degree of concentration, the level of product differentiation, and government policies, including statutory controls. To what extent can vocational education and training be regarded as an ordinary industry? How much competition can and should there be within the vocational education and training sector? What differences in competitive position does convergence in provision in the sector permit? How will the conflict evolve between institutional uniformity on the one hand and internal diversity within the sector on the other?

The institutional structure approach relates to the interplay between the internal organisational structure of the institutions, the vocational education and training sector as a whole and the external environment. In this approach, the primary focus is on the way the institutions function at the level of the entire vocational education and training sector.

Institutions can also take action themselves and try to influence the environment, either individually or (more usually) via coalitions with other types of institutions. In this control-oriented world-view, institutions openly exploit the opportunities that exist to control or influence particular bodies in their environment.

We can categorise this into control of four main kinds of bodies: resource providers, client groups, competitors and regulatory bodies.

Control of resource providers concerns access not only to funds and material provision, but also to work experience placements and educational resources. Control of client groups is a matter of fostering good relations both with potential future employers and with groups who can help ensure a steady supply of students and perhaps of contracts and consultancy. Control of competitors can take various forms - familiar in those in the business world - driving competitors out of the market, pricing agreements and cartel formation. Influencing regulators is less easy for individual institutions, but can be undertaken collectively. For example, associations of institutions or boards of institutions are far from powerless in this respect.

3.2.2   The sector as a collection of organisations

The different systems of vocational education and training in Europe can be viewed as communities of organisations that share the same aims and values and are subject to the same regulatory and endorsement procedures.

What weight should we attach in this respect to inter-sectoral relationships within vocational education and training? And how much weight to relations with other parts of the educational world, such as industrial training, the privately run institutions, educational publishers, and institutions which disseminate knowledge via modern media like cable television or the Internet?

Relations with industry organisations are essential. They represent the main potential employers of trained labour and in some countries also have a powerful say in the formulation of the training curriculum and examination syllabuses. But industry organisations also play a role in technology transfer and in helping to promote knowledge transfer. They undertake activities relating to research, knowledge transfer, training, public information and the stimulation of innovation. Some industry organisations and networks conduct joint technological activities. This calls for the educational institutions to review their position. The question is how this network of relationships surrounding the vocational education and training institutions has taken shape in the different European Union countries.

3.3 The institutional aspect of vocational and adult education

3.3.1 Institutional approach

Within the broad system of vocational education and training, there is a complex relationship between the public and the private sector. This relationship can include the provision of education and training, the production of learning materials (ranging from textbooks to multimedia packages), physical infrastructure including buildings and equipment, and audio-visual, computer and telematics applications as well as 'human capital' (teachers, support staff etc.). The nature of these relationships can also vary from client, producer, competitor, or partner.

In many cases there is co-operation between the sectors. Private institutions make substantial (paid) use of teachers and buildings, which are part of the public infrastructure, while private institutions are regularly 'bought in' by public bodies for the sake of their specific expertise. Much less is known about the public/private sector relationship regarding the development, production and sale of learning materials (books, software) and different forms of hardware (computers, network connections etc.).

3.3.2 Markets and systems

Vocational and adult education and training can be analysed both as a 'system' and as a 'market'. The latter approach has become more dominant in recent years. While a 'market' approach may be apposite in order to study vocational and adult education 'markets' no country in Europe operates a completely free market system. Institutions are central to vocational and adult education 'markets' in at least three different ways. First, the operation of a market mechanism itself presupposes certain institutional arrangements, for instance contractural arrangements. Second, markets are just one of several viable mechanisms that can and do govern human transactions and interactions: hierarchies, the state, associations and networks are others. The latter are alternative governance mechanisms that shape the way in which market mechanisms operate in the field of vocational and adult education in particular countries. These particular market mechanisms in turn influence the subsequent choices of different (individual as well as collective) actors within that field. Thirdly national institutions shape the way in which various types of individual and collective actors in the field of vocational and adult education tend to perceive alternative strategies.

Strategic management means management with regard to issues of longer-term importance and the main aims of the organisation. The term also relates to the way the organisation focuses on its environment. These three areas - the external environment, longer-term issues and main aims or mission – comprise three major facets of strategic management. The first of these facets centres on the question of the future prospects of the system and how the system can respond to these. Strategic management is then a matter of planning, and of translating those plans into key approaches which the system can adopt to deal with future problems. The second facet centres on the question on what results the vocational education and training system chooses to regard as really important. What kind of system do the parties involved want to produce? Strategic management is then a matter of drafting the main aims. The third facet concerns the management of those aspects that are crucial to the survival of the institutions. Strategic management means ensuring that the system can preserve and strengthen a relatively independent position vis à vis the environment. This includes maintaining and developing the capacity for change and development. Strategic policy can then be understood as a matter of guaranteeing the position of the system of vocational education and training within its environment; preserving and strengthening a relatively independent position vis à vis the environment; and managing those aspects which are crucial to the survival of the system of vocational education.

3.4 Instructional aspect of vocational and adult education

3.4.1 Working and learning

Recent reforms in different countries in Europe have aimed at achieving a more 'practice-oriented' approach to learning. This is intended both to create an improved interface between education and the labour market, and to provide better motivation for those who feel less at home with the theoretical orientation of much vocational education. The question is which combinations of initial training and work are the most productive? It should be emphasised that we are not thinking here only of 'formal' combinations of theoretical and on-the-job training, but also of work experience gained through 'Saturday jobs', mini-businesses etc. A confirmation of the efficacy of combined learning and work might have far-reaching consequences for the funding of education, and in particular for student grants and loans.

Finally, there is the investment argument. Investment in workplace learning and training have been shown to produce good returns both for individuals and for companies. These developments have given the workplace a more central role in training. Participation in 'formal' industrial training courses has increased greatly over recent years, even if the distribution of such participation is so inequitable. Participation is heavily dependent on the size of the company, the particular industry and trainee characteristics. About the nature and extent of less formal learning activities (workplace learning, on-the-job training) much less is known. In all these different forms of combined learning and work, the question is which particular combinations are the most productive and to what extent government should be involved in activating and stimulating their use.

A central theme of this book is that continual changes in technology and work organisation, and new demands for quality control in production (efficiency, flexibility, product quality), as well as an orientation to changing consumer demands, require higher standards of skills and flexibility in the work force. In order to meet these standards it is necessary to deliver more training to the work force. Training of employees in general, and learning in the workplace in particular, can be regarded as a major challenge for Human Resource policies in the company. In the contribution from Jerome Onstenk it is argued that informal and integrated 'On-the-job-Learning' (OJL) at all levels of the organisation should be an important characteristic of new organisational paradigms. OJL is structured by the characteristics of work activities. It takes place if and when the work situation (task, task management and work organisation) provides a learning environment. Depending on the strength of this learning environment OJL can contribute to the acquisition of task-specific skills, and also key-qualifications and broad competence. What are the conditions for developing the workplace as a 'rich learning environment'? Do new production concepts and the organisation of autonomous work groups offer new and more favourable conditions for improving the learning potential of production level jobs?

3.4.2   Knowledge creation and transfer

A growing number of working people are being called upon to respond almost daily to technological advance, changing competitive relationships, and organisational innovation resulting in a demand for new skills.

Human Resource Development and vocational education and training are increasingly seen as an integral part of company management. Likewise in activities directed at improving the quality of work, increasing attention is being paid to workplace training. It has, however, proved difficult to develop the relationship between new organisational concepts, such as the learning organisation and new social and technical forms of production, and educational concepts at the level of the individual or (small) group.

Alongside the traditional training paradigm based on didactic teaching, mostly aiming at formal qualification, there is the need for a new learning-based paradigm, based on the application of new skills and knowledge in the workplace. This paradigm embraces both individual learning and the idea of organisational learning. Within this paradigm, training can be considered as a function which transcends the transfer of knowledge. It has a main purpose in facilitating knowledge transformation and production through a series of processes during which knowledge takes on different aspects and values, passes through various states and is exchanged by a multitude of actors.

Such a new way of looking at learning and training has gained considerable theoretical support from approaches and concepts formulated in a number of different contexts. The first approach, drawn from management theory, focuses on the relationship between explicit knowledge and tacit knowledge within the knowledge-creating company. A second approach to the question, conceived by psychologists and anthropologists interested in the social dynamics of knowledge, is related to the development of communities of practices in the context of skilled work.

The focus on knowledge transformation processes underlines the importance of new kinds of participatory training interventions. There is less a focus on 'training contents' but rather on the formulation of proposals and solutions, on identifying constraints, on learning and re-interpreting situations collectively and, last, but not least, on acquiring the specific technical skills needed to develop innovation. This new focus could also be the basis for new approaches in the field of initial training. It is no longer sufficient to rely on the acquisition of so-called core skills or key competencies, instead it is necessary to develop new models geared to anticipate future developments, to the acquisition of work process knowledge and to dealing with unforeseen and unpredictable situations.

3.5   The returns of vocational and adult education

3.5.1   Performance of the vocational education and training system

There has recently been growing interest in the cost-effectiveness of vocational and other forms of education. There are various reasons for this. There is a growing desire to know whether government policies are actually achieving their objectives (in a measurable way) and whether they are doing so with an efficient use of resources. Vocational education and training institutions are being forced to a greater extent to demonstrate the returns on their efforts or to determine the price of their educational products. Individuals and employers want information about the returns on their investments in education. One reason why individuals and employers sometimes invest too little in training is thought to be lack of information, or the uncertainty surrounding the returns to be expected. In almost all cases, an accompanying background factor is a stronger realisation that the current scarcity of resources, accompanied by heightened demand, increases the need to make careful spending decisions.

At the moment, the interest in performance-related issues is inspired mainly by considerations of an economic nature. However, educational performance can also be measured in other terms, such as the contribution made to more equality in access to positions in society. The idea of 'performance' or 'results' is not monolithic and must be broken down into a number of sub-meanings. The question of how far the system of vocational education and training is achieving its objectives (i.e. its effectiveness) can be answered at several different levels: that of the individual, of the education system or parts of it, and the aggregate level of society. At the level of the individual, the question is what social opportunities have been created through education. In this respect, thoughts usually turn to measurable returns like occupational status and income, but less easily measured returns such as personal development and social and cultural participation can also be taken into account. It should be noted, however, that returns like income and occupational status are generally strong determinants of the less tangible returns.

At the level of the education system, effectiveness can be gauged by factors like output: how many participants leave the education system or parts of it with what qualifications. A negative formulation of the question is how many participants leave the education system prematurely. This is known as internal effectiveness. It is precisely in this respect that some parts of the vocational education and training system frequently fail to perform satisfactorily. The drop-out rate from publicly provided vocational education and training is frequently high. It must, however, be remembered that there is some conflict between the desire to make education widely accessible and the demand for high internal effectiveness.

The question of whether people later, for example, find jobs appropriate to their qualifications is called external effectiveness. The external effectiveness of education is an aggregate of the individual 'effects' mentioned earlier.

Finally there is the issue of effectiveness at the level of society as a whole. The question here is whether the system of vocational education and training helps to achieve objectives defined at collective level. Major objectives in this respect are the contributions made to economic growth, the maintenance and growth of employment and an acceptable distribution of incomes and other goods.

Adult education and training are moving to the centre stage of the educational and even the societal system. As economics are to an increasing extent dependent upon the knowledge and skills of its adult population, there is a growing need to update and restore levels of knowledge and skills during a single lifetime. The outcome of supply and demand characteristics of adult education and training is a major force in shaping these skills levels.

There is increasing concern in many countries about whether adults are sufficiently well able to read and understand vital information, which they encounter in their everyday lives. Safety regulations in the workplace, instructions for using new technology, payment procedures, directions for the use of medicines, maps, graphs and diagrams, travel documents, government information and such like, all present large sections of the population with what may be insuperable problems.

The question of literacy can no longer be seen as black and white, but rather as a continuum of skills which people may possess to a greater or lesser degree. This is illustrated by a recent survey of a sample of the adult population in eight 'advanced' countries involved looked at language and numeracy skills. A follow-up study is working on the development of tools to measure other areas of skills, such as problem-solving, writing, mathematics and science and continuous learning.

3.5.2   Cost-benefits of employer-paid training

Each year untold numbers of companies make substantial investments in staff knowledge. For many companies, expenditure on human capital is at least as important as spending on physical capital. Even so, there is still much that is unclear about industrial training. Who pays for such training? This may be easy to see as regards the direct costs, but a good deal more difficult as regards indirect costs in the form of lost production. Does the employer bear these costs, or does the worker also contribute by accepting a salary which is lower than might be earned elsewhere? Who benefits from training? Is it the worker, who can sell his or her knowledge to other companies, or is it the employer who, after all, knows more about the worker than other companies? Many studies have found that the returns on industrial training are extremely high. But is that really so, or are we dealing here with an artefact?

In the economics of education there is a long tradition of calculating the financial returns on investments in education. Access to training is not the same for everyone. Some workers are offered more opportunities for investment in training than others. As investments in human capital such as training create inequality between workers, these differences in training participation increase social inequality (wage inequality, employment opportunities, etc.). It seems that on-the-job training becomes an increasingly more important source of human capital investment. If training opportunities are not the same for all workers, the increase in investments in on-the-job training will result in an increase in social inequality.

The high effects of training may reflect risk-premium, rent sharing, liquidity constraints on the part of the worker and may indicate that training is not completely firm specific human capital. All this may result in training levels which are less than efficient. Market failure in training may call for government intervention.

The risk-premium might be reduced, and the participation increased, if the government would step in, with schools and subsidies. The rent-sharing could only be attacked with general competitive policies. With partly specific training and liquidity constraints collective action by the industry may solve the problem under-provision of training.

Training may be provided by firms themselves, industry associations, private training institutions or the government. The initiative to train workers may come from the employee or from the firm. It may be available for all employees of a firm, or it may be organised as a programme for new employees only. Financial arrangements may also differ. Depending on the type of training, it may be financed by the worker, the firm, or the government. The government may restrict itself to providing free or cheap training, it may pay the opportunity cost (i.e. lost wages), or it may give tax deductions to employees. Costs of training (instructors hired, fees to training institutions) are considered labour cost, which can be fully deducted in the year in which they are incurred before profit taxes are levied. Hence, cost for investment in human capital has a preferential tax treatment relative to investment in physical capital. Opportunity cost (production lost) is deductible if the employer carries the burden (as wages paid for non-productive time), but is not deductible if the employee bears the burden in terms of reduced wages while in training. Opportunity costs may easily outrun the direct cost. But they are not easily verified. Hence, for purposes of stimulation through tax facilities one may apply a multiplier on direct training expenditures as a deductible for profit taxes. Increasing the multiplier in a recession may be a method to counteract employers' cutbacks on training.

The value of the training investment is usually mainly observable to the participants themselves - i.e. the worker and his/her current employer - and not to any other employer. The National Vocational Qualifications (NVQs) in the United Kingdom serve as a certification and standardisation of training investments. This form of certification may decrease uncertainty among employers about the value of the training. It may, on the other hand, increase poaching, as information about the quality of training the worker has undertaken becomes more widely available.

MARKETS AND INSTITUTIONS IN VOCATIONAL AND ADULT EDUCATION

Chapter 2

Introduction to Section 1
Markets and institutions in vocational and adult education

Fons van Wieringen
University of Amsterdam

In this first section of the book, we set the scene for vocational and adult education in Europe and place it in the debate over state versus market. Can vocational and adult education be seen as a market, or is it mainly a state regulated affair. Does vocational and adult education operate as a market? This section shows that between market and state there exist several other arrangements, such as communities and associations.

Looking at the vocational and adult sector one can distinguish at least five sub-sectors, such as the private and the para-public sector. Some argue that we should see the functioning of this sector as a quasi-market.

From an economic point of view, this section shows that market failures and equity are the main argument for interfering in the sector. In the area of lifelong learning, several interventions are analysed in relation to their possible effects on certain market failures.

Lifelong learning can be seen as an educational strategy for the future of the vocational and adult education sector. There are other strategies, and these are discussed in this section.

Knowledge and skills are, as Crouch states, to be seen as presenting opportunities: individuals who acquire advanced levels of education are more likely to secure prosperous futures for themselves. Everyone in the work force has a source of occupational pride in their skills and knowledge; income differentials are compressed through the market-compatible device of reducing the relative scarcity of high skill.

Is it so that policy-makers increasingly look to individual profit-maximising firms for solutions to collective problems? Considerable reliance is placed on individual firms; there is little confidence that public policy can make an autonomous contribution. Private collective action by firms can be achieved quickly and flexibly. The move from national government policy to the firm is an escape from the reach of public collective action. Or are there meaningful positions between the state and the market? With what consequences for vocational and adult education?

Other arrangements can be situated between market and state. Van Lieshout proposes a typology of five governance mechanisms. Starting with human capital theory, he applies it to the analysis of operation of systems for vocational and adult education. The human capital theory states that the benefits of investments in general training will accrue to the worker. The worker will also pay for the cost of investment in general human capital. The costs of and revenues from specific training will be shared between the worker and the firm. If the firm retains part of the worker's gains from the investment in general human capital, the worker will leave for another job in which his/her skills are more fully rewarded. If on the other hand the firm pays for the investment in general human capital, it faces the risk that the worker will leave after completing the training. In that case, the firm will lose its investment. For similar reasons, the firm will not be willing to pay all the costs involved with investing in specific training.

As suppliers of training, schools and firms have different advantages and disadvantages to offer. The advantage of schools is that they generally train (prospective) workers of more firms, which enables the achievement of economies of scale and scope in education and training that surpass those that are possible within (in particular small and medium-sized) firms. The disadvantage is that schools will not be as keenly aware of the actual type of skills a prospective worker will need as the firm that will employ him. In this sense, firm-based training may increase efficiency by focusing on the supply of skills. Firms will concentrate on training exactly for those skills that are directly necessary for the satisfactory accomplishment of a particular job.

Broader basic skills (also referred to as key qualifications) tend to be positively related to the potential for self-learning. Subsequently, it may be more efficient to invest substantially in the acquisition of such key qualifications early on, in order to save on training costs later. As individuals and their parents may lack the necessary funds to pay for such training themselves - and may find it impossible or too risky to take out a loan to pay for such training - states tend to substantially subsidise education and training for such skills in the initial education system.

> What balance of funding between the state and individual firms would be the most efficient? If firms have to fund all education and training themselves, this may damage their international competitiveness. But if the state too generously funds education and training, the same may happen due to the resulting tax burden on citizens and/or firms.

From this question, Van Lieshout arrives at a five-part typology of governance mechanisms, market, clan/community, association, concern, and state. Whereas pure market approaches distinguish only individual actors, governance theory adds other types of collective actors. This five-part typology provides a suitable basis for an analysis of the operation of systems of vocational and adult education.

This chapter presents a more detailed picture of the structure of the providers of vocational and adult education. How is the vocational training sector organised? Can it be analysed as a quasi-market? Personnaz & Mehaut are examining how relationships between training organisations and various categories of those seeking training are organised. What are the principal characteristics of the training organisations, and what are their activities?

Five sub-sectors can be identified:

- The public sector. This sector contains all the organisations under the control of public authorities and exercised through various ministries.
- The para-public sector. This sector groups together chambers of commerce and industry with chambers of agriculture and trades. Initial training, like vocational training, for the artisan, industrial and market sector is one of the traditional vocations of these para-public institutions.
- The company sector. Part of this sector consists of employer organisations, inter-professional organisations or professional organisations and the other part of associations created or controlled by one or more companies. These associations are generally in a process of outsourcing training in their former internal centres.
- The association sector. The organisations in this sector are generally involved in political, social, religious or trade union movements.
- The private, profit-making sector. This set of organisations is the most heterogeneous and is composed of organisations that legally are limited liability companies and have developed training as their sole or additional activity.

Despite the specialities of certain organisations and strong institutional patterns in certain segments, the large number of training programme suppliers and the services they offer most often to both companies and the state attest well to a form of quasi-market in which a form of competition - even if it is not predominately expressed by pricing - operates.

It is often claimed that there is under-investment in training. Two pieces of evidence have been put forward to support this claim. First, potential market failures in the field of training have been identified. Such market failures may cause under-investment. Secondly, empirical work indicates that rates of return from firm training exceed rates of return from formal education. If this is the case, investments in training should increase relative to investments in formal education.

Oosterbeek first lists possible market and non-market failures in the field of lifelong learning. Next he considers credible instruments to repair these failures. In addition he discusses possible side effects of these instruments. The resulting framework can be used to evaluate actual proposals for enhancing lifelong learning. A problem is how to allow identification of the contribution of different market failures to the under-investment in training. To enhance the policy relevance of such studies, it is desirable to start measuring the actual importance of different failures.

Probably the most important reason for governments to intervene in the education and training market is, however, not the presence of market failures, but the widely supported view that participation in learning activities should depend only on characteristics that are relevant to education and training. In many countries, much effort is put into realising equal opportunities. Equity considerations are prominent when dealing with initial and formal education. But such considerations can also be important in adult education and training. Whereas educators sometimes defend the thesis that adult education and training offer second chances to those who were less successful in initial education, practice shows that more highly educated people are much more likely to participate in adult education and training than those with low levels of initial education. Thus, instead of compensating, adult education and training magnifies the differences produced by the initial education system. From an equity point of view, this may be rather undesirable.

To remedy the market failures discussed in the previous section, some forms of government intervention may be implemented. A list of credible remedies for market failures is discussed. This list is an inventory of policy instruments which promote lifelong learning. Each policy instrument is evaluated by considering which failure is most likely to be repaired by it, and also by discussing side effects that may emerge in terms of other market failures, implications for equity and government failures. All instruments are partial solutions as they are meant to repair a single market failure. Successful policy intervention should be based on combining a set of non-conflicting, complementary instruments that solve the most pressing failures. Which combination of instruments is most appropriate will depend on circumstances that differ across periods and countries.

Instruments can be part of a strategy, such as a strategy towards lifelong learning. Such strategies offer a response to changes in the social environment of vocational training and adult education. What strategies would provide an appropriate response to them? Which strategic responses will be adequate?

In this chapter, four educational strategies are discussed. In the first, education is primarily an instrument used to achieve other aims of society, or education has primarily set its own goals and striven to achieve them. In the second, education is either pre– or post–structured. At present, government educational policies and legislation in all European countries are based mainly on the idea of pre–structuring, but this is certainly not the only possible educational strategy. The following four educational strategies are constructed:

1. Basic education (pre–structured, determining its own goals).
2. Independent education/learning (post–structured, determining its own goals).
3. Recurrent education (pre–structured, instrumental).
4. Integrated education (post–structured, instrumental).

Public sector vocational education focuses on foundation training and the first stage of further training for the workplace. This initial training is heavily structured, with set attainment targets and learning pathways leading to nationally approved qualifications. The education system knows best and formulates its own objectives. Although it does of course take account of the requirements of society, the fact that this form of education is intended to provide a lasting basis means that priority is given to the system's own teaching aims.

Public sector vocational education concentrates on initial training, with the aim of giving pupils and students the best possible preparation for a first job, in order to ensure a smooth transition from school to the workplace. The level of ambition is high: the best possible initial qualification so that college leavers are well trained when they enter the labour market. The initial qualification is not job–specific, but is tailored to a particular industry or occupational area. It offers entry to a range of occupations.

Independent education/learning

Under this educational strategy, pre-planned programmes and courses are relatively unimportant, other than in initial vocational training. It is often only apparent in retrospect which programme is relevant and the best person to decide that is the trainee or client. There is little point in establishing an extensive system of consultation and communication. The important thing is to ensure a broad, flexible range of provision from which the consumer or client can choose whatever seems most useful.

Public sector vocational education is active in both the initial and the post–initial phase.

With this strategy, unlike the previous one, the public sector vocational education system also has a strong focus on post–initial education. It sees workers seeking further training as a growing market. In both initial and post–initial training, the higher professional education and vocational training and adult education fields focus on, and are strongly influenced by, the business market - individual companies, industries and professional associations. The role of the national bodies at the interface of industry and education is extremely important in this respect.

Recurrent education

The key terms for public sector education are 'modularity' and 'lifelong learning'. Education, whether initial or post–initial, is instrumental in whole–life planning and in ensuring a smooth transition between the different phases of life and an easy alternation of periods of working, learning and caring.

Both initial and post–initial education are based on socio-economic needs and are instrumental in reforming business processes and the structures of production. With a view to the rapidly changing labour situation, initial education sees it as part of its responsibilities to lay the foundations for lifelong learning. To achieve this, pupils and students must be taught the necessary interest, attitude and learning skills. Learning to learn is therefore an important concept during initial training, learning the skills required for the independent acquisition of new knowledge and skills.

In addition, public sector education creates a set range of courses designed to assist people at a particular stage in their lives. These may be directed at entry or re-entry to the labour market, providing further training for those in work or improving general education and assisting personal development (for example, literacy, civics or a second language). The relevance of the courses is clearly indicated in advance.

Integrated education

Education, including initial and further training, is organised in such a way that it offers countless, retrospectively valuable opportunities to respond both to the rapid, vigorous economic changes taking place and to the present and future personal situations of trainees. The education system gears its learning paths to this and serves both economic and social purposes.

With this strategy, there is less emphasis on fixed initial qualifications than under the other three. Education, including both further and initial training, is organised as flexibly as possible in order to provide a rapid and satisfactory response to the changing needs of society and of individuals.

Due to market forces, education becomes heavily demand–oriented: that is, industry and individual students have a strong influence on programmes.

At curriculum level, this produces individualised learning paths designed to meet the needs of a variety of target groups.

As can be seen from the four strategies, the belief in the operation of the market forces differs to a large extent.

Chapter 3

Skills-based full employment: the latest philosopher's stone[1]

Colin Crouch
Oxford University and European University Institute, Florence

1. SKILLS, KNOWLEDGE AND EMPLOYMENT

The acquisition of knowledge and skills is increasingly seen as both the main challenge and the central opportunity for achieving a return to full employment. It is considered a challenge because it is feared that people without appropriate knowledge and skills will in future be unable to find work. There are two main reasons for this. First, most though by no means all the jobs that have been destroyed through technological progress in recent years have been low-skilled ones, and the educational levels demanded for most occupations seem to be rising; in nearly all societies unemployment is highest among those with low levels of education (OECD, 1994: ch 6). Second, it is generally assumed in the existing advanced countries that the challenges posed by the rise of new low-cost producers in other parts of the world can be met only if labour in the former countries has high levels of skill which will differentiate it from the capacities of workers in the newly industrialising countries.

More positively, knowledge and skills are seen as presenting opportunities: individuals who acquire advanced levels of education are more likely to secure prosperous futures for themselves. At its most ambitious this perspective refers to the utopian vision of the 'learning society', a society almost without unskilled, low-productivity people, in

[1] This paper first appeared in the British Journal of Industrial Relations 35 (1997) 367-84 and is reprinted with the kind permission of the publishers, Blackwell

which all mindless and physically damaging jobs have been robotised; everyone in the work force has a source of occupational pride in their skills and knowledge; income differentials are compressed through the market-compatible device of reducing the relative scarcity of high skill. In such a society the number of those remaining who could not attain a high skill level would be so small that the rest of the community would be able to subsidise the wages earned by their low-productivity labour, ensuring that their standard of living would not fall too far behind the rest. While this vision is utopian, it is a utopia towards which there has been real progress. In many countries two particular forms of low-skilled work - back-breaking rural labour and domestic service jobs which combined personal subservience with hard work and long hours - declined massively during the process of industrialisation. The globalisation of many activities continues to produce an increasing shift to high-skill production in the advanced countries: technological advance mainly replaces unskilled work[2]. Also, populations in the advanced countries take increasing advantage of educational opportunities in order to improve their employment chances. There is a constant upward shift in the skill profile of the working population.

Policies to encourage continued up-skilling are almost certainly *necessary* to both social and economic advance. Many, especially in the political world, also hope that these policies will also be *sufficient* for such an advance: that the abolition of low-skilled work will reduce to a minimum the need for social policy. As the British Labour Party expressed the point in its successful 1997 general election campaign (Labour Party, 1997): resources should be shifted from welfare to equipping the population with competitive skills. This is seen as a supply-side collective action successor to a Keynesian demand management strategy and a welfare state that are no longer regarded as viable. High expectations have therefore been invested in education in general and vocational education and training (VET) in particular. The purpose of this article is to raise certain critical questions concerning the viability of this strong form of the skills strategy.

First, only a minority of the working population is involved in producing internationally traded goods and services. Indeed, if competitive niches are gained through the increased productivity of highly skilled labour, the size of work force required for a given unit of output will continue to decline. Very large increases in production and sales are needed to secure significant advances in employment. This imparts a quality of, at best, 'two steps forward, one step back' to any attempt at improving employment opportunities by means of educational advances.

---

[2]   The so-called Hekscher/Ohlin effect (Ohlin 1967).

A few clearly high-skill export sectors can be identified: information technology, pharmaceuticals and some other branches of chemicals, aircraft manufacture (Crouch, Finegold and Sako, forthcoming: ch. 3). No country has been able to base more than a small amount of its export activity in these. Even if skills increase in the areas of medium-high skills, such as various areas of machine tool production, they are (especially as productivity advances) unlikely to employ large numbers of people. Some important service industries employ highly skilled workers and are internationally traded, especially some aspects of finance and insurance. The range of these will expand as trade barriers are reduced, especially within groups of nations like the European Union. However, given the direct nature of much service delivery, many services need to have large numbers of their staff employed in (and usually from) the countries where the service is being delivered, even if ownership and top management are located in the home country.

Ironically, as world trade grows, the proportion of a high-productivity nation's *work force*, as opposed to capital, which is engaged in internationally traded activity probably declines (Deutsches Institut für Wirtschaftsforschung, 1996). Sectors which provide employment and those which provide advantages in international trade are by no means identical. In most countries the biggest single employers of highly educated labour have been the health, education and welfare sectors, which are only marginally involved in international trade and usually mainly in public ownership (Crouch, (forthcoming): ch. 2).

Second, by no means all new employment opportunities require high skills; jobs that require low or even reduced skills might be smaller in number within an advanced economy than those that require higher skills, but they are usually easier to create and more readily address the situation of the hard to employ. If one were to be given a large sum of money and told to use it to create some employment for the young unemployed as quickly as possible, it would be better to open outlets for selling imported T-shirts than to launch a soft-ware laboratory.

Third, at least in the short run the fact that the educationally successful tend to be occupationally successful is the result of a competitive process; if everyone becomes educationally successful according to some existing criteria, then those criteria shift to a higher level. Improving education can be an individual solution because it assists one in the competitive process, but that very characteristic means that it cannot be a general or a collective solution. If education standards are generally rising, then the educational level of the persons engaged in any particular occupation will be seen to rise. It does not necessarily follow from this that the skill level of the work has risen. In the long run it is possible and often likely that employers will notice the increased capacities among their work force and start to make use of them in new activities: this is the assumption on which the whole up-skilling strategy rests. However, the long term might be very long, with considerable disillusion being experienced meanwhile among those who find that their increased education has served only to submit them to increased competition for jobs.

Fourth, since in almost all countries new, secure jobs making use of advanced skills are not expanding fast enough to absorb those liberated from low-skilled agricultural, factory and menial service work, running parallel to enskilling strategies have been those for creating jobs of the opposite kind: low-productivity, menial work in poor conditions. This strategy advocates the deregulation of labour markets - in particular in order to make it easier for employers to dispose of employees - and reduction of living standards to ensure avoidance of unemployment among those who fail to improve their productivity (OECD, 1994).

A deregulation approach and an enskilling one tend to embody opposing logics. In the former case all emphasis is on ease of disposal; for the latter it is important that employers regard employees as a long-term investment resource, a high rate of inter-firm labour mobility usually making employers reluctant to carry out much training. The problem is solved by a growing segmentation of labour markets and divergence in the occupational fates of different sections of the working population. However, the fact that many succeed in the competition for attractive employment makes it particularly tough for those who fail, whether because they are outsiders in the sense of being unemployed, or because they remain in poor, marginal jobs which are available to them only because they accept low wages and highly insecure and uncongenial conditions. The two countries in which this form of employment has expanded most, the UK and the USA, have experienced an extraordinary polarisation in their income distributions in recent years, with the bottom 10 per cent of the *working* population in the USA now being absolutely poorer than they were at the end of the 1970s (OECD, 1996). Job creation of this kind has to be very sensitive to costs, and is likely to take place only if security, protective measures and social insurance costs as well as wages are reduced.

Finally, while the pursuit of a high level of vocational skills for a society is a collective goal, it is increasingly found that the principal sources of these skills are individual firms, and governments have to defer to firms for judgements about what skills should be provided and through what means. This is one of the major changes caused by the move from the Fordist mass-production economy, the move which itself creates the main opportunities for the learning society. The most innovative corporations today are those which try to shape a distinctive whole-firm strategy for both the way in which they produce their output and in the content of the output itself. This point is intensified in the case of services, which account for an increasing proportion of economic output, since there is not the same distinction between production process and product as in agriculture or manufacturing: the process is the product. These factors make it increasingly important that skills suit the specific needs of companies. There are therefore severe limits to what governments or any other collective actors can do alone to engineer appropriate improvements in vocational training.

Business firms are not equipped to maximise collective objectives, but their own profitability. In doing this they will certainly provide training and retraining for large numbers of employees; there is however no reason why company decisions and market forces will maximise the level of vocational ability for a whole society except through a largely serendipitous fall-out. There is therefore a dilemma: achievement of what is coming to be defined as the main collective goal of economic policy depends increasingly on actions by private actors who have no necessary incentive to achieve that goal.

While all these problems of a skills strategy are important, many recent developments in approaches and policy have been particularly concerned with this last one of the implications for public policy of the growing importance of the individual firm. This therefore merits particular attention.

2. THE PARADOX OF COLLECTIVE ACTION IN A FIRM-DOMINATED ECONOMY

At the heart of the paradox that policy-makers increasingly look to individual profit-maximising firms for solutions to collective problems lies a second one: the same processes that are taking the decisive actions 'down' into individual companies are also taking them 'up' into global levels. In a world of rapidly changing and highly competitive markets, considerable reliance is placed on individual firms finding new niches; there is little confidence that public policy can make an autonomous contribution. Trust in firms' ability to achieve their goals is increased by the growing size of transnational corporations, who are able to make strategic alliances with each other for certain shared purposes, making possible action on a global scale. Achieving a capacity for collective action at a cross-national public level is slow and painful, as the stilted progress of western European integration shows. *Private* collective action by firms, in contrast, can be achieved quickly and flexibly. Therefore, the apparent move down from national government policy to the firm is often also a move up to the global level. Both the firm and the global economy are levels which escape the reach of public collective action.

2.1   Dilemmas of apprenticeship

The most constructive response that one finds to this conundrum is the
return to apprenticeship models of VET in several countries, including
France, Italy and Sweden, which which had in earlier decades abandoned the
model as a mediaeval survival in favour of more state-directed approaches
(Crouch, Finegold and Sako, forthcoming: ch 5; Rault, 1994).
Apprenticeship, by systematically linking firms and the state education
system in a partnership for the initial training of young people, both
preserves the collective good component and makes VET sensitive to both
individual firms' needs and rapid changes in skill needs as reflected in
process and product development within the market place. Even then, the
apprenticeship model has only flourished fully in contexts like the German
one, where powerful representative organisations of firms play a further part
in linking the individual company to the collective good of skill production
and in linking firms and teaching institutions in maintaining standards if
proficiency and the quality of curricula (Backes-Gellner, 1996; Streeck,
1987).

There are however even problems with this approach. Systems
maintained by representative organisations can be slow to adapt to change
because a large number of interests have to be consulted before a major
adjustment can be undertaken. The German system is currently having
difficulty adapting to the needs for social skills and to a more service- rather
than manufacturing-oriented economy (Backes-Gellner, 1996; Regini, 1996).

Since the German economy is undergoing problems of competitiveness,
resulting mainly from the costs of the unification of East and West Germany
in 1991, many firms are arguing that they cannot afford the costs of
sustaining the apprenticeship system and the representative organisations
(the *Kammern*[3]) that sustain it. The *Kammern*, although part of the business
community, are seen as embodying collective concerns, sometimes also
government concerns, and thus can be criticised by firms as imparting cost
burdens which weaken the international competitiveness of German firms
compared with those from countries where there are no such obligations.

It is unlikely that German business will destroy a VET system that has
given it so many competitive advantages. It is however likely that current
problems will prevent the system from developing as it now logically
should. One implication of rapidly changing skills and technologies is that

---

[3]   In full, *Industrie- and Handelskammern*. Although this translates as chambers of
commerce and industry, the German institutions are quite different from British chambers
of commerce, in that they have a formal status in law which both requires firms to belong
to them and accords them specific rights to participate in certain areas of policy.

workers need frequent retraining and up-skilling. The German and indeed all other apprenticeship systems are heavily weighted towards the initial training of young people, and should probably now be considering ways in which elements of the co-ordination mechanisms used for this VET could be extended to further training. However, German employers are arguing that, precisely because they bear such a burden of collective action at the apprenticeship stage, they should be left completely free to act autonomously over further training (Crouch, Finegold and Sako, forthcoming: ch. 5). Adaptations *could* be made to the German apprenticeship system. It has changed much in the past; and in principle the dual system could be extended to further VET. If these changes do not happen, it will be because firms do not want external intervention in their affairs, not because apprenticeship and interest associations are inherently incapable of adaptation.

A further problem is that, in a period of uncertainty, young people face a difficult dilemma in choosing between applied courses of the apprenticeship type as opposed to general, academic education. For those who succeed at it, the latter form enjoys more prestige and is potentially more flexible in terms of the job opportunities it offers. On the other hand, for those who pursue it unsuccessfully general education is far more likely to lead to dead-end and low-skilled employment than specific skills training. *Ceteris paribus*, for the individual there must be a bias in favour of conserving the possibility of aiming high, and therefore of taking more general courses. However, for the many who will not be among the more successful, this will turn out to be poor advice.

2.2 Business expectations

Related to this problem is a frequent inconsistency in the business sector's expectations of the education system. There are some difficulties in establishing firms' preferences here. On the one hand they increasingly want good general standards of education rather than highly specific skills. This is a reflection of two major changes taking place in the character of work: the frequency of change itself, change in the skills required to perform a job and the need for flexibility and adaptability; and the growing importance, even in the manufacturing sector, of service skills, skills of personal communication. These changes lead employers to seek in new recruits an ability to learn and what they usually call 'social skills' (Regini, 1996), which might mean anything from ability to co-ordinate and secure co-operation, through ability to communicate effectively, to simple willingness to obey orders. With the exception of the last mentioned, these are the kinds of abilities that general education is best at providing. On the other hand, firms are often very critical of general education systems, saying that they want an education more closely geared to the world of employment. Their position is not necessarily contradictory. This may be a matter of different employers, or employers of different types of labour, having different requirements; firms may be seeking a general education but of a different kind from that being provided by educational institutions; or firms may want people with the adaptability that a general education can give, but articulated according to a specific corporate culture.

Firms can resolve the dilemma of the relationship of their specific needs to employees' general educational background in three contexts. The first is apprenticeship, provided this can respond sufficiently rapidly to their needs. The second, which corresponds to the position in the USA or, to some extent, the UK, is for the general education system to provide a vast, unstructured diversity of opportunities, some of which will be wasted and misguided, but others of which will hit the target of providing employers with their needs. Third, the Japanese large-firm model represents a particular combination of the other two: general educational provision of a US kind, but within a more 'German' context of a clear indication of the likely successful routes.

The second form may well be preferred by many employers, in Germany and Japan as much as in the USA, as it meets some of their current preoccupations. On the one hand, little is required from firms in terms of interaction with governments, agencies, schools, even business associations or *Kammern*, interactions which might add to firms' costs and slow responses at a time when labour costs and speed of response are a priority. The model also assumes a large supply of potential labour from which some can be selected and many rejected - a characteristic which would not commend itself to employers at a time of consistently high employment as in the 1950s and 1960s, but quite acceptable in a prolonged period of slack labour markets.

If we view the situation through the eyes of a young person on the other side of the market, such a system may look less attractive. Suppliers of own labour power differ from suppliers in most other markets. Especially if we take the position of young potential suppliers of labour, deciding on what courses to take in order to appear attractive on the market, they suffer from a number of disadvantages. Virtually by definition they are poorly informed and unable to appraise the variety of courses knowledgeably. They must however make decisions that will not be easily reversed but which must predict accurately the state of labour market opportunities in a future time period - that after they have completed their educational preparation. They must also make extensive investments of time, energy and possibly money. Also, they cannot afford to make mistakes, since when all one is taking to market is one's own labour, one is offering only one item for sale, and one which has taken a lengthy period of preparation.

In many circumstances there are no reasons why firms, left to themselves, will not engage in a large amount of vocational training, especially the increasingly important reskilling of existing workers - though the new emphasis on dissolving the employment contract into labour sub-contracting and a shortening of the length of time that workers spend with a particular firm contradicts the idea of a growing emphasis on further VET for an existing work force. Company-led VET is likely to be exceptionally adaptable and seems to be associated, at least in the strong if different cases of Japan and the USA, with high performance in particularly highly skilled and innovative areas. However, it remains doubtful whether, by itself, an approach of reliance on firms can in any way produce the frequently stipulated requirement of an up-skilling of most of a working population - even where, as in the USA, that reliance is linked to a public policy and general cultural bias in favour of extensive general education. It cannot be claimed that in any country relying primarily on autonomous company initiative the majority of firms is operating at this standard. Even where firms do make a major contribution to training and retraining their employees, the evidence suggests that all except true leading-edge firms with a strategy of incorporating all their employees within their corporate concept do so for only a minority of their staffs, and limit further training to firm-specific skills which do not contribute to labour-market flexibility[4] . Similar problems are reported of firm-level further VET in Germany, where as we have noted the collective co-operation of initial VET system is not carried over into further training.

The current period is one of uncertain product markets and intensified global competition in which firms need to reduce their costs wherever possible, but in which a combination of rising educational standards and high unemployment are making skilled labour a plentiful commodity. In this context firms have strong incentives to move from a 'voice' to an 'exit' approach in their labour-market behaviour[5], stressing the need for complete ease and freedom in hiring and firing policy while reducing their engagement in all institutions that require interaction and communication. In

---

[4] Becker (1975) argued that skills could be divided between the general (which would be financed by students themselves or a public education system) and the firm-specific (which firms would provide without fear of poaching because other firms could not make use of them). Therefore, he claimed, the often discussed collective action problems of providing VET did not really exist. However, Stephens (1996) has pointed to the existence of 'transferable skills' which are too specific to be provided easily by general education but which can be used by a number of different enterprises.

[5] In the sense of that distinction developed by Hirschman 1970.

this environment the pursuit of the learning society as a general collective goal or object of public policy cannot be fully delegated entirely to firms. The growing paradox of the simultaneous demand by firms for both higher general education and VET to provide greater adaptation to the milieu of the individual firm requires change from all forms of VET system: greater adaptability on the part of apprenticeship systems; far more effective advice to young people facing the deceptively helpful diversity of so-called free market systems; some fundamental reconsideration of systems that provide rather narrow, public VET schemes with little contact with industry itself.

2.3   Company cultures or the end of the employment relationship?

Further ambiguities in firms' definitions of their needs are embedded in an issue which has already been mentioned above: the tension between employers saying that they want on the one hand to engage employees in long-term commitment and skill development, and on the other to make labour more disposable. When firms say they want a general, educated adaptability, but defined and articulated according to a specific corporate culture so that new employees will identify with the firm and its goals, they are usually prepared to provide such an acculturation themselves, avoiding the usual collective action problems. However, while employers increasingly stress the specificity of their cultures and their desire to inculcate their employees in them, they also increasingly stress the need for greater ease of hiring and firing and tell employees that they must expect to change jobs more frequently than was common in the past. The short, and declining, length of time spent with a particular employer by the average US employee is today often seen as a mark of the superiority of that country's employment system (OECD 1994) - even if there is evidence that some of the very brief periods that young people spend with employers are not so much examples of flexibility of employment as inefficient job matching caused by failures of communication between general education and vocational needs. A decline in employment length is meanwhile being recorded in Japan, Germany and other nations which in the past had lengthy average employment periods (ibid).

Even more challenging to the company culture idea is the trend towards ending the concept of employment altogether and replacing it by a series of contracts between a customer firm and a mass of small labour-contracting firms, temporary agencies, or, in extreme cases, individual providers of labour services. These can be accompanied by the growth of supplier communities as in Japan, in which case they are compatible with a culture model. However if, as is often the case, they are advocated as cost-cutting and commitment-reducing strategies, this is unlikely to occur. This will be particularly the case if, as in the UK, sub-contracting and franchising are not really examples of small-firm formation but of self-employment without infrastructural support.

It is likely that often these paradoxes are resolved by segmentation, with firms retaining a long-serving group of key staff who are inculcated into a culture and a larger number of other, marginalised kinds of employees (part-time, temporary, casual), franchisees, sub-contractors, suppliers of independent labour-services who are outside that circle. However, it is also possible that, in the present context of intensified competitiveness, some firms are seeking to discover how far they can proceed with a policy of 'eating one's cake and having it': seeking strong but *unreciprocated* commitment and loyalty from staff. Anxieties about the constant pressure to demonstrate to shareholders adequate achievements in down-sizing and delayering leads managers to do this, these managers themselves being vulnerable to redundancy through these processes. There will be those who respond positively to this situation: people confident in the scarcity of their skills and of their chances of gaining new employment once the current contract ends. This will be common among people with particularly rare skills, able to charge high fees for their services which provide them with security during any temporary periods of unemployment. Many modern technological occupations embody elements of this. Such people are most likely to be found at the sharp edges of new technology or science-based innovation, where the high morale produced by being involved in exciting innovation can provide that combination of total dedication to the task in hand with willingness to accept a high level of insecurity which is, for contemporary employers, makes the ideal worker.

However, even these qualities may have collective and institutional components. It will be easier for a highly skilled person to accept insecure employment in one firm if that enterprise is part of a network of similar firms whose managers and staff know each other well, since there will be a reasonable chance that the end of a contract at one firm will be quickly replaced by one at another with whom the worker may already be in contact. It will be very different for employees of isolated companies not so mutually connected. These are among the advantages of industrial districts, including those in the USA of high-tech firms.

2.4   The loss of confidence of government agencies

A further consequence of the lead passing to firms is that government agencies try increasingly to work close to firms' needs. This can resolve some of the problems of remoteness and rigidity that has often characterised the bureaucratic mode of public economic intervention, producing some new creativity in relations between government and business, especially at local level. However, some of the circumstances that have accompanied the move have produced a kind of crisis of self-confidence in public agencies which limits their competence to make a contribution. In general, the state, even the French state, is losing its claim to be able to guide firms that have not found dynamic new paths for themselves into appropriate courses of action (Crouch, Finegold and Sako, forthcoming: ch. 4). Are any institutions today in a position to carry out such a task? As recent responses of Swedish employers have made clear, even when business leaders share the objectives of improving skills, they do not want this to proceed at a pace any faster, or under a direction other, than those of individual companies (ibid; Sweden, 1992). On the other hand, governments cannot pursue skill maximization strategies unless they are in close touch with business interpretations of what this means in practice. Once their officials and professionals retreat to a role of deregulating in order to leave space for company autonomy, and to the residual role of caring for social casualties, they cease to be plausible participants in the development of a high-skill economy and lose the possibility of acquiring and maintaining the expertise necessary to function as well informed participants in the provision of advanced skills. They also thereby lose the capacity to improve the skill positions of their populations beyond the extent to which the companies operating within the borders of their states find to be in their own interests.

Government action then tends to become primarily associated with the care of social casualties and failure. This raises very difficult questions. Governments retain responsibility for the hard-to-employ, and develop special schemes to equip unemployed young people as well as the long-term adult unemployed with skills that will improve their job chances. In virtually all countries this is the biggest single role for government in the VET field. There is then a dilemma. Should this work be kept in special agencies set apart from the rest of VET strategy? Or should it be integrated with measures to advance 'state-of-the-art' skills? If the former route is followed, work with the unemployed becomes restricted to a clearly labelled ghetto, the training institutions involved will be stigmatised as dealing with failures and they will be quite cut off from all areas of advance.

Probably for this reason, most government have integrated work with the unemployed with strategies for advanced VET. However, this is often unrealistic as the two sets of activities are very different. There is then a danger that the stigma attached to remedial VET extends to the whole public-policy component and government agencies are simply not taken seriously within advanced areas. They then become cut off from important developments and lose both confidence and eventually real competence.

This then harmonises with the prejudices towards to most kinds of government action of current neo-liberal orthodoxy in a self-reinforcing way: the state's role having been residualised to one of a safety net for the welfare casualties of the economy, it is then residualised further because it has become associated with such tasks and is therefore seen as inimical to innovation.

3.   POLICY IMPLICATIONS

Growing dependence on the individual enterprise rather than general public policy as the source of major initiatives in work skills raises a major paradox: the acquisition of skill has become a fundamental public policy issue, being almost a requirement for future guarantees of effective citizenship if the price of poor or inappropriate educational preparation for work is likely to be a low-paid job in a low-productivity sector with diminished security; but for its provision we are increasingly dependent on the private sphere of the individual firm which can have no responsibility for general needs. In conclusion it is possible to point to certain possible policy responses to these trends and concerns.

3.1   Reasserting the role of public agencies for pursuing high skills

Public agencies (including business associations) must be able to play an effective part in trying to maximise the role of advanced skills in the economy if we are to transcend this dependence on individual firms. To do this they will have to be equipped with appropriate and rapidly changing knowledge. This does not lead to the increasingly fashionable solution of public agencies working with companies through a mode of 'market' provision of advice like any other consultancy, since this merely follows firms' existing perceptions. Public VET bodies must certainly work far closer with firms than in the classic mode of, say, French or Italian state provision, but they must do so from positions of authority, based partly on being channels of funds allocated authoritatively, and partly on the fact that their decisions are rooted in extensive knowledge, so that they will win the respect of firms. They must therefore be well resourced and well staffed with professional experts with long-term commitments to this field of work. The model of short-term employee contracts with agencies fighting for their own survival and more worried about possible bankruptcy than becoming major sources of expertise on skill requirements that has been imposed on British

Training and Enterprise Councils (TECs) - following the rather unsuccessful model of British small firms in general - is not a helpful guide (Crouch, Finegold and Sako, forthcoming: ch 7). A neo-liberal residualised concept of public service, in which all attractive activities have been hived off to private consultancies, leaving public policy in the hands of a rump agency with poor quality staff, scant resources and low prestige cannot provide the basis for an authoritative service.

In particular the role required will not be achieved by agencies which have as their principal responsibility catering for the unemployed, especially where responsibility for placing the unemployed in jobs is linked to that for disciplining them and requiring them to accept work offers. When these strategies are employed, the public service cannot then become associated in employers' minds with advanced developments in VET. King (1995) has recently described how, during the 1970s, employment placement services in many countries adopted a path of moving up-market, delivering high-quality services from High Street premises, and extending their appeal to a wide range of potential employees. This was part of an up-grading of public labour-market policy in order to help people maximise their match to career opportunities. A central aspect of this task was the complete separation of this career guidance service from that of paying unemployment benefit and checking on the job searches of those registered as unemployed.

King then describes how this strategy has been completely reversed since the late 1980s, initially in the UK and the USA but through a policy which has now become central to the employment strategy of the Organisation for Economic Co-operation and Development (OECD) and recommended to all member countries (OECD, 1994). There are two reasons for this. First, job-placement services are being privatised as part of the general contemporary strategy of stripping back public activities. Clearly, private job placement agencies want to take over the task of advising and placing those for whom it is easy to find employment. The remaining state service therefore becomes again a residual one, the staff of which will not gain experience in tracking high-quality labour needs. Second, in order more closely to monitor the behaviour of the unemployed, services of benefit payment, job search and policing are all concentrated in the one residual employment department.

The story is an interesting case of how perceptions of the employment problem among government departments in a number of countries have changed, away from trying to ratchet up the skill needs and practices of firms and towards finding low-wage jobs towards which the unemployed can be encouraged. TECs in the UK have had a similar experience affecting, not job-placement services, but agencies designed originally to be the spearhead of Britain's challenge to German and Japanese skill levels.

It is legitimate to conclude from this that public agencies in this field need to be able:

(i) to relate closely to individual firms; but

(ii) to advise firms on the basis of an authority based on constantly updated knowledge, so that competences can be ratcheted up and so that educational institutions and relevant government departments can be kept in touch with what is required; and

(iii) to be able to influence firms' further VET efforts as well as their participation in initial training.

This has a number of implications for the design of policy and policy agencies. They must be well resourced and able to develop high-quality expertise so that they can become associated with success. They will probably be best equipped to operate authoritatively if working closely with business networks and neo-corporatist associations, the state must be endowed with sufficient authority to counter cartelistic tendencies within these networks. Such requirements could be embodied in a number of different institutional forms, depending on what most suits local political cultures, but care needs to be taken with the precise design: departments of central government, provided they are capable of responding genuinely with local initiative; less formally structured agencies, provided not compelled to act in a passively responsive market mode; chambers or similar representative bodies of business, provided free to support innovation and new industries; community colleges linked with local economic development agencies. It is particularly important that, however training is provided, a public agency has responsibility for standard-setting and monitoring.

Such policy instruments need to be kept separate from the task of dealing with mass unemployment. Their role is necessary to competitiveness in any business community which does not seek to find its market niches by stripping down its labour and other social standards to the point where it can compete with the new industrialisers; and if they are successful they will and do produce employment opportunities of good quality. Even a country like the UK, which has had as a self-proclaimed policy trying to compete by reducing labour standards, finds its export successes at the top ends of the market. If the UK were to improve its international performance it would be by increasing the number of firms capable of competing in this way, not by entering new low-quality markets.

3.2   Reasserting publicly funded general education

The current trend towards low taxation and concomitant reduced public services that has become near-universal in the advanced world has unavoidable implications for skills and employment. In virtually all countries there are major inputs of public spending into education, usually concentrated on the young. There are strong public-goods aspects of education, which make it impossible to treat it like just another consumption or even investment good. A commitment to a learning society requires more and constantly improving education at all levels, and it is difficult to see how this can occur without concomitant increases in educational spending. Individuals might be expected to make some contribution to the costs of their own education, but the scope for this is limited.

At younger age levels the expenditure is that of parents rather than individuals themselves. Since children can rarely be expected to repay their parents' expenditures on them, such spending does not take the form of rational investment expenditure in anticipation of individual gains on the part of the investor. It is far more likely to be determined by parents' current income and wealth. A shift towards increased parental contributions to educational spending would therefore produce a strong shift in the take-up of educational opportunities towards young people from wealthy families. Such a development would ease the problems of governments based on parties drawing much of their support from such families, as their voters would feel less anxious than at present that their children will face competition from others for what promises to be a declining proportion of well rewarded secure positions in the economy of the future. It would however not only be incompatible with the promise of equality of opportunity which remains a universally accepted educational slogan among all shades of political opinion in most societies, but it would also be incompatible with the concept of a learning society. This requires a maximisation of the use of human intellectual abilities, not their restriction to those from wealthy families.

At older ages more use can be made of individuals' willingness to invest in their own skills, as the US model shows. However, scope here is also limited. First, the inequality effect of differential parental wealth still operates. If young people from the bulk of the population are to finance their own advanced education they have to do so by working part-time during their studies. Large numbers do this in the USA, the Netherlands, Denmark, the UK and elsewhere (OECD, 1996). In many ways this can be a useful development, giving people work experience and providing a supply of workers who do not seek security or full-time work while able to bring to the routine tasks they perform, mainly in the retail and catering sectors, a level of alertness and ability that would not otherwise be available to employers in those fields. Beyond a certain point however simultaneous study and paid work will affect academic performance and therefore lower the quality of the educational enterprise.

Alternatively, firms might be expected to make more of a contribution to subsidising general education, as many of them are doing in such countries as Sweden, the UK and the USA. But again the scope is limited. If there is a free-rider problem about firms providing vocational education, leading virtually all countries to develop policies for encouraging them to do this, it will be that much more difficult to persuade more than a number of them to assume a growing share of the task of funding general education. If one reason for trying to move to a low-tax economy is to reduce the cost burden on companies that must complete globally with countries that impose few costs on firms, there is little to be gained from replacing taxes by direct contributions from firms to fund the same services.

It is difficult to see any major democratic alternative to a prolonged and intensified commitment by governments society strategy. to publicly funded education at most levels as part of the learning

4.   REASSERTING THE ROLE OF PUBLIC-SERVICE EMPLOYMENT

However, it follows from many of the foregoing arguments that an important minority of the work force will be unable to participate in the employment provided by the learning society; even specific skill-upgrading agencies will not be the route through which the majority of the unemployed will find work. Indeed in their work for further VET they will be helping those already in employment, not even labour-market entrants; and, as we have seen at a number of points, involvement with work for the mass of unemployed diminishes at least the image and probably the substance of agencies' attempts to operate at the top end of the skills range. This challenges the position of those who posit improvements in VET as an alternative to the growth of low-productivity jobs, and also that of those who claim that deregulating labour markets and leaving firms free within the market will both reduce unemployment and encourage improvements in quality in VET and elsewhere.

For many years to come many members of the work force will be unable, as a result of both demand and supply factors, to gain high-quality places in the labour market. It should not be pretended that, if they only showed adequate initiative and respond to the education opportunities available, most people would be able to do so. Many will be forced to compete for the low-productivity opportunities that will not require high levels of education except as the filtering device through which, by definition, many will not pass. Either people in this position will be required to face low wages and high insecurity by competing for jobs in deregulated private services as their long-term prospect; or an expansion of public services will provide them with secure but still low paid work.

Such choices are beyond the scope of this article, but in any event consideration needs to be given to the future of public services as sources of employment. The primarily public social and community services sector of the economy has been the principal employer of highly educated labour in all countries (Crouch, 1998: ch. 4). (Even where, as in the USA, a large part of the sector is counted as private, that includes a good deal of charitable and publicly subsidised provision; the amount of pure market activity in this area is limited.) That sector and the services it supplies, some of which make a central if indirect contribution to competitiveness, have therefore been a fundamental component of the high-skill economy. A concentration of public policy preoccupation on reducing the size of the public service would not of course lead to a complete loss of all occupations and services currently being performed there; some would thrive under privatisation and marketisation. There would however be a large net loss: to take only the example closest to our current concerns, a complete marketisation of education would lead to a decline in its up-take by poor and moderate-income families, with a large loss in both high-skill teaching jobs themselves and in the economic contribution that results from an educated work force.

At the same time, public services have been important sources of employment for low-skilled workers too, as several services with a public-goods component require only low-skilled labour (ibid). One thinks immediately of the whole range of environmental cleansing services: refuse collection, street-cleaning, maintenance of public spaces; also of elementary child care and some hospital employment. These services have often made a distinctive contribution to the structure of employment available in the advanced societies: work that required little skill, paid rather low wages, but offered security of employment and (because of the commitment of most public employers to concepts of 'the good employer') freedom from the brutalisation often associated with low-skilled and low-paid work. The anxiety to reduce the size of public employment and taxation has recently led most national and local governments to make working conditions for this kind of employment more closely resemble that to be found at the low end of the private sector, either by privatising it or changing its regime through marketisation within the public service.

If we must accept that a sizeable number of people is destined to remain in low-skilled employment, the former public-service model will require rehabilitation. A dilemma currently preoccupying the OECD is that while wages should fall at the lower end of the skill range in order to increase the supply of jobs, poor and insecure working conditions and frequent job changes have a demoralising effect (OECD, 1996). The public-service model of low pay combined with decent conditions, which it is difficult to achieve in the down-market private sector, can square that circle and did so for many years in most countries. It may well be possible to achieve efficiency savings from a committed, permanent work force even at these low skill levels, but overall it must probably be conceded that this is not the cheapest form of public service: at the lowest skill levels where there is little to be gained from 'investing in people' that can be best achieved through harsh conditions and frequent dismissals in order to find ever cheaper workers.

REFERENCES

Backes-Gellner, U. (1996), *Betriebliche Bildungs- und Wettbewerbungsstrategien im deutsch-britischen Vergleich*, Rainer Hampp, Munich.

Crouch, C. (forthcoming), *The Social Structure of Western Europe*, Oxford University Press. Oxford.

Crouch, C., Finegold, D. and Sako, M. (1999), *Are Skills the Answer? The Political Economy of Skill Creation in Advanced Industrial Countries*, Oxford University Press, Oxford.

Ohlin, B. (1967), *Interregional and International Trade (rev. ed.)*, Harvard University Press, Cambridge.

King, D. (1995), *Actively Seeking Work*, University of Chicago Press, Chicago.

Labour Party (1997), *New Labour because Britain deserves better*, Labour Party, London.

OECD (1994), *The Jobs Study: Evidence and Explanations*, OECD, Paris.

OECD (1996), *Employment Outlook*, OECD, Paris.

Rault, C. (1994), *La formation professionelle initiale*, La documentation française, Paris.

Regini, M. (Ed.) (1996), *La formazione delle risorse umane*, Il Mulino, Bologna.

Streeck, W. (1987), *The Role of the Social Partners in Vocational Training and Further Training in the Federal Republic of Germany*, CEDEFOP, Berlin.

Sweden (Arbetsmarknadsdepartementet) (1992), *Kompetensutveckling, SOU 1992:7. Final report of Kompetensutredningen*, SOU, Stockholm.

Chapter 4

Enhancing the Operation of Markets for Vocational Education and Training

Harm van Lieshout
University of Amsterdam

1.   MARKETS AND SYSTEMS

While there are merits in a 'market' approach to analyse VET, such a paradigm shift should not be implemented in a way that ignores some important lessons of a 'systems' approach. Both approaches are basically one-sided in their interpretation of human (inter)action. The 'systems' approach tends to overrate stability in that it stresses the fact that human beings in various societies show a remarkable preference for doing many things in a basically similar way to their ancestors. The social discipline of cultural anthropology provides a vast body of literature that documents this fact, and contains many striking examples. The 'market' approach tends to overrate change in that it basically conceives of human beings as basing all of their action on an inherently rational choice that best serves their personal interests. The discipline of economics provides a vast body of literature that has been quite successful in explaining important facts this way. Both perspectives are thus important. Each on their own, however, entails a considerable risk of near-sightedness in the explanation of human behaviour and its aggregate effects.

While this risk may be negligible for the study of some problems, I contend that it is quite relevant when it comes to the analysis of VET - which is the theme of this paper. Policymakers have generally conceived of VET as a system, but over the last years some appear to have traded this in for a market conception. This paper asks the question as to which theoretical approach is the best candidate to study human interactions in this field? It does not seek the answer in a choice between markets or systems, but in a theoretical framework that integrates both approaches.

The paper makes its argument along the following lines. Section 2 first discusses the paradigm shift from 'system' to 'market' in science and politics. Section 3 then discusses one recent application of a 'market' approach to the field of (Dutch) VET, and points out some important analytical weaknesses from which this suffers. The key problem is that it uses an incomplete typology of the important governance mechanisms. Section 4 subsequently offers a theoretical criticism of neo-classicism. Section 5 presents an alternative conceptual framework that does not suffer from these flaws: governance theory. This proposes a typology of five governance mechanisms to study the co-ordination and interactions patterns in specific socio-economic fields: markets, state, hierarchies, associations and networks. Section 6 shows how this general framework can be applied to the field of VET.

2.   HOW SYSTEMS BECAME MARKETS

During the nineteen fifties and sixties, functionalism played a dominant role in sociological theory (e.g. Parsons, 1951; Merton, 1968). Functional theory can be seen as the sociological counterpart of anatomy and physiology in biology. It views patterns of human interaction as integrated in social systems, and focuses on identifying and labelling the system's parts. Functionalists emphasise four elements in their analysis of social systems (cf. Wallace and Wolf, 1986, p. 11-12):

*   the general inter-relatedness of the system's parts;

*   the existence of a 'normal' state of affairs, or state of equilibrium, comparable to the normal or healthy state of an organism;

*   the way that all the parts of the system reorganise to bring things back to normal;

*   the central role that shared values of actors or generally accepted standards of desirability play in sustaining this 'normal' state of affairs.

One important criticism of functionalism is that it stresses consensus and co-operation over conflict in its analysis of human interaction. This particularly applies to its older forms and formulations, but may still be appropriate for some newer forms. The core problem with (this type of) functionalism is that it presents an over-socialised view of human action in that it seeks to explain stability in human interaction patterns, and uses shared values as a crucial explanatory variable. Such values are passed on from one generation to another through socialisation processes in which individuals internalise the values from the group/society from which they are a member.

Mainstream economics has provided an important alternative to this functionalist concept: the market. Neo-classical economics is the specific economic paradigm that has (re-) located markets at the centre of economic attention. Over the last decades, this paradigm has steadily become the prevailing economic orthodoxy. It is hard to narrowly define the territory of neo-classicism, as there are important differences between individual neo-classicists. Nevertheless, it is safe to say that the following elements form the core of the neo-classical market conception (Hodgson, 1988):

*   methodological individualism: contrary to the functionalist attempt to explain phenomena from the 'needs' of a collective system, it tries to explain phenomena in terms of statements about individuals;

- rational choice: it analyses human action by economic actors as rational and maximising their individual interests, not as the result of socialisation processes;

- at the same time, it sees actor's preferences as exogeneously given;

- the premise that chronic information problems are absent.

- a theoretical focus on movements towards or attained equilibrium - an attribute which it shares with functionalism.

This neo-classical approach to human (inter)action has steadily gained dominance over the functionalist approach, both in academic research and in policymaking. But there has been a considerable time lag between changes in the theories favoured by academics and those by policymakers. This is exemplified by the fact that the neo-classical economic approach to human activity has only gained real prominence in European and American policy-making since the rise of Thatcherism and Reagonomics in the late seventies and early eighties. In addition, there have been important national differences in the timing of such paradigm shifts. Even today, the rise of the market paradigm and its theoretical twin of rational choice theory have been stronger in some countries than in others. Among European politicians and policymakers, it has, for instance, been particularly prominent in the U.K. Its early roots can be traced to the start of the long reign of the Conservative Party in English national politics, from the mid-seventies until 1997, and the rise of Thatcherism within that party.

A more recent rise of the market paradigm in policymaking has occurred in the Netherlands. This is exemplified by the project 'Market Operation, Deregulation and Legal Quality (MDW)', currently sponsored by the Dutch Department of Economic Affairs. The doctrine behind this project can be summarised as follows:

- market competition is generally congenial to both economic performance and social welfare;

- deregulating markets is an attractive guideline for state policy towards markets in general;

- such deregulation will usually improve the quality of legal frameworks that regulate these markets.

The MDW enterprise consists of a number of research projects on specific sectoral markets that are suspected of needing a deregulatory cure. Examples are the taxi market, the pharmacy market, and - although this project has received considerably less attention - the market for intermediate skills (see next section).

The time lag between paradigm shifts in science and in policymaking also applies to the field of education and training. In most countries, more or less functionalist approaches to the analysis of national education and training systems have dominated policy-making and government sponsored research in this field throughout the nineteen-eighties, and often do so even today. This is not due to neglect of this field by economists. Economists have provided a number of crucial contributions to the analysis of VET over a long period – at least since Becker's classical work on human capital (Becker, 1964). And this line of research and analysis obviously has had an impact on policy-makers' perception of problems and their proposals for improving systems. For a long time, however, the basic perspective of VET that guided most policymakers continued to resemble the 'system' metaphor more closely than it did that of the market. More recently, this balance appears to be shifting, and more policymakers appear to be guided by a market metaphor in their approach to VET. Usually, such an approach is significantly influenced by mainstream neo-classical theory.

To some extent, this last fact is somewhat paradoxical. Both labour economics and the economics of education share the same economic historical and intellectual roots that have also equipped them with a 'market' approach. As in other economic sub-disciplines, this approach has been reinforced by the rise of the neo-classical paradigm. But at the same time, strict neo-classical approaches to markets play a much smaller role in the economics of education and labour economics than in most other economic sub-disciplines. Many labour and educational economists concede that the neo-classical utopia of a perfect market will in practice supply insufficient skills. State intervention to combat this specific market imperfection is readily accepted, certainly more so than in most other markets. Many policy proposals from educational economists propose a specific institutional form for *public* funding of vocational education and training. Thus, such economists have generally been aware of the possible dysfunctionality of VET markets. With this in mind, we turn to a discussion of the research project into the Dutch market for intermediate skills conducted as part of the MDW project of the Dutch Department of Economic Affairs.

3.   MARKET APPROACHES TO VET: A DUTCH EXAMPLE AND ITS FLAWS

Where it comes to VET, the Netherlands provides a recent example of an attempt to apply a neo-classical market approach to the analysis of the sector. One of the research projects stemming from the MDW project of the Dutch Department of Economic Affairs has tried to address the efficiency of the operation of the Dutch VET market. The final report of this project was published last year (Vrancken and De Kemp, 1996). The report has not stimulated a lively debate. This is a pity, as such a debate can help clarify the issues at stake in the operation of markets for intermediate skills. This paper is intended as a contribution to such a debate.

Whilst this paper is critical of the approach used in the study, and proposes an alternative, the project does represents an important contribution to the body of literature in this field. The researchers have attempted to apply general economic analytical tools to the field of VET. That this attempt suffers from some serious flaws should not, on its own, be held against it. It is exactly these flaws that enable a thorough appreciation of the merits and limits of such a straightforward application of these tools to this field. In the medium and long term, this might prove more important than the extent to which this project was more or less correct in its conception of VET markets. And, to be sure, the project was certainly on the mark in some respects. What is striking, though, is that it simultaneously neglects some aspects of markets for intermediate skills that are at least as important as the ones it does deal with.

The first chapter of the project final report discusses the central questions that the research sets out to analyse. The main question is to ascertain whether it is possible to enhance the efficiency of the Dutch VET market. The chapter does acknowledge that - contrary to extreme versions of neo-classical theory - state regulation in markets for intermediate skills may be welcome at various points.

Chapter two then offers an analysis of the supply-side of the market formed by schools. It distinguishes three market segments (full-time initial VET, part-time initial VET and post-initial training) and four dimensions in the regulation of the supply-side:
- rules regulating the public financing of this supply;
- rules regulating the entrance of providers into this market;
- rules regulating the conditions of the skill production by schools;
- rules regulating the transparency of this supply.

Chapter three tries to establish the static and dynamic efficiency of the operation of this supply-side. It uses a quantitative method to establish the relative static efficiency of public investment in VET schools. It concludes that the static efficiency of the Dutch school-based supply of VET is not exceptionally low, but that there appears to be room for improvement. It also concludes that the dynamic efficiency - which is measured as efficiency of the school-to-work transition - is not always optimal.

Chapter four of the report discusses the institutionalisation of the supply-side of American, English and (West) German VET markets. It concludes (Vrancken and De Kemp, 1996, p. 66):

- that none of these countries have perfect solutions for the prevention of 'market failures' in markets for intermediate skills;
- that - even they did - a perfect and immediate imitation of their institutional arrangements in the Netherlands would not be possible;
- and - finally and to some extent despite the first conclusion - that a regulated approach to strengthening the role of the market mechanism on the supply side appears a logical consequence of this international comparison.

Chapter five points out opportunities to enhance the operation of the Dutch market for intermediate skills. On a general level, its suggestions are to further reduce the amount of government intervention in this market, to increase the transparency of the supply of VET, and to stimulate market behaviour by potential participants. On a more practical level, the advice is to stimulate competition between publicly funded VET schools. One way of achieving this would be to entitle private-for-profit training institutions to receive public funding. In the light of the general outlook of the MDW operation, of which this research project is a part, these suggestions are not surprising. But they are not backed up by convincing argument.

Most VET experts will not find it hard to point out several important weaknesses of this project. First, it narrows its discussion of the Dutch market for intermediate skills to the supply-side of this market and the changes that could be made there. But a large body of research in the economics of education has proposed the enhancement in the operation of educational markets through changes on the demand-side, in particular through the introduction of some kind of voucher system. In his critique of the report, Kuipers (1996) suggests that a shift from public funding of schools to public funding of pupils through vouchers may be a more promising avenue for enhancing the operation of the Dutch VET market. As it is likely that different forms of public funding for VET will require a different organisation of the supply-side of this market, this implies an important limitation of the project. In itself, it may, of course, be appropriate to focus the analysis on the supply-side. But this does require at least a brief discussion of the extent to which supply-side changes are more promising than demand-side changes, the reasons for this, and some empirical evidence, or at least explicit assumptions, about the operation of the demand side. De Jager (1996) criticises the implicit assumptions of the report on the latter. The report focuses on tuition fees as a key incentive for (potential) students, and equates a substantial differentiation of fees, and student response with a well-functioning market. De Jager (1996, p.8) accurately points out that education should not be treated as a cost but as an investment, and that students themselves actually do treat it that way. While it is true that they pay little attention to tuition fees in their choices, they pay considerable attention to the 'life-time' benefits that a particular track appears to offer. This is evident when one looks at the consistent popularity of the preparatory tracks for college in the educational system among subsequent generations of youth. This is not explained by differences in the cost of education but by differences in expected benefits over a life-time. From a labour market perspective, such benefits provide a more promising rationale for educational choices by youth than educational costs per se.

This brings us to a second objection. The report only discusses the part of the supply-side of the education and training market formed by publicly and privately funded VET schools. Firstly it neglects the fact that these compete with senior secondary schools offering college-preparation tracks, and thus underestimates the extent of competition between schools on the market for students. Secondly it neglects the fact that firms also offer VET. This is particularly important, as a core conclusion of the international VET literature is that apprenticeship systems - where companies are the main supplier of training - constitute a effective and efficient form of VET market (e.g. CEREQ, 1994). The admirable performance of the German apprenticeship system serves as the most important case in point. It is striking that the discussion of the German dual training system in the Dutch report is quite up to date and basically positive in its assessment (Vrancken and De Kemp, 1996, pp. 62-63 and 64-65), but does not result in a positive assessment of company-led VET in its conclusions (Vrancken and De Kemp, 1996, p. 66), nor to the inclusion of apprenticeship as a viable alternative to school-based VET in the analysis of the Dutch VET market. The report simply neglects the work-based component of apprenticeship, and lumps together the school-based component of apprenticeship with part-time school-based VET. This is all the more surprising as about a third of current Dutch enrolments into initial VET concern apprenticeship and important Dutch committees have pleaded for a larger share of work-based learning in general and apprenticeship-type tracks in particular (Open Overleg Wagner; 1984; Tijdelijke Adviescommissie Onderwijs and Arbeidsmarkt, 1990). There in fact is substantial competition between school-based and work based apprenticeship VET tracks (PEIL, 1996).

Third, the neglect of firms implies a second way in which the demand side of the market for intermediate skills is neglected. There is not only a demand side formed by youth and young adults looking for training, but also one formed by firms looking for young workers with a certain combination of skills. Firms are the other important customer of VET schools, but they are absent from the report. Only their demand for VET graduates at an aggregate level is implicitly discussed when the report summarises data on school-to-work transition in the Netherlands. This demand is treated as given. But a host of international comparative research shows that similar firms in different nations in fact *need* very different amounts and combinations of intermediate skills due to international differences in work organisation (Prais, 1995a; Prais, 1995b; Mason and Finegold, 1995; Wagner and Finegold, forthcoming). In fact, this insight has led to the accepted practice of distinguishing different equilibrium in markets for intermediate skills. Some countries (e.g. the U.S.) are seen as a so-called low-skill equilibrium, whereas others (e.g. Germany) are seen as a high-skill equilibrium (Finegold, 1991; Soskice, 1994a; Van Lieshout, 1997). As higher skills correspond with higher wages, the social and economic effects of both types of equilibrium differ. Thus, one potential way of enhancing the operation of the Dutch VET market would be to stimulate firms to adopt so-called 'high performance workplaces', and thus stimulate the demand for VET.

These first three objections deal with the identification of the relevant actors in VET markets. The general argument is that the Dutch research has neglected some relevant actors in VET markets (firms) and inadequately conceptualised others (students). This has consequences for the definition of efficiency in the research, which brings us to a second objection: that the project incorrectly defines and measures efficiency. It conceives of efficiency as the cost efficiency of public investment in schools. The research was based on the concern that inefficiencies may flourish in publicly funded VET schools because of the lack of competition in the VET market, and thus focuses on the measurement of the cost-efficiency of those schools (Vrancken and De Kemp, 1996, p. 29). But this is much too limited a conception of the efficiency issues involved in VET markets and public investment in them. As De Jager (1996) pointed out, education and training are investments, which means one should assess costs in the light of the *benefits* they produce. If less cost-efficient schools produce higher benefits because their training is of a superior quality, they may very well be more efficient from the standpoint of the state. And in that case competitive elimination of less cost-efficient schools may in fact lead to efficiency losses at the macro-level. The report neglects the fact that competitive elimination in a market does not necessarily occur according to criteria that would contribute most to macro-level efficiency. Competition may, for instance, favour schools that are good in attracting students, rather than those that are good in equipping them with the skills they need.

Thus, a fourth objection to the report is that it focuses on the cost-efficiency of publicly funded schools but neglects the overriding question of the efficiency of the public investment in the VET market at an aggregate level. One vital question that needs to be addressed here is whether there is an under- or over-supply of intermediate skills in the labour market. There is an abundant literature that tries to settle this issue (see, for example, Freeman, 1976; Hartog, 1985; Stern and Ritzen, 1991; Theeuwes, 1993). As labour markets are segmented, an under-supply in one segment may co-exist with an oversupply in another. Consequently, the smoothness of the school-to-work transition is one important indicator of efficiency, and Vrancken and de Kemp correctly treat it this way. But this indicator is neither the only one relevant, nor necessarily the most important one. State intervention in education and training aims to provide youth with more than just skills for their first job: namely, with a decent skill basis for their career. This is why general, academic tracks dominate most educational systems. Even if graduates from academic, general tracks face a more cumbersome school-to-work transition than VET graduates, the resulting efficiency losses may be offset by the higher benefits in the long run. Consequently, it is inadequate to measure the static efficiency of publicly funded VET schools exclusively by the extent to which they enable a smooth school-to-work transition. This should be accompanied by an assessment of the extent to which these schools have succeeded in providing students with the skills that will help them in the medium and long run (e.g. the level of computer literacy with which they equipped their students). While, today, initial VET cannot be expected to supply its graduates with all the skills they will need over their career, we do and should expect it to lay a solid skill foundation for a productive career. But Vrancken and de Kemp avoid this important question.

Fifth, the distinction between two types of efficiency in the report is problematic. Vrancken and De Kemp (1996, p. 29) correctly criticise efficiency research that exclusively focuses on static efficiency (cost efficiency at a given point in time). They properly argue that this should be accompanied by an assessment of dynamic efficiency: the extent to which product and process innovation takes place, and suppliers accommodate to changing circumstances and technologies. But they incorrectly translate dynamic efficiency in VET markets as the smoothness of school-to-work transition. As we discussed above, the latter is not a form of dynamic efficiency, but of static efficiency, as it exclusively measures the performance of the VET market at a given point in time. Instead, the dynamic efficiency of a VET market should be assessed by its *responsiveness*: the extent to which education and training systems adapt the contents of their supply flexibly over time. We already mentioned one element of this above, under the heading of static efficiency: to what extent does VET provide students with a solid skill basis for their career (rather than just their first job). One could argue whether this should in fact be considered as static or dynamic efficiency; it seems to combine elements of both. What certainly falls under the heading of dynamic efficiency is the question as to what extent the structure of training occupations is still adequate in the light of the way in which labour market developments alter such structures. For instance, are new emerging occupations and sectors of employment translated into corresponding VET tracks? In such labour market segments - e.g. information technology - we might even strive for an oversupply of graduates, as the core skills acquired in such a track will certainly also benefit graduates and their employers if they find employment outside the computer industry. The report, alas, fails to deal with the issue of responsiveness.

Sixth and finally, the report fails to fully acknowledge the potential for state failure next to market failure. This is curious, as the reports basic inclination to state intervention is indeed sceptical, as it is based on the premise that markets are efficient. To its benefit, this Dutch report does realise that this premise is not always legitimated by the actual performance of markets in real life. There, they sometimes show important inefficiencies. But in the instances where the report suspects potential inefficiencies in VET markets, it routinely calls for state intervention. It is, however, questionable whether state intervention always provides the best answer to a particular market failure. In fact, the state is ill-equipped to perform particular tasks on its own because it lacks the relevant expertise. Besides, or instead of, state intervention, voluntary co-operation between actors might also help overcome market failures. Formal or informal self-organisation of relevant actors may sometimes be a more adequate response to market failure than state intervention. State actors face substantial information problems when intervening in particular markets that can only be dealt with through help from insiders; insiders' organisations may supply such information. In actual VET markets, various forms of self-organisation have emerged (e.g. sectoral training funds) and proven worthwhile, and states have tended to sanction and stimulate it. But Vrancken and de Kemp completely neglect the possibility of the (self) organisation of relevant actors as a policy option.

The strange combination of a basic scepticism toward state intervention on the outset, and a routine call for state intervention in the light of any potential market failure makes Vrancken and de Kemp's proposals appear paradoxical. To give some examples, while the report's basic call is for less state intervention, it does not challenge the core form of state intervention in providing public funding for VET. It takes for granted the current level of public funding for VET, and the share of it that is attributed to schools. The report calls for state intervention in increasing the transparency of supply and the 'market behaviour' of (potential) participants in VET tracks (Vrancken and De Kemp, 1996, p. 67). But it does not adequately analyse the main types of state regulation, assess their impact, and develop a coherent proposal from this. For instance, it shies away from a straightforward attack on one important aspect of Dutch state policy concerning VET schools over the last decade. Over this period, the Dutch government has consciously changed the 'schoolscape' through a sequence of mergers from a large number of relatively small and specialised schools into roughly fifty large educational centres. This reduction may reduce competition, as most Dutch students tend to choose a school in their own region and will probably continue to do so. This merger policy has spurred an intensive debate over the last decade, and it is striking that the research did not take up this state policy so vital for school competition, when the latter is the theme which it seeks to analyse.

A similar paradoxical character applies to assigning responsibility for efficiency. On the one hand, the report sticks to the root of neo-classical theory and assumes that market competition will let the 'best' schools emerge. This way, it in effect decentralises the full responsibility for market efficiency to publicly funded schools. But, as we noted before, it is by no means certain that competition between schools will result in macro efficiency. Alternatively, one could - and maybe should - hold the state responsible for the institutionalisation of market incentives for schools so that most of them opt for the 'right' strategy. The report's recommendations do in fact sometimes do so, and propose the Dutch government should institutionalise particular incentives for schools. For instance, the report allows the Dutch state to retain the current practice of defining the minimum contents of publicly funded VET tracks through a system of binding national skill standards (Vrancken and De Kemp, p. 70). And it complains about the lack of incentives for publicly funded schools to enter the market for post-initial training (Vrancken and De Kemp, 1996, p. 69). But these and other proposals lack a thorough theoretical or empirical justification, nor do they come close to providing a full discussion of the issue. This is a pity, as the big question for states today is exactly if, how, and to what extent they should intervene in VET markets. To what extent do they need to invest in education and training at all? And, within this broad category of investment, to what extent should they invest in general education, initial VET or post-initial training? Should they direct their investments to the supply-side of the market or to the demand side? These are, as we noted before, are questions not addressed in this report.

4.   A CRITIQUE OF A NEO-CLASSICAL APPROACH TO MARKETS

The critique of the Dutch report on the national VET market in the previous section at the very least suggests that the application of neo-classical economic theory to this field requires a better field-specific translation than was presented in that report. The report neglects important micro, meso and macro level insights from the economics of education and other disciplines. The first thing needed to improve it is a theoretical approach to VET markets that is more versatile and does more justice to such valuable insights.

This brings us back to the debate on markets and systems. It should be noted that this debate is not equivalent to that on the merits of economic versus sociological approaches. Specific economic theories may have more in common with certain sociological ones that with other economic theories. For instance, the rise of a rational choice paradigm in economics - neo-classical economics - has inspired the growth of a sociological version of rational choice theory. Both assume that actors try to make optimal decisions that maximise their utility, and share methodological individualism as a core premise. Methodological individualism prescribes that the collective results of human action be explained by the choices that individual actors make. An extreme version of this (that has been particularly strong in economics) takes this prescription literally. Less extreme versions (more popular with sociologists) admit that it may be appropriate to interpret groups as an individual actor for research into macro or meso level problems (e.g. Boudon, 1979). These versions allow an analysis of groups as if they were individual actors, when they are well organised and have clear institutional arrangements that can take collective decisions for their members (Boudon, 1979, p. 52). In practice, even most economists stick to this looser version of methodological individualism as they treat firms as if they were individual actors (e.g. top managers) (Finegold, 1991). In this light, the remaining basic difference between standard economic and sociological approaches is in the strictness of the rationality assumption and the extent to which rationality depends on the institutional environment. 'Pure' versions of neo-classical economics conceive of actors as inherently free in their choice. On the other hand, scholars as Boudon (1979) explicitly acknowledge that not each course of action is equally accessible to individual actors. Institutions influence the accessibility of various options for individuals, and the benefits and disadvantages associated with them.

Methodological individualism can be considered the most important gain rational choice theories had to offer over old functionalist theories that presented an over-socialised view of human behaviour and neglected actor's considerable scope for free choice. At the same time, neo-classical economics has generally preserved an important flaw of the old functionalist school. The latter has long thrived on the assumption that human interaction constitutes coherent systems at an aggregate level, and that such systems have a 'natural' state of equilibrium to which they automatically tend. When we merely substitute 'markets' for 'systems', we have translated this in a key assumption of (traditional) neo-classical economics. This position neglects the potential for dysfunctional and inefficient current practice and for the existence of disequilibrium. Both functionalism and neo-classical economics have subsequently been criticised for a conservative bias, as they tend to interpret today's status quo as an equilibrium that should be evaluated positively. To be sure, this criticism does not apply to all applications of functionalism or neo-classicism. There are, for instance, neo-classical theories that allow for the existence of disequilibrium. And, as the research discussed in the previous section shows, neo-classical analysis often starts from the assumption that a particular market is currently not perfectly efficient. In fact, neo-classicism deserves praise for turning our attention to the possibility of inefficiencies in today's practice, and to the possibility that competitive elimination of less efficient actors may contribute to a more positive equilibrium than that of today. But this implies that there are different equilibria which (from a macro standpoint) have different advantages and disadvantages. For instance, most neo-classicists have tended to analyse European labour markets as suffering from 'Eurosclerosis', that there are too many rules that prevent these markets from achieving a 'better' equilibrium with less unemployment.

But while neo-classicists thus may evaluate the (dis) equilibrium in actual markets quite differently, their analysis and evaluation of such equilibria is led by an utopian view of a perfectly free market. It is, however, highly questionable whether such a utopian market does in fact always lead to the optimal type of equilibrium. Many economists acknowledge that markets do not always result in efficient outcomes. Market failures may occur, particularly because of the consequences of economic transactions on third parties. In these instances, many neo-classicists allow for state intervention to provide public goods that else would be under-supplied. Consequently, many neo-classicists bring in the state as an alternative governance mechanism in most of their analyses. This entails a remarkable paradox, as neo-liberals in general and neo-classical economists in particular are generally sceptical of state intervention because of their reliance on 'free' markets for achieving efficiency, and subsequently call for a state that is strictly limited in its role (cf. Cohen and Rogers, 1992). But if they admit that a particular market has failures, most fall back exclusively on that same state as an alternative for the market.

The immediate call for state intervention neglects, however, a less drastic and stressful solution: voluntary co-operation between individual actors based on trust and/or legal contracts. The most obvious form of human co-operation is when different individuals team together in formal organisations based on legal contracts. In labour markets, firms are an obvious and key example, an example pointed out by economists earlier in this century (e.g. Coase, 1937). Again, it should be noted that most neo-classical economist do in fact discuss firms as key actors in product, labour and other markets. From a formal standpoint this suggests that, in practice, they adopt a more sociological version of methodological individualism. But, in effect, they tend to treat firms as black boxes that can be equated with top managers whose preferences are exogenously given. The reason behind this is that rational choice theories share an emphasis on the profit-maximising behaviour of individual actors. As far as they do focus on institutions, it tends to be on external institutions that provide a particular incentive structure that is thought to influence these actor's rational calculations,

But institutions are not only important because they influence the availability and attractiveness of various options for actors. They also influence actor's perceptions. The basic problem with methodological individualism is its a-historical view of actors. It analyses them, as if they entered a situation with an open mind. But in real life, actors have a specific history. Past experiences influence present perceptions, for instance on what are possible and appropriate courses of actions, and what is efficient. If actors come from different backgrounds and were subsequently influenced by different institutional contexts, their views will differ. In sociology, this is known as 'socialisation': actors that grow up in a similar context tend to develop shared values and accepted standards of desirability that help to sustain a 'normal' state of affairs in a society. This crucial root of functionalism has generally been neglected by rational choice theory. Subsequently, the latter has been criticised as merely substituting the over-socialised view of human activity inherent in the old functionalist approach by an under-socialised one. In addition, neo-classical economists often make an assumption as to the extent to which a particular market can be considered in equilibrium, and how positively such an equilibrium should be evaluated. A short reference to the theoretical norm of a utopian free market is often thought to suffice, rather than a solid empirical analysis of such markets and a thorough, field-specific, view on what would be optimally efficient. And third, neo-classicism often tends to mystify the actual mechanisms along which a positive readjustment of a system/market to a 'better' equilibrium may occur. It often *assumes*, rather than thoroughly analyses:

- which particular type of actor (individual or organisation, customer or supplier) is in the best position to change its behaviour in a way that enhances efficiency most;
- which changes in the behaviour of this actor seem more worthwhile in this respect than others;
- how and why market selection will be along the criterion that contributes most to long-term efficiency, rather than along criteria that benefit suppliers that are (from a macro standpoint) less efficient.

While these weaknesses may be minor for some types of analyses, and 'purer' forms of neo-classicism can consequently be considered appropriate tools for them, they represent major flaws in others. This is certainly the case with education and training, and it is along these lines that the Dutch report was criticised in the previous section. There are two main arguments here. First, education and training are themselves a core example of socialisation processes. Thus, the particular institutions in a particular country and economic sector may be expected to lead to a particular set of shared values and accepted standards among actors that are socialised within their context. The German apprenticeship system provides a nice case in point. The fact that many training and production managers have themselves satisfactorily completed apprenticeship training and subsequently risen to their current position, provides an important argument for the preference of those firms to continue apprenticeship training. The lack of such training experience by American managers with a college background makes them generally more sceptical of apprenticeship training. Second, it is highly questionable whether markets alone may lead to optimal efficiency in education and training markets. The economics of education acknowledges that perfectly competitive education and training markets may lead to under-investment in education and training in general, and that this threat is particularly apparent in markets for intermediate skills (Ryan, 1991). The question of who should pay for training represents a problem for co-ordination with a distribution conflict. If the (prospective) worker pays for training himself, the employer does not have to, and vice versa. In addition, there is a related distribution conflict concerning the benefits of training. Human capital has feet and may subsequently walk to a competitor that can then reap the benefits of training investment by a previous employer. In this light, it would be paradoxical, at the least, to solely rely on the market mechanism to enhance efficiency in education and training markets. To expect efficiency gains exclusively from increased competition is to neglect the fact that too much competition can damage efficiency, and that efficiency may also emerge from increased co-operation between specific actors.

Within neo-classical economics, the best available solution to these problems is to allow a considerable role for state intervention in VET markets, and to attribute a key role to firms in the supply of training. This solution combats some of the problems associated with the Dutch report discussed in section 2. But it would not solve all of the previously discussed weaknesses of neo-classical analysis and it neglects other possible, less drastic solutions to these problems than direct state intervention. Neo-classical economics tends to neglect or underestimate the relevance of other governance mechanisms as viable alternatives for, and additions to, competitive markets, and the importance of such alternative governance mechanisms for the operation of markets in real life. Thus, the question is whether there is a more suitable paradigm available to guide the analysis of VET markets.

5.   **RECONCILING MARKETS AND SYSTEMS: TOWARDS AN INSTITUTIONALIST APPROACH TO MARKETS**

There are, and always have been, competing paradigms for rational choice theories within both economics and the other social sciences. These are based on a more socialised view of human behaviour, and go by the name of institutionalism. Over the last decades, the literature in both disciplines shows the rise of a 'new institutionalism', that simultaneously combats many problems associated with functionalism and neo-classicism. Mayntz and Scharf (1995, p. 40-43) distinguish five types of neo-institutionalism. To begin with they distinguish an organisational-sociological institutionalism that criticises neo-classical economics for primarily seeing organisations as production/exchange systems shaped by technologies and the transactions they are involved in, and that alternatively stresses symbolic and cognitive elements within organisations such as opinions, ideologies and myths (e.g. Powell and DiMaggio, 1991). In addition, they distinguish two versions of neo-institutionalism that stem from the political sciences. The first concentrates on a criticism of the reductionist and utilitarian character of neo-classical economics, that exclusively explains political phenomena as aggregate effects of utilitarian behaviour by individuals, and neglects organisational structures and normative and symbolical causes of individual behaviour (March and Olsen, 1989). The second version concentrates on the consequences of political processes and their organisation, that influence the aggregation of behaviour into collective effects, and the neglect of this in rational choice approaches (Mayntz and Scharpf, 1995). Finally, Mayntz and Scharpf distinguish two economic versions of neo-institutionalism. The first is an 'economic institutionalism' that tries to explain institutions by a 'relaxed' version of rational choice theory (Williamson, 1975; 1985; North, 1981). The second is an 'institutional economics' that aims for an institutional explanation of economic facts (Granovetter, 1985; Streeck, 1992). As our concern here is with the economic effects of education, I will concentrate on these last two versions below.

The 'economic institutionalism' is perhaps better known by the name of 'transaction cost economics'. Its main advantage over neo-classicism is that it explicitly acknowledges that not all economic transactions take place in markets. Rather, some individual actors tend to co-operate in firms or, as transaction cost economics calls them, hierarchies. Most neo-classical economists merely see firms as actors, who could be analysed as if they were individual managers. Transaction cost economics recognises that firms/hierarchies in effect are an alternative governance mechanism that substitutes for markets in connecting various individuals. The basic argument is that hierarchies emerge to co-ordinate transactions when the costs of co-ordination through the market are too high (Williamson, 1975; 1985). It adds a cost category to the ones recognised by traditional neo-classicism: transaction costs. To satisfactorily engage in market transactions calls for extensive monitoring of the attractiveness of the offers of various suppliers, and of the satisfactory fulfilment of concluded contracts. When such costs are high, it may be more efficient to provide the products or services in-house, under one's own (hierarchical) authority. A second difference with neo-classicism is that transaction cost economics explicitly assumes bounded rationality rather than the stricter forms of rationality assumed by most (other) neo-classicists. And third, transaction cost economics more adequately understands the important role that institutions play in enabling an efficient operation of markets in the first place. Markets can only function if it is clear who has the ownership of a particular good or service. North (1981) showed that the basic unit that constitutes markets is the institution of the contract, which attributes property rights to specific actors. The state ultimately guarantees the fulfilment of these contracts by its monopoly on the use of legitimate force.

Transaction costs economics itself has, however, also met with substantial criticism (Hodgson, 1988; Lindberg et al., 1991). These critics consider the typology of governance mechanisms within transaction cost economics still incomplete, and its conception of human choice still too rational and efficiency-driven, as it sees the balance between hierarchies and market as the necessarily efficient result of a selective competitive process. This has inspired a body of literature that Mayntz and Scharpf (1995) refer to as institutional economics, but that is also referred to as the 'governance' approach (Streeck and Schmitter, 1985; Campbell et al., 1991; Hollingsworth, 1991; Hollingsworth et al., 1994a; Van Lieshout, 1996; Van Waarden, 1997). These authors share the view that transaction costs economics still underestimates the role of co-operation, socialisation and institutions. The argument goes two ways. First, the three-part typology of market, state and firms as governance mechanisms is still not comprehensive enough, and should be expanded by two others: associations and networks. Second, while the bounded rationality used by transaction cost economics is an improvement over the neo-classical assumption of more or less unbounded rational choice, it is not enough.

Governance theory has been criticised for failing to clearly demarcate the various types of governance mechanisms. Mayntz and Scharpf (1995, p. 60) state that governance theory suffers from the multi-dimensionality of the underlying classification. They certainly have a point here, which is illustrated by the fact that different authors have in fact proposed different typologies. These differ both in the number of governance mechanisms proposed, their names and definitions, and the underlying dimensions -if any- from which they are derived.

Streeck and Schmitter (1985)[1] distinguish four types of governance mechanisms: community, market, state and association. They list twelve dimensions of difference between them. The core difference is that each has a distinctive guiding principle of co-ordination and allocation: spontaneous solidarity (community), dispersed competition (market), hierarchical control (state) and inter and intra-organisational 'concertation' (association). Lindberg et al. (1991) list seven governance mechanisms. Six of these are derived from two underlying dimensions: the degree of formal integration (low, moderate or high) and the range of interaction (bilateral or multilateral). In addition, they devote much attention to the state. But as this does not fit in their scheme based on the aforementioned two underlying dimensions, they choose to conceptualise and theorise on the state in its own terms. Most authors, however, have opted for a five-part typology (Hollingsworth et al., 1994a; Van Lieshout, 1996; Van Waarden, 1997). In the words of Hollingsworth et al. (1994b, p. 5-7) these are markets, states, hierarchies, associations and networks. While there remain differences between the typologies presented by the authors, there appears to be an emerging consensus on the optimality of a five-part typology over those with four or seven types. Streeck and Schmitter's typology lacks the category of hierarchies (or firms), whose relevance has been shown by transaction cost economics. The typology of Lindberg et al. (1991) appears attractive as it spells out a limited number of underlying dimensions from which the various types are derived. Closer scrutiny, however, reveals two important weaknesses. First, they do not derive the state from their two underlying dimensions, which deprives their typology of much of its face-value theoretical elegance. Second and more importantly, the fact that they distinguish between bilateral and multilateral forms of co-ordination is highly problematic, in particular with the interpretation of markets and hierarchies. This way, markets are reduced to bilateral contracts, whereas the crucial aspect of markets from a governance viewpoint is indeed the multilateral co-ordination between actors that can be achieved through their engaging in bilateral contracts. Similarly, hierarchies also interpreted as bilateral- typically co-ordinate the behaviour of more than two individuals, as most firms employ more than one person.

As mentioned, above, there remain differences between various authors that use a five-part typology in their specific terminology (e.g. whether they

---

[1]. Streeck & Schmitter (1985) did not use the word 'governance', but their article can be considered one its the important roots.

call the fifth governance mechanism network, community or clan). Also, not all of them try to spell out underlying dimensions from which these types are derived. Hollingsworth et al. (1994), for instance, use a more Weberian typology in which the five types are described rather than strictly defined. Van Waarden (1997) derives his five-part typology from three underlying dimensions. The first is (as with Lindberg et al.) the degree of formal association. Contrary to Lindberg et al., Van Waarden limits himself to just two categories: informal and formal. Van Waarden's second dimension characterises the internal structure of organisations, and distinguishes horizontal organisations from vertical organisations. His third dimension distinguishes private from public organisations. This leaves us with the following scheme:

Table 1. Van Waardens Three Dimensions of Organisations (1997)

Governance Mechanism	Formality	Internal Structure	Public / Private
Clan / Community	Informal	Horizontal	Private
Association	Formal	Horizontal	Private
Concern	Formal	Vertical	Private
State	Formal	Vertical	Public

The first weakness of Van Waarden's version is the same as with Lindberg et al. (1991): there is an odd man out that is not derived from the same dimensions as the other four types. With Lindberg et al. this was the state, with Van Waarden it is the market. Should one try to define the market in terms of the underlying dimensions, one would probably arrive at the trilogy private, horizontal and informal. But then markets and networks provide the same score on the three dimensions, which appears a weakness. Second, his three dimensions should constitute eight categories instead of four, and it is not clear why only four of them are worked out as governance mechanisms. Why should the other four combinations not also constitute separately identifiable governance mechanisms?

Paradoxically, combining this five-part typology of governance mechanisms with Mayntz and Scharpf's own proposal for an actor-centred institutionalism points us into the right direction to combat their criticism of the former. To begin with, it is important to note that Mayntz and Scharpf propose to preserve methodological individualism. But they propose a relaxed version of methodological individualism in that it allows the treatment of groups as individual actors. When groups have clear-cut institutional arrangements to take collective decisions for their members, or when the orientation of individual group members is substantially and consciously aimed in the same direction (e.g. a social movement), these may be modelled as a collective actor for analytical purposes (Mayntz and

Scharpf, 1995, p. 51). As the introduction of methodological individualism did provide an important improvement of neo-classical economics over the older versions of functionalism, it is possible to agree with Mayntz and Scharpf that the preservation of methodological individualism in an institutionalist approach is an important advantage.

Mayntz and Scharpf (1995, p. 44) correctly note that the use of such corporate actors (groups) does not imply that an explanation can always discard the various individual actors of which they consist. Corporate action can be analysed as the aggregate result of the behaviour of these individuals; in fact, rational choice theory has been applied to such analysis with a considerable amount of success. Even in hierarchies, no top manager actually commands complete authority over all individuals. In political science, this topic is analysed as the principal-agent problem. The basic lesson is that any collective actor simultaneously constitutes an arena in which individual actors (or smaller corporate actors) compete and co-operate. Thus, a collective actor is a governance mechanism of its own in that it co-ordinates the behaviour of individual actors within its ranks. Mayntz and Scharpf correctly conclude that this implies adopting a multi-level view of governance. In principle, there are more levels that could be taken into account in a particular analysis. Whether it is important to actually include all of them, including separate individual actors within organisations, explicitly into the analysis will depend upon the issue at hand.

Where Mayntz and Scharpf's basic lesson is that there is such a thing as collective actors and that this implies a multi-level view on governance, it appears paradoxical that they later criticise governance theory for its multi-dimensionality. This is not a problem, but an asset of the framework. What can be criticised is that there has been a considerable amount of confusion of the definition of governance theory. The five-part governance typology presents what I consider a minimum variety of basically different types of actors that can be distinguished along the lines of Mayntz and Scharpf's version of methodological individualism. Where pure market approaches distinguish only individual actors, governance theory adds four basic types of collective actors. The first was already acknowledged by neo-classicism: the state. It distinguishes itself from other actors in that all individuals in a given society are a member of it, not by free choice but by legal force.

The second actor is a hierarchy. Neo-classicism does discuss hierarchies - particularly firms - but usually only as an actor in a market, and not as a governance mechanism of its own. Transaction cost economics correctly acknowledges that they simultaneously are a governance mechanism of their own. Hierarchies are formal organisations from which individuals become a member of their free choice. But when they enter, they are bound to the hierarchy by a contract that can be enforced by the state, and subsequently cannot leave at any time they prefer. Also, the contract implies subordination to the authority of (top) management, which has the authority to prescribe the appropriate behaviour of workers and lower levels of management. Thus, individual actors take up basically unequal positions in hierarchies, and therefore hierarchies are a basically vertical form of organisation.

Contrary to transaction cost economics, a governance approach does not stop here. It offers three important criticisms for the transaction cost paradigm. First, the basic objection is that transaction cost economics limits itself to hierarchies as the only form of governance that is based on co-operation. But hierarchies are only one specific form of co-operation. There is an alternative model of formal organisation that differs fundamentally from the hierarchical model - the association. The prime difference with hierarchies is that associations have members. These members provide the core reason for the existence of associations. Management and workers of associations are supposed to serve their needs, and to adhere to the outcome of collective decision processes between those members - what Streeck and Schmitter (1985) call 'organisational concertation'. And as these members are considered equal peers, associations are basically horizontal rather than vertical. Governance theory stresses the role of associative behaviour in general and of associations in particular. Not surprisingly, an important part of its roots lies in the neo-corporatist tradition of the eighties. In particular Streeck and Schmitter's classical work put forward associations as an important alternative form of governance (Streeck and Schmitter, 1985). They see 'organisational concertation' as a fourth guiding principle of interaction and allocation, next to 'dispersed competition', 'hierarchical control' and 'spontaneous solidarity'. Cohen and Rogers (1992, pp. 424-425) name four useful functions that associations can fulfil for societies. First, they can provide information for policy makers on their members' preferences. Second, they can help remedying inequalities in material advantage by permitting individuals with low per-capita resources to pool these through organisation. Third, they can function as 'schools for democracy' in that they can help citizens develop competence, self-confidence and a broader set of interests than they would acquire in a more fragmented political society. Fourth (and this is the crucial point for governance theory) they can provide a distinctive form of social governance, alternative to markets and hierarchies, that permits society to realise the important benefits of co-operation among citizens.

The second criticism on transaction cost economics was also already embedded in Streeck and Schmitter's classical work (Streeck and Schmitter, 1985). They list 'spontaneous solidarity' as another guiding principle to be distinguished from hierarchical control and dispersed competition. Spontaneous solidarity implies informal co-operation: co-operation that is not embedded in a formal organisation. The governance mechanism associated with this has been alternatively referred to as community, clan or network. For reasons discussed below, I prefer the last term. Both networks and markets relate to independent individual units that voluntarily engage in an exchange. But the 'market' category exclusively studies the situation shortly before the exchange occurs, when various candidates for the exchange compete to achieve the best possible exchange. Axelrod (1984), however, showed that even in a market where a multitude of actors cannot be trusted, co-operation can emerge as long as individuals know they can meet again during future market exchanges. His innovation was to bring time into the analysis. The network concept refers to the more or less stable patterns of exchange that may arise between various individual actors that prefer to trade with one another because of a satisfactory past experience and trust in a continued co-operative relation. Thus, the category of networks points out that an exchange may involve more than money and a good; it also brings along expectations that are raised, realised or shattered.

Third, governance theory criticises the use of bounded rationality by transaction cost economics. It acknowledges that this is an improvement over the use of less-bounded forms by neo-classical economics, but maintains that it does not adequately combat all the latter's flaws. In this sense, it agrees with the criticism put forward by Mayntz and Scharpf (1995, p. 52-53). The weakness of rational choice theory is that it capitalises on egoistic-rational maximisation of utility. But human behaviour is not only guided by an orientation on personal utility, but also influenced by institutions. These define an actor's position among other actors, and may give him certain rights and obligations. When rational choice theory does include institutions into the analysis, it tends to treat them as external restrictions. This way, institutions are linked to the Weberian category of normative action, and individual actors to the category of goal-rationality behaviour. But actors do not exclusively use the scope left by institutions to maximise their own utility, and institutions may prescribe utility maximising behaviour as appropriate. Thus, one cannot strictly say which type of rationality stems from which source. Actors have both a self-orientation and an orientation to a collectivity to which they belong. As actors usually participate in more than one collectivity, there can not only be conflict between self-orientation and group-orientation, but also between orientations of different groups. Therefore, it is important to check empirically which orientation is actually decisive for particular actions. And finally, human behaviour is not merely influenced by personal utility and by the relevant institutional context at that time, but also by socialisation and history. The next section will show how incorporating these insights leads to a fundamentally different approach to markets.

This version of governance theory helps us to resolve the confusion surrounding differences in labels and in underlying dimensions from which the types are supposedly derived. This confusion stems from the attempt to define the types as in some sense posing a monopoly on a certain kind of behavioural category - competition, co-operation and authority. Such efforts are bound to fail, as the same relations/interactions/transactions can simultaneously have competitive, co-operative and authoritative aspects. An actor can voluntarily co-operate with a competitor, but (as the notion of market leadership shows) such voluntary co-operation between individual actors may include differences in power and hence give one leverage over the other. If we pick a particular market to analyse, all other governance mechanisms simultaneously are collective actors. Each of these collective actors entails a particular combination of co-operation and authority. The typology of Van Waarden (1997) and its legitimisation in effect tries to define these four "collective actor" governance mechanisms by the nature of the co-operation within them: formal or informal, and public or private, legal status. It goes wrong in attempting to interpret these four governance mechanism as one unique combination of scores on these three dimensions. For instance, labelling the state as vertical denies its horizontal and thus associational character that is the result of democratic parliamentary elections. This latter aspect of the state is often referred to as a 'community'. But these two aspects are inherently connected and should not be separated in this typology. This, by the way, is exactly the reason why I prefer to label the fifth governance mechanisms 'networks' rather than 'community'[2]. Similar remarks can be made for associations, hierarchies and networks. For instance, labelling associations as private neglects that they often perform public functions which the state has installed in them (Streeck, 1992); the same goes for hierarchies (e.g. publicly funded private schools!). And associations are not exclusively horizontal; they not only have a 'logic of membership' but also a 'logic of influence'. They may use the argument of gaining political influence to get their members to agree with decisions that fail to fully maximise these member's personal utility. Hierarchies are, on the other hand, not exclusively vertical; the rise of teams in the organisation of production introduces an associational aspect.

This way, the five-part typology of governance mechanisms cannot only be used to distinguish which actors operate in a particular market, but also to analyse the particular character of the collective actors within this market as governance mechanisms in their own right. For instance, one can first

---

[2]. I prefer 'networks' to 'clans' as the former is most neutral in this respect, while the latter also evokes a community image to some extent, due to its roots in the study of non-western societies in cultural anthropology.

ascertain that employers' associations are important actors in a particular labour market, and then ascertain that these appear to have a considerable amount of hierarchical control over their members (or not). When it is necessary to include two (or more) levels of analysis, this is an appropriate course of action, as long as one carefully distinguishes them from one another. In the previous example, the fact that these associations have a considerable amount of hierarchical control over their members does not mean that they should be analysed as hierarchies. They are and should be studied as associations. But the fact that they have a considerable amount of hierarchical control over their members is important to explain why they may choose one particular course of action rather than another (to which an association with considerably less hierarchical control might be inclined). The point is that collective actors actions are not only influenced by the incentive structure they face in the external market, but also by political processes on their internal market. To give another example, if one treats Dutch VET schools as 'black boxes' (as the Dutch research project discussed in section 3 did) one does not adequately realise that these may adopt basically different policies. For instance, they may capitalise on apprenticeship tracks or school-based tracks in their policies. Surely, to an important extent they will choose between these two different strategies according to the opportunities and constraints offered by their external environment (e.g. whether firms are willing to supply apprenticeship positions). But to some extent, they are also the result of internal political processes. Teachers may fear that an apprenticeship strategy may endanger their job security in the long run. The internal political process in a school may subsequently lead to the adoption of a school-based strategy, even if external incentives would appear to make an apprenticeship strategy more attractive.

To conclude, empirical markets differ in the mix of governance mechanisms that governs them, as well as in the particular operation of any of these. This implies that it is crucial to *empirically* ascertain which mix of governance mechanisms actually governs a particular market or field. To allow such empirical analysis, governance theory puts forward the notion of governance *regimes*. Regimes of economic governance differ in the way in which these five elements are configured (Hollingsworth and Streeck, 1994, p. 270). The object of comparative, empirical research is to determine the relative importance of the various types of governance mechanisms in different contexts, to describe how they are articulated with one another, and to assess the extent and direction of change in regimes over time (Hollingsworth et al, 1994b, p. 8). Regimes of economic governance vary with spatial-territorial location as well as between functional-economic sectors (Hollingsworth and Streeck, 1994, p.271). Variance by location is a consequence of the fact that social institutions are rooted in local, regional and/or national political communities. Variance by sector is caused by the fact that each sector has specific technological and economic properties, which influence its industrial organisation. Just as sectoral differences in technology and market conditions give rise to differences in industrial order within countries, national differences produce different governance regimes within similar sectors in different countries.

It is possible to agree with proponents of the three-part typology of markets, hierarchies and the state that it may be superfluous for each individual research project to include the other two governance mechanisms to track down the basic aspects of a particular governance regime. It is contended, however, that this choice needs to be based on solid theoretical and empirical arguments, which means that the five-part typology is the appropriate benchmark against which any deviation should be measured. It is also contended that with VET it is crucial to include at least associations and possibly networks into the analysis because of their important role in current VET markets. This point will be elaborated in the next section.

6.   A GOVERNANCE APPROACH TO VET
MARKETS

From the perspective of governance theory, VET is not exclusively provided through the market. It is crystal-clear that VET requires a (often formal, but at least informal) training contract that binds a trainee to one or more training organisations(s), a firm or a school. This implies that there is (at least in an analytical sense) a market where both parties search for one another to conclude such contracts. But the organisation of such markets differs between countries. I doubt, for instance, that any German research would use a similar approach to analyse its market for intermediate skills as the one used in the Dutch research discussed in section 3. The supply-side of the German market is dominated by firms that offer apprenticeship positions to youth, which would imply that German research would confine itself to firms rather than schools if it would choose to narrow its analysis of the supply-side down to one type of actor. In addition, it is doubtful whether any German policymaker would see a lack of competition among these training suppliers as an important problem. Even if youth have already narrowed down their choice for a training firm to one specific occupation, there are various training firms within their region that offer apprenticeship positions for this occupation, and where they can - and typically do - apply.

The important insight that governance theory has to offer is that the specific mix of (collective) actors that populate a particular market influences the way it operates. So do the orientations of these actors, influenced by their history and socialisation. As a consequence, any market analysis should spell out the types of actors populating them and their specific orientation, as well as the incentive structure that it should constitute for each type of actor. Fligstein (1996) offers an approach to markets that meets this framework of governance theory. He calls this a political-cultural approach. He uses the metaphor 'markets as politics' to create a sociological view of action in markets (Fligstein, 1996, p. 656). This metaphor has a double meaning. First, it sees the formation of markets as part of state-building. Second, it sees markets as reflecting two kinds of political processes: within the organisations that participate on the market, and across these organisations. Fligstein proposes the idea of a 'conception of control' to summarise the core orientation of actors in a market. By this, he means (Fligstein, 1996, p 658):

> "...understandings that structure perceptions of how a market works and that allows their actors to interpret their world and act to control situations. A conception of control is simultaneously a worldview that allows actors to interpret the actions of others and a reflection of how the

market is structured. Conceptions of control reflect market specific agreements between actors in firms on principles of internal organisation (forms of hierarchy), tactics for competition or co-operation, and the hierarchy or status ordering of firms in a given market. A conception of control can be thought of as 'local knowledge' (Geertz, 1980)".

Fligstein develops 16 propositions regarding markets. The first four of these do not necessarily imply a view of organisations that is limited to firms, and further clarify the difference between his political-cultural approach to markets and a rational choice or transaction cost approach (Fligstein, 1996, p. 661-662):

" *Proposition 1*: The entry of countries into capitalism pushes states to develop rules about property rights, governance structures, and rules of exchange in order to stabilise markets for the largest firms.

Proposition 2: Initial regulatory institutions shape the development of new markets because they produce cultural templates that affect how to organise.

Proposition 3: State actors are constantly attending to some form of crisis or another. This is because markets are always being organised or destabilised, and firms are lobbying for state interventions.

Proposition 4: Laws and accepted practices often reflect the interests of the most organised forces in society. These groups support wholesale transformations of institutions only under crisis circumstances like war, depression, or state collapse."

This political-cultural view of markets helps explain the fact that markets for intermediate skills show more or less stable national (and often regional) differences over time, as it brings in the notion of the path-dependency of national institutions and thus markets. This notion tells us that "History, so to speak, solidifies into structures which constrain future development." (Dosi, 1994, p. 12). To a large extent, such structures are organisations – hierarchies - that govern the actual provision of training itself. They do so within the constraints and opportunities offered by general and specific, formal and informal rules that guide their behaviour. These rules may be set by various actors; the state, employers' associations and unions are prime examples.

Dosi (1994, p. 11-12) lists seven reasons why one should expect path dependency by institutions, the first four of which he derives from David (1992):

1. they incorporate shared conventions and mutually consistent expectations grounded in shared historical reasons and conscious perceptions of the shared past;
2. they provide role-typing and acculturation mechanisms which is a sort of sunk capital of organisations;
3. they embody codes for communication and information processing;
4. the inter-relatedness of different organisational functions self-reinforces specific organisational structures;
5. there may occur a competency trap whereby increasing skill at the current procedures makes experimentation with alternatives less attractive (Levinthal, 1992);
6. organisational routines are by their very nature a source of organisational inertia;
7. entrenched, socially shared expectations underlie the reproduction over time of behavioural patterns.

The notion of path-dependency particularly applies to institutions concerning education and labour. These have developed quite separately across nations over the last centuries (De Swaan, 1989). This means that, on the one hand, organisational capacities for quality VET have developed quite differently across countries. In Germany, they are concentrated predominantly in firms; in most other countries, they are concentrated predominantly in schools. According to Dosi's fourth proposition, this means that even if the German dual system would be as superior as some have thought, other countries with a predominantly school-based educational history may be better off (at least in the short and intermediate run) by continuing this strategy. Various authors have in fact made such an argument, for instance in the context of the debate on the transferability of German-style institutions in this field to the U.K. (e.g. Soskice, 1994b; Wagner, 1997). On the other hand (and even more importantly) path-dependency implies that civic culture in various countries will have different expectations of how VET should be organised, and what rights and entitlements this should imply for various actors concerned. As these expectations will somehow be mirrored in voter choices in elections, the societal basis for various policies will also differ across nations. So will, as a consequence, the potential for implementation of various policies.

This all leads to the conclusion that one cannot adequately study a VET market without paying attention to the particular mix of actors that populate them, their 'conceptions of control', and the external institutions that influence them. This paper will conclude with a discussion of how each of the five governance mechanisms is important for VET, which actors should be distinguished in VET markets, and how each of the five governance mechanisms can contribute to macro efficiency, as well as endanger it.

Neo-classical economics attributes to *hierarchies* the possibility to increase efficiency through economies of scale and scope. This is as important in the production of vocational qualifications as with other types of production. As long as particular skills are important for a substantial group of individuals, it will be economic to co-ordinate their training. This is an important reason why we concentrate education in schools. These, then are a first type of hierarchy that is important for VET. Firms are a second type of hierarchy that is important. They also supply VET, be it as part of the formal educational system (apprenticeship or internship), in the form of formal post-initial training, or as informal on-the-job training. These various types of supply offer different advantages and disadvantages. To begin with, schools and firms have different advantages and disadvantages as suppliers of training. The advantage of schools is that they generally train (prospective) workers of more firms, which enables the achievement of economies of scale and scope in education and training that surpass those that are possible within, in particular, small and medium-sized, firms. The disadvantage is that schools will not be as keenly aware of the actual type of skills a prospective worker will need than a firm that will employ him/her. In this sense, firm-based training may increase efficiency by focussing the supply of skills. Firms will concentrate on training exactly for those skills that are directly necessary for the satisfactory accomplishment of a particular job. The danger of this is, however, that this leads to an under-supply of broader basic skills. As human capital may leave the firm, firms are less inclined to pay for the acquirement of such broad skills (Becker, 1993). This may limit the potential for intra- or inter-firm mobility of a worker, which does not contribute to an efficient operation of a labour market. Also, acquiring skills is cheapest when people do not have to be trained for them but learn them gradually along the way. Broader basic skills (also referred to as key qualifications) tend to be positively related with the potential for self-learning. Subsequently, it may be more efficient to substantially invest in the acquirement of such key qualifications early, in order to save on training costs later. As individuals and their parents may lack the necessary funds to pay for such training themselves, and may find it impossible or too risky to loan them, states tend to subsidise education and training for such skills in the initial education system.

In sum, firms and schools each have their benefits and disadvantages as suppliers of education and training. It is clear that we want individuals to start with the acquisition of broad basic skills in schools, and subsequently move on to firms for the acquirement of firm- and job-specific skills. The question is how the transition from one to the other can best be organised. Should youth directly move from full-time participation in schools to full-time employment in firms? Or is it better to include an intermediary period in which students/workers participate in both (an apprenticeship or internship)? Should schools concentrate on general education or should some of them also offer vocational education and training? Does the increasing speed with which the relevance of particular skills decay not necessitate either a more rapid change in the basic skills we teach in initial education and training, and/or substantial public investment in a basic skill update halfway through peoples' careers? Also, it is crucial to note that training offered by firms and by VET schools may be functionally equivalent. This implies that the more firms invest in the supply of broad skills, the less the state has to, and vice versa. This is why most countries envy Germany, where firms do substantially invest in broad-based training for a significant proportion of youth. But what balance in funding between the state and individual firms is most efficient? If firms have to fund all education and training themselves, this may damage their international competitiveness. But if the state too generously funds education and training, the same may happen due to the resulting tax burden on citizens and/or firms. And, as was pointed out before, the state may not be able to supply students with the right packages of skills. States that come up with the right answers to these questions will more substantially increase the efficiency of their VET market than those that merely stimulate efficiency by enlarging price-competition between schools.

But states have only a limited capacity to alter the behaviour of firms and schools. Note, for instance, that today VET schools in the Netherlands, Germany and the American state of Wisconsin share the characteristic that they supply both school-based VET and the related school-based instruction for apprenticeship tracks. National laws do not prescribe a particular balance between them. Nevertheless, apprenticeship tracks account for the large majority of student enrolment at German 'berufliche Schulen' and school-based tracks for the large majority at Wisconsin's technical colleges. The Netherlands finds itself somewhere in between, with apprenticeship accounting for about a third of total enrolment. While differences in state policies may offer an important explanation for these differences, differences in firms' 'conceptions of control' regarding training appear the more important factor. Comparative research shows important international differences in the organisation of labour in matched plants in various economic sectors (Prais, 1995a; 1995b; Mason and Finegold, 1996; Wagner and Finegold, forthcoming).

Associations can also increase efficiency in VET markets. The role of unions and employers associations has rightfully gained prominence in the European conception of VET markets through a series of 12 national casestudies sponsored by CEDEFOP. The German case-study has probably attracted most interest, both because of the importance of German unions and employers associations for the governance of training and because of its theoretical soundness (Streeck et al, 1987). Streeck et al. (1987, p. 4) distinguish four basic ways in which associations are directly involved with initial VET and with post-initial training in Germany:

- regulation: the determination of objectives, subjects and standards of training;
- financing: the mobilisation of financial resources for training;
- implementation and administration;
- supervision and control.

In addition, employers' associations and unions are indirectly involved in the operation of the German VET market. They jointly negotiate binding minimum wage levels for their members in collective bargaining agreements, which are typically extended to non-members in the same sector. Soskice (1994a) points out that it is exactly these high wages that necessitate larger and international firms to effectively train their new recruits in order to allow them to acquire a high level of productivity that warrants these high wages. At the same time, the comparatively low apprenticeship wages make it worthwhile to direct an important share of firms' training investments to apprentices rather than to regular workers, as the formers lower wages helps to keep down training costs.

Similar advantages and disadvantages may also stem from *networks*. The prime difference between networks and associations is whether co-operation is formalised in an organisation, which may have the means to force compliance of its members to collective decisions. Such a safeguard may be an important reason why associations might be a preferred form of co-operation among firms when it comes to the actual supply of training, because of the need to limit the risk of poaching of trainees. An association may use informal or formal means to discourage such poaching among its members; networks are more likely to lack such an authority. On the other hand, Japanese networks of firms do not appear to have suffered from substantial poaching due to the culture of life-time employment. And, networking between firms allows for co-operation over the boundaries of specific associations that may lead to additional benefits (e.g. sharing of facilities). Networks of workers may increase efficiency by easing the re-employment of unemployed workers, as they can inform them of relevant vacancies, and employers of skilled applicants, and thus help to combat information problems in the labour market. But this may also lead to inequality and inefficiency, in that it favours insiders over outsiders. For instance, it is sometimes considered a disadvantage of apprenticeship that it is not equally accessible for all youth. Relatives and friends of already employed workers often have a better chance of acquiring an apprenticeship position. German firms, for instance, sometimes show a certain preference to hire children of their workers ('Mitarbeiter-Kinder' or 'Miki's') and customers ('Kunden-Kinder' or 'Kuki's') as apprentices.

Within a neo-classical framework, the *state* is usually already attributed various responsibilities regarding the provision of VET. It should guarantee a satisfactory operation of the market mechanism in VET, and it should take care of some tasks (e.g. the funding of initial education and training) itself. The range of possible and legitimate state interventions is even larger within the context of governance theory. It can not only be held responsible for its direct intervention in VET and for the satisfactory operation of the market mechanism, but also for the satisfactory operation of the other three governance mechanisms - hierarchies, associations and networks. As some examples of state intervention in these were already mentioned above, it is not necessary to further elaborate here.

Put differently, we can say that the state is responsible for the choice of how the VET *market* should actually operate. The recognition that various actors play important roles in such markets implies that market mechanisms can be present at various points and in various ways. For instance, the state can stimulate competition between firms, competition between schools, competition between both, and competition between associations to attract students to their tracks (or, for associations, to tracks within their sector). But schools can also compete for other reasons (for instance to achieve the optimum supply of skilled workers for the regional labour market) and along different dimensions (the quality of their training). In addition, they may interpret such benchmarks in various ways.

This five-part typology provides a much more suitable basis for an analysis of the operation of VET markets and possibilities for its improvement than the (more or less implicit) framework used in the Dutch report criticised in section 3. VET markets are more complicated than that report would have it; hence, more options exist for its improvement. Most neo-classical analyses neglect some (though many fare better than the Dutch report). This is not only a weakness in itself; it also has repercussions for the analysis of the remaining governance mechanisms it does consider (such as the market). Increased school competition is indeed a policy option to consider. But realising that most skill acquisition takes place in firms should point policy makers in the direction of other questions and options that, at the dawn of the 21st century, seem more important. First and foremost, they have to realise that market mechanisms in general and competition in particular operate quite differently in markets where firms are the most important actor than in those where schools are.

How to stimulate firm-sponsored training? How to achieve life-long learning? Surely, neo-classical economics has very important insights to contribute to these and other questions. But the important advantage governance theory has to offer, is that it allows the incorporation of such insights, while connecting them with insights from other scientific branches. The recent changes within neo-classical economics itself help to ease this process. Perhaps one day the twain shall meet.

REFERENCES

Axelrod, R. (1984), *The evolution of co-operation*, Basic Books, New York.
Becker, G. (1964), *Human capital. A theoretical and empirical analysis, with special reference to education*, The University of Chicago Press, Chicago, IL/London.
Campbell, J., Hollingsworth, J.R. and Lindberg, L. (Eds.) (1991), *Governance of the American economy*, Cambridge University Press, Cambridge.
Coase, R. (1937), "The nature of the firm" *Econometrica* 4, pp.386-405.
Cohen, J. and Rogers, J. (1992), "Democratic governance and secondary associations" *Politics and Society*, pp.393-472.
CEREQ (1994), *Apprenticeship: which way forward?*
David, P. (1992), "Why are institutions the carriers of history? Notes on path-dependency and the evolution of conventions, organisations and institutions", working paper, Stanford University, Department of Economics, Stanford.
Dosi, G. (1995), "Hierarchies, markets and power: foundational issues on the nature of contemporary economic organisation", *Industrial and corporate change*, Vol.4, No.1, pp.1-19.
Finegold, D. (1991), "Institutional incentives and skill creation: preconditions for a high-skill equilibrium" in Ryan, P. (Ed.), *International comparisons of vocational education and training for intermediate skills*, The Falmer Press, London/New York/Philadelphia, pp.93-116.
Finegold, D. and Mason, G. (1996), "National training systems and industrial performance: US-European matched-plant comparisons", ILR-Cornell Institute for Labour Market Policies Conference. Paper presented at the ILR-Cornell Institute for Labour Market Policies Conference 'New empirical research on employer training: Who pays? Who benefits?' Cornell University, November 15-17, 1996, Ithaca, NY.
Fligstein, N. (1996) "Markets as politics. A political-cultural approach to market institutions" *American sociological review*, Vol.61, No.8, pp.656-673.
Freeman, R. (1976), *The overeducated American*, Academic Press, New York.
Geertz, C. (1983), *Local Knowledge*, Basic Books, New York.
Granovetter, M. (1985), "Economic action and social structure: the problem of embeddedness", *American journal of sociology*, Vol.91, No.3, pp. 481-510.
Hartog, J. (1985), "Overscholing?" *Economisch statistische berichten*, Vol.13, No.2, pp.152-156.
Hodgson, G. (1988), *Economics and institutions. A manifesto for a modern institutional economics*, Polity Press, Oxford.
Hollingsworth, J.R. (1991), "Die Logik der Koordination des verarbeitendes Gewerbes in Amerika" *Kölner Zeitschrift für Soziologie und Sozialpsychologie*, Vol.43, No.1, pp.18-43.
Hollingsworth, J.R., Schmitter, P. and Streeck, W. (Eds.) (1994a), *Governing capitalist economies. Performance & control of economic sectors*, Oxford University Press, New York/Oxford.
Hollingsworth, J.R., Schmitter, P. and Streeck, W. (1994b), "Capitalism, sectors, institutions, and performance", in Hollingsworth, J.R., Schmitter, P and Streeck, W. (Eds.), *Governing capitalist economies. Performance and control of economic sectors*, Oxford University Press, New York/Oxford, pp. 3-16.
Hollingsworth, J.R. and Streeck, W. (1994c), "Countries and sectors. Concluding remarks on performance, convergence and competitiveness", in Hollingsworth, J.R., Schmitter, P. and Streeck, W. (Eds.), *Governing capitalist economies. Performance and control of economic sectors*, Oxford University Press, New York/Oxford, pp. 270-297.

Jager, G. de (1996), "Werkt de markt voor beroepsonderwijs?", in Gerbrands, P. and Oudshoorn, C. (Eds.), *De toekomst van het secundair en tertiair beroepsonderwijs*, OCFEB, Rotterdam, pp.4-11.

Kuipers, M. (1996), "Marktwerking in het secundair en tertiair beroepsonderwijs: een particuliere visie", in Gerbrandsd, P. and Oudshoorn, C. (Eds.), *De toekomst van het secundair en tertiair beroepsonderwijs*, Rotterdam, pp.12-17.

Levinthal, D. (1992), "Surviving Schumpeterian environments: an evolutionary perspective", *Industrial and corporate change*, Vol.1, No.2, pp.417-443.

Lieshout, H. van. (1996), "Governance of vocational education and training. A comparison of apprenticeship Systems in (West) Germany and Wisconsin (U.S.)", paper presented at the WESWA Conference, Utrecht, 12/13 November 1996, Utrecht, AWSB Netherlands School of Social and Economic Policy Research.

Lieshout, H. van (1997), *Een internationale vergelijking van de school-to-work transition in Nederland, Duitsland, de VS en Japan*, Utrecht University, AWSB Netherlands School for Social and Economic Policy Research, Utrecht.

Lindberg, L., Campbell, J. and Hollingsworth, J.R. (1991), "Economic governance and the analysis of structural change in the American economy", in Campbell, J. Hollingsworth, J.R. and Lindberg, L. (Eds.), *Governance of the American economy*, Cambridge University Press, Cambridge, pp.3-34.

March, J. and Olsen, J. (1989), *Rediscovering institutions. The organizational basis of politics*, The Free press, New York.

Mason, G. and Finegold, D. (1995), *Productivity, machinery and skills in the United States and Western Europe: precision engineering*, National Institute of Economic and Social Research. London.

Mayntz, R. and Scharpf, F. (Eds.) (1995), *Gesellschaftliche Selbstregelung und politische Steuerung,*. Campus, Frankfurt/New York.

Merton, R. (1968), *Social theory and social structure*, New York: The Free Press.

North, D. (1981), *Structure and change in economic history*, Norton, New York.

Open Overleg Wagner (1984), *Op weg naar een gezamenlijk verantwoordelijkheid. Eindrapport van het Open Overleg inzake de voorstellen van de commissie Wagner inzake het beroepsonderwijs*, 's-Gravenhage.

Parsons, T. (1951), *The social system*, The Free Press, Glencoe.

PEIL (1996), *Op het kruispunt van leerwegen. Eindrapport en advies van het Projectteam Extra Impuls Leerlingwezen*, PEIL, Rijswijk.

Powell, W. and DiMaggio, P. (Eds.) (1991), *The new institutionalism in organizational analysis*, University of Chicago Press, Chicago.

Prais, S. (Ed.) (1995a), *Productivity, education and training: Britain and other countries compared*, National Institute for Economic and Social Research, London.

Prais, S. (Ed.) (1995b), *Productivity, education and training: an international perspective*, National Institute for Economic and Social Research, London.

Ryan, P. (Ed.), *International comparisons of vocational education and training for intermediate skills*, Thew Falmer Press, London/New York/Philadelhia.

Soskice, D. (1994a), "Reconciling markets and institutions: the German apprenticeship system", in Lynch, L. (Ed.), *Training and the private sector. International comparisons*, University of Chicago Press, Chicago/London, pp.25-60.

Soskice, D. (1994b), "Social skills from mass higher education: rethinking the company-based paradigm", *Oxford review of economic policy*, Vol.9, No.3, pp.101-113.

Stern, D. & Ritzen, J. (Eds.) (1991), *Market failure in training? New economic analysis and evidence on training of adult employees*, Springer, Berlin.

Streeck (1992), *Social institutions and economic performance. Studies of industrial relations in advanced capitalist economies*, SAGE, London.

Streeck, W., Hilbert, J., Kevelaer, K.H. van, Maier, F. and Weber, H. (1987), *The role of social partners in vocational training and further training in the Federal Republic of Germany*, CEDEFOP, Berlin.

Streeck, W. and Schmitter, P. (1985), *Private interest government: beyond market and state*, SAGE, London/Beverly Hills.

Swaan, A. de (1988), *In care of the state. Health care, education and welfare in Europe and the USA in the modern era*, Uitgeverij Bert Bakker, Amsterdam.

Theeuwes, J.(1993), "Het rendement van scholing en training" *Economisch statistische berichten* 78 (3928), pp.845-849.

Tijdelijke adviescommissie Onderwijs-Arbeidsmarkt (1990), *Onderwijs-arbeidsmarkt: naar een werkzaam traject*, Samson H.D, Tjeenk Willink, Alphen aan den Rijn.

Vrancken, P. and Kemp, A. de (1996), *Marktwerking in het secundair en tertiair beroepsonderwijs. Een verkenning*, Ministerie van Economische Zaken, s'Gravenhage..

Waarden, F. van (1997), "Vakopleiding in de procesindustrie een collectief goed?", in Opleidingsfonds Procesindustrie (Ed.), *Een reisje langs de Rijn. Visies op organisatie en financiering van opleiden in de procesindustrie*, Opleidingsfonds Procesindustrie, Haarlem, pp.73-91.

Wagner, K. (1997), "Costs and other challenges for the German apprenticeship system after unification", paper presented at the EU Conference on Knowledge Production and Dissemination to Business and the Labour Market organised by the Max Goote Expertisecenter, Amsterdam, 23-25 April.

Wagner, K. and Finegold, D. (1997), "Der Einfluss der Aus- und Weiterbildung auf die Arbeitsorganisation - eine Untersuchung in der Fertigung US-amerikanisher Maschinenbauunternehmen", Unpublished manuscript.

Wallace, R. and Wolf, A. *Contemporary sociological theory. Continuing the classical tradition*, 2nd Edition, Prentice Hall, Englewood Cliffs.

Williamson, O. (1975), *Markets and hierarchies: analysis and antitrust implications*, The Free Press, New York.

Williamson, O. (1985), *The economic institutions of capitalism. Firms, markets, relational contracting*, The Free Press, New York.

Chapter 5

Market and Institutional Patterns in the Development and Activities of the French Vocational Training System

Elsa Perzonnaz and Phillipe Méhaut
French Centre for Research and Qualification(CEREQ)

1. VOCATIONAL EDUCATION AND TRAINING IN FRANCE

In the past twenty-five years vocational training has experienced significant growth in France, stimulated in part by business demand and also by demand from the public sector through its unemployment policies. In response, a supply has developed, combining players from the public and private, profit-making and non-profit-making sectors. How is the vocational training sector organised? Can it be analysed as a quasi market (Glennerster, 1991)? These are the main issues discussed in this paper. It is based on a survey conducted in 1993 by the Cereq using a representative sample of the largest training companies in France (those with an annual turnover greater than one million French francs). Consequently, the analysis below does not take into consideration individual trainers or 'small' training organisations, although it is known that numerically they are a majority of training organisations yet account for only about 20% of the sector's activity.

After examining how relationships between training organisations and various categories of those seeking training are organised we shall analyse the principal characteristics of the training organisations and then their activities before formulating a few hypotheses about such a market's functioning.

2.   DEMAND AND ITS RELATIONSHIPS TO SUPPLY

2.1   Definitions and field of study

First of all, we must specify what we call further vocational training. It is all the training activities for professional or non-professional purposes that affect:
– young people, who have left school but do receive a professional
   insertion assistance through government measures (apprenticeships
   excluded);
– adults, consisting of unemployed or non-working people who benefit
   from government training measures assisting them in going back to work
   (women wanting to go back to work again for example) or in their exit
   from unemployment;
– those undertaking training at their own initiative or on that of their
   employers. In the former situation, some of them receive support from
   government sources or mutual benefit funds (for example within the
   framework of individual training leave).

Then we should not forget to mention a particular point of the French institutional setting concerning private enterprises. Since 1971, they have been required to allocate funds to training their employees based on a certain percentage of their labour costs. At the present time, this legal obligation is 1.5%, but on an average, companies spend 3.3%. There exist, however, great disparities depending on company size and the sector (Bentabet & Zygmunt, 1996). Beyond the obligation to provide financial support for training, businesses are free to choose the procedures that determine and implement their training policies, subject to consultation with works councils. They may choose the categories of employees to receive training and decide whether the training takes place through an in-house department or is provided through services purchased from an outside provider. Similar procedures exist in the public sector whether the employer is the French State or a public hospital for example. Furthermore, companies may partially discharge their obligation by contributing to mutual benefit insurance organisations, most often on an equally shared basis, that behave like 'assurance funds'.

Over the long term, in-house training has declined, with an increase in the purchase of outside training services. Hence, vocational professional training, like other service activities, is becoming out-sourced, a process that goes hand in hand with the development of market exchange. In the following pages, our analysis of the supply will be limited to its transactions which result in a market or quasi-market relationship between training organisations and one or more organisations seeking training, thus excluding in-house company training.

2.2   Market exchange and the service relationship

In the last years, debate about the nature of certain service activities has grown, particularly for those services dependent on personal relationships. Aside from the issue of the product's physical substance, two guiding themes emerge (Gadrey & De Bandt, 1994). On the one hand, there is the idea of co-production: certain service activities can not be conceived without a strong two-way relationship between the service provider and the client, who is involved not only in defining the product but also in developing it. This co-production presupposes that a relationship of trust is established and often militates against product standardisation. Furthermore, the uncertainty of the 'result' is stressed. This uncertainty about the result may explain the interest in in-house training and also the client's search for a permanent relationship or institutional mediation, in order to be able to reduce this uncertainty. Hence, the debate is less centred on the virtues of the market as a 'normative' principle that one often finds in political declarations and more on the effectiveness of constructs that are not shaped purely by the market as the term is traditionally understood or are based on other regulations.

The nature of the buyer-seller relationship (or market relationship) established and those involved will vary considerably depending on the originator of the demand and the financing of the training. And the service relationship (trainer/trainee) could be partly disconnected from the market relationship. Let us look at the most frequent situations.

2.2.1   Demand from individuals

- Situation no. 1. A self-financed demand (financing by an individual or an individual training voucher still quite rare in France) places the market relationship and the service relationship in direct contact.

- Situation no. 2. A demand financed by a third party (insurance funds in the case of individual training sabbaticals, for example, or training costs borne by a government agency for unemployed people). The service and market relationships are separated.

2.2.2   Demand from companies (or the French State as employer)

- Situation no. 3. The presence of a company immediately sets up a triangular relationship with a market relationship between the company and the training organisation and a service relationship between the training organisation and the trainees/company.

- Situation no. 4. This relationship can become more complex when a "third party payer" is brought into it as with insurance funds.

2.2.3   The 'public' demand

This demand is found mainly among government-aided clienteles, essentially job seekers. In most of these situations, the relationship is triangular, but it can also be set up by very different mechanisms:

- Situation no. 5. A set grant to a training organisation (frequently a public provider) in order to provide free or almost free training (without prior bidding among training providers for the grant).

- Situation no. 6. Set financing based on bids in which the training organisations compete to receive the set sum and then provide free or almost free training.

- Situation no. 7. Mutual agreement, which close to situation no. 3.

MARKET RELATIONSHIP IN DIRECT CONTACT

Situation N° 1

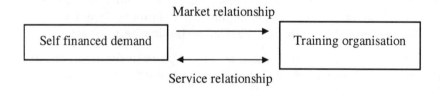

Situartion N° 3

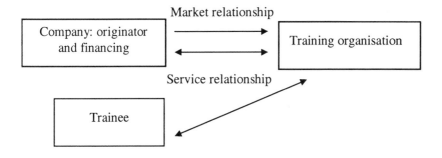

Situation N° 7

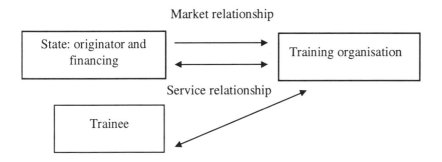

MARKET RELATIONSHIP WITH THIRD-PARTY

Situation N° 2

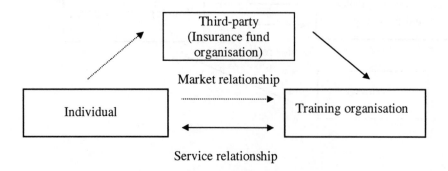

Situation N° 4

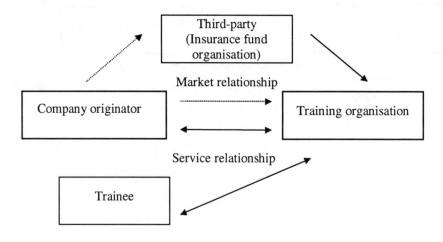

Situation N° 6

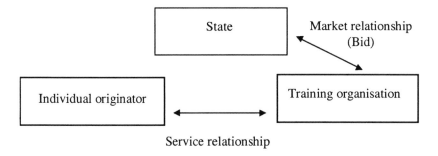

ADMINISTRATED RELATIONSHIP

Situation N° 5

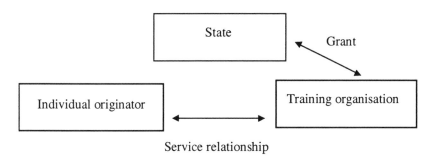

Figure 1. Service and buyer-seller relationship

As we can observe, the nature of the relationships varies considerably depending on the specific situations. The 'buyer-seller' relationship can range from the 'traditional' market relationship (situations no. 1, 2 or 7), to a regulated relationship (situation no. 5). But this relationship can bring in a 'paying third party' (situations no. 2, 4 and 6) that may not be neutral in the choice of the training organisation. Some insurance fund organisations, for example, have networks of preferred training organisations and can bring their weight to bear on the company's selection of a training company (for example in situation no. 4).

If we were to pick out the dominant trends, we could say that:

–   for the demand from individuals, situation no. 2 predominates with an
    attempt to develop situation no. 1, a voucher system;
–   for the demand from companies, situation no. 3 predominates, especially
    for large organisations. Situation no. 4 is rather more developed for small
    companies;
–   for the public demand, the trend is away from situation no. 5 towards
    situations no. 6 and no. 7.

3.   PATTERNS IN SETTING UP AND DEVELOPING
A TRAINING SUPPLY SYSTEM

The rapid growth of funds available for further vocational training
brought about by the 1971 law and the French State's heavy involvement in
this area has encouraged the gradual development of a training system
characterised by strong growth in the number of training organisations. At
the end of the 1980s, the number of active organisations increased from
17,000 in 1989 to 32,000 in 1993. These organisations are characterised by
their heterogeneity in terms of legal status, size and types of activity, all of
which contribute to an unclear and complex picture of vocational training in
France.

The training system, such as it presently exists, is not only the product of
this growth of funding, but is based on a heritage of vocational training
policies and practices predating the 1971 law. These practices were based
mainly on acquiring basic and cultural knowledge and technical expertise.
Although the first initiatives in this direction were taken in public
establishments, the spread of these objectives then presupposed the support
of associations and institutions, which were for the most part of religious,
trade-union or humanitarian. For this reason, among the 20% of the
organisations created before the 1971 law, we note a clear majority of public
and associate organisations.

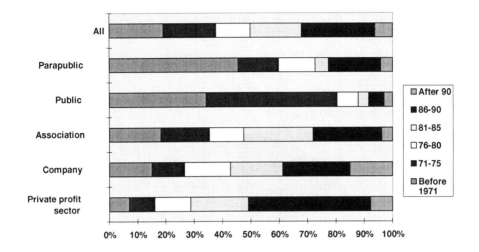

Figure 2. Distribution of organisations by creation date and type

Although the law stimulated vocational training policies in companies during the first half of the 1970's, expenses stabilised in 1976 and increased again only at the beginning of the 1980s, propelled by the largest companies, which were providing the most training. The funds allocated by companies to vocational training increased from 2.8 billion francs (in current francs) in 1972 to 44.5 billion francs in 1994. Expenses for outside training supporting this training market were 35% of this figure at the end of the 1970's and have reached 45% today. Hence the growth in expenses has gone hand in hand with a process of outsourcing thus stimulating development of the market.

A similar growth of vocational training expenditure by the public authorities, concentrated on managing unemployment and in particular on the social and professional insertion of young or adult job seekers, has also been observed. Thus, the expenditures of the French State (and the Regions since 1983) have increased from 1.7 billion francs in 1972 to 33.3 billion francs in 1994 (a little less than half of this figure is directly allocated to funding vocational training initiatives).

Based upon a foundation of older training practices, the vocational training system has developed in response to the growth of this demand and has been organised around a limited number of sectors, grouping together organisations with common characteristics, especially when considered in terms of the social institutions that control them. This diversity of institutions is also expressed by the fact that the majority of the organisations build their training capacity on other activities such as initial training, social initiatives, dissemination of cultural knowledge or even the production of goods and services.

Hence, five sectors can be identified (see Figure 3):

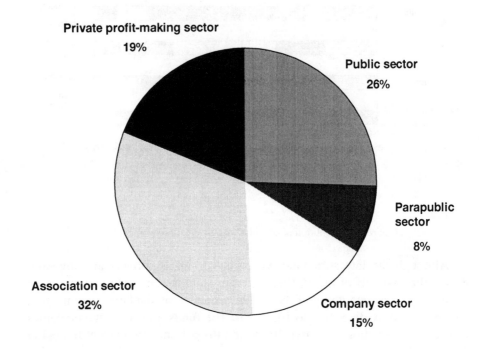

Figure 3. Distribution of global turnover by type

3.1.1   The public sector

This sector contains all the organisations under the control of public authorities exercised through various ministries. Among those involved are the Ministry of Education (vocational training centres associated with groups of lycées), the Ministry of Labour (AFPA), the Ministry of Agriculture and also regional government agencies. The high percentage of organisations created during the period directly after the 1971 law attests to the French State's strong commitment to be involved as a provider of vocational training. But this impulse to create organisations declined markedly beginning in the middle of the 1970s when the State positioned itself more as a financing agent than a direct provider.

The organisations in this sector generate a little less than one quarter of the total turnover.

3.1.2   The quasi-public sector

This sector groups together the Chambers of Commerce and Industry, and the chambers of agriculture and trades. Initial training, like vocational training, for the artisan, industrial and market sector is one of the traditional vocations of these quasi-public institutions. In a large part, they were created before the 1971 law. The Chambers of Commerce and Industry were also able to create, more recently, organisations that they control but that are devoted exclusively to vocational training.

The organisations of this sector generate a little less than 10% of the sector's total turnover.

3.1.3   The company sector

Part of this sector consists of employer organisations, inter-professional organisations or professional organisations and the other part of associations created or controlled by one or more companies. These associations are generally in a process of out-sourcing training in their former internal centres. The first group appeared during the 1960s with the involvement of professions in the training process of their employees, but their involvement really began when they started the practice of putting their resources into insurance funds for vocational training. The creation of ASFO (Associations for Training) was a part of this movement. The establishment of alternating work-study programmes at the beginning of the 1980s also explains the relatively strong growth of organisations in this sector from this period onwards.

The organisations of this sector generate about 15% of the total turnover.

3.1.4   The association sector

The organisations in this sector are generally involved in political, social, religious or trade union movements spread throughout France and maintain strong ties with their founding principles. Some were already present before 1975, but most of them were created in the series of measures taken to deal with unemployment after 1980. Organisations with this legal status that have not-for-profit but no ideological orientation are also included in this sector.

This sector is the largest with 38% of the organisations and 32% of the turnover.

3.1.5   The private profit-making sector

This set of organisations is the most heterogeneous and is composed of organisations that legally are limited liability companies and have developed training as their sole or an additional activity. Half of them were created after 1986, following the increase in funds going into vocational training. This sector also has a high turnover with many organisations created but few surviving over the long term.

This sector accounts for 19 % of the total turnover.

4.   THE CHARACTERISTICS OF THE PRODUCERS

4.1   Low concentration reduces clear understanding of the supply situation

Vocational training suppliers are quite numerous in France. But the business sector that they constitute is also extremely unconcentrated. Eighty-two percent report an annual turnover of less that one million French francs and only generate about 20% of the total turnover, which, in 1993, came to 33.8 billion French francs.

Remember that these organisations are not included in the survey that produced the data and conclusions below.

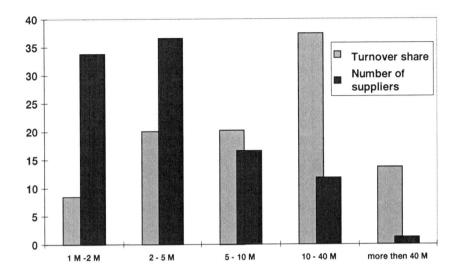

Figure 4. Concentration degree

The low concentration of the sector also is found with organisations generating a turnover of more than one million French francs. Three-quarters of these organisations generate turnovers of less than 9.5 million French francs. The concentration is the lowest for organisations in the association sector and the private, profit-making sector, although the largest organisations are also found in the latter sector. The organisations in the public and quasi-public sectors are substantially larger and are strongly represented in the 5 to 10 million franc and 10 to 40 million franc categories.

The large number of small-sized organisations in the market is an additional factor in reducing clarity in the supply situation and increases the uncertainty about product quality. The existence of more or less formal networks among the organisations is one way by which these organisations increase their visibility. These networks develop common training methods and one of their main objectives is the development of common criteria for training service quality.

A trend towards organising the sector professionally in the form of initiatives by the service providers structuring the sector is taking shape along the same objectives. The Federation of Professional Training, an employer organisation of private training organisations was created in 1991. A collective bargaining agreement for training organisations was signed in

1988, standardising the labour market and working conditions. At the same time, the use of charters, quality labels and official quality standards (ISO standards or network or internal charters) has been developing. The main challenge is to clarify the situation of the supply, which is trying to come to grips with the growing number of providers and also to overcome the co-ordination difficulties between providers and decision makers.

4.2   Vocational training as a supplementary activity

Vocational training does not constitute the sole or main activity of many organisations. Hence, the vocational training system mixes both companies specialised in vocational training with various economic and social institutions whose main business activity is not vocational training.

Less than half of the training organisations report vocational training as their sole activity. This percentage is substantially the same in every institutional category, except for government organisations in which the figure is 60%. Some organisations, by their vocation, are active in many areas. This is the case, for example, for the Chambers of Trades, which maintain consulting and management activities for self-employed tradesmen.

The idea of vocational training as a combined product covers, however, two distinct aspects. The first aspect applies to the training organisation in the narrow meaning of the term, independently of its institutional environment. Vocational training activity is non-exclusive because the organisation has other business activities. The most common are consulting and management activities and human resources studies. Involved in several relatively close fields, this type of service company is common in the private profit-making sector. But additional activities may also involve initial training and personal services in the association sector, or more generally the production of good and services (in this respect, data processing is probably one of the most common). In the latter case and in extreme cases, training is a service that accompanies the sale of another product. The professional reputation of the organisation will then not be based first of all on vocational training but on its skills in another field from which it will rely to develop its training activity.

An organisation can nevertheless report vocational training activity as an exclusive activity and still rely on other resources in its immediate environment. This is the case of training services associated with lycées that have developed further vocational training in addition to existing initial training. This type of structure relies on internal resources such as the premises, the personnel and teaching and equipment. This is also the case for industrial companies that produce consumer goods or equipment and have out-sourced vocational training.

A clear grasp of the market will vary according to the activities developed by the organisations. Although we can not verify this assertion at this point in the survey, we can nevertheless formulate the hypothesis that three types of client-product relationships can be schematically identified:

- if vocational training is the sole activity of an organisation, the client will look for a professional provider of vocational training;
- if the training is a support activity for another activity in the organisation, the primary expertise of the organisation in its main activity will guide the buyer's choice;
- if the producer develops a set of service activities for companies in comprehensive human resources management, the client will then probably look for a comprehensive service and more customised training.

5.   CHARACTERISTICS OF THE ACTIVITY AND RELATIONSHIP TO THE DEMAND

One can then identify three forms of organisation for the supply/demand relationships. The first one is a pattern of specialisation by clienteles and financing. This provides the first approach to market mechanisms. A priori for example, an organisation totally dependent on funds from business will be more under immediate market pressure than an organisation totally dependent on government funds. A second pattern is one of specialisation by training content. There again, an approach by way of content provides an approximation of some of the pressures encountered in building relationships to demand (issues of standardisation, training customisation etc.). Finally we will try to formulate a few hypotheses about the ways in which trust is built between organisations and clients.

5.1   Unequal degrees of specialisation depending on the clienteles and financing

As we have seen, training funding come from two main clienteles: employers who want training for their own salaried personnel and public authorities working within the framework of pre-qualification and qualification policies and designed for professional insertion of the unemployed. Financing from individuals who directly finance their own training as individuals still remains relatively marginal, between 1.5% and 8% depending on the sector. Only certain organisations specialised in these training services have large amounts of funding from individuals.

Although the size of public and private financing is substantially equivalent on the whole, the situation is much less balanced when the survey results are examined by institutional category. In private organisations and company training centres, companies provide more than half the funds, closely associated with intra-company training programmes. In the private profit-making sector for example, private financing is more than 80% of the turnover for about 60% of the organisations.

As for the association sector, it is clearly dependent on government financing, developing in response to government policies for training and professional insertion of the unemployed. Hence, this sector fluctuates according to the French State's expenditure and policies. Termination of a programme can mean the end of many associate organisations.

Although we can note relatively strong specialisation in the types of financing, there is, however, no direct congruence between institutional categories and the funding agents. Government organisations, in particular, are not involved exclusively in public funds and tend also to solicit funding from businesses. Conversely, soliciting French State funds is common among profit-making organisations.

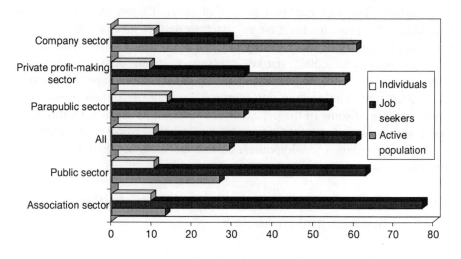

Figure 5. Distribution of trainee hours according to the beneficiary public situation on labour market

The proportion of the various financing generally follows the various clienteles. In terms of total numbers, the salaried clientele is the majority.

Trainee hours demonstrate, however, a predominance of job seekers in the overall organisation activity.

Variations appear between the numbers of trainees and the trainee-hours and financing, revealing big differences in the length and price of training programmes. The-trainee hour indicator seems to be the most accurate measurement of the activity volume of the organisations; the longest training programmes, often for the unemployed, can involve small numbers of individuals but account for a large proportion of organisation activity. But using this indicator introduces an incoherent element in studying funding agents. For example, job seekers account for a third of the trainee-hours in the private profit-making sector, a substantial proportion, but appear smaller when the funding structure is studied. These training programmes are substantially less expensive than those for salaried employees.

5.2   Specialities and training levels

The levels at which training programmes are delivered are also informative of the activities by institutional category. Consequently, the private profit-making sector, which is largely oriented towards training for salaried clienteles, combines this type of clientele with so called 'transversal' training programmes, which are not attached to a particular level and are typically foreign language or information technology programmes. Secondly these programmes deliver high level training for company managerial staff. Their content is more often oriented towards the administration and service sector (data processing, office automation, sales, management, communication, etc.).

Company sector organisations also serve a salaried clientele, but the training programmes are more for manufacturing workers and office workers. Although training programmes for the administration and service sector predominate, the large size of training programmes for production should be noted. Hence, these programmes are produced by organisations closely associated with a company environment and able to take advantage of equipment already on site or to make heavy investment.

On the other side is the association sector, which delivers training programmes for job seekers at a low training levels. These are frequently pre-qualification or refresher programmes, oriented towards personal development or personal services, specialities that fit into the framework of usual association activities.

The quasi-public and public sectors stand out for training a more diversified clientele, composed predominately of job seekers in government organisations and quasi-public organisation. The diversity of legal status is reproduced in terms of the level of the clienteles trained. As far as training specialities are concerned, there are production training programmes in the public sector and administration and services programmes for the quasi-public sector.

5.3   A tentative interpretation of the three training families

A factor analysis and a classification enable us to show forms of specialisation for the suppliers in certain market 'niches', defined along three lines: training speciality, clientele status and training level. Based on this analysis (Aventur et al., 1995) we can suggest the following ideas. Firstly personal development and professional insertion training programmes are provided by about 20% of all organisations. In this field, employer organisations are almost absent, and private ones very rare. However, as we have seen, a significant percentage of associations operate in this area. These programmes are directed towards individuals, most often unemployed and frequently obliged by public authorities to accept trainees on a permanent basis, which presupposes much customisation to individual demand. On the other hand, these programmes do not lead to certification (diplomas) any more than others and the organisations that do award them use quality procedures (ISO standards or quality charters) less. Standardisation, thus, appears to be weak. Given the characteristics of the applicants, who often have a low training levels and are experiencing professional or social adjustment difficulties, evaluating the quality of programmes is difficult. The relationships to the demand are most probably situations no. 6 and 7 (see chart 1), and the evaluation of quality (expertise, selection by bids, etc.) will be based for the most part on the power of the public sector.

Secondly, on the opposite side of the spectrum, foreign language and information technology training programmes are concentrated among private profit-making organisation. Private financing (mostly by employers) predominates. These training programmes can be grouped with management and sales training programmes. In this case also, the clienteles are largely composed of salaried employees (and thus financed for the most part by employers). There also, private profit-making organisations, company sector organisations and also the quasi-public sector are heavily involved. The training more frequently takes place in companies (one programme for a group of trainees from one company only) on the average. These organisations do not award diplomas as a rule. With the exception of language training programmes, they do not use quality standards very significantly either. The relationship to those seeking training is probably situations no. 3 and 4 (see chart 1). The model of standardisation is probably by the market, in which confidence is built on the one hand by experience and on the other by the reputation of the organisations, based perhaps on their other activities (services in the case of information technology, for example). Thirdly, training programmes for production techniques (automation and robotics), industrial transformation techniques (metallurgy, and plastics technology) for factory workers and skilled workers seem to be more diversified. They involve both salaried employees and job seekers. For salaried employees, these training programmes can take place either inside or outside companies. In both cases, the training organisations are relatively large compared to the organisations in the first two categories. This can be interpreted as an indication of the level of investment required (a barrier to entry) to conduct these training programmes. As a tendency, government organisations and organisations from the quasi-public and company sectors are over-represented for this type of programme, but all types of organisations deliver training. The use of official standards is more frequent whether diplomas or quality standards (ISO or charters). This area is one in which the nature of the training assumes certain technical equipment and consequently organisational stability. The relationship to the demand may mix various situations depending on the institutional category of the organisation. Confidence is built both on the reputation of the organisations as related, for example, to their initial training activity and the standardisation by official standards and/or institutional links to companies.

6.   CONCLUSION

In conclusion, it is appropriate first of all to stress the limits of the analysis presented above. Although certain indicators allow us to understand the heterogeneity of the training programme supply (in institutional terms, the nature of the supply and the relationship to financing), they enable us only indirectly to approach constructs of the supply/demand relationship, and especially the procedures used by potential clients to reduce the uncertainty about the 'result' of the service. These procedures may, though infrequently, be connected to the product (in the case of diploma-granting training programmes), the production process (through quality standards) or the establishment of long-lasting relationships (institutionalised or not) with the training organisation. In the present state of affairs, the last situation is the most difficult to determine, as it pertains to the more or less permanent character of the relationship between a certain company and certain organisations or the nature of the selection procedures or quality control exercised by the State.

It appears that in the field of service activities and more particularly training, only an analysis conducted in conjunction with the nature of the market and the service relationship would be able to fully clarify the functioning of the so called market.

In spite of these limitations, we shall draw these two main conclusions:

The first is that, despite the specialities of certain organisations and strong institutional patterns in certain segments, the large number of training programme suppliers and their services offered most often to both companies and the French State attest well to a quasi-market in which a form of competition, even if it is not expressed predominately by pricing, does operate.

The second conclusion deals with the quality of the service. Concerning public demand (notably for the training the unemployed), we have seen that the trend is unquestionably towards customising training. Concerning companies, trends show pressure towards designing training more closely on work situations and building links between professionally acquired skills and formal training, which reinforce the demand for co-construction of the training product. Training organisations activities may then evolve not towards standardisation, a trend that would reduce this co-production dimension and bring training programmes into line with industrial patterns, but rather towards what Gadrey (1996) calls a professional streamlining in which the dimensions of human relationships, information and trust predominate.

REFERENCES

Aventur, F., Charraud, A.M., Méliva, A., Personnaz, E. and Rincent, J.C. (1995), "Les activités des organismes de formation continue", Bref Céreq, n° 115.

Bentabet, E. and Zygmunt, C. (1996), "La formation professionnelle continue financée par les entreprises", Document observatoire, Céreq, N°116.

Gadrey, J. (1996), *Services: la productivité en question*, collection sociologie économique, Desclée de Brouwer.

Gadrey, J. and De Bandt, J. (1994), *Relations de services, marchés de services*, Editions du CNRS, Paris.

Glennerster, H. (1991), "Quasi market for education?" *The economic journal* 101, pp.1268-76.

Hatchuel, A. (1996), "La relation de service", *Informations sociales* 52, pp.60-65.

Margirier, G. (1994), "Le marché de la formation professionnelle des salariés", *RFE* 4 pp.45-84.

Merle, V. and Gesse, C. (1991), "Marché de la formation et typologie des organismes de formation", *études et expérimentations* 11, pp.5-8.

Stankiewicz, F. "Politiques de l'emploi et marché de la formation délivrée aux chômeurs: modèle de l'offre de formation administrée et modèle de quasi-marché", Formation Emploi.

Chapter 6

Reasons and policies to stimulate lifelong learning

Hessel Oosterbeek
University of Amsterdam and Max Goote Kenniscentrum

1. INSTRUMENTS FOR LIFELONG LEARNING

Due to rapid technological change and increasing international trade, less educated workers in OECD countries face poor labour market prospects. In the US this shows up in lower earnings for the low skilled, while in Europe their probability of unemployment has increased. Wood (1994, p.347) distinguishes four different ways to attack this problem: firstly raising barriers against imports from the south; secondly the reducing relative supply of low skilled by education and training; thirdly boosting the relative demand for low skilled by public works or employment subsidies; fourthly taxes and transfers to redistribute income. There seems to be a growing consensus that the second strategy aimed at increasing skills levels for the low skilled is the most promising policy (OECD, 1996) although there are also some sceptics with regard to the 'skills-hype' e.g. Shackleton (1995). As Wood (1994, p.361) notes the education and training solution is attractive since it could be beneficial from both an efficiency and an equity point of view.

For this reason the notion of lifelong learning has attracted renewed attention amongst policy makers (OECD, 1996). There also seems to be almost universal consensus about the fact that some form of government intervention is required to establish a situation where lifelong learning is a reality for all. But consensus breaks down once the choice of particular modes of intervention is under consideration. Some people argue for instance that a payroll tax for training as is in France, is a good solution (TUC, 1995), while others favour compulsory apprenticeships for young people who leave full-time education (e.g. Layard, Robinson and Steedman, 1995).

In its recent study the OECD (1996) argues that lifelong learning for all requires two ingredients. In the first place all people need a minimum platform of skills that enables them to enter the labour market and to benefit from future exposure to learning environments.[1] Secondly, lifelong learning for all requires that adult education and training is not a privilege for a selective group, but instead should be available to all adults.

In a thoughtful analysis Booth and Snower (1996) develop the following argument. If the acquisition of skills is left to the marketplace, an efficient amount of skills will be produced only if there are no uncompensated benefits or costs. If for one reason or another there emerge benefits or costs that are not compensated, the agent that causes these benefits or costs will not take these into consideration when deciding upon the level of skills. In such circumstances it is said that the market 'fails'. Many different forms of market failures can possibly arise in the case of education and training. According to Booth and Snower, the form of government intervention should be related to the type of market failure. A similar line of reasoning is followed by Stern and Ritzen who argue that "the public role in training should be based on the reasons why the market may fail"(1991, p.6).

In addition, the potential benefit from repairing a market failure should be weighed against the costs and also against possible failures associated with the government intervention.

This line of argument leads to a framework in which a specific intervention is connected with a specific market failure; the desirability of the intervention thus depends on the occurrence, importance and magnitude of the associated failure. This is an attractive framework, but has one important drawback. Judging a specific intervention only in terms of the failure it is supposed to repair, ignores the possible negative effects that the intervention might have. These negative effects may belong to the category 'government failures' but may also cause or strengthen other market failures. This is especially important if one realises that in practice it is often quite difficult to abandon an established programme. Some programmes or interventions may be aimed at market failures that turn out to be temporary; but once the failure disappears the programmes may still exist and have negative side-effects. In other words, the partial evaluation implicit in the framework is incomplete. The aim of this

---

[1] According to Doeringer (1994), however, "raising foundation skills is a much over-rated solution to the kind of productivity problems facing high performance firms. The foundations of productivity that are valued by such firms are not those of knowledge and skills, but involve work force qualities such as flexibility, adaptability, teamwork, and problem-solving capacity. These are not the qualities that schools are used to training for ... "(p.102). This point of view supports a shift away from cognitive skills towards other job skills (sometimes labelled 'life' skills).

paper is to present a more complete evaluation of different instruments that have been proposed to promote lifelong learning.[2]

The plan of the paper is as follows. Section 2 identifies and discusses all possible failures in the markets of education and training. This section also discusses failures connected to government intervention in the field of education and training. Presented in section 3 is an exhaustive list of remedies for the market failures. This list is an inventory of policy instruments to promote lifelong learning. Each policy instrument is evaluated by considering which failure it attempts to repair, and also by discussing likely side-effects of the instrument in terms of other market failures, implications for equity and government failures. Section 4 concludes.

2.   WHY OR WHY NOT?

In this section we identify and discuss possible failures in the markets of education and training. Many of the failures are well-known and are mentioned in numerous publications. Others have only been identified very recently. The recent books edited by Booth and Snower (1996) and Stern and Ritzen (1991) are especially valuable sources of such 'new' failures. This section also discusses possible failures connected to government intervention in the field of education and training.

Probably the most prominent potential market failure related to the training of employed adults is the *poaching problem*. This refers to the possibility that the worker leaves the firm who provided the training in order to work for another firm. To the extent that the first firm shared in the cost of training, this firm incurs a loss, while the second firm attracts a trained worker without paying the cost for this. Because the first firm paid part of the cost while the second did not, the second firm is able to pay the worker a higher wage than the first firm. As a result firms are not prepared to pay for the costs of training when (part of) this training is believed to be useful in other firms as well. This causes an under-investment in training.

Although the problem of poaching seems real, the dominant economic theory with regard to training - the human capital theory - argues that the problem should not occur. Middleton, Ziderman and Van Adams (1993, p.109) even state that the poaching argument is flawed. The reasoning is based on Becker's celebrated distinction between general and specific training (Becker,

---

[2]   An earlier version of this paper was prepared for the OECD project on lifelong learning.

1962). General training produces skills which are equally useful in many firms, whilst specific training generates skills which raises a worker's productivity only in the firm that offers the training. Because a worker can reap the full benefits from general training, s/he will also incur the full costs. In the absence of liquidity constraints (see below), the worker will be prepared to do so. Hence, the firm does not pay for a worker's general training. With specific training, economic theory predicts worker and firm to share the costs and benefits according to a rule that maximises the expected net revenues (Hashimoto, 1981). Here too, the parties will settle at the investment level that is optimal from the social point of view; there is no poaching externality.

A series of recent contributions (Stevens, 1994; 1996) disputes the general-specific dichotomy and offers a theoretical basis for the poaching problem. She shows that not all forms of training need to be either general, or specific, or even some linear combination of these two extremes. Instead some forms of training may produce skills that are useful in a limited number of firms, and perhaps more useful to some of these than to others. Such so-called transferable training creates a market form that is neither monopsonistic (as with specific training) nor perfectly competitive (as with general training). Some of the benefits from training will fall to the firms that can poach the workers, and since neither the worker nor the current firm will take these benefits into account, there will in general be under-investment in transferable training.

The cost of an investment typically precedes the benefits. This is also the case with investment in education and training. Bearing the cost of an investment requires the availability of sufficient financial resources, either in the form of own wealth or by being able to borrow. If the party that could benefit from an investment can not command these resources, that party is said to be *liquidity constrained* (among many others this point is made by Acemoglu, 1996; Bartel, 1994; Stern and Ritzen, 1991; Wood, 1994, p.53). Especially in the case of individual investments in education or training, liquidity constraints are believed to be relevant. The main cause of this is that the future returns to the investment are too uncertain to serve as collateral.

Education and training may produce positive effects which exceed the returns to the worker and the firm. Generally the involved parties do not take such effects into account when making their decisions and will therefore under-invest. The poaching effect discussed above is an example of such a so called *externality* (in the case of poaching the parties ignore the poaching firm's benefits).

Ulph (1996) discusses externalities related to skilled workers because of their greater flexibility to adapt new technology. In a formal model he derives an expression for the social marginal product of skilled workers that includes a term that reflects the gain to society from having more successful firms. According to Ulph, "markets typically fail to reward flexibility adequately since it is hard to write long term contracts that ensure that firms perceive no cost to actually using or retaining a skilled worker as the consequence of its Research and Development decisions" (p.106). As a result, firms invest too little in Research and Development.

Snower (1996) discusses two related and reinforcing externalities that can lead to what he calls a "low skills, bad job trap". The first externality is a 'vacancy supply externality'; when firms create a skilled vacancy, this does not only raise the firms expected profit, but it also raises the returns that workers can expect from training. The more skilled vacancies there are, the higher the probability that a skilled worker is matched to a skilled vacancy. Likewise, a 'training supply externality' emerges when a worker acquires education or training. Such training does not only produce a private return to the worker, but also increases firms' expected gain from supplying vacancies, because the probability that the vacancy is filled with a skilled worker has gone up.

But perhaps the externalities that attracted most attention from economists during the past decade are the external effects of human capital on output that drive the so-called endogenous growth models. As Lucas (1988, p.19) notes: "human capital accumulation is a social activity, involving groups of people in a way that has no counterpart in the accumulation of physical capital" (quoted in Shackleton, 1995, p.23), see also Romer (1986).

Especially in the context of the US and UK labour markets, *high turnover* of workers may be the cause of under-investment in training (Bartel, 1994: Stern and Ritzen, 1991; Prais, 1995, p.12). If workers leave their firms frequently, the probability that an investment in training will turn into a loss for the firm is quite large. When training is general or transferable, this problem is equivalent to the poaching problem; although the cause might be different. Poaching refers to actions of non-training firms, but turnover may also be high for other - non-economic - reasons. But the presence of high turnover may frustrate investment in specific training as well, because this type of training is not threatened by poaching. In his formalisation of Becker's model, Hashimoto (1981) derives an expression in which the sharing of the cost of specific training between firm and worker depends on the probability of a 'quit' and the probability of a dismissal. If a 'quit' is likely and a dismissal not, the worker bears the largest share of the cost (and benefit) of training, whereas the opposite holds if a dismissal is likely and a 'quit' is unlikely. In the extreme case of zero probability of a 'quit' (dismissal), the worker (firm) does not contribute to the costs of specific training and receives no benefit from it.

A natural way for workers to bear their share of the training cost is in the form of a lower current wage. Workers and firms may agree upon a wage rate below the workers' potential marginal productivity. Such an agreement can be frustrated by *minimum wage legislation* (Leighton and Mincer; 1981; Stern and Ritzen;1991). If the level of the minimum wage is high relative to the worker's productivity, subtracting the worker's share of the training costs from his/her wage, may result in a wage rate below the legal minimum. If below-minimum wages for trainees are not permitted, the training may not occur.

To the extent that training is not specific, it is also useful in other firms. But these other firms will only reward a worker for their training if they can observe its contents. In many cases there may be *imperfect information* regarding these contents which may cause transaction costs to signal the outcomes of general training (Bartel, 1994; Stern and Ritzen, 1991). This makes investment in non-specific training less attractive for workers and therefore they are believed to under-invest in such forms of training.

Opposed to this is a mechanism suggested by Katz and Ziderman (1990). They argue that the asymmetry of information about the contents of training, make it possible for the current firm to bear a larger part of the training costs (even if the training is completely general), thereby reducing or even eliminating the negative effects of poaching, liquidity constraints or minimum wage legislation. In a sense, the information asymmetry makes the general training specific. Or, as Acemoglu and Pischke put it, "... the line between what is general and what is specific may not be technologically drawn, but rather determined by frictions in the market" (1996, p.2).

Bartel (1994, pp.119/20) makes the point that under investment in training in the US may be due to *poor basic skills*. If the general level of basic skills in a country is poor, firms in that country may opt for technologies that rely on automation and low skilled labour instead of skilled labour (Stevens, 1996, p.39). This argument reveals that a minimum platform of learning is not only important from the perspective of an individual worker because more highly educated workers are more likely to participate in training, but also because it affects the type of jobs firms create. In that sense, the target of a minimum platform is related to Snower's training supply externality.

It is generally acknowledged that the returns to education and training are rather high on average, but the dispersion of the returns is relatively large. Hence a considerable amount of *risk* is involved (Ritzen, 1991). For most investors (firms and workers) returns will exceed costs, but for a certain (non-negligible) proportion net returns may turn out to be negative. For workers, the risk element is likely to lead to under-investment in training. The usual assumption is that economic agents are *risk averse* - that is, with a given expected return they prefer prospects with lower dispersion. This does not imply that workers will never invest in a risky type of training, it just says that their level of investment will fall short of the socially optimum level. Firms, on the other hand, can pool the risks of training different workers, as long as the returns to the training of different workers are uncorrelated. For their share in the training investment, the presence of risk need not be a problem. This holds as long as the firm's pool of trainees is sufficiently large, but for smaller firms this may not be the case. In addition to this, smaller firms may also face some other special problems with regard to training: it may be quite difficult for them to organise internal on-the-job training programmes and they may be less well informed about the contents of external off-the-job training programmes. In other words small and medium size firms cannot benefit from economies of scale in training. Therefore special arrangements may be required for such firms (Middleton, Ziderman and Van Adams, 1993, p.113).

Many countries have special subsidised training programmes aimed at the unemployed. The rationale for these programmes is straightforward. Unemployed workers are likely to possess skills that have become obsolete and in order to renew or upgrade their current stock of skill, some retraining is required. Such training is subsidised because the unemployed workers usually do not have sufficient financial resources. For society it may be beneficial to pay for such training if it reduces expenditure on unemployment benefits because the unemployed find a job sooner due to the training (for more on this, see below). An undesirable side effect of this policy, however, might be that employed workers may *defer upgrading* or renewing their skills until they are unemployed, because in that case they benefit from the government's subsidy. In other words public subsidies for training of the unemployed give employed workers a cost disadvantage in training (Stern and Ritzen, 1991). This may lead to crowding out of employee training by unemployed training.

Workers have an incentive to acquire new skills if their investment in training costs falls short of the expected returns to training. For that to be the case, their earnings have to be linked to their level of skill. According to Stern and Ritzen (1991) the compensation schemes in many firms are based on other principles than rewarding skills. In particular in many contracts wages are based on seniority instead of actual performance or productivity increases. Related to this, there is a more general concern that *skill wage differentials are too narrow*. Due to unions, minimum wage legislation and social security income floors, wage differentials by skill do not accurately reflect productivity differences (Wood, 1994, p.349; Prais, 1995, p.12, also makes this point).

Firms have an interest in renewing and upgrading the skills of their workforce as long as current workers are not replaced by new workers. But when it is easy for firms to *replace* their current (old) workforce when their skills have become obsolete by new (young) workers who have been educated recently, firms may benefit from doing so. Whether it is beneficial for firms to adopt this strategy depends on the costs they incur to attract educated young workers and to dismiss their old workforce. If firing is easy and unemployment benefits are readily available, it is less likely that firms pay for maintaining the skills of their current workers (Stern and Ritzen; 1991). To the extent that *labour and capital are complementary factors* of production, under investment in skills acquisition for one or more of the above reasons can be amplified (Acemoglu, 1996). The argument is that under investment in skills will reduce the profitability of investments in physical capital. The resulting deficient investment in physical capital will lead to an even more deficient level of training. This mechanism is sometimes referred to as the 'low-skill, low-tech trap' (Snower and Booth, 1996, p.342)

So far we have discussed market failures in the market for education and training. Probably the most important reason for governments to intervene in the education and training market is, however, not the presence of market failures, but is based on the widely supported view that participation in learning activities should only depend on characteristics that are relevant to education and training. Such characteristics are motivation and effort and ability, as opposed to other factors such as social background, gender and race. In many countries much effort is put into realising equal opportunities.

Equity considerations are prominent when dealing with initial and formal education. But also in adult education and training such considerations can be important; whereas educators sometimes defend the thesis that adult education and training offer second chances to those who were less successful in initial education, actual practice is that more highly educated people have a much higher probability of participating in adult education and training than those with low levels of initial education. Thus, instead of compensating, adult education and training magnify the differences produced by the initial education system. From an equity point of view this may be undesirable.

In relation to equity in education and training, it is important to distinguish between static and dynamic measures of equity. In the static case it is only current income positions that matter, whereas in the dynamic case, one takes a lifetime perspective. Put differently, with the static equity concept it matters that individuals from poorer social backgrounds have equal access to education and training. Whereas from a dynamic point of view it matters that those who have attained the highest levels of education and training are among the richest of their birth cohort. Thus, for the evaluation of subsidies it does not only matter whether these subsidies are received by individuals from poor families, but also whether these subsidies take the lifetime position of the recipients into account.

The preceding paragraphs listed market failures in the training market and discussed equity. The obvious next step is to investigate which policy instruments may help to fix these failures. This may suggest too high a level of trust in government intervention, because government intervention may lead to non-optimal results. Since we are aware of this potential problem, we first discuss possible *government failures* in the field of training and adult education, and go then on to discuss policy instruments.[3] The following government failures in the field of training can be identified.

To the extent that intervention in the training market requires government expenditures, taxation is necessary. With the exception of lump sum taxes, all forms of taxation distort the functioning of markets and that causes a *deadweight loss*. The estimated taxation of the GDP in the US economy is 30%. That means that each dollar of tax levied has a welfare cost of 1.30 dollars. Since the welfare costs per dollar of taxation increase with the level of taxation, and taxation is relatively low in the US when compared to other developed countries, this estimate is likely to be the lower boundary of the actual costs of taxation in other OECD countries. Thus, where recipients of education subsidies may feel that their education is 'free', this argument implies that it is not only not free, but actually more expensive to pay with public instead of private money. (And this still ignores possible efficiency gains from private expenditures.)

Government officials will not always act in the public interest (Booth and Snower, 1996, p.10). This is a straightforward application of the *principal-agent problem*. If bureaucrats have objectives that deviate from the objectives of the public, and if they have a certain amount of private information, the actual outcome is likely to differ from the socially desirable outcome. The design and implementation of policy instruments should aim at minimising this deviation. Others refer to this non-market failure as 'internalities' or 'difficulty in defining and measuring outputs' (Hansen, 1991 p.226; Finegold, 1996, p.238). Agreement on output of the programme is required to address this problem (Hansen 1991, p.225). An interesting and relevant empirical application of principal-agent theory to public training programmes is found in a recent study by Heckman, Smith and Taber (1996). In this study it is tested whether bureaucrats "cream-skim", by selecting the most employable applicants into a training programme. The evidence suggests that this is not the case.

For good reasons governments and civil servants operate in an environment that includes many regulations and procedures (red tape). But at the same time these regulations and procedures restrict *the flexibility and efficiency* of

---

[3] Important contributions to the literature on government failures in general include Wolf (1979; 1984).

government intervention in the training market (Booth and Snower, 1996, p.11). In this context Finegold (1996, p.241) mentions the absence of bottom line and termination mechanisms.

Another reason for government failure (in training) is the *high time preference of politicians*. The primary aim of politicians is to be re-elected. All programmes that have long term instead of short term benefits are therefore less attractive to politicians (Booth and Snower, 1996, p.11; also Finegold,1996, p.244).

A final potential government failure relates to the case where government intervention takes the form of government provision. In that case the market is served by a single source (Finegold, 1996, p.240). A single supplier may act like a monopolist, who has no rivals and therefore lacks an important incentive to operate efficiently.

3.   HOW?

To remedy the market failures discussed in the previous section, some forms of government intervention may be implemented. In general, government intervention can have three different forms: provision, funding and regulation. Most of the instruments discussed in this section relate to funding, but some other forms of intervention are discussed as well.

A list of credible remedies for the market failures discussed in the previous section is presented in this section. This list is an inventory of policy instruments to promote lifelong learning. Each policy instrument is evaluated by considering which failure is most likely to be repaired by it, and also by discussing side effects that may emerge in terms of other market failures, implications for equity and government failures. All instruments are primarily partial solutions as they are meant to repair a single market failure. Successful policy intervention should be based on combining a set of non-conflicting, complementary instruments that solve the most pressing failures. Which combination of instruments is most appropriate will depend on circumstances that differ across periods and countries. At the end of this section we discuss one specific combination of policy instruments that has recently been proposed in the context of the British situation.

An intervention that attracted considerable attention and also support in recent years is one or another version of a *voucher* or entitlement scheme (Le Grand and Estrin, 1989; Levin, 1983; Booth and Snower, 1996, p.343; Shackleton, 1995, p.50). When discussing this form of intervention it is worth bearing in mind that many different proposals go under this heading. The basic idea is that prospective consumers receive a bundle of vouchers to buy education services instead of subsidising educational institutes directly. Due to this, consumers are believed to exercise consumer sovereignty and to operate with more care and caution when spending their own vouchers than when they spend public resources. Moreover, it is believed that with vouchers, suppliers will shift their focus from satisfying government bureaucrats towards the needs of their consumers.

Thus, vouchers are primarily proposed to repair the government failure of a single supplier. Which market failures are fixed in addition to that, depends very much on the precise contents of the scheme. If the voucher scheme consists of a grant that is uniform for different individuals (but which may vary across different types of education), it is primarily aimed at internalising external effects. If the value of the voucher bundle that people receive depends on individual characteristics, then the instrument can also be used to serve equity goals. This is the case if people from poorer social backgrounds or with lower levels of initial ability are given larger bundles. Furthermore it is possible that vouchers are not a full grant, but contain also a loan component. In that case, the voucher instrument may also repair imperfections in the capital market and thereby fixes the liquidity constraints.

The accreditation of programmes (Booth and Snower, 1996; Bartel, 1994, and Stern and Ritzen, 1991) is the most straightforward instrument to address information problems regarding the contents of education and training courses. In many countries efforts are undertaken to set up a procedure for the accreditation of programmes. But this instrument has some potential disadvantages that fall into the category of government failures. Firstly, the system has to have a procedure for accrediting new programmes and for 'discrediting' old programmes. But given the established positions of the people involved, the discrediting procedure is likely to be rather conservative; this renders the instrument inflexible. Secondly, the instrument requires a substantial administrative effort along with the resources that go with such an effort. Thirdly, the instrument runs the risk of being biased towards formal training and against informal training. Finally, to repeat the argument developed by Katz and Ziderman (1991), a slight amount of asymmetry of information might be beneficial in the training market because it allows the firm to bear a larger share of the cost of general or transferable training. With accreditation this asymmetry vanishes.

Special *apprenticeship contracts* are advocated by Snower and Booth (1996, p.343) as an answer to the 'high-wage, low-skills trap'. The idea is that youngsters combine, during their first years in the labour market, on-the-job training with off-the-job instruction. For such contracts to be attractive for employers the training wages have to be set at a low level or otherwise training subsidies have to be given to employers (Stern and Ritzen 1991, p.7). Moreover, these contracts may be a solution to the problem imposed by a minimum wage. Apprenticeship systems play an important role in Germany,

Denmark, Austria and Switzerland. A possible drawback of such systems is that changes in the content of the programmes are adapted rather slowly.

Stern and Ritzen (1991) mention as a reason for skills shortages wage structures based on seniority rather than on skills and productivity. Also Snower and Booth mention the removal of institutional obstacles to widen wage differentials between skilled and unskilled workers as a possible solution. In particular they refer to certain aspects of job security legislation and the monopoly power of labour unions. In a sense this argument attributes failures in the skills market to failures in the labour market. Accordingly, the role of the government is to *re-establish competitive forces in the labour market*. One may question, however, whether the outcomes of this measure are not too drastic in terms of, for instance, its effects on earnings inequality. An important argument for increasing the supply of skilled workers is that the position of unskilled people is rather bad. Increasing the proportion of skilled people by enlarging the difference between the positions of skilled and unskilled people makes the remaining poor workers even worse off.

Related to this, Wood (1994, p.357) identifies two opposing effects in strategies aimed at reducing the number of unskilled. On the one hand, the supply of skilled workers can be boosted by spending public resources on education and training, but on the other hand, to finance these expenditures, taxation is necessary which reduces the net skilled-unskilled wage differential as long as the unskilled are exempted from this taxation. Which of the two effects dominates depends on the success of the programme on which the public resources are spent and on the elasticity of the supply of skilled relative to unskilled labour.

In the presence of positive externalities the textbook solution is to provide *public support*. In the field of education and training public support is widespread. Subsidies should be given to workers if the 'training supply externality' is relevant, and to employers to the extent that the 'vacancy supply externality' is important. For other externalities, the party that causes the effect should receive the subsidy.

Several remarks are in order here. First, in case of public subsidies there is always the possibility that the subsidy is a windfall gain to the receiver if they would have invested in skills acquisition without the subsidy. Second, the argument of the dead-weight loss from taxation is prevalent here; to provide subsidies, taxes have to be levied which causes an excess burden. Third, it is rather easy for firms to misuse the subsidy provision by just 'selling' certain activities as being training whereas actually they are different. A remedy for such misuse is to monitor the activities, but obviously a cost is related to that (Bartel, 1994; Stern and Ritzen, 1991, p.7). Finally, it should be noted that subsidies are not a good instrument to repair liquidity constraints because this also benefits those who are not constrained, who will therefore over-invest (Acemoglu, 1996, p.59).

Some instruments that are in use in the field of adult education and training may seem at first sight rather different from a subsidy to employers or workers, but are in fact close substitutes for a subsidy, or are sometimes really equivalent. Some examples follow.

A specific measure aimed at giving firms an incentive to invest in their workers' skills is the provision of investment *tax credits and depreciation allowances* (Snower and Booth 1996, p.344). A related point is raised by Miller (OECD, 1996) who advocates adequate accounting of the stocks of human capital that a firm has contracted. Such accounting may provide firms with superior information about the input and output of training and thereby improve their decision making in this area. Good accounting practices are also a prerequisite for giving tax credits and depreciation allowances.

Similarly, some observers have advocated more generous *tax deductions* for employees with respect to the cost they make for training (Bartel, 1994). But obviously, there is not much of a difference between giving a subsidy to employees or allowing tax deductions. The only difference is that a subsidy causes a real expenditure while tax deductions cause so called tax expenditures. Tax expenditures might be more attractive to politicians who care about the public share in national product, but no different effects can be expected in terms of education and training outcomes.

Related to subsidies for firms in general is the policy instrument of giving *government subsidies for the creation of employer training collectives* (Bartel, 1994). The special feature of such subsidies is that they are directed towards the problem that small and medium size firms may have in the provision of training. But as Bartel mentions, there is a concern about the sharing of private information and the possibility of free-riding behaviour.

Different models of government provision in the form of *loans* are aimed at repairing liquidity constraints (Booth and Snower, 1996; Bartel, 1994). A version that attracted a lot of interest and support in recent years is the form of 'income contingent loans' or ICLs (Barr, 1993; Barr and Falkingham, 1993; Chapman and Harding, 1993). In this model, no grants are given but only loans with income dependent repayment. During their studies students receive a loan, which they repay in the form of a percentage of their earnings. It is also possible to give those who earn below a certain threshold a dispensation. Compared with the mortgage type loans schemes which are operative in, for instance, the UK, repayment is more evenly spread over the graduate's professional career. That is, the costs of the investment in schooling are repaid when the returns materialise. Compared to the graduate tax system, where all graduates pay a special tax, the important difference is that a person never repays more than the sum of the loan and interest. Therefore, the disadvantage of the graduate tax system, that there is no direct link between costs and benefits, does not apply to the system of ICLs.

A separate issue relates to the interest rate students should pay. From the point of view of the lender it is desirable that the interest rate includes a premium for defaulters. This is feasible if an individual's probability to default is as uncertain to the borrower as it is to the lender. That is, however, not very likely; borrowers probably know more about their own characteristics and therefore about their own risk than lenders do. As a result those posing bad risks will drive the good risks out of the market. The relevance of this mechanism increases with the heterogeneity of the student population. Since enrolment in post-secondary education has increased in most countries over the past decades, student populations may indeed be quite diverse. The important message from this is that the government has to be very careful when determining the default premium included in the interest rate. A low default premium is equivalent to providing a subsidy. The size of this 'subsidy' can be reduced by screening students. Academic records are likely to be a good indicator of the students future default probability, and it may therefore be desirable to deny student with poor academic records loans.

Both in the UK and Australia, simulation models have been used to predict the effects of the system of ICLs in terms of the amount repaid and the average repayment period. Assuming a zero income growth and a zero real interest rate (that is interest equal to the rate of inflation), the amount repaid is the same as in a mortgage type loans system in which repayment is due within ten years. The average repayment period in the income contingent loan system is between 25 and 30 years. To the extent that the growth rate of earnings exceeds the real rate of interest, the income contingent loan system will be advantageous.

As mentioned earlier, liquidity constraints occur because people cannot use their own knowledge and skills as collateral. This is because there is too much risk involved. In other areas, risk is covered by insurance. Referring to that Stern and Ritzen (1991, p.7) label a system of ICLs 'inverse insurance'.

As another solution to the problem of liquidity constraints Booth and Snower (1996) mention the possibility of conditional loan guarantees. Instead of governments lending the money themselves, private banks provide the loans but the government covers the risk of default by giving banks a guarantee. Whether this is an attractive option depends on the relevance of government failures in the direct provision of loans. If private banks can organise a loans system efficiently while preserving access, loans guarantees are preferable. Otherwise the government earns the rent that would fall to private banks.

In a recent report the Trades Union Council (TUC) (1995) advocates a levy system (see also, among others: Booth and Snower, 1996; Bartel, 1994; and Shackleton 1995, pp.53-60). The basic idea is that firms are obliged to pay a certain amount of money (a percentage of their payroll for instance), which is collected at an aggregated level (industry or national) and is earmarked for training expenses. Firms that can prove that they already spent a certain amount on training expenses can deduct that amount from their levy payment. A system along these lines is operative in France. The primary aim of this system is that it circumvents the poaching problem and that free-riding is impossible. Firms that do not train their own employees may still poach trained workers from other firms, but due to the levy system they also incur a cost for that.

Although often advocated, the levy system has a number of disadvantages. First, there is no incentive to spend more on training than the agreed percentage. Second, if the amount of the levy is based on a percentage of the payroll, the system is likely to favour large firms, since they benefit from economies of scale in training. Third, the levy system focuses completely on formal training and ignores informal training. This is a disadvantage for firms who rely more heavily on informal forms of transmission of knowledge and skills. Fourth, and related to the problem with informal training, is the measurement problems. Firms can easily claim that certain expenses cover training costs and it requires close monitoring to prove it if that is untrue. Fifth, the levy system ignores the fact that different firms may have different training needs. These may differ between industries, but also between, for instance, newly established and 'old' firms within the same industry. Sixth, the levy system ignores the degree that the burden of the levy can be shifted to workers. The extent to which this is possible depends on labour demand and supply elasticities. Firms whose demand is elastic and/or face an inelastic supply curve, can easily shift the burden of the levy, which gives them a competitive advantage at the expense of its workforce. Finally, the levy increases the price of labour, thereby making investment in physical capital relatively more attractive.

Snower (1994) has proposed to *link training subsidies to unemployment benefits* and other welfare programmes. The idea is to activate the use of transfer expenditures. Such a policy has been adopted in Sweden where income support is conditional on participation in training. The Swedish system of income transfer is characterised by a high percentage of so called workfare programmes as opposed to income programmes and poverty trap programmes. According to Bjorklund and Freeman (1995) this characteristic enables Sweden to combine a relatively high level of labour force participation with a relatively equal distribution of income.

Nevertheless, this approach has limitations. As Wood (1994, p.362) notes, a problem is that many unemployed persons lack the potential for advanced training. In relation to this, he refers to the low success rate of recent UK efforts to train the unemployed. Only thirty-six per cent of the persons who completed the Employment Training scheme went into jobs, self employment, or full time training (Wood,

1994, p.364). Shackleton (1995, p.53-60) is also critical about the this type of intervention. LaLonde (1995) gives an overview of evaluation studies of US training programmes. He concludes that unless policymakers can develop more intensive high-cost services, the promise of public sector programmes to improve the skills of economically disadvantaged and dislocated workers is limited (p.150). Even a doubling of government-funded training services is unlikely to improve the workforce's skills significantly (p.165). The reason for this pessimistic view is that current expenditure on these programmes very low relative to the problems which they are attempting to cure.

As mentioned above, government training programmes for the unemployed are likely candidates for government failures. Examples are 'creaming' and displacement effects.

According to Bartel (1994, p.122/3), even *without intervention* it is also likely that training will increase in the near future. She argues that this will happen as a simple by-product of technological change during the next decade. Indications of that are drawn from her own research, which reports that in industries with higher rates of technological change employees are significantly more likely to receive company training (Bartel and Sicherman, 1995). She quotes Tan in saying that "the marginal cost of producing a unit of human capital investment decreases with technological change" (Tan, 1989). This point of view deviates considerably from the pessimistic view that technological change leads to a higher rate of depreciation of skills and that a lack of skills may hinder innovation.

A simple solution to the poaching problem, is to write *training contracts* that oblige the worker to repay the training costs when they leave. The repayment may depend on the amount of time elapsed between the end of training and the moment of leaving the firm. Although this solution seems simple and quite efficient, and is probably widely used in practice, it received little attention in training literature. Only Stevens (1996, p.22) gives a reference to a report by the British Employment Department that proposes to allow employers to enforce a training contract providing for the individual to work for a specified period after training or to repay some of the costs.

A straightforward answer to the problem that firms may adopt the strategy of replacing their old workers by hiring new ones instead of maintaining the skills level of their current workforce, is *to differentiate the rate for unemployment insurance.* Employers are then more directly confronted with the causes of their hiring and firing practices. The problem with this solution is that firms may have to dismiss employees for totally different reasons, reasons that may be beyond the control of the firm. It seems rather undesirable to shift the full burden in these cases to the firms. Moreover, differentiated unemployment rates for firms may have perverse effects in hiring practices.

Recent Dutch experience points in that direction. Firms become very reluctant in to give new workers permanent contracts; instead they extend probation periods or hire workers on temporary contracts. This, in turn, is not beneficial for the incidence of training as employees with permanent contracts are more likely to participate in training programmes than workers with temporary contracts (Oosterbeek, 1996).

After a discussion of the limitation of programmes aimed at raising the skills level of the lower skilled, Wood (1994, p.365) advocates *improving the quality of basic education.* He claims that such a shift may be more cost effective. It should be noted, however, that solid studies to support this thesis do not exist. Moreover, improving the quality of basic education requires public funding and will thus be accompanied by a dead-weight loss.

All the proposals discussed above are partial solutions; they are summarised in Table 1. Each solution aims at curing one specific market failure, but does not constitute a comprehensive policy. A mixture of instruments is therefore required. But which instruments are exactly required and in what mixture depends on the actual relevance and magnitude of market failures. And these are country and period specific. For that reason it makes little sense to come up with a uniform proposal for all countries independent of the actual situation. A proposal for a specific mixture of instruments has to be judged in the context of the circumstances pertaining to the country that being adopting it.

A concrete proposal to enhance lifelong learning - combining different instruments from Table 1 - has recently been formulated by Layard, Robinson and Steedman (1995). Their proposal relates to the specific characteristics of the British education system and labour market in 1995. The attractive feature of the plan is that it includes both the creation of a learning platform for young people and further education for adults. The plan captures elements of some of the instruments listed above. The main ingredients of the proposal are the following (Layard, Robinson and Steedman, 1995, p.4):

1. All employed young people under 19 should be employed as trainees, with compulsory off-the-job vocational education.
2. Like full time degree students, all other adults studying for recognised qualifications should have their fees paid from state money. Maintenance grants for full time degree students should be progressively changed into loans.
3. Costs where possible should be met from well-defined sources.
4. A Learning Bank should be established to provide loans to all students of 18 and above studying for degree and pre-degree qualifications.
5. A University for Industry should be established to provide high quality teaching materials for the new expansion of education, including distance learning.

6. The teaching profession should be upgraded, as a long term contribution
   to skill formation in primary and secondary schools.

The first element of this proposal coincides with the instrument of apprenticeship contracts included in Table 1. The second and fourth elements relate to the instruments of public support and loans, whilst the third element reflects the authors concern about an excess burden from taxation. The fifth and sixth elements can be interpreted as ways to improve the quality of basic education. According to the analysis in this section, the authors main concerns are externalities, liquidity constraints and poor basic skills. Of lesser concern in the current British setting are apparently the information problem and the poaching problem. The importance of liquidity constraints for the British skill shortage is questioned in a paper by Greenhalgh and Mavrotas (1994), who find no statistically significant effect of income level on the probability to participate in individually arranged training (p.592/3). The fact that information problems are of no concern is probably related to the British system of National Vocational Qualifications. This example shows the usefulness of the scheme in Table 1 for evaluating specific plans.

4.   CONCLUSION

It is often claimed that there is under-investment in training. Two pieces of evidence are put forward to support this claim. Firstly, potential market failures in the field of training are identified. Such market failures may cause under-investment. Secondly, empirical work indicates that rates of return to firm training exceed rates of return to formal education. If that is the case, investment in training should go up relative to investment in formal education.

This paper contains a survey of the literature on market failures in the field of training. Furthermore, it relates these failures to possible policy instruments to cure these failures. Our discussion of the policy instruments in the field of work related training reveals that an instrument is typically suited for a particular market failure, but may at the same time enhance other market failures or can be attended by non-market failures. This finding, which is summarised in Table 1, suggests that for practical purposes this framework is only applicable if the relative importance of different market failures is known. Only in that case is it possible to design a policy (consisting of a combination of instruments) that is likely to be successful. Otherwise a policy may be introduced which might have been suitable in other circumstances, but will fail in the situation in which it is introduced. The literature discussing market failures is, however, in most cases not specific enough to allow identification of the contributions of different market failures to the under-investment in training. To enhance the policy relevance of such studies, it is therefore desirable to start measuring the actual importance of different failures.

REFERENCES

Acemoglu, D. (1996), "Credit constraints, investment externalities and growth", in Booth,
    A.L. and Snower, D.J. (Eds.), *Aquiring skills; Market failures, their symptoms and policy
    responses*, Cambridge University Press, Cambridge.
Acemoglu, D. and J.-S. Pischke (1996), "The structure of wages and investment in general
    training", MIT, mimeo.
Barr, N. (1993), Alternative Funding Resources for Higher Education, *The Economic Journal*
    103, pp.718-728.
Barr, N. and Falkingham, J. (1993), *Paying for Learning*, WSP/96.
Becker, G.S. (1962), Investment in Human Capital: A Theoretical Analysis, *Journal of
    Political Economy* 70, pp.9-49.
Bartel, A.P. (1994), "Workplace training in the United States", in Asefa, S. and Huang, W.C.
    (Eds.), *Human capital and economic development*, W.E. Upjohn Institute for Employment
    Research, Kalamazoo.
Bartel, A.P. and Sicherman, N. (1995), "Technological Change and the Skill Acquisition of
    Young Workers", NBER Working Paper Series 5107.
Bjorklund, A. and R. Freeman (1995), "Generating Equality and Eliminating Poverty the
    Swedisch Way", Centre for Economic Performance Discussion Paper No. 228.
Booth, A.L. and Snower, D. (1996), "Introduction: does the free market produce enough
    skills", in Booth A.L. and Snower, D.J. (Eds.), *Aquiring skills; Market failures, their
    symptoms and policy responses*, Cambridge University Press, Cambridge.
Chapman B.J. and Harding, A. (1993), "Australian Student Loans", ANU Discussion Papers
    287.
Doeringer, P.B. (1994), "Can the U.S. system of workplace training survive global
    competition", in Asefa, S. and Huang, W.-C. (Eds.), *Human capital and economic
    development*, W.E. Upjohn Institute for Employment Research, Kalamazoo.
Finegold, D. (1996), "Market failure and government failure in skills investment", in Booth,
    A.L. and Snower, D.J. (Eds.), *Aquiring skills; Market failures, their symptoms and policy
    responses*, Cambridge University Press, Cambridge.
Greenhalgh, C. and Mavrotas, G. (1994), "The role of career aspirations and financial
    constraints in individual access to vocational training", *Oxford Economic Papers* 56,
    pp.579-604.
Hansen, W.L. (1991), "Nonmarket failure in government training programmes", in Stern, D.
    and Ritzen, J.M.M. (Eds.), *Market failure in training? New economic analysis and
    evidence on training of adult employees*, Springer, Berlin/Heidelberg/New York.
Hashimoto, M. (1981), "Firm-specific human capital as a shared investment", *American
    Economic Review* 71, pp.475-482.
Heckman, J.J., Smith J.A. and Taber, C. (1996), "What Do Bureaucrats Do? The Effects of
    Performance Standards and Bureaucratic Preferences on Acceptance into the JTPA
    Programme", NBER Working Paper Series #5535.
Katz, E. and Ziderman, A. (1990), "Investment in general training: the role of information and
    labour mobility", *Economic Journal* 100, pp.1147-1158.
LaLonde, R.J. (1995), "The Promise of Public Sector-Sponsored Training Programmes",
    Journal of Economic Perspectives 9, pp.149-168.
Layard, R., Robinson, P. and Steedman, H. (1995), "Lifelong Learning", Centre for Economic
    Performance, Occasional Paper No.9.
Le Grand, J. and Estrin, S. (1989), *Market Socialism*, Clarendon Press, Oxford.

Leighton, L., and Mincer, J. (1981), "The Effect of Minimum Wages on Human Capital Formation", in Rottenberg, S. (Ed.), *The Economics of Legal Wages*, American Enterprise Institute, Washington DC.

Levin, H.M. (1983), "Individual Entitlements", in Levin, H.M. and Schütze, H.G., *Financing Recurrent Education*, Sage, Beverly Hills/London/New Delhi.

Lucas, R.E. (1988), "On the mechanics of economic development", *Journal of Monetary Economics* 22, pp.3-42.

Middleton, J., Ziderman, A. and Van Adams, A. (1993), *Skills for Productivity; Vocational Education and Training in Developing Countries*, Oxford University Press, New York.

OECD (1996), *Lifelong learning for all*, OECD, Paris.

Oosterbeek, H. (1996), "A decomposition of training probabilities", *Applied Economics* 28, pp.799-805.

Prais, S.J. (1995), *Productivity, education and training: an international perspective*, Cambridge University Press, Cambridge.

Romer, P.M. (1986), "Increasing returns and long-run growth", *Journal of Political Economy* 94, pp.1002-1037.

Ritzen, J.M.M. (1991), "Market failure for general training, and remedies", in Stern, D. and Ritzen, J.M.M. (Eds.), *Market failure in training? New economic analysis and evidence on training of adult employees*, Springer, Berlin/Heidelberg/New York.

Shackleton, J.R. (1995), *Training for employment in Western Europe and the United States*, Edward Elgar, Aldershot.

Snower, D.J. (1994), "Converting unemployment benefits into employment subsidies", *American Economic Review Papers and Proceedings*.

Snower, D. (1996), "The low-skill, bad-job trap", in Booth, A.L. and Snower, D.J. (Eds.), *Aquiring skills; Market failures, their symptoms and policy responses*, Cambridge University Press, Cambridge.

Snower, D. and Booth, A.L. (1996), "Conclusions: government policy to promote the acquisition of skills", in Booth, A.L. and Snower, D.J. (Eds.), *Aquiring skills; Market failures, their symptoms and policy responses*, Cambridge University Press, Cambridge.

Stern, D. and Ritzen, J. (1991), "Introduction and overview", in Stern, D. and Ritzen, J.M.M. (Eds.), *Market failure in training? New economic analysis and evidence on training of adult employees*, Springer, Berlin/Heidelberg/New York.

Stevens, M. (1994), "A theoretical model of on-the-job training with imperfect information", *Oxford Economic Papers* 46, pp.537-562.

Stevens, M. (1996), "Transferable training and poaching externalities", in Booth, A.L. and Snower, D.J. (Eds.), *Aquiring skills; Market failures, their symptoms and policy responses*, Cambridge University Press, Cambridge.

Tan, H.W. (1989), "Technical change and its consequences for training and earnings", manuscript RANS Corporation.

TUC (1995), *Funding Lifelong Learning; A Strategy to Deliver the National Education and Training Targets*.

Ulph, D. (1996), "Dynamic competition for market share and the failure of the market for skilled labour", in Booth, A.L. and Snower, D.J. (Eds.), *Aquiring skills; Market failures, their symptoms and policy responses*, Cambridge University Press, Cambridge.

Van Lieshout, H. (1997), "Enhancing the operation of markets for vocational education and training: a governance approach", paper prepared for the EU seminar Knowledge Production and Dissemination to Business and the Labour Market, Amsterdam, April 23-25.

Wood, A. (1994), North-south trade, employment and inequality; changing fortunes in a skill-driven world, Claredon Press, Oxford.

Instrument	market failure directly aimed at	effects on other market failures	implications for equity	related government failures
vouchers	external effects; possibly liquidity constraints		if differentiated	solves single supplier problem
Accreditation	information problem	biased towards formal training		inflexible; administrative effort
Apprenticeship contracts	external effect of high wage low skills trap	Slow adaptation; reduces minimum wage problem		
Re-establish competition in labour market	widen skill wage differential		increases inequality	
Tax credits and tax allowances for firms; public support; tax deductions	externalities	windfall gain; not directed towards liquidity constraints	from tax payers to receivers of support	dead-weight loss; misuse
Subsidies training collectives	small firm problem			free riding problem
ICL's	liquidity constraints		more equitable than grants	Administrative burden
Conditional loans guarantees	liqiduity constraints	rent for commercial banks	more equitable than grants	

Levy system	poaching	disadvantage for small firms; benefits formal training; affect capital/labor price	burden shifted to workers	Measurement problems
Linking training subsidies to unemployment benefits	activate unemployment benefits	displacement	aimed at bottom group	Cream-skimming
Training contracts	poaching			
Differentiated unemployment premia	replacing old workers	hiring practices	protects insiders	too general
improve quality basic education	poor basic skills			dead-weight loss of taxation

Table 1 Evaluating policy instruments

Chapter 7

The Future of Vocational Education and Training

Fons van Wieringen
University of Amsterdam

1.   CHANGES IN THE ENVIRONMENT AND STRATEGIC RESPONSES

What changes are occurring in the social environment of vocational training and adult education and what strategies would provide an appropriate response to them? It would be nice if we knew. Unfortunately, we cannot tell what changes the future will bring, we have little idea what strategic responses will be possible and we simply do not know whether those strategic responses will be adequate. Scenarios can be used to gain a better insight into the many uncertainties of the future. This does not make the uncertainties disappear, but it enables them to be given a name and connected with other uncertainties, and even now and then with certainties. Drafting scenarios can make it easier to deal with potential future problems. They can be used to explore the future and sharpen vision, making it possible for those involved to see events as part of a greater whole and therefore to identify their implications more readily.

Can scenarios be explicitly incorporated in the process of formulating strategies? Scenarios can form a variety of contexts for strategies for vocational education and adult education. It is fairly essential to grasp the difference between a strategy and a scenario. Scenarios are an extremely useful tool for strategy formulation. Scenarios describe possible trends, whereas strategies present options for action in response to these potential developments. Scenarios provide a testing ground for strategies or, to put it another way, they are the wind tunnels in which different strategic options can be tested out. The aim is to work out the various possible strategies within the different scenarios (van der Heijden 1996).

It is a question of elaborating the different strategies within the different scenarios. Every possible strategy can be translated into every scenario. The extent to which scenario and strategy are treated in an integrated fashion may vary. A strategy which only works well in one of the scenarios and in none of the others is certainly hazardous. Strategies indicate ways of dealing with the different futures. An ensemble of scenarios can form a common framework for the development of a strategy that is more sensitive to changes in the environment.

For each draft scenario it is possible to establish more important links than the number that are worked out.

Scenarios must be drafted in such a way that they are all about equally probable. It is important, therefore, when designing strategies, not to look for the most appropriate scenario, but to set the various strategy proposals in the context of all the different scenarios. 'Wind tunnelling' means using the various futures (scenarios) to provide test conditions to reveal the strengths and weaknesses of each of the possible strategies. For this reason, it is important that the various scenarios should be regarded as equal and be given equal weight as test conditions. To do justice to interactive developments, scenarios must satisfy a number of criteria:
– a scenario must be hypothetical; it must be based on unforeseen events, reactions to those events, and combinations of events;
– a scenario must have a plural construction to enable comparison;
– a scenario must cover the entire time-span from the present to the future situation;
– a scenario is a sketch; it describes the main features and does not go too deeply into details. In addition, it indicates the crucial moments of choice - the moments at which points for embarking on a different direction in the future are situated;
– a scenario is multi-faced and holistic - it relates to the interaction between developments and events or other kinds of discontinuities which may occur in the future.
– Scenarios serve a number of purposes (Van der Heijden 1995, Schoemaker 1995):
– they are useful in catering for changes which are hard to detect, they identify early warning signals;
– they help in the determination of the robustness of the qualities of vocational education and of the vocational education policy system;
– they help to instigate better strategic options;
– they assess the risk/profit profile of each strategic option in the light of uncertainties;

– they communicate messages within the system.

The scenarios and strategies can be used as tools to improve understanding of the vocational education and training systems and their social environments. The use of the scenarios and strategies in a 'strategic dialogue' can produce a better basis for the decision–making process.

2. METHODS FOR DEVISING SCENARIOS

There is no fixed method for devising scenarios, but various steps have been taken in this direction. Schoemaker (1992) distinguishes the following stages:

– Determination of the range, for example the time-span.
– Determination of the major stakeholders, such as resource suppliers, employers, customers, competitors, allies, regulators and supervisors.
– Identification of basic trends in the environments.
– Identification of key uncertainties: what events, whose outcomes are uncertain, will significantly affect the issues of the vocational and educational training sector? Next we want to identify relationships among those uncertainties about the future environment of vocational and educational training.
– Construction of initial scenario themes: the various outcomes are arranged in terms of continuity, level of preparedness, and turbulence. Select the two major uncertainties. Place the positive and negative outcomes of the uncertainties in different scenarios to obtain the extremes and add a middle of the road scenario.
– Check for consistency and plausibility: are the trends compatible with the chosen time-span? Do the scenarios combine outcomes which can logically be combined? Are the major stakeholders placed in a position that they find unattractive and can change? If so, try a different scenario that is more stable.
– Develop learning scenarios: general themes emerge from the simple scenarios and from checking them.
– Identify research needs.
– Develop quantitative models.
– Think up decision-orientated scenarios: are the scenarios relevant? Are the scenarios internally consistent? Are they archetypical, do they present generically different futures rather than variations on a theme? Does each scenario provide a situation in which the system can continue to exist for a longer period?

On the basis of years of practical experience with scenarios for Royal Dutch Shell, Van der Heijden (1995) provides a number of instruments to help in the development of scenarios:
- Classification of variables as predetermined and uncertain;
- Identification of patterns and trends in events;
- Arrangement of variables on the basis of importance and predictability;
- Research on what makes a fundamental difference for the client;
- Practical aids for linking and grouping concepts, such as magnetic hexagons;
- Causal diagrams and computer resources to handle them efficiently.

A commonly used method in the construction of scenarios is the structured consultation of experts. One way of doing this is by means of a questionnaire. These questionnaires concern a particular subject and are filled in by experts selected for the research. If there is a second or third round, the experts receive a summary of the results of the previous round, including a statistical indication of the group responses and of the degree of consensus.

The project resulting in the scenarios and strategies for vocational and adult education was phased as follows:
- Collection of data on trends in vocational and adult education.
- Collection of data on trends in four designated social environments.
- Identification of approximately 300 relevant experts, drawn from all the different social and economic environments.
- Initial round of questionnaires to experts on environments.
- Seminar for policy makers, based on results of initial questionnaire.
- Seminar for experts on environments, based on results of initial questionnaire.
- Second questionnaire (environments together).
- Separate round of questionnaires to experts on policy and administration environment
- Development of dimensions for scenarios and strategies and initial draft of scenarios and strategies.
- Seminar for policy makers - further elaboration of scenarios and strategies.
- Seminar for experts on environments - further elaboration of scenarios and strategies.
- Final draft text of scenarios and strategies.
- Scenario workshop for broad - based group of social experts and policy makers.

2.1   Four social environments

In order to develop scenarios and trends for vocational and adult education trends affecting the system of vocational and adult education were broken down into a number of different social and economic environments. Four of these were selected for further study and inclusion in the project. They were designated the labour system, the economic and technological environment, the training and knowledge environment and, finally, the policy and administrative environment. The first two terms require little explanation. The training and knowledge environment is based on the assumption that the system of vocational and adult education operates in a world where training and knowledge are widespread and influence education. The policy and administration environment has been included because policy making is an essential context for the development of the system of vocational and adult education. From the point of view of the system, policy and administration is an obvious social environment.

Labour system context	Economic/technology context

Vocational training/adult education
Higher professional education

Training/knowledge context	Policy/administration context

Figure 6. The four selected environments

2.2   Selection of trends

Some 100 trends were collected which various experts rate as important for development in the vocational education and adult education environment. We reduced these 100 to approximately 50 trends. We then presented them to groups of experts from each of the four environments, each comprising some 70 individuals.
– What is a trend? We have used five criteria for the further specification of trends:
– a trend is potentially or actually active, it leads to more than marginal changes
– a trend is discrete and capable of being delimited
– a trend is persistent

- a trend has a network of experts with a minimal level of organisation and reporting on the trend
- a trend has a recognised or suspected important connection with the education and training system.

The fifth criterion is necessary because it is not the intention to develop scenarios for the economy in general, for example. Scenarios of that kind are already available. What matters here is to formulate the educational facets of general trends.

Even after these criteria have been applied, the problem remains that it is difficult to make a pronouncement on the comparability of the trends. We used reductive techniques to arrive at a smaller number of trends which are probably more comparable with one another.

A selection was made of some fifty trends regarded by various experts as important factors shaping the social and economic environment of vocational training and adult education.

These included, for example:
- Greater flexibility;
- The ageing population;
- Increasing importance of labour mobility and training;
- Industry's increasing willingness to contribute to education;
- Selective participation in training;
- Growing knowledge intensity;
- Increasing use of technology as an economic instrument;
- Technology and internationalisation;
- Changing structure of employment;
- Increasing importance of regional structures.

These fifty trends were presented to groups, each of about seventy experts. This meant that experts on each of the environments were presented with a set of around twenty trends and that the set of questions differed from one environment to another.

2.3 Consultation of experts

We observed the following criteria in the selection of experts:
- assumed expertise in the field of environmental changes that may be of importance for vocational education and adult education
- assumed expertise in the field of the macro determinants, particularly the labour market and technological developments, in relation to vocational education and adult education
- assumed capacity to formulate motivations concerning future developments that are relevant for vocational education and adult education, including firm-based training courses

– selection from the circles of government, vocational education, firm-based training courses, employees, employers and the academic world
– the participants must be able to grasp the changes in their field and to have a clear picture of what those changes mean for their organisation.

Experts were sought from the following circles: industry organisations; employers' organisations and trades unions; Chairpersons / Directors of the 25 largest sector organisations; Research and Planning Division of small and medium companies; research bureaux attached to independent or semi-independent foundations, universities and research institutions; professors of strategy, corporate development, economic development, labour organisation, adult education, secondary vocational education, higher vocational education; editors of relevant journals; the Vocational Training/Adult Education Departments of educational support institutions; officials of the EU, Cedefop, ETF (Turin), ILO, Leonardo and BIBB; senior consultants in specialist divisions of firms of management consultants; the executive boards of regional training centres and colleges of higher professional education; members of the Higher Professional Education Council and the Vocational and Adult Education Council; directors, deputy directors, and heads of department / senior members of the Adult vocational Education and Higher vocational Education boards of the Ministry of Education, Culture and Science; members of the education/industry committee for apprenticeship systems and directors of private sector training institutions.

A total of 228 experts from the environments of labour and employment; economy and technology; training and knowledge were approached for the first round of the written questionnaire.

Experts from the fourth environment – policy and administration - were handled in a different way and were only questioned once.

Of the 228 experts 108 returned the questionnaires (n=108). The average response was 47%.

48% of the total group of respondents work in the private sector and 42% in the public sector. 10% of the respondents work in both sectors. Many of the respondents are involved in the education sector through an employer or employee organisation (28%). More than one-fifth (21%) of the total group of respondents are female, while 79% are male. 85% of the group of respondents are aged 40 or older.

In addition to the written questionnaires, small-scale seminars were organised: one with policymakers, and one with experts. The policymakers were from the Adult Vocational Education and Higher Vocational Education boards of the Ministry of Education, Culture and Science and from the Adult Vocational Education Council and the Higher Vocational Education Council.

The group of experts was drawn from the private education sector or they were experts in the environmental segments concerned.

The analysis of the first round aimed to provide an empirically reliable and theoretically meaningful reduction of the 50 trends. Factor analysis was carried out for each group of respondents in combination with homogeneity analysis of the resulting factors. We found eight factors in each environment after the first round. These eight factors cover 20 of the original almost 50 trends. They are the following trends:

The 20 trends linked with these 8 factors were put to the respondents during the second round. As mentioned above, 108 experts were approached, and the response was 65%.

Variants of factor analyses of the 20 statements or selections from them and homogeneity analyses yielded a number of scenario dimensions that are relevant for scenario construction. We here present the five dimensions with the environmental segment(s) concerned:

Economy and Technology Environment
Dependence of economy on knowledge interaction structure.
Employment Environment
Employability life (work-training-care) cycle/alternation.
Economy and Technology / Employment
Decreasing company responsibility for educational investment.
Employment and Education and Knowledge Environment
Difficult to place migrants.
Education and Knowledge Environment
Education outside the school / the school under threat / ICT competitors.

We used the first two dimensions for the construction of initial scenarios. These two main factors which emerged from the analysis of the second questionnaire were used as dimensions for the scenario model. The 'economic dependence on knowledge interaction structure' became the horizontal axis and 'flexible periods of working, caring and training' the vertical axis.

Dependence of the economy on knowledge interaction structure			
		low	high
Flexible periods of working, caringand training	weak	The aloof society	The dual society
	strong	The secure society	The pick–'n'–mix society

Figure 7. Model for social scenarios

Based on this model, four social scenarios were constructed: the aloof society, the dual society, the secure society and the pick–'n'–mix society

2.4 The aloof society

Society ascribes to the education system a powerful role in the initial phase. Beyond this, however, it sees no significant role for education in social, economic or technological development. This is not seen as part of the education system's core business. Bodies like companies, industry organisations and social security agencies are quite capable of providing the necessary specialist knowledge and expertise for themselves. Demanding this sort of contribution from the education system would jeopardise its basic functions. Business and social organisations are clear about what they want from the education system. It should provide a firm foundation for individuals to play their part in society and in the world of work. They see the establishment of this foundation as the core business of education. In their eyes, it is a difficult enough task to do this successfully and it is not sensible or realistic to expect education to do anything else.

Vocational education is expected to deliver high-calibre basic training to equip young people with a solid basis for their further personal and professional development within society.

Nothing is expected of the education system with regard to social developments such as the combination of work, learning and care responsibilities. In this scenario, the increasing flexibility of the pension system and differentiation in social security arrangements aimed at permitting career breaks and a better distribution of work throughout life have negligible consequences for education.

2.5 The dual society

Society has two separate sets of expectations regarding the education system. It expects a proper foundation and at the same time active participation in setting up training courses to reflect specific developments in the workplace. These two sets of expectations are not presented in an integrated form. It is up to institutions to devise an adequate organisational structure to cope with them.

Individual companies and industries are very alert to changes in their skill requirements and very ready to call on the education system to provide these skills. Society expects higher professional education and the adult education and training fields to play their part by setting up regional networks with small and medium enterprises and by delivering young talent with the knowledge and skills required by the local labour market. The education system is also expected to contribute to the local economy, for example by steering students into work experience placements and research activities in local (mainly small and medium) enterprises, and by undertaking contract development activities and contract education.

Companies expect higher professional education and the adult education and training systems to keep in close touch with developments and to take account of them in their courses. The education system is expected to contribute both basic initial education and specific training in response to specific changes in practices within particular companies, industries or occupational groups. Society expects education constantly to adapt to changes in the workplace and in the economy.

Society regards education (both initial and further training) as important, but primarily in relation to clearly defined economic goals. Expectations of the education system do not extend to combinations of working, learning and caring. More flexible pension arrangements and differentiation of social security to facilitate the independent development of career breaks and a better distribution of work throughout life are not part of this scenario. They may occur, but if so will do so primarily in an economic context. Education plays no part in them.

2.6   The secure society

Developments in the social security field make education an increasingly important component of social security. The social security system is directed less at simply providing incomes and more at equipping people for employment. In this scenario, however, this is confined to general qualifications. There is no actual structure to optimise interaction between companies and schools. Education is primarily regarded as important in relation to social aspects of the combination of working, learning and caring. Education is, as it were, the link or glue between work and family responsibilities, and is viewed in the light of that function. The education system is not seen in the first instance as contributing directly to the economy in co-production with companies.

Society expects the education system to be open-minded about the place of education in the lives of individuals and requires it to target all the various phases of human life. The business world is not particularly interested in a direct partnership with education.

The reform of the welfare state brings a marked change in emphasis from the passive provision of incomes for the unemployed to an active stance on the labour market. This results in a tripartite social consensus and co-operative action aimed in part at getting the low–skilled into subsidised employment. This policy is backed up by limited cuts in employment-related benefits and a stepping-up of financial incentives. The educational facets of this approach relate primarily to social security and are not to any great extent formulated or structured in response to economic developments.

The education system is expected to provide a solid basic training (broad employability) and to formulate a range of further training opportunities and individual care/work arrangements based on the educational aspects of combinations of care and work.

Collective labour agreements made by the social partners with government backing include provision for training facilities for people in work. Government acquires a greater role and responsibility regarding the training of people in work and is heavily involved in efforts to improve the quantity and quality of work/care/training combinations.

Individuals are also expected to invest in their own development. Workers interrupt their careers or reduce their hours of work in response to the presence of working partners, family responsibilities, pressure of work or a desire for sabbaticals. Working and learning are combined or alternated.

2.7   The pick–'n'–mix society

The emphasis in the previous scenario was on social and educational security. Government played an important part in this. In this fourth scenario, however, there is no standard solution. Society offers many kinds of solution side by side and these are of varying use to consumers. Variation and diversity are more important than security.

A much more flexible and individualised pension system is created to promote worker mobility and facilitate the alternation of working, learning and caring. This system is primarily geared to current and expected future trends in industry. Differentiation in social security provides additional encouragement for individuals to operate as active agents in the labour market and to alternate periods of work, education and care. It is left to individuals to decide what combination they prefer, and government has no role in this.

An essential feature of this scenario is that economic and social aspects are in no way separate. However varied, expectations form an integrated whole. Economic and social demands blend together and must be co-ordinated within education (including initial and further vocational training). Precisely because of this interaction between economic and social demands, expectations regarding education are extremely diverse.

Workers themselves are responsible for keeping their knowledge and skills up to standard and so increasing their own employability. This is particularly true of workers taking career breaks or switching temporarily or permanently to part-time employment, for example to spend more time with their families. Variety is the name of the game.

The diversity of the education on offer is also reflected in contracts drawn up by companies with regional training centres, colleges of higher professional education and private sector providers (increasingly including temporary employment agencies). Employment agencies play a major role in co-ordinating supply and demand. In addition to their traditional intermediary role, they focus increasingly on improving the skills of potential and current staff through the provision of counselling and support in the training field.

2.8   Construction of educational strategies

The development of the educational strategies was based initially on the reasons given by respondents during the first and second round of questionnaires for the scores they awarded to developments relevant to the two dimensions of the scenarios. In other words, the basis was provided by the reasons given concerning those trends which were among the factors used in the process of constructing the scenarios described above.

These reasons were reduced to two dimensions. In the first, education is primarily an instrument used to achieve other aims of society, or education has primarily set its own goals and striven to achieve them. In the second, education is either pre- or post-structured. At present, government educational policies and legislation in all European countries are based mainly on the idea of pre–structuring, but this is certainly not the only possible educational strategy. Diagram 3 shows the four possible educational strategies.

	Institutional structure	
	Pre–structuring	Post–structuring Instrumentality
Sets own goals	1. Basic education	2. Independent
Instrumental to other aims	3. Recurrent education	4. Integrateable education

Figure 8. Educational strategies

The following four educational strategies were constructed on the basis of this model:
1. Basic education (pre–structured, determining its own goals).
2. Independent education/learning (post–structured, determining its own goals).
3. Recurrent education (pre–structured, instrumental).

4. Integrated education (post–structured, instrumental).

Unlike the societal scenarios, the educational strategies are of course drafted from the point of view of the education system. This means that they address the nature of the education provided and the identity of the provider.

2.9   Educational Strategies

2.9.1   Basic Education

Public sector vocational education focuses on foundation training and the first stage of further training for the workplace. This initial training is heavily structured, with set attainment targets and learning pathways leading to nationally approved qualifications. The education system knows best and formulates its own objectives. It does, of course, take account of the requirements of society, but the fact that this form of education is intended to provide a lasting basis means that priority is given to the system's own teaching aims.

The aim of public sector vocational education is therefore firstly to guarantee students a good start in their careers and secondly - and less importantly - to equip them to cope with changes in the labour market. Higher professional education and vocational and adult education and training are the initial forms of training, a basic form of social provision required to create the best possible chances for all. A high level of participation in education is also important to maintain the economic prosperity of the Netherlands. Access for all is a primary aim. Young people from underprivileged backgrounds need more attention and support but must also be enabled to enter the labour market with good basic qualifications. That is a social function which the market cannot fulfil. The institutions expect government to continue to fund this kind of initial vocational education.

2.9.2   Independent education/learning

Under this educational strategy, pre-planned programmes and courses are relatively unimportant other than in initial vocational training. It is often only apparent in retrospect which programme is relevant and the best person to decide this is the trainee or client. There is little point in establishing an extensive system of consultation and communication. The important thing is to ensure a broad, flexible range of provision from which consumers or clients can choose whatever seems most useful.

Public sector vocational education is active in both the initial and the post-initial phase.

Under this strategy, unlike the previous one, the public sector vocational education system also has a strong focus on post-initial education. It sees workers seeking further training as a growing market. In both initial and post-initial training, the higher professional education and vocational training and adult education fields focus on, and are strongly influenced by, the business market including individual companies, industries and professional associations. The role of the national bodies at the interface of industry and education is extremely important in this respect.

An on-going dialogue between the education system and the various industries ensures the development of a flexible supply of post-initial training courses which can be taken in many different ways and which reflect the rapid changes occurring in the workplace. At curriculum level, this leads to the introduction of modular programmes, more flexible choice of subjects and individual learning paths.

2.9.3   Recurrent education

The key terms for public sector education are 'modularity' and 'lifelong learning'. Education, whether initial or post-initial, is instrumental in whole life planning and in ensuring a smooth transition between the different phases of life and an easy alternation of periods of working, learning and caring.

Both initial and post-initial education are based on socio-economic needs and are instrumental in reforming business processes and the structures of production. With a view to the rapidly changing labour situation, initial education sees it as part of its responsibilities to lay the foundations for life-long learning. To achieve this, pupils and students must be taught the necessary interest, attitude and learning skills. Learning to learn is therefore an important concept during initial training: mastering the skills required for the independent acquisition of new knowledge and skills.

In addition, public sector education creates a set range of courses designed to assist people at a particular stage in their lives. These may be directed at entry or re-entry to the labour market, providing further training for those in work or improving general education and assisting personal development (for example, literacy, civics, or a second language). The relevance of the courses is clearly indicated in advance.

With regard to the knowledge economy, vocational and adult education and training and higher professional education see no major role for themselves. They co-operate with industry on the development of post-initial training designed to keep the knowledge and skills of workers up to standard, but are more reactive than proactive in this area. The pre-structuring of education means almost by definition that curriculum development plays a more or less reactive and reflective role.

2.9.4   Integrated education

Education, including initial and further training, is organised in such a way that it offers countless retrospectively valuable opportunities to respond both to the rapid and vigorous economic changes taking place and to the present and future personal situations of trainees. The education system gears its learning paths to this and serves both economic and social purposes.

Under this strategy, there is less emphasis on fixed initial qualifications than under the other three. Education, including both further and initial training, is organised as flexibly as possible to provide a rapid and satisfactory response to the changing needs of society and of individuals.

Due to market forces, education becomes heavily demand-oriented: that is, industry and individual students have a strong influence on programmes. At curriculum level, this produces individualised learning paths designed to meet the needs of a variety of target groups.

Education seeks not only to play a role in the transfer of existing knowledge, but also to contribute to the development and dissemination of new knowledge designed to promote economic growth. It feels itself instrumental in and co-responsible for economic innovation. To this end, the education system co-operates with other knowledge institutions, industries and innovative companies in the region.

At a system level, this strategy more than any other produces sharp competition, both within public sector education and between public and private sector providers. The vocational and adult education and training and higher professional education fields have to compete with a host of private sector providers developing courses to meet the educational needs of both companies and individuals. These providers target the entire market, including both initial and post-initial education. The industry organisations have their own training institutions to guarantee a supply of good staff. The companies are also keen to keep control of training via in-company courses.

2.10   Construction of administrative strategies

Experts from the fields of policy and administration were asked to rate trends in this area in terms of certainty and importance. Analysis of the answers revealed a number of dimensions for the construction of administrative strategies.

The administrative strategies were based on the one hand on the implementation of functions regarded as essential either by the market or by government, and on the other on a view of policy as starting either with the individual or with the institution or institutions. Expressed as a figure, this gives us the following.

Figure 4 Administrative strategies

	Starting–point for strategies: Individual/Consumer	*Starting–point for strategies: Institution*
Functions guaranteed by government	1 Controlled consumption of education	2. Promotion of autonomous institutions
Functions guaranteed by the market	3. Free consumption of education	4. Leave to administrative bodies

The four administrative strategies can then be categorized as follows:

1. Controlled consumption of education

Policy starts with the participants/target groups; the focus is on individual participants and the state guarantees basic functions.

2. Promotion of autonomous institutions

Socially responsible institutions; the focus is on institutions and government guarantees basic functions.

3. Free consumption of education

Competition is the ordering principle; the focus is on the individual consumer and basic functions result from market forces.

4. Leave to administrative bodies

Functional administrations for different parts of the country - the focus is on institutions, there are no central guarantees for basic functions and the administrative structure is based on functional administrations for different parts of the country.

2.10.1   Controlled consumption of education

Under this administrative strategy, policy starts with the individual consumer, but there are also central government guarantees for basic functions. In that sense, there is strong central government control. The Education Ministry plays a major role. It remains responsible for ensuring an adequate uptake of education. A proportion of educational funding is transferred from institutions to participants (for example, via education vouchers or training credits). This means that institutions providing higher professional education, vocational training or adult education must prove their worth by supplying products which represent good value for money.

But education is not left entirely to market forces. The Ministry has a very direct interest in seeing that certain target groups are properly served. A considerable amount of centralised control by the Education Ministry remains necessary to ensure satisfactory educational provision for the disadvantaged. This kind of socially desirable initial and further training is primarily in the hands of the regional training centres.

The change to funding participants may lead to a form of 'performance–related' system (earning credits). The disadvantaged must also be given access to good education. Policies for this have to be developed. Political control via the purchasing of services for the weaker sections of society will be extremely important. A government exercising more selective control will continue to see this as its responsibility.

2.10.2   Promotion of autonomous institutions

This administrative strategy assumes the development of socially responsible institutions. Over the last decade, this kind of strategy has been given heavy emphasis by the Ministry of Education, Culture and Science. Institutions are comparatively autonomous and set their own socio-political priorities with regard to the groups they wish to target within society. The institutions are aware of their own importance to the regional economy. They focus on the demands of the market, but also set socio-political priorities with regard to target groups within society. Consequently, they offer a varied range of educational provision in response to perceived needs.

The Education Ministry supports and monitors these processes on the basis of its supervisory responsibilities, ensuring in particular that institutions actually fulfil the basic functions for which they are responsible.

The institutions are responsible for their own management expertise and develop strong regional links. Their supervisory boards include members with a broad range of social experience as well as management specialists and representatives of the main regional bodies. Social liaison within the region is also organised via a regional consultative structure or advisory committees from the different sectors of industry.

2.10.3   Free consumption of education

Under this administrative strategy, the Education Ministry pursues a type of educational policy which has much in common with the general policies of the Ministry of Economic Affairs with regard to other goods and services. That is to say education is no longer regarded as in any way special, but rather as a set of goods and services like any other. The only remaining matters for government policy are economic aspects such as promoting competition, preventing monopolies, guaranteeing freedom of information and protecting consumers.

Should government decide to intervene at all in the market, it will do so purely as a regulatory authority and not in pursuance of its own aims. The Education Ministry will probably continue to be the main contractor/client in a few areas. Via this role, it will retain a number of responsibilities, such as safeguarding ethical standards and access, providing for the disadvantaged and preventing premature school-leaving. Otherwise, market forces will tend to dominate.

Higher professional education colleges and adult education and training institutions are no longer subject to educational legislation, but operate as companies and have that legal status. As such, they implement programmes, which may be contracted and funded either by the Education Ministry or by participants and companies.

2.10.4   Leave to administrative bodies

There is a steady increase in the scale of administration. Eventually, there will be separate administrations for different parts of the country, each governing a number of regional training centres or higher professional education colleges. Such centres and colleges will be less schools in the traditional sense than combinations of schools or teaching units under one roof. They will be governed by functional administrations for particular parts of the country. This may eventually have the side-effect of creating monopolies which will inhibit flexibility.

To promote the free play of market forces, it will be desirable to involve clients in this development, for example via tripartite administrations.

Rather being for a particular part of the country, some administrations might be organised along denominational lines or as cross-border authorities. The latter could be particularly important for the border areas.

Funding no longer goes to individual institutions, but to the administration for the particular part of the country. The Education Ministry liases with these bodies and some of its responsibilities are transferred to them.

This type of administrative arrangement requires some degree of supervision at national level. The Ministry continues to play a part in monitoring developments but the division of the country into area authorities means that many of its present tasks will disappear or be transferred to these functional administrations for the different parts of the country

2.11 Using scenarios to test strategies: do-it-yourself matrix

As part of the project, a workshop was organised in the autumn of 1997 for people from the vocational education and adult education and training fields. The workshop had two aims. Firstly, to expose the draft scenarios and strategies to critical scrutiny by the field, in order to make them clearer. Secondly, to see whether 'wind–tunnelling' would work. Were the scenarios a useful way to test the tenability and robustness of the educational and administrative strategies? And could the scenarios and strategies be used to launch a strategic dialogue?

One can try this exercise by studying the matrix below and making a serious attempt to complete the cells. Better still, complete the matrix together with a couple of colleagues: that way, a strategic dialogue can be stimulated. And that, after all, is the whole point of drafting scenarios and strategies.

Figure 5. Educational and administrative strategies based on scenarios

	Scenario 1. The aloof society	Scenario 2. The dual society	Scenario 3. The secure society	Scenario 4. The pick-'n'–mix society
Educational Strategy: 1. Basic education	Is this strategy an appropriate response to this scenario?	Is this strategy an appropriate response to this scenario?	Is this strategy an appropriate response to this scenario?	Is this strategy an appropriate response to this scenario?
Educational Strategy: 2.Independent education/learning	Is this strategy an appropriate response to this scenario?	Is this strategy an appropriate response to this scenario?	Is this strategy an appropriate response to this scenario?	Is this strategy an appropriate response to this scenario?
Educational Strategy: 3.Recurrent education	Is this strategy an appropriate response to this scenario?	Is this strategy an appropriate response to this scenario?	Is this strategy an appropriate response to this scenario?	Is this strategy an appropriate response to this scenario?
Educational Strategy: 4.Integrateable education	Is this strategy an appropriate response to this scenario?	Is this strategy an appropriate response to this scenario?	Is this strategy an appropriate response to this scenario?	Is this strategy an appropriate response to this scenario?
Administrative Strategy: 1. Controlled consumption of education	Is this strategy an appropriate response to this scenario?	Is this strategy an appropriate response to this scenario?	Is this strategy an appropriate response to this scenario?	Is this strategy an appropriate response to this scenario?

Administrative Strategy: 2. Promotion of autonomous institutions	Is this strategy an appropriate response to this scenario?	Is this strategy an appropriate response to this scenario?	Is this strategy an appropriate response to this scenario?	Is this strategy an appropriate response to this scenario?
Administrative Strategy: 3. Free consumption of education	Is this strategy an appropriate response to this scenario?	Is this strategy an appropriate response to this scenario?	Is this strategy an appropriate response to this scenario?	Is this strategy an appropriate response to this scenario?
Administrative Strategy: 4. Leave to administrative bodies	Is this strategy an appropriate response to this scenario?	Is this strategy an appropriate response to this scenario?	Is this strategy an appropriate response to this scenario?	Is this strategy an appropriate response to this scenario?

3.   CONCLUSION

Experiences with the scenarios and strategies thus far reveal that the main features of the scenarios and strategies were credible to the field, and further details were added to them in the course of the dialogue. This is likely to happen in all further discussions and, in that sense, the scenarios and strategies will never really be complete. The assessment of the strategies in the light of the scenarios has, as was intended, produced a clearly structured strategic debate. The confrontation between the societal scenarios and the educational and administrative strategies helps to increase and sharpen understanding both of changes in the social environment and of possible strategic responses to them.

The relevance of the different strategies can be worked out in more detail within the four scenarios. In this way both strategies and scenarios can acquire a sharper focus and more reality value. The pictures that we construct like this can be used as a compass for the organisation of vocational education and adult education.

REFERENCES

Becker, H.A. (1982), "Methodische aspecten van scenario's" in *Beleidsanalyses,* 1982-4, pp.7-12.
Centraal Planbureau. (1992), *Nederland in Drievoud,* Sdu, Den Haag.
Centraal Planbureau. (1993), *Bevolking Opleiding en Participatie tot 2015: drie scenario's,* CPB, Den Haag.
Hartog, J. (1996), "Kennis van de toekomst" in *Kennis voor morgen,* Min van OC&W, pp.49-85.

Hart, S. and Banbury, C. (1994), "How strategy-making processes can make a difference", *Strategic   Management Journal* 15, 251-269.

Heijden, K. van der (1996), *Scenario's: the art of strategic conversation*, John Wiley & Sons Ltd., Chichester.

Martinand, J.L. (1995), "The purposes and methods of technnological education on the threshold of the twenty-first century", *Prospect*, Vol.XXV No.1, pp.49-56.

Mintzberg, H. (1994), *The rise and fall of strategic planning* ,Prentice Hall, Hemel Hempstead.

OECD (1991), *Technology in an changing world*, OECD, Paris.

OECD (1994), *Science and technology policy; review and outlook 1994*, OECD, Paris.

OECD (1995), *Learning Beyond Schooling*, OECD, Paris.

OECD (1996), *Education and training; learning and working in a society in flux*, OECD, Paris.

Researchcentrum Onderwijs Arbeidsmarkt (1996), *De arbeidsmarkt naar opleiding en beroep tot 2000*, Universiteit Maastricht, Maastricht.

Schoemaker, P.J.H. (1995), "Scenario Planning: a tool for strategic thinking", *Sloan Management Review*, Winter 1995, pp.25-39.

Schoemaker. P. and Van der Heijden, K. (1992), "Integrating scenarios into strategic planning at Royal Dutch/ Shell", *Planning Review*, Vol.20 No.3.

Wieringen, A. M. L. van (1996), *Onderwijsbeleid in Nederland*, Samsom Tjeenk Willink, Alphen aan de Rijn.

LEARNING AND ORGANISATION IN
VOCATIONAL AND ADULT EDUCATION

Chapter 8

Introduction to Section 2
Learning and Organisation in Vocational and Adult Education

Graham Attwell
University of Bremen

The five different contributions to this section provide an overview of many of the key debates on the future development of adult and vocational education in Europe. In particular they focus on the role of education and training in developing new knowledge, innovation and jobs. This in turn leads to a need to question the relationship between technology, work organisation and education and training.

Graham Attwell and Alan Brown address this theme through their study of new requirements for education for VET professionals. This work arises out of a two year European Union sponsored Leonardo project 'New Forms of Education of Professionals for Vocational Education and Training (EUROPROF). In the chapter they discuss why the EUROPROF project has excited so much interest form vocational education and training researchers. The first reason, they say, is the growing recognition of the centrality of VET professionals to the teaching and learning process. Second is the collaborative research methodology developed by the project for transnational programmes. Thirdly is its design, in eschewing traditional curriculum approaches based on technical rationality, and has instead sought approaches based on the concept of 'Gestaltung' or shaping of work and technology.

The paper, based on surveys and studies undertaken through the EUROPROF project, looks at the 'cross cutting themes' in the education of VET professionals. These include the social shaping of work and technology, the importance of work related knowledge and the need to professionalise vocational education and training. It then advances a model for Continuing Professional Development based on the development of communities of practice. The major components of the model are developing practice, developing expertise and developing a research capacity. The ability to design and carry out authoritative research into aspects of professional practice individually or as part of a team is seen as an integral part of practitioners developing a research capacity.

They conclude by pointing to the need to develop new processes to identify the parameters and nature of the work-process knowledge applied in a profession or occupation, and the necessity for new tools to develop and expand the learning processes integral to such a curriculum. The aim should be to develop a dynamic community of active reflective learners.

Jeroen Ostenk builds on aspects of this contribution by looking at learning in work teams as a tool for innovation. He stresses the importance of learning at work to meet the challenge of continual changes in technology, organisational renewal, optimisation of the quality of production and an orientation to changing customer demands. He argues that informal and integrated on-the-job learning is an important characteristic of the new organisational paradigm.

Ostenk advances a model of the learning potential of jobs. On-the-job learning is not structured by specific pedagogical activities but by the structural characteristics of the work activity itself. It takes place if and when the work situation constitutes a learning environment. Whilst both job content and work environment can open up learning possibilities a workplace has to fulfil certain conditions in order to qualify as a strong learning environment. In discussing the learning potential of the work environment he identifies two central dimensions: the social-communicative environment and the information environment. The first dimension refers to the potential for collective and mutual learning and the second to the relevant information available in the job situation.

On-the-job training, organised by the enterprise, constitutes the second important opportunity for employees to learn in the workplace. On- the-job training concerns all those activities which are explicitly aimed at training employees by supporting, structuring and monitoring their learning. Whilst every job triggers learning, not all learning will lead to the desired results. Every learning intervention is intervening in an ongoing process of learning and sense making.

A major strategy to improve learning possibilities on-the-job is a combination of job enrichment and autonomous work tasks. The introduction of semi-autonomous work teams may be seen as an important strategy for learning, as well as developing more flexible production and enhancing motivation and commitment. Working in teams can lead to the enlargement or enrichment of the job especially through the enlargement of opportunities for decision making and solving production problems. Teams also enlarge the learning potential by reinforcement of collective learning processes in the group.

Ostenk goes on to analyse the problems and risks associated with the introduction of work teams. He concludes that the innovation of work is as much of a challenge to on-the-job-learning as a means in the development of a company culture geared to the integration of working learning and innovation.

Massimo Tomassini focuses his paper, 'How the Learning Organisation Evolves', on an examination of new theoretical contributions which help to give an evolutionary interpretation to the notion of the learning organisation. The hypothesis is that the learning organisation is a concept which can be used to cover aspects other than those typical of change at intra-organisational and interpersonal level, intended to achieve a systematic view and overcome resistance to change. The learning organisational can also be taken as a metaphor to develop the potential of situated knowledge and to exploit the opportunities for the social construction of knowledge in work communities. Compared with traditional models, this metaphor is far more open to inter-organisational dynamics of dialogue and sense-building by various communities equipped with specific models of interpretation and language codes.

In the first section of his paper Tomassini looks at the dominant approaches to the learning organisation and in particular to contributions to the filed of organisational learning and its application. He asks how the concept of the learning organisation can be continue to be used in conditions of constantly evolving innovation and learning needs. What does the concept mean in relation to complex and shifting forms of organisation?

He gores on to examine the value of knowledge and diffuse organisation. He counter-poses the idea of rethinking the enterprise as a knowledge platform to business process re-engineering. In putting forward new forms of organisational transformations he proposes the need to update classical learning organisational models. This in turn requires 'perspective taking', a process of exchange, evaluation and integration of the knowledge of a given community with that of other interacting communities.

The final section looks at the emergence of learning networks; forms of learning which involve strengthening knowledge within the community and at the same time improving interactions between the knowledge possessed by different communities. The theory of the learning organisation, he says, should be developed in this direction, taking account of the multitude of possible forms acquired not only by communities of practice and knowing themselves and internally, but also by their inter-relations.

Fons van Wieringen, in his paper 'VET systems and criteria for effectiveness', states that there is no single standard of effectiveness by which to judge vocational education in Europe. The systems differ in terms of the function and especially in the way they are designed. Systems can be classified and differentiated in terms of steering, funding, suppliers and the functional exclusiveness of the institution in which vocational education is provided. Following an analysis of these dimensions he goes on to outline work to develop a new conception of an educational system.

This is followed by an examination of different approaches to investigate the effectiveness of vocational education services. Four approaches are explored: the 'balanced score card, qualification targets, social functions and measures of organisational effectiveness. Analysis of the different systems can be combined in a matrix approach with different methods of evaluation. This allows a choice of different processes and techniques for measuring the effectiveness of vocational education.

It is clear from the analysis that there is no such thing as one ultimate criteria for the quality of European VET systems. However all the systems do have to find a balance between internal processes and external groups. Like Jan Ax's following contribution van Wieringen looks at the interests of different stakeholders in vocational education. An organisation like vocational education can be viewed as an organised collection of internal and external stakeholders. In such a multiple constituency perspective different stakeholders will hold different views of effectiveness. Stakeholders and support groups will form a series of overlapping coalitions to impose a dominant view of effectiveness on the organisation. Although vocational education serves a number of different, and sometimes counter-posed purposes, the two components crucial for delivery of the outcomes are the qualification of the teachers and the way knowledge is organised within the institution.

In his contribution, entitled 'Searching for Educational Quality: A Stakeholder Approach', Jan Ax explores perceptions for measuring quality in matching secondary vocational education and the demands posed by society. He examines the re-organisation of the Dutch vocational education and training system in terms as to what extent these structural and organisational changes bring about sufficient change in the way the institutions function to meet prior expectation. The contribution describes an explorative, descriptive inventory in the form of a field study of the external relations of the new Regional Training Centres as perceived by key witnesses.

The study, based on a series of open interviews, is preceded by a discussion of the stakeholder approach, which focuses on external relations. This formed the basis for the design of the interviews.

Ax advances the position that ultimately the efficacy of an organisation is determined by the sum of its stakeholder and that the Regional Training Centres, in pursuing a demand led strategy, need to have a proper understanding of the interests of their stakeholders. Stakeholders, he says, are all those who have an interest in the functioning of the organisation. His study deals with the external stakeholders, with those interested actors who are not part of the organisation. He analyses the different interests of this group and distinguishes different methods to identify stakeholders. He goes on to examine the meaning and implication of a stakeholder approach. The stakeholder approach is seen as a decision making oriented evaluation procedure to obtain information relevant to policy.

The next section of the paper examines the findings from the Dutch survey. The paper looks at the different views of the different groups of stakeholders including administrative bodies, customers in respect of school leavers, institutions with similar responsibilities of a parallel function, providers of resources, information providers, access providers and representatives of the target groups. These are analysed in terms of policy implications.

Chapter 9

Cross Cutting Themes in the Education of VET Professionals in Europe

Graham Attwell, and Alan Brown
University of Bremen : University of Warwick

1. THE EUROPROF PROJECT

In February 1996 the Leonardo Surveys and Analysis project 'New Forms of Education of Professionals for Vocational Education and Training' (EUROPROF) was launched at a workshop in Bremen, Germany. The project, which initially involved some thirteen partners from different European Member States, aimed to identify new occupational profiles and develop new Masters Degree programmes for teachers, trainers and planners in vocational education and training. Whilst the initial phase of Leonardo da Vinci funding has now ceased, the project partnership has reformed itself as the EUROPROF network with over 30 members in every European Member State, the countries of Eastern Europe, the USA and Australia. The partners are now editing their second English language book, the Finnish language book is in a reprint and a Greek language book is awaiting publication. Over eighty reports, papers and other documents have been produced. The network is awaiting evaluation of four new funding proposals, and 1998 is the third year running that EUROPROF has organised a symposium at the European Conference on Educational Research (ECER). Despite this the project can only be said to have been partly successful in its original aims. The new Masters programmes were seen as a central plank in professionalising Vocational Education and Training and thus in moving VET towards recognition as a discipline in itself, rather than its present 'half life' between and drawing on different academic traditions and disciplines. Despite considerable progress over the last two and a half years this development is some way off, if indeed the original proponents would still choose to formulate their objectives in such a way.

1.1   Background: the need for EUROPROF

In this short paper we will examine some of the barriers to those goals and discuss the further steps that need to be undertaken in the development of a new framework for the professionalisation of VET. It is worth reflecting on the reason that the EUROPROF project has generated such a volume of activity and attention. First is the growing recognition of the centrality of VET professionals, especially in the context of the 'new paradigm' of lifelong learning, to the teaching and learning process. Pedagogic research has shown that far from replacing the role of teachers ad trainers, new forms of learning, including the use of open and distance learning materials and work-based learning, require an active intervention in planning, designing and mediating the learning process (see, for example, Attwell, 1997; Engeström, 1995; Mjelde, 1995; Brown, 1997a; Guile and Young 1997; Kauppi, 1998). Second is the question of methodology. The growing recognition of the importance of VET to innovation and economic competitiveness, allied to the European integration process, has led to an increase in European VET research, largely funded through the European Commission (Bynner and Chisholm, 1998). This in turn has focused attention on the methodologies required to carry out studies on a transnational basis. The EUROPROF project has developed the idea of collaborative research as an additional tool to the more traditional comparative approach which has characterised previous project development (Attwell, 1998), and has participated in the debate around an action research approach to transnational development (Nyhan, 1998). Furthermore the EUROPROF development has focused attention on the question of differences in culture and their impact and meaning for attempts to establish VET at a European level (Attwell and Hughes, forthcoming; Heikkinen, forthcoming). The third reason for the interest in the EUROPROF project lies in its wider implications for VET in Europe. In its design EUROPROF has eschewed traditional curriculum approaches, based on technical rationality (Edwards, 1995; Attwell and Brown, forthcoming). Instead it has sought approaches based on the concept of Gestaltung[1] (Heiddeger, 1996), and aiming to overcome the fragmentation of existing provisions in

---

[1] The German word "Gestaltung" has caused some problems for researchers in seeking an adequate English translation. The most commonly used word is `shaping' – in the sense that workers develop the skills and knowledge to co-shape the work organisation and the use of technology.

education for VET professionals (Kauppi, 1996). Such an approach has applicability for the wider field of VET in Europe as a whole, especially given the preponderance of new curriculum projects within the portfolio of EC funded VET programmes (Ant, 1998).

In this paper we will firstly consider a number of 'cross cutting themes' that have emerged through the life of the EUROPROF development. Secondly we will outline the model of continuing professional development developed to respond to these themes. Thirdly we will reflect on the new questions such a model poses for vocational education and training research in Europe. The paper is based on an analysis of the different surveys and studies undertaken through the EUROPROF project and on a number of other 'related' Leonardo projects, notably the INTEQUAL and Post 16 Strategies projects. In undertaking this analysis a central concern is how to close the gap between research and practice in VET, in other words how to build a community of practice which can assist in the professionalisation of VET through an articulation of the outcomes of research in practice. It should be noted that this approach differs significantly from the concerns of the European Commission with project 'impact'.

2.   THE EXISTING EDUCATION OF VET PROFESSIONALS

In a forthcoming publication (Attwell and Hughes, forthcoming) we explain how the process of collaboration has enabled the EUROPROF project to identify a series of trends and directions in the role and education of VET professionals in the different member states, and reveals a complex and apparently paradoxical situation of simultaneous convergence and divergence.

Firstly, there is a broadening in the role of VET professionals in most countries in Europe. Perhaps of greatest significance is the increased attention being paid to continuing vocational training. Whereas previously the main focus for continuing training lay in the area of management development, the acceptance of ideas such as lifelong learning and the changes in work organisation are extending continuing training to include wider sections of the workforce and to encompass a broader curriculum. This means new responsibilities for traditional human resources development (HRD) specialists but also leads to a blurring in the division of roles between what was seen as the work of VET practitioners and that of HRD professionals.

Secondly, as a result of this trend, there is a new emphasis on organisational learning leading to new roles for both VET and HRD professionals in organisations and enterprises and in initial vocational education and training. The third area where roles have broadened is in the provision of vocational education and training for the unemployed. The task of retraining the workforce is seen as a major task in most EU states. There is a movement away from lower level, narrowly focused instructional activities to a more holistic model which includes counselling, work placement and monitoring as well as the planning and management of more demanding retraining programmes.

Fourthly, the trend towards decentralisation of vocational education and training provision is leading to new roles in management. At the same time the emphases on situated learning and work process knowledge are leading to deep seated changes in the form and delivery of VET provision. There is a move away from instruction and classroom provision towards a new focus on the management of the learning environment and the identification, design and structuring of learning activities. This in turn is highlighting activities such as mentoring, coaching, simulating and facilitating rather than instruction and didactic teaching. Once more, the trends indicate that reform of initial vocational education and training towards more work process related activities rather than just classroom learning, is both broadening the role of VET professionals and, at the same time, leading to a convergence between the traditional roles of VET and HRD specialists. The primary role of both is now the management of the learning process.

However, if these changes are running in parallel in most member states, the way the effects of these changes are manifested in different cultures and their impact on national systems is not only complex, but often divergent. For example, whilst occupational profiles are converging across member states, whilst the national labour markets are moving in similar directions and whilst (because of globalisation) new models of work organisation are being widely disseminated, the relationship between these elements and the relationship of these changes to different socio-cultural contexts is diverging. It is outside the scope of this paper to analyse fully the reasons for such divergence. For this readers are directed to the forthcoming publication (Attwell and Hughes, forthcoming). Our aim in this paper is to identify the cross cutting themes and suggest ways in which these may assist in the development of research and models to reconcile divergence in practice.

However, it is apposite at this juncture to consider the underpinning theory and practice which is central to much of the education of VET professionals in Europe. Traditional definitions and explanations of professional competence or expertise have been based on theories of technical rationality - on the basis that learning can be applied in predictable and repeated ways (Edwards, 1993). Vocational education and training curricula and processes have traditionally been based on imparting a fixed body of knowledge and skills required for identified tasks within occupational roles. Furthermore the Taylorist work organisation which not only has dominated industrial and commercial practice, but also the organisation of vocational schools and work-based training, has led to the division of roles between different specialists in the field of education and training. Thus the existing provision for the education of VET professionals tends to reproduce a division of labour between 'teachers', 'trainers', 'designers and developers' and 'training managers' (Kämäräinen, 1998). In this way the existing provisions split the integrative idea of 'work process knowledge' to particular aspects for which different categories of VET professionals can claim an exclusive ownership (e.g. command of the knowledge-basis of 'vocational subjects', experience in organised learning within enterprises and training centres, and so on).

3. CROSS CUTTING THEMES

The brief survey above provides a background for the identification of cross cutting themes. The picture of diversity and divergence does not in itself provide the basis for common European development, other than a comparative analysis. Nethertheless the EUROPROF project has been able to identify a series of themes, which although they are reflected in different ways in different countries and regions, allow the identification of models for further common development. These themes were first identified as a series of project 'cornerstones' (Attwell, 1997).

3.1 Social shaping as a goal

There is a growing critique of the European vocational education and training agenda as being economistic in viewing qualifications as necessary for adaptation to technological and economic demand (Attwell and Hughes, forthcoming). Heidegger (1997) argues it is not enough for skilled workers to be able to respond to the changing requirements of our society. Instead they need the skills and knowledge to be able to shape the application of technology and the social form of work for themselves, thus emphasising the dialectical relationship between education, technology and work. Rauner (1998) also points to the inadequacy of existing taxonomies of knowledge, seeing the need to overcome the duality between academic knowledge (brain work) and vocational skill (hand work) which he traces back to the Renaissance. In the 21st century he suggests, work-related knowledge will become central to both profitability and social community. This theme provides a basis for identifying the new kinds of knowledge required of VET professionals, including both technical and pedagogic competence, as well as the ability to shape their own work.

3.2   The importance of work-related knowledge

The cognitive side of occupational competence is key to the development of context-related expertise: with work-related knowledge providing the link between knowledge, which is not context related, and experience at work, which may not necessarily be used in a generalisable way. This implies both the need for active reflection upon experience and a shift from information to knowledge: expertise cannot be developed through simple although extended information acquisitions, but only through continuous and subtle cognitive experiences related to putting knowledge into action, co-developing personal and professional knowledge, and integrating individual knowledge into the larger dimensions of knowledge held by groups and whole organisations.

3.2.1   Need to focus upon learning and knowledge development

In terms of VET innovation the `enjeux' are very relevant: a shift of emphasis is required from training to learning and from the mere transmission of knowledge through training interventions to the facilitation of learning (i.e. the creation, use and circulation of knowledge), through more complex interventions in which training is mixed with other HRD practices. In particular, it seems as if VET has to ensure that individuals are able to contribute to the processes of knowledge development within organisations. Accordingly there is a need to overcome the division between VET orientated teachers and HRD orientated trainers.

3.2.2   Knowledge development as a key factor in innovation

The focus upon particular kinds of knowledge development has been identified as a key factor in innovations designed to increase the supply of creative knowledge value: "what is important for the production of knowledge value is not so much facilities or equipment in the material sense, but the knowledge, experience, and sensitivity to be found among those engaged in its creation" (Sakaiya, 1991, p270). This way, knowledge is assumed as the real driving force of our era, but also strictly linked with day-to-day problem-solving and problem-setting in working situations, and more generally with the development and use of professional competencies and expertise.

3.3　The Professionalisation of VET

It is arguable that the themes identified above could be applied to any professional or occupational expert. In this way the challenge in developing new occupational profiles and new qualifications for VET professionals reflects the challenges facing the development of VET in Europe today. However it is also argued that the drive to 'professionalise the professionals' must be placed at the centre of European curriculum development concerns in the field of VET. Given the themes outlined above, and compared with the policy and practice in present education of VET professionals, the task is indeed daunting. The EUROPROF project originally posited the development of new Masters programmes as a step towards the recognition of VET as a discipline in itself. Given the intensity of the debate over the past two years we would develop this argument further. There have been concerns expressed that the term discipline, with its connotation of university departments and traditional forms of knowledge fails to meet the challenges facing VET. Our own research has pointed to the need for a new taxonomy of knowledge based on work processes (Attwell et al, 1997). In this context the term 'community of practice' (Brown, 1997b) may offer a more clear meaning of what we are striving to achieve, as could Young and Guile's (1997) formulation of a 'community of connective specialists'. All these formulations share the central concepts of a body of self-reflexive experts, able to apply knowledge and skills in a work related context. To this extent it remains a critical concern that the barriers between university based research and learning and the applied practice of VET teachers and trainers is broken down in developing a new relationship between theory and practice in action in VET.

3.4　Models for Continuing Professional Development

Our analysis of the failings of the present education of VET professionals has led us to the need to develop new models. Such models should include the initial education of teachers and trainers, but also need to develop a broader perspective in order to encompass continuing learning. The models should be based on the development of new knowledge through the application of expertise. Such a model needs to be robust at the level of pedagogy and design whilst providing the flexibility for its implementation in different cultural and social settings. The Continuing Professional Development (CPD) of professionals needs to be reflective, forward-looking and dynamic. It needs to equip professionals with the ability to support the development of skills, knowledge and understanding of others as well as of themselves, in a commitment to lifelong learning, as well as seeking to accommodate requirements for complexity and flexibility. Such a task is only achievable with a commitment to continuing professional development within a culture which acknowledges the importance of developing practice, expertise and a research capability in an inter-related way (Brown, 1997a), so as to be able to support the generation of new forms of knowledge (Engeström, 1995).

3.4.1 Communities of Practice

The Continuing Professional Development of professional communities of practice needs to incorporate current concerns, but also have the ability to look beyond these, and this is possible only if, as Ellström (1997) argues, practitioners develop a broad developmental and interactive view of occupational competence. This would complement a focus upon the significance of work-related knowledge and work process knowledge in the Continuing Professional Development of professional communities of practice. A fuller explanation of our model for the CPD of VET professionals is provided elsewhere (Attwell and Brown, 1998). Here we will limit ourselves to a summary of the major components of the model.

3.4.2 Developing practice

Initial competence as a professional is often associated with the ability to 'survive' and gradually assume a full position within particular 'communities of practice' (Lave, 1991). However, practitioners need to have a continuing commitment to explore, reflect upon and improve their professional practice (Schön, 1983; 1987). This in turn means that practitioners have to develop the understanding, skills and knowledge necessary to evaluate and review their professional practice, recognising that such practice often takes place in complex and dynamic contexts.

3.4.3 Developing expertise

The initial key to going beyond competent practice lies in the ability to transfer skills, knowledge and understanding from one context to another (Eraut, 1994), so Continuing Professional Development has to be able to support this process, including through helping practitioners to perform effectively when they work with colleagues and in groups with different kinds of expertise (Engeström, 1995).

Another aspect of developing expertise lies in the ability of the professional to handle the complexity and inter-relatedness of issues. There is clearly not a precise moment when one can identify a shift from 'competent practitioner' to 'expert', not least because it requires a degree of self-acknowledgement as well as recognition by others (Brown, 1997c). Expertise rather lies at the conjunction of research, theory and practice, such that the practitioner can be considered 'reflective', not only upon action, but also upon 'reflection in action' (Schön, 1987). In order to develop expertise it is important for practitioners to develop their research skills and be able to apply them to their professional practice. In an important sense then expertise is itself partly generated through research.

It should also be noted that understanding and, if appropriate, application of theory has a role to play within developing expertise. While the value of practical theory or 'theorising' in the sense of reflecting upon his or her own practice is central to the process of becoming an experienced professional (Schön, 1987), this on its own is insufficient. Rather because it is locked into current modes of practice, it is important that 'theoretical learning' is also developed (Guile and Young, 1996). Theoretical learning provides the concepts for analysing the problems that arise for professionals at work and for making explicit the assumptions underlying existing practice (Guile and Young, 1996). This conceptual knowledge can then be used to underpin reflection upon practice at a deeper level than just 'theorising' practice. Such conceptual knowledge can have both explanatory power and be applied to (changes in) practice. It therefore complements the development of practical learning, based upon reflection on practice. Crucially, however, the development and application of theoretical learning also facilitates a forward-looking perspective: enabling thinking about how practice might be developed in future.

3.4.4   Developing a research capability

Teaching and nursing are recent examples of professions where there have been explicit attempts to move more towards making these research-based professions, where practice is not only informed by research, but new knowledge about practice is capable of being generated by the professionals themselves. This entails explicit recognition that practitioners have a key role to play in how new knowledge is generated and applied in practice (Engeström, 1995). Further this could be linked with an attempt to create wider communities of practice that embrace research as a guide to both policy and action (Brown, 1997a). The ability to design and carry out authoritative research into aspects of professional practice individually or as part of a team is an integral part of practitioners developing a research capability. However, possession of research skills will also be valuable in helping professionals analyse, interpret, evaluate and, if appropriate, apply the research findings of others.

3.4.5   The ability to communicate effectively

Personal change and development are central to the educational process, and professionals have to be receptive to challenges to their ideas and existing patterns of thought and action. Reflecting upon and responding to change will also involve complex social processes in which the ability to communicate effectively is essential.

3.4.6   Inter-relationships

Professional knowledge can itself be regarded as a personal synthesis of received occupational knowledge and situational understandings, derived from experimental learning, which are capable of being further transformed through a process of critical reflection (Hammond and Collins, 1991). As expertise develops, and new contexts are utilised in the performance of practice, so the processes of research, review and reflection can lead to the creation of new forms of knowledge (Engeström, 1995). Continuing professional development can play a role in making these processes explicit such that others too can share in the developmental process. Hence Continuing Professional Development has at its core a number of inter-related commitments. The most obvious is a commitment to personal development. The others include:
- exploration of, reflection upon and improvement of professional practice;
- development of skills, knowledge and understanding (of critical reflection) necessary to evaluate and review professional practice;
- need to understand processes of change (as practice increasingly takes place in complex and dynamic contexts);
- ability to create new knowledge;
- development of theoretical knowledge to underpin and complement reflection upon practice;
- study of the interplay between theory and practice;
- need to be able to transfer skills, knowledge and understanding from one context to another;
- the generation of expertise through research;

- ability to handle complexity and inter-connectedness of issues (including through the formulation of mental models, schemas or networks);
- development of contextualised understandings;
- translation of understanding into action, as appropriate;
- further development of communication skills;
- attempt to create a wider community of practice that embraces research as a guide to both policy and action;
- ability to design and carry out authoritative research into aspects of professional practice;
- ability to analyse, interpret, evaluate and, if appropriate, apply the research findings of others.

3.5   Cross Cutting Themes in Practice

We are convinced that our model is robust enough to be applicable in different historical, cultural and social settings. However, the model poses new questions in terms of curriculum design and implementation. Traditional curricula, based on criteria of technical rationality, have been designed around the identification of outcomes, albeit with differing taxonomies and assessment regimes. In higher education curricula have been derived from the identification of a corpus of knowledge associated with a particular subject or discipline. In vocational education curricula are most frequently derived from some process of functional analysis, through examining the skills and knowledge required for a particular occupational profile and then deriving a list of objectives or outcomes, with the greater or lesser participation and influence from social partners. Our exploration of cross cutting themes, and the development of a model for continuing professional development, indicates a need to develop new processes. Firstly there is the need to identify the parameters and nature of the work process knowledge applied in a profession or occupation. In recognising that knowledge and learning play a central role in the development of innovation then it must be seen that there are choices in how such knowledge is defined. It is possible to develop different scenarios for the future of work and technology in different occupational fields. The very form of education will influence the ability for different scenarios to be enacted.

Secondly, and more importantly, attention needs to be focused upon the centrality of learning to our model. If learning is, as we believe, situated, then this gives an increased importance to the provision of a range of rich learning situations and the ability and support to reflect on that learning. Thus the new curriculum may be better understood as a series of processes, rather than a series of defined outcomes based on a limited corpus of knowledge. This in turn leads to two observations. First there is the need for new tools to develop and expand such learning processes. In this way the world of education and of VET may once more benefit from the experiences of those working in the field of HRD and organisational learning. Second is the need for a dynamic process where the VET community itself plays a central role in defining and developing the goals and design of its own professionality – in other words a dynamic community of active, reflective learners.

However, the development of such a community itself demands the forging of a new relationship between VET researchers, policy makers and planners, and VET practitioners. The present divides in Member States are reflected at a European level. A first evaluation of the impact of the new European programmes in VET and in education which followed the Maastricht agreement must raise concerns over the way research has been integrated within the programmes, and as to the effectiveness of the programmes outcomes. The professionalisation of VET demands not only the development of new pedagogic processes but new methodologies and processes for VET research itself. In this respect there is a need to develop rigorous tools and methodologies for comparative VET research as a tool for the identification, trialling and development of a VET pedagogy at a European level.

REFERENCES

Ant, M. (1998), "Surveys and Analyses in Vocational Education and Training: results and trends" in Dietzen, A. and Kuhn, M. (Eds.), *Building a European Co-operative Research Tradition in Vocational Education and Training*, Bundesinstitut für Berufsbildung, Berlin und Bonn.

Attwell, G. (1997), "Towards a community of practice for vocational education and training professionals", in Brown, A. (Ed.), *Promoting Vocational Education and Training: European Perspectives*, University of Tampere Press, Tampere.

Attwell, G. (1998), "New Forms of Education of Professionals for Vocational Education and Training", in Dietzen, A. and Kuhn, M. (Eds.), *Building a European Co-operative Research Tradition in Vocational Education and Training*, Bundesinstitut für Berufsbildung, Berlin und Bonn.

Attwell, G. and Brown, A. (1998),"Work Related Knowledge and the Education of VET Professionals", paper presented to 1998 ECER Conference, Ljubliana, 17-20 September.

Attwell, G. and Brown, A. (forthcoming), "The acquisition of skills and qualifications for Life Long Learning - trends and challenges across Europe", in *CERETOQ Directory*, CEDEFOP, Thessaloniki.

Attwell, G. and Hughes, J. (forthcoming), "Researching VET - from Collaboration to Comparative Approaches", in Lauterbach, U. and Sellin, B. (Eds.), *Comparative Vocational Education and Training Research in Europe, Policy Links and Innovation Transfer*, CEDEFOP/ DIPF, Frankfurt.

Attwell, G., Jennes, A. and Tomassini, M. (1997), "Work related Knowledge and Work Process Knowledge", in Brown, A. (Ed.), *Promoting Vocational Education and Training: European Perspectives*, University of Tampere Press, Tampere.

Brown, A. (1997a), "Valuing the development of practice, expertise and research int continuing professional development of vocational education and training professionals", paper presented at European Conference on Educational Research (ECER 97) Frankfurt, September 1997.

Brown, A. (1997b), "A dynamic model of occupational identify formation", in Brown,A. (Ed.), *Promoting Vocational Education and Training: European Perspectives*, University of Tampere Press, Tampere.

Brown, A. (1997c), "Becoming skilled during a time of transition: observations from Europe", paper presented at Sixth (US) National Career Development Conference on 'Careers and Technology', Daytona Beach, Florida, January 1997.

Bynner, J. and Chisholm, L. (1998), "Comparative Youth Transition Research: Methods Meanings and Research Relations", in *European Sociological Review*, Vol. 14, No. 2, pp.131-150.

Edwards, R. (1993), "Multi-Skilling the Flexible Workforce in Post-Compulsory Education and Training", in *Journal of Further and Higher Education*, Vol.17 No.1.

Ellström, P.E. (1997), "The many meanings of occupational competence and qualifications", in Brown, A. (Ed.), *Promoting Vocational Education and Training: European Perspectives*, University of Tampere Press, Tampere.

Engeström, Y. (1995), *Training for Change*, ILO, London.

Eraut, M .(1994), *Developing professional knowledge and competence*, Falmer, London.

Guile, D. and Young, M. (1996), "Connecting work, learning and higher level qualifications: a new role for theory and practice in Masters degrees", unpublished paper, Post-16 Centre, Institute of Education, University of London.

Hammond, M. and Collins, R. (1991), *Self-directed learning: critical practice*, Kogan Page, London.

Heidegger, G. (1997), "Key considerations in the education of vocational education and training professionals", in Brown, A. (Ed.), *Promoting vocational education and training: European perspectives*, University of Tampere, Tampere.

Heikkinen, A. (1997), "How to study apprenticeship collaboratively", in Heikkinen, A. and Sultana, R.G. (Eds.), *Vocational Education and Apprenticeships in Europe*, Tampereen Yliopisto Kasvatustieteiden Laitos Julkaisusarja, Tampere.

Kämäräinen, P. (1998), "In search for the educational relevance of 'work process knowledge'- Insights in current research and reflections on educational consequences", paper presented to 1998 ECER Conference, Ljubliana, 17-20 September.

Kauppi, A. (1996), "From Fragmentation to Collaboration in vocational teacher education", in *LlinE Life Long Learning in Europe*, Vol. 2, No. 2.

Kauppi, A. (1998), "Curriculum Development for Integrating Work and Learning", in *LLinE Lifelong Learning in Europe*, Vol.3 No.2, pp.76-85.

Lave, J. (1991), "Situated learning in communities of practice", in Resnick, L., Levine, J. and Behrend, S. (Eds), *Perspectives on socially shared cognition,* American Psychological Association, Washington DC.

Mjelde, L. (1994), "Will the Twain Meet? The World of Work and The World of Schooling (Vocational and General) in Relation to Upper Secondary Educational Reforms in Norway", in Heikkinen, A. (Ed.), *Vocational Education and Culture – European Prospects from History and Life History*, Tampereen Yliopisto, Tampere.

Nyhan, B. (1998), "Promoting a European Vocational Education and Training Resercah Tradition – the role of the surveys and analyses measure of the LEONARDO da Vinci programme", in Dietzen, A. and Kuhn, M. (Eds.), *Building a European Co-operative Research Tradition in Vocational Education and Training,* Bundesinstitut für Berufsbildung, Berlin und Bonn.

Rauner, F. (1998), "Human Resource Pathways for the Year 2000; the Future of Vocational Education and Training", paper presented at International Federation for Training and Development Conference, July 21-24, Dublin.

Sakaiya, T. (1991), *The knowledge value revolution*, Kodansha International, Tokyo.

Schön, D. (1983), *The reflective practitioner*, Basic Books, New York.

Schön, D. (1987), *Educating the reflective practitioner*, Jossey Bass, London.

Young, M. and Guile, D. (1997), "New possibilities for the professionalisation of UK VET professionals", in *Vocational Training and HRD in Europe: research and traditions, Journal of European Industrial Training*, Vol.21 No. 6/7, pp.203-212.

Chapter 10

Learning in Work Teams as a Tool for Innovation

Jeroen Ostenk
SCO Kohnstamm Institute, Amsterdam

1.   THE IMPORTANCE OF LEARNING AT WORK

Continual changes in technology, organisational renewal, optimisation of the quality of production (efficiency, flexibility, product quality) and orientation to changing consumer demands require higher standards of skills and flexibility in the work force. In order to meet these standards it is necessary to deliver more training to the work force and define training in terms of investment rather than costs. Training of employees in general, and learning in the workplace in particular, can be regarded as a major challenge for Human Resources Development. In a recent White Paper on Lifelong Learning (OCW, 1998) the Dutch government stressed the importance of learning at work as an essential contribution to lifelong learning. Apart from opening up better possibilities for the recognition and accreditation of prior learning, however, there were no specific policies proposed to enhance this kind of learning processes. So a lot is expected from companies themselves in this respect.

In a way it could be said that companies do already respond to this call, despite the government doe not ask them to do so. But companies themselves feel a growing need for strengthening their core competencies on a competitive market where people make a difference (Kessels, 1996, Onstenk, 1998). It will be argued in this chapter that informal and integrated on-the-job-learning (OJL) at all levels of the organisation can be seen as an important characteristic of the new organizational paradigm.

In the next paragraph the model of the learning potential of jobs is introduced. In the third paragraph semi-autonomous work groups are discussed as the basic organisational unit of new production concepts. In paragraph 4 learning in work teams will be discussed in terms of their for the learning potential and innovation strategies.

2.   THE LEARNING POTENTIAL OF JOBS

A distinction can be made between on-the-job learning (OJL) and on the job training (OJT). OJL is not structured by specific pedagogical activities, but by the structural characteristics of the work activity itself.

Figure 1   The Learning Potential of Jobs (Source: Onstenk, 1997)

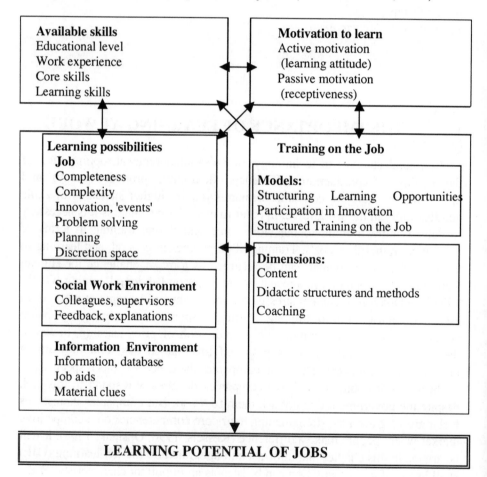

It takes place if and when the work situation (task, task management and work organisation) constitutes a learning environment. OJT is characterized by explicit pedagogic structuring: explicit training objectives and plans, printed course material, computerised job guides or active involvement of a trainer.A workplace has to fulfil certain conditions in order to qualify as a strong learning environment (Onstenk, 1994, 1995a, 1995b, 1997). Adopting and developing the terminology of Baitsch and Frei (1980), these can be analysed in terms of the learning potential of jobs. The model, as elaborated by Onstenk (1994, 1995b, 1997), see fig. 1, is based on activity theory (Engeström, 1987; 1994) and constructivist theories of practical knowledge (Scribner, 1984) and situated learning (Lave and Wenger, 1991).

The learning potential refers to the likelihood that learning processes will occur in a particular job situation. This likelihood depends on

1) the available skills and learning abilities of the employee;
2) the willingness to learn of the employee;
3) the learning opportunities on the job;
4) the availability of training on-the-job;
5) relationships and mutual influences of these factors.

Learning processes and the development of competence result from the specific combination of the workers skills and qualifications (formal education, work experience, learning skills), their ability and willingness to learn and develop competence and the learning possibilities on the shop-floor (tasks, co-operation, control, autonomy, training policies, organisational change etc.).

Both job content and work environment can open up learning possibilities. With regard to the *job content* (scope and variation), the amount of problems to solve and the autonomy to deal with these problems are essential. Jobs differ greatly in content and variation. A company has a lot of organisational choice in this respect: the same kind of job can be designed in different ways, allowing for more or less learning opportunities. Learning possibilities can be enlarged by putting people in different posts in the production process, enabling them to broaden the range of skills which can be themselves still rather narrow (multi-skilling). Much more effective and consequential is a redesign of jobs whereby complete jobs are created: jobs which include preparing, executing, controlling and steering tasks (Projectgroep WEBA, 1989). This greatly enlarges the chance that people in their job meet on a regular - and recognised ! (compare Kusterer, 1976) - basis do discuss new situations, problems and 'events' (Zarifian, 1991), in which they can learn about new methods, technologies or products. Work problems become learning problems when existing solutions are not effective and solutions completely satisfactory ones do not yet exist. Encountering serious work problems, developing interest to solve them and having the opportunity for reflection are strong incentives to learning (Engeström, 1994). The only way to learn by solving problems is to actually have enough autonomy, skills, means and support to be able to solve the problem (De Sitter, 1994). An organisation must stimulate and accept searching for answers, including the possibility to make mistakes. Employees should be allowed to experiment and take the relevant decisions. The organisation must guarantee the conditions for this. Employees must have as much influence on order, tempo, methods and task variation as is needed in order to solve the problems they meet in the job. If problems cannot be solved alone, it must be possible to look for support from colleagues or support staff (Projectgroep WEBA, 1989). This can include organising specific developmental research activities supporting workers/learners to reach for the zone of proximal development (Engeström, 1987). If these conditions are not met, encountering a problem does not result in learning but in stress (Karasek and Theorell, 1990).

Also the *work environment* can be more or less conducive to learning. Two dimensions can be distinguished: the social-communicative environment and the information environment.

The first dimension refers to the potential for collective and mutual learning. This connects closely to the problem richness of the job and refers to learning from and with others in the work place as a community of practice (Lave and Wenger, 1991). Social clues for learning/problem solving are given by experienced colleagues, experts and supervisors. Collective problem solving, giving and taking support and feedback, but also telling work related stories, are strongly favoured learning (Raizen, 1989). Experienced colleagues and supportive supervisors must be present and they must be accessible. Mutual learning can be organised in quality circles or weekly work meetings, where employees and supervisors discuss daily work problems, aiming at improving performance and solving problems. But also a lot of learning is done in informal talk during coffee breaks. Research shows how repair mechanics of photocopier machines solve problems by discussing with clients and by telling 'war stories' in which specific machines and customers are discussed (Raizen, 1989). In this way participating in the community of practice (Lave and Wenger, 1991) is essential in developing competencies. Employees learn and 'teach' together solving complex, specific and situated problems. This is especially important because of the fact that the machine manuals, produced by the company, in many cases was not of much help. The amount of communication is not only important for the support of problem solving, but is also important for giving meaning to working life and to develop the commitment which has gained such a high esteem in the learning organisation. If critical-reflective learning is expected of employees the work environment needs to listen to and to make use of the proposals.

The second dimension refers to relevant information that is available in the job situation. Information can be available in the form of job aids (Bastiaens, 1998), databases, handbooks, manuals etc. or as information produced in the production process itself, i.e. as an effect of automatisation and informatisation (Zuboff, 1988), but can also be embedded in the physical set up of the work situation (Scribner, 1984). Learning strategies used on the job are specific and situation bound. They are determined by the attempt to handle the job with minimal efforts and maximum results. Available information and clues, given by the social and physical work environment, are actively used. This is not only true for knowledge workers (Kessels, 1997), but also for so called unskilled jobs.

2.1   On-the-Job Training

On-the-job-training (OJT), organised by the firm constitutes the second important opportunity for employees to learn in the workplace. It can be defined as intentional, structured and organised OJL. All dimensions of learning possibilities identified above could be applied to OJT too. But in OJT learning is an explicit objective (for employee and company) and, to varying degrees, the organisation, structure and management are geared to learning and there is an educational strategy underlying it. OJT can be regarded as a kind of continuum, reaching from a minimal educational intervention to structured training. OJT concerns all those activities which are explicitly aimed at training employees by supporting, structuring and monitoring their learning. It is not always possible or meaningful to draw a strict dividing line between provisions for learning and training in the workplace. The distinction between implicit and explicit learning is a question of degree. There is a continuum which ranges from learning in the workplace by OJT to off-the-job training. Training in the workplace includes characteristics of learning in the workplace, as well as characteristics of a training course. OJT concerns a specifically organised activity, or series of activities, which is characterised by a planned structure, explicitly formulated learning goals to be achieved, a form of evaluation and a clear demarcation in terms of time. It ranges from minimal educational intervention to in-depth structuring. OJT may vary from giving an employee a particular job with a view to learning to structured training and explicit learning in places of work which are designed as a (multimedia) learning environment. Three main forms of OJT can be distinguished (Onstenk, 1994, 1995a, 1997):

1)   the structuring of learning opportunities in the workplace (getting to know the job, job rotation, allocation of jobs with learning in mind);

2) participation in innovation processes and quality circles (i.e. a innovation laboratory), (Engeström, 1996);
3) structured training in the workplace (structured OJT).

The models can further be analysed along three dimensions: objectives, goals and contents (technical, social, communicative, organisational skills; declarative, procedural and conditional knowledge); didactic structures and methods; guidance and coaching.

2.2 Learning as Interplay of Employee and Work Situation

Much discussion on learning, training and HRD concentrates on organising specific learning events. The model of the learning potential of jobs offers another perspective. It is not aiming primarily at designing a course which happens to be delivered on the job, but stresses the fact that any learning at the workplace is in fact part of a chain of planned and unplanned learning events. It also focuses attention on optimising learning opportunities at the actual job.

The concept of the learning potential differs from other definitions which concentrate either on job characteristics (Karasek and Theorell, 1990) or, on the ability of individuals to learn. The model proposed here defines a learning situation as a learner in a specific learning/working environment. Both dimensions of the learning potential are important. A specific job does not offer the same amount of learning opportunities to every worker at any moment. This is not to deny that one job can have more or less learning opportunities than another, on the contrary; it is one of the aims of this exercise to plea for designing jobs which are richer in learning opportunities. On the other hand one employee is able and willing to learn more than another. But that should not be a reason to make learning abilities the most important screening point or to expect to improve learning in the organisation (only) by enhancing willingness to learn.

The model indicates possibilities to enhance learning by aiming at different dimensions. Measures and projects to foster learning should focus directly on shaping and changing both the subjective dimension, i.e. employees' willingness and ability to self- and work-directed learning and the objective dimension, that is the supply of learning opportunities and factors which either promote or impede learning. Only in that way can the workplace qualify as a strong learning environment. Innovation of the organisation and the labour process should be geared towards the learning potential of jobs. This can include designing broader jobs with learning opportunities as well as the fine tuning of steering necessities (solving production problems) and steering opportunities (both in terms of autonomy and qualification). The work environment should be made inducive to learning by establishing small work groups and by emphasising the training and teaching roles of managers and key workers (Evans and Brown, 1994). These however are only effective when they 'trigger' learning activities either directly by posing challenges or indirectly by stimulating employees to learn.

It should be stressed that every job triggers learning, although not all learning will lead to the desired results. A job with few opportunities to develop competence can have very powerful learning effects leading to learned helplessness (Leyman and Kornbluh, 1989). But also unskilled jobs can offer opportunities for learning although they demand no recognised skills. Much working knowledge (Kusterer, 1976) is demanded in order to keep production processes rolling. Recognition of prior learning and practical competence acquired in this way is very important when embarking on a training or learning trajectory with regard to new production concepts. Every learning intervention is intervening in an ongoing process of learning and sense making.

2.3   Autonomous Work Teams

A major strategy to improve learning possibilities on-the-job is a combination of job enrichment and autonomous task groups. In new sociotechnical production concepts (Kern and Schumann, 1984; De Sitter, 1994; Boonstra and Jongeneelen, 1996) the learning potential can be enhanced by reinforcement of the learning opportunities at the job. Jobs become broader and multi-dimensional, decision making and latitude amplify, social contacts are becoming more frequent, more intensive but also sometimes more indirect and remote (e.g. by using phones or computers). At the same time the availability of information and information processing devices at the workplace (computers) is growing rapidly. This kind of change can be analysed at the level of the individual job. In many cases however it seems more fruitful to analyse these changes at the level of the department or work group. It is typical for the new model that the (semi)-autonomous work group or team is made a central principle of the organisational and at the same time an important learning strategy. The old Taylorist model leads to a complex organisation with simple and isolated jobs, steered by managers and planning specialists. The new model entails relatively simple organisational structures, with complex and more complete jobs (De Sitter, 1994). Learning on the job entails multi-skilling, the level and quality of which depends on the content of the newly designed job itself and on the possibilities for situated learning offered by the social work environment (colleagues and supervisors).

Introducing work groups as a leading organisational principle has several objectives, not necessarily reinforcing each other. Different countries vary considerably in the degree and kind of task groups and other forms of small work group organisation. In countries like Sweden or Germany the organisation in small work groups is geared primarily towards democratisation of the workplace and enhancing the quality of labour. In Japan the main objective is intensifying the contribution of employees to the decision supporting process, without affecting the right of the management to make final decisions. In the UK or USA work groups have a more classic objective of enhancing worker participation and satisfaction (Cole, 1989). In Germany and the Netherlands the concept of work groups has a close relationship to new production concepts. The Dutch WEBA-instrument (WEBA, 1989; Christis, 1998) is inspired by socio-technical organisation theory and aims at renewal of jobs and solving welfare problems by the redesign of the organisation of production, including work groups (Onstenk, 1997).

The first and most important objective in introducing small work groups is the productive function. The work group must open up opportunities for organising the labour process more flexibly, by integrating tasks and by making employees multi-usable so that switching of tasks becomes easier.

Production problems are becoming harder to predict and larger in consequences because of smaller batch sizes, fast renewal of technology and products and the drive for continuous improvement. These can be better solved when and where they occur (De Sitter, 1994). Employees have a broader view on the production process and of the place of their own work in the whole system. Also more opportunities are offered for discussing problems and mutual support in solving them (Haug, 1994).

Another important function of the small work group is work planning at the level of the work process itself. Employees work flexibly so absenteeism can be dealt with much easier. Sudden changes in product specifications can be dealt with like last minute orders. In this way decentralised planning, made possible by modern information technology is used to the maximum. This also allows learning events to happen on the shop floor, as problems have to be solved collectively and proposals for innovation can be discussed and tested.

A second objective for introducing small work groups has to do with enhancing motivation and commitment. In fact this is historically the most common argument for group work. Small work groups are introduced in order to improve the quality of labour and to lower absenteeism. This objective has been especially important in older attempts to introduce work groups. It is dominant in the USA. The small work group is supposed to solve motivational problems. Job enlargement and enrichment is not so much aiming at improving the work process but at stimulating motivation, responsibility and self esteem of employees. In a later stage the group is also used to improve production. Working in small groups or quality circles is supposed to strengthen group cultures in the company. This form of organisation in small groups is important in enhancing learning processes leading to socialisation and developing social-communicative skills.

A last objective, which is becoming more important recently, entails using small work groups as an explicit learning strategy. A distinction can be made between the small work group as a strategy for improving individual competencies of employees and for the strengthening of the organisation (the concept of the learning organisation). The small work group as a strategy for development of competencies is aiming at promoting the learning of employees by job rotation and task enrichment, by collectively solving problems and by enlarging steering opportunities on the shop floor and by intensifying mutual learning processes. The organisational principle of the small work group can also be geared primarily to process improvement, as is the case in the Japanese style quality circle. The most important objective of group activity is making proposals for improvement, for avoiding process problems and for the identification and elimination of 'superfluous' movements and actions (Cole, 1989; Weber, 1994). In Japan work group meetings often happen in free time. Production problems, but also simple techniques for quality control (i.e. statistical methods) are discussed. This can, however, result in intensification of the working day and elimination of learning opportunities in the work itself.

2.4 Small Work Groups as Learning Strategy

Working in teams can enlarge the learning potential by enlarging learning opportunities in the job. These may result from enlargement or enrichment of the job. In many cases, by introducing working in teams the job is broadened by learning to perform more tasks, e.g. by rotation to work posts within the group. Also enrichment takes place by the integration of simple repair and quality control tasks in the job. In order to make possible problem solving on the spot, both the necessity to make steering decisions and the authority to do so at group level is enlarged.

In production functions job rotation is (re) discovered as a learning route for multi-skilled expertise. Rotation over the different work posts within the work team can be organised. In a period of some months or years a combination of introductory training and a period of practice on the job can be repeated several times, for new jobs within the small work group or production line. Well paced training trajectories and differentiated work levels are connected and every employee can learn by doing at their own level (Onstenk, 1997; Onstenk and Van Woerkom, in preparation).

Probably the most important contribution to the learning potential of the small work group is the enlargement of the opportunities for making decisions and solving production problems in the group. Characteristically for the small work group is collective planning of work and problem solving.

Both the necessity and latitude for employees to take decisions are enlarged. In decision and choice processes like this the collective competence of the group can be used and developed. Both problem solving and decision making while working and more specific communication and reflection promoting events, like work meetings or quality circles, can play an important role in this respect.

Teams also enlarge the learning potential by reinforcement of collective learning processes in the group. Employees work more and more closely together, exchange information or discuss the planning of work, work problems and opportunities for improvement. This can be more powerful if employees have different backgrounds and expertise, although at the same time this can be a specific barrier to learning, because communication problems can occur (Zarifian, 1995). An important aspect is the structural enhancement of opportunities for mutual learning. Employees learn from each other the tricks of their work in the process. By organising team meetings and discussion opportunities, both while working and at specifically assigned moments, problems are mutually discussed, which not only enables people to learn from each other, but by forcing people to formulate problems also makes possible learning by critical reflection (Haug, 1994; Engeström, 1994). An important learning effect can result from collectively discussing problems and improvement proposals by experienced workers from different departments together with professionals (designers and planners). In designing small work groups this dimension can explicitly be designed by combining employees with different qualifications (content and level) in the work group. This is of special importance when integrating tasks from different areas (e.g. integrating mechanical maintenance and repair in the work of electro-engineers or operators).[1]

In many cases the learning and teaching of colleagues is expected but not recognised as a specific task. Facilities are lacking, but improvements can be found. One possibility would be to allocate this as a specific task for older, experienced employees. Another approach (Onstenk and Voncken, 1995;

[1]   In a Dutch textile printing company a good example was found (Onstenk and Van Woerkom, in preparation). Every team, responsible for a whole production line, included not only machine and process operators, but also a maintenance technician and someone form the R&D department. These experts shared their specific knowledge and learned about the 'daily' problems of the machines, but also supported at team level a more thorough discussion on innovation and improvements. The company, which has an active policy on competence development and up-skilling as well as up-scaling (recognition of improved skills by certification and pay structures), regarded this set up as very satisfactory, both because indeed skill levels were rising, product quality and process reliability improved and innovations took off more easily.

Onstenk, 1997; Onstenk and Van Woerkom, in preparation), to make the coaching of colleagues or team members an explicit part of job descriptions. In a Dutch paper coating and printing factory (Onstenk, 1997) the ability to explain one's own work to others was expected of, and rewarded by higher pay levels within the team. So, although the number of management levels was reduced (flattening of the organisation), within teams a structured rise in pay levels was connected to both improving skill levels and coaching capabilities.

This was supported by developing specific job descriptions and work instructions (mostly made by experienced workers themselves) which made clear what the company expected of a specific job, but at the same time also offered effective learning material. Both workers and management considered this a very effective and satisfying strategy. Team members recognised that being able to explain things to others was not only an effective way of helping newcomers to become experts, but also helped the experienced worker him/herself to understand better what he/she was doing. Not only was the system a successful replacement of an earlier up skilling attempt using external training facilities, but also this proved to be a successful framework for innovation and for tailoring and adapting new machinery. This strong internal organisation of learning processes was supported by specific external training interventions. e.g. employees could be sent to a regional training centre, which offered process simulation facilities. Also, learning was an integral part of investment decisions: when looking for new machinery, not only was cost and technical efficiency and performance looked at, but also at the quality of (self) learning material for technical machine descriptions, manuals, handbooks and instruction guidelines offered by the vendor.

Another important learning possibility is the establishment of representative responsibility. In many groups there is the post of group representative, which can be formally described, but which also can be rotating, as in the more autonomous work groups. In this kind of task social-communicative as well as planning skills can be developed and also insights to the whole of the production process can be attained. In a Dutch industrial bakery, analysed by Verhallen and Onstenk (in preparation) general job descriptions at team level were extended to multi-skilling (e.g. able to work at different stations in a whole process from dough preparing to baking and packing) and also broadened in scope: not only was competent performance of production tasks expected, but also active awareness of quality care, quality control and first line maintenance (solving small problems, accurate description and seeking support for larger problems). A package of self study material (i.e. work instructions made by experienced workers) was developed, supported by remedial programmes for the low skilled and mostly non-Dutch speaking employees. Within each team specific key roles were described, asking from specific team members activities for specific themes like quality improvement, process innovation, mentoring/coaching, health and safety or maintenance problems on the shop floor (without making them responsible or accountable in managerial terms). These key people had regular contacts with company staff services (Research and Development, Training Department, Personnel Department, Maintenance etc.) with regard to these themes and were expected to report on these issues at regular work meetings. This policy showed good results as far as the learning processes of these key persons were involved. At team level some contradictory tendencies occurred, which had to do with establishing differences between 'good' and 'bad' jobs within the teams, but also with communication problems within the teams.

2.4.1   Problems and Risks

Small work groups offer more learning opportunities to employees. At the same time however they demand more from people. Improvement of the quality of jobs, combined with a rise in level, can increase the risk of being moved to work in another job of poor quality elsewhere. Many cases show a reduction of the number of people employed in production jobs, even while production output has risen (Onstenk and Voncken, 1995; Onstenk, 1997; Onstenk and Van Woerkom, in preparation). Also, required skills levels have risen, sometimes considerably. Because of labour protection regulation and social negotiating this does not necessarily mean that only low skilled workers are thrown out, although they do make a large proportion. In order for low skilled employees to stay employable it is important that not only learning possibilities at the job, but also the learning abilities of employees must be enlarged and integrated in careful career policies. By giving tailor made training interventions, including training in basic skills like language and arithmetic, and also social, communicative and team skills, companies try to improve learning skills of employees. A rise in informal learning opportunities includes and in this respect sometimes presupposes specific embedded training interventions This however does not completely solve the problem companies experience when they get to the limits of the learning and development capacities of employees. Although most companies recognise that they have, by far, not yet done everything that could be done with regard to the amount and quality of training, coaching and supporting, nevertheless this is a real problem, asking both for a more sophisticated learning strategy, i.e. involving explicitly depicting zones of proximal development (Engeström, 1987; 1994; Onstenk, 1997b), and for giving room for different levels and speed of development within a team. Of course this is very delicate, as also it should not be made too easy for supervisors or more easily learning and developing team members to leave fellow workers behind, doing 'the job they are good at' and not giving them opportunities to learn, be it at a slower speed.

More generally, heterogeneity in work teams with regard to ethnicity and language, but also to age, occupational or social and cultural backgrounds, is becoming an essential problem for organisations when teams become the basic organisational unit, both for productive tasks (importance of co-operation and communication; dealing with a growing amount of information), but also as a learning situation (Verhallen and Onstenk, in preparation).

Employees have to learn to participate in group processes (communication, co-operation) and to recognise learning opportunities. Both are a necessary pre-condition for learning to take place (and also to do the job!). OJL is structured by the organisation of labour, but also by guidance and support of the learning process by managers, trainers and colleagues. Learning and learning opportunities depend not only on the design of the job, but are also closely connected to changes in style of leadership and responsibilities, to the trajectory of change and more generally to skill formation processes in the company. The consequences of this for the integration of a welfare policy in the company policy as a whole are still not recognised enough. The structural role for learning processes as stimulated by work organisation and guidance and support of the learning process by managers and colleagues is still underestimated in most innovation and organisational renewal processes (Onstenk, 1997b). The small work group can, combined with integration of maintenance and quality control in production jobs, enhance considerably the learning opportunities on the shop floor. But in many cases qualification processes are not central. Because the qualification function is not the first objective of the small work group, a tension with formal qualification trajectories can be expected. Training by rotation or mutual support can be threatened by work pressure or personnel shortages. In many cases not enough attention is paid to the role of managers as 'facilitators' of learning processes. The same is true for the development of and instrumentation as the 'colleague as trainer'. Management often still lacks imagination for an integration of learning and working.

Learning issues can become crucial when earlier innovation attempts prove to be unsuccessful (Hogerwerf, 1997). Onstenk and Van Woerkom (in preparation) show how, because in another company belonging to the same holding, a radical attempt to introduce self steering teams was aborted, the above mentioned Dutch textile printing company decided to choose less ambitious objectives with regard to self steering of teams, but to concentrate designing a structure suitable for and promoting learning and development processes towards a gradual rise more self steering and independence of teams, but allowing for differences in speed and depth of changes between teams as a consequence of differences in skill level and production processes. This proved to be successful strategy. Some teams are already a de facto self steered team (that is reporting directly to the production manager and not to an appointed team leader or supervisor), others are still managed by a team leader or supervisor, but taking on gradually team responsibility for specific tasks like maintenance, planning or quality improvement. All teams show a tendency to multi-skilling and increased learning at team level.

Actual results in terms of acquisition of skills and competence of job rotation and working/learning in a small work group are judged very differently. On the one hand there seems to be a development of a higher level of skills, when for example maintenance tasks or quality control is integrated in the job. In autonomous work groups workers are invited to become more autonomous and to discuss problems and improvements with designers and planners. On the other hand learning in the group, especially in lean production concepts, can be restricted to learning a series of low level, short cycle tasks just by mere repetition. Although continuous improvement is aimed at, this is restricted to details, leading to more efficiency and avoidance of unnecessary movements, which in turn leads in many cases to higher work pressure. In this case there is no real rise in skill level, but more a broadening of the available range of low skills tasks, which enhances the flexibility of production and usability of labour power, but not the level of competence (and the market value!) of the employee. The quality of OJL depends on the sequence of problems and 'critical events ' (Zarifian, 1991) occurring in day to day work practice. So differences in design and organisational choices in the same job and work process can have large consequences for learning opportunities. For example, learning opportunities in working with CNC-machines depend on the integration of separation of programming tasks (and the complexity of the programming needed). If programming does not take place at the shop floor, learning opportunities in the small work group remain restricted.

Informatisation, flexibility, quality assurance and working in small work groups lead to a greater importance for employees to have social communicative, organisational and core skills (Onstenk, 1992; 1995, 1997). At the same time these kind of skills can be learned very well on the job, although some support by specific training interventions can be useful (see above)

A very important problem can be the integration of OJL in personnel and allocation policies. The optimal use of small work groups and multi skilled jobs implies also job security, long term contracts for the core staff and clear career paths. Systems of job rotation are aiming at broadening skills and the development of multi-usability. These systems are connected to a career model, which opens up the opportunity to do more interesting and varied work, more responsibility and higher pay. This can be connected to a trajectory of experience based learning and training. But many classification and pay systems are not adequately geared to working in groups. Also lower supervisor jobs are disappearing, which can lead to a break in traditional career patters for production jobs (compare the eroding role of the German Meister). These problems are encountered by all cases. There is a reaction to try and change or extend the job classification system (which can be difficult if they are not the system holder themselves), and building stepwise trajectories within the team rather than a traditional job ladder. The problem of severing connections between different management levels (the distance between a production job and the first management level becoming much wider) is not solved in this way, making it sometimes difficult for companies to keep their most skilled production workers.

3. CONCLUDING REMARKS

Innovation of work is as much a challenge to OJL as a means. This is reflected in the often-misused concept of the 'learning organisation'. Most companies have no real idea of organisational changes that are necessary, partly because this often represents a complete break with tradition and there are few ready-made strategies and examples to hand. There is a role for the government to play here in promoting pilot projects and providing information. OJL is closely associated in this sense with innovation within companies, both with a view to strengthening and revitalising the Dutch economy and improving the quality of labour. There is still a gulf, however, between innovation in work organisation (key word: new concepts of production) and changes in training provision.

The model of the learning potential of jobs is both a descriptive and a conditional model. As a descriptive model it states the influence of characteristics of the different dimensions on the likelihood of learning. This depends both on the dimensions itself as on their interrelationship and interaction. Learning occurs in an interaction between employees and the opportunities for learning presented by the job, mediated by skills and receptiveness to learning of employees. The model proposes possibilities to enhance learning by aiming at the different dimensions. Looking at both the literature and examples it seems that measures and projects to foster learning focus in many cases more directly on shaping and changing the subjective (employees' willingness and ability to self and work directed learning) dimension, than the actual learning opportunities in design and organisation of jobs. Innovation of the organisation and the labour process should be geared more clearly towards the learning potential of jobs. New production concepts and work teams offer a good perspective for broader jobs with learning opportunities; fine tuning of steering necessities (solving production problems) and steering opportunities (both in terms of autonomy and qualification) and a work environment inductive to learning. These are only effective when they indeed 'trigger' learning activities either directly by posing challenges or indirectly by stimulating employees to learn. Learning, discussion and critical reflection do not occur automatically if jobs become broader and more challenging, but should be organised, making use of new models of training on or close to the job. This also requires a redefinition of training, i.e. making use of ICT (open learning, multi-media), which should be used to support the learning potential, rather than replacing or ignoring it. The same goes for a company culture geared to an integration of working, learning and innovation.

REFERENCES

Baitsch, C. and Frei, F. (1980), *Qualifizierung in der Arbeitstätigkeit*, Hans Huber, Bern.

Cole, R.E. (1989), *Strategies for Learning. Small-Group Activities in American, Japanese, and Swedish Industry*, University of California Press, Berkeley and Los Angeles.

Cole, R.E. (1993), "The Leadership, Organization and Co-determination Programme and its evaluation: a comparative perspective", in Naschold, F., Cole, R.E., Gustavsen, B. and Beinum, H. van., *Constructing the New Industrial Society,* Van Gorcum/The Swedish Center for Working Life, Assen/Maastricht/Stockholm.

Engeström. Y. (1987), *Learning by expanding. An activity-theoretical approach to developmental research* Orienta-Konsultit Oy, Helsinki.

Engeström, Y. (1994), *Learning for Change: New Approach to Learning and Training in companies*, ILO, Geneva.

Fruytier, B. (1994), *Organisatieverandering en het probleem van de Baron van Münchhausen*, Proefschrift, Nijmegen.

Karasek, R.A. and Theorell, T. (1990), *Healthy Work: Stress, Productivity and the Reconstruction of Working Life*, Basic Books, New York.

Kusterer, K.C. (1976), *Knowledge on the Job: Workers' Know-How and everyday Survival in the Workplace*, Washington University Ph.D.

Laur-Ernst, U. (1989), *Schlüsselqualifikationen - innovative Ansätze in den neugeordneten Berufen und ihre Konsequenzen für Lernen*, BIBB, Berlin.

Lave, J. and Wenger, E. (1991), *Situated learning. Legitimate peripheral participation*, Cambridge University Press, Cambridge.

Leymann, H. and Kornbluh, H. (1989), *Socialization and the world of work*, Gower, Aldershot.

Onstenk, Jeroen (1992), "Skills needed in the workplace", in Tuijnman, A. and Kamp, M. van de, *Learning in the lifespan. Theories, research, policies*, Pergamon Press, London, pp. 137-156.

Onstenk, J.H.A.M. (1994), *Leren en opleiden op de werkplek. Een verkenning in zes landen*, MGK, Amsterdam.

Onstenk, J.H.A.M. (1995a), "Skill Formation, On-the-Job Learning and On-the-Job Training", paper for the Expert Conference on On-the-Job Learning, 28/29 September 1995, Amsterdam, SCO-Kohnstamm Institute, Amsterdam.

Onstenk, J.H.A.M. (1995b) "Human Resources Development and learning on the job", in Mulder, M., Nijhof, W.J. and Brinkerhoff, R.O. (Eds.), *Corporate Training for effective Performance*, Kluwer, New York.

Onstenk, J.H.A.M. (1997a), "Technologie en Leren op de werkplek in een papier coating fabriek. [Technology and Learning on the job in a paper coating and printing company.]", unpublished Case study for the research project on New Technology and learning on the job. Summary of case studies in Le Blansch, K. and Onstenk, J.H.A.M. (1997), *Technologische ondersteuning van leerprocessen in de werkomgeving.* [Technological support of OJL] Senter, Den Haag.

Onstenk, J.H.A.M. (1997b), *Lerend leren werken. Brede vakbekwaamheid en de integratie van Leren, Werken en Innoveren.* [Learning how to combine work and learning. Broad occupational competency and the integration of working, learning and innovation. Thesis], Proefschrift, Eburon, Delft.

Onstenk , J.H.A.M. and Woerkom, M. van (in preparation), *Coaching and Team Learning in two Dutch companies*, Casestudies for the Leonardo-project Toolkit Quality 2000.

Projectgroep WEBA (1989), *Functieverbetering en organisatie van de arbeid. Welzijn bij de arbeid (WEBA) gelet op de stand van de arbeids- en bedrijfskunde*, Directoraat van de Arbeid van het Ministerie van Sociale Zaken en Werkgelegenheid, Voorburg.

Raizen, S. (1989), *Reforming Education for Work: a cognitive Science Perspective*, National Center for Research in Vocational Education, Berkeley.

Scribner, S. (1984), "Studying Work Intelligence", in Lave, J. and Rogoff, B. (Eds.), *Everyday Cognition: its Development in Social Context*, Harvard University Press, Cambridge.

Verdonck, G. (1995), *Keeping up competence. Leermogelijkheden op de werkplek*, Stichting Technologie Vlaanderen, Brussel.

Zarifian, Ph. (1991), *Organization qualifiante et flexibilité*, Certes, Paris.

Chapter 11

How the Learning Organisation Evolves
Notes on Some Conceptual Issues about Learning Networks

Massimo Tomassini
ISFOL, Rome, Italy

1. DEFINING THE LEARNING ORGANISATION

The idea of the learning organisation is widely shared by all those who study the phenomena of change in organisations and intervene in them, even though its meaning is still not clearly defined. The learning organisation is a concept that is not usually used in a technical sense but mainly as a metaphor for flexible, effective forms of organisation, capable of encouraging the participation and empowerment of human resources. Whereas approaches such as re-engineering and total quality are based on well-established techniques of action, the learning organisation continues to be a reference which is open to a variety of interpretations and forms of action for change based on shared assumptions and values within systems of varying breadth.

Far from being a limitation, this openness is a strength, even when providing counselling and training services. It is not surprising that the learning organisation is constantly brought into play, precisely where the background of this concept is broadest, in terms of tools and techniques (and customers), i.e. in the myriad of consulting firms and research institutes, firmly established in enterprises in the widest variety of sectors and in public institutions belonging to the Society for Organisational Learning (founded by Peter Senge as an off-shoot of the Centre for Organisational Learning of the Massachusetts Institute of Technology). At the Society's 1997 annual conference ("From Learning Organisations to Learning Communities", Orlando, Florida) - in which over 800 guests from the United States and many other countries took part - the learning organisation continued to be regarded as an evolving notion, to be pushed beyond the thresholds of the traditional organisational dimension (based on the large corporation) and towards more complex dimensions: from the micro-social dimension of communities of practice to the macro dimension of networks and local communities. At these levels, too, the concept of the learning organisation can be useful for organisational analysis and intervention, but it needs to undergo a series of transformations and updates (System Thinking in Action, 1997).

The present article seeks to make progress in this direction by briefly examining some of the contributions which help to give an evolutionary interpretation to the notion of 'learning organisation'. The hypothesis is that the 'learning organisation' is a concept which can also be used to cover aspects other than those typical of traditional organisational learning models based on the dynamics of change at intra-organisational and interpersonal level, intended to achieve a systemic view and overcome resistance to change.

The learning organisation can be also taken as a metaphor designed to highlight the "autopoietic" (Maturana, Varela, 1980) characteristics of organisational contexts, to develop the potential of 'situated' knowledge, and to exploit opportunities for the social construction of knowledge in work communities. Compared with traditional models, this metaphor is far more open to inter-organisational dynamics of dialogue and sense-building by various communities equipped with specific models of interpretation and language codes.

In this perspective, activating different types of learning network, which are discussed in the closing section, is a necessary trend if new forms of learning organisation are to be created and also a strength from the viewpoint of extending and updating some essential concepts in this field.

1.1   The Dominant Approaches to the Learning Organisation

A recent survey has shown that during the past five years there has been an extraordinary increase in the number and complexity of contributions to the two fields, in some respects parallel, of organisational learning and learning organisation, the second being the 'application' area of the first (Easterby-Smith, 1997).

These two fields incorporate different disciplinary approaches and traditions of thought: the author has singled out six for organisational learning and three for the learning organisation. In the first case, they are psychology and organisational development, management science, sociology and theory of organisations, strategy, management of production and cultural approaches. There are overlaps between these approaches, but each maintains a fairly rigorous separation of interests and theoretical assumptions. The second set is the result of an encounter between two main schools, management science and psychology-organisational development, which are often combined for practical purposes: the learning organisation is a field where ideas tend to be evaluated in terms of their applicability and where a close link exists between making the change and studying its processes and nature (Easterby-Smith, 1997).

In the field closest to management science, learning is mainly conceived as the acquisition, sharing and use of knowledge. Schemes based on this type of knowledge dynamics can be used to plan actions which seek, for instance, to develop facilitating factors for learning organisations, as in the case of the learning audit method of P. Nevis, or to establish links with total quality in terms of measuring learning, as in the approach of R. Garvin.

P. Senge and his followers occupy a specific position in this school, and have developed various types of intervention based on the famous five disciplines of the learning organisation (bringing to light the mental models which determine the action of the members of the organisation, sharing knowledge among the members - with special emphasis on the visions of members in positions of leadership, developing personal mastery of the organisational situation through lifelong learning and testing of views, facilitating group learning based on awareness of the dynamics of group interactions and generalising systemic thought as the learning factor which links all the others and reveals the determinants and effects of isolated actions within overall patterns).

Senge's contribution favours the utmost integration between two aspects largely taken into account by the literature in this field: the management needs for human resource management and planning, on the one hand, and the concepts and tools derived from the schools of applied psychology, on the other.

When the latter predominate, according to Easterby-Smith we are within the second field of the learning organisation, linked to social psychology and organisational development, in which models defined 'cyclical' and 'evolutionary' prevail. In cyclical models (which all can be seen as deriving from the well-known learning model of Kolb as a succession of phases of experience, reflection, conceptualisation, experimentation) moments of view and practice alternate, and also individual and collective moments. In evolutionary models, which all derive more or less from the work of Argyris and Schön (and indirectly from Bateson's theory of learning), what is of value is the passage from stereotyped forms of learning to innovative and creative forms. The problem which all address, starting with the 'founding fathers', is how to develop the collective action of the members of the organisation: error correction based on simple correction of learnt routines (single-loop learning) is often not enough and needs to evolve towards a change of the cognitive patterns underlying the theories of action of individuals and organisations (double-loop learning). The different evolutionary models give different interpretations of these two basic moments of learning, but in all of them the aspects of synchronisation between individual images of the organisation and socially shared maps remain central. For all of them, the central problem is basically that of innovating the behaviour of the organisational actors, after having understood the mistakes and their causes and overcome the impasses and organisational resistance to change embedded in single-loop learning.

Thus, although the survey briefly examined here tries to adopt a different approach, it is once again evident that a very close link exists between the approach of Argyris, being part of the disciplines derived from psychology, and the more eclectic and 'ready-to-wear' approach of his pupil, Senge. In both cases, the theory supports practices of change designed to create systemic views of organisational problems and to trigger processes of change towards more conscious and shared forms in the background of relationships which constitute the organisation.

Easterby-Smith's survey of learning organisation theories (which is far more extensive than can be shown here) has the clear merit of placing these approaches within a more complex context. It contains references to other approaches akin to the learning organisation, although with different assumptions and objectives, and includes the one devised by Nonaka and colleagues of the knowledge-creating company, which falls within the 'cyclical' models (because it assumes a combination of tacit and explicit knowledge) as well as within the 'cultural' approaches to organisational learning (because it compares western and Japanese management). Mention is also made of the school of the resource based view of the firm, whereas that of knowledge management is ignored, even though it deals with important learning dynamics.

Nevertheless, the survey emphasises the dominant position of classical theories of organisational learning and learning organisation and their psychological derivation (albeit adjusted by the practice of organisational action and by crossing with other schools), as well as the fact that their scope is basically intra-organisational (although geared towards awareness of external changes) and interpersonal (since organisational learning is taken to be the product of reciprocal adjustments of individual images and maps).

It is not appropriate here to discuss the completeness of the survey or whether the positions of the various schools are correct. What is necessary is to raise some more complex and practical questions: how can the concept of the learning organisation continue to be used in conditions of constantly evolving innovation and learning needs? How can it be used in contexts which display the implicit potential, often unclear to the actors themselves, to generate new solutions and improvements even in contradictory situations? What does this concept mean in relation to complex and shifting forms of organisation (networks, cobwebs, virtual organisations, etc.)?

2.	2. THE VALUE OF KNOWLEDGE AND DIFFUSE ORGANISATION

In posing such questions the intent is not to raise doubts about the usefulness of the concept of learning organisations but rather to revive its interest in terms of re-thinking organisational situations, from a more profitable angle than those so widely (and often usuccessfully) practiced of re-structuring and re-engineering (Keidel, 1994). It also means putting it to the test of emerging phenomena such as:

- the increasing value attributed to knowledge as a crucial resource for the development of the organisation, which must be recognised as sometimes having a tacit nature, embedded in the action of individuals and, in parallel, must be recognised as having a quality which cannot always be traced to psycho-social dynamics;
- the renewed dislocation of prevailing organisational forms, with the spread of federalist, network, virtual organisations or others which differ structurally from centralised or functional models focusing on the need for dialogue between different contexts, rather than for solutions within each;
- the increasingly important role in these organisations, and potentially in all organisations, of poorly formalised micro-structures centred on communities of practices with autopoietic capacity, where learning appears to stem from the intrinsic characteristics of the respective contexts rather than from complex interpersonal dynamics.

The first of these factors which calls for an update of the concept of learning organisation is therefore linked to knowledge. "Re-thinking the enterprise as a knowledge platform" (De Leo, 1995) is one of the main alternatives today to actions which focus on the search for optimum solutions within given constraints and, as in the case of business process re-engineering, are more in danger of creating rigidity than achieving optimisation. The objective of knowledge-based organisation approaches is therefore to trigger value-generating mechanisms by speeding up the process of making explicit and disseminating the latent knowledge which has built up within the organisation. This method of centring the link between organisation and knowledge is very akin to the efforts made by economists to consider the consequences of the dual nature, simultaneously dynamic and relational, of the resources of knowledge: dynamic, because its value declines within time and can only be kept up if the knowledge is regenerated and extended by learning. It is at the same time relational, because the production of knowledge is the result of an effort of interpretation which places phenomena in a conceptual network of schemes, expectations and memories embedded in individuals and social systems and gives them meaning in relation to past experience and the contexts of action (Rullani, 1994). Many organisational approaches to knowledge, especially in the knowledge-management school of thought, try to develop further these relational and 'emersion of the submerged' aspects of social dynamics which economic theory merely mentions, with the exception of a few interesting works.

The problem is that most engineering-based approaches to knowledge management threaten to minimise certain crucial aspects of the nature of knowledge, a complex resource unsuited to any form of forced emersion, and which, in order to be used, demands an understanding of the complexity of the phenomena of learning and social-symbolic interaction which can generate it.

Nonaka and colleagues (Nonaka and Takeuchi, 1995) have made some crucial contributions in this regard by clarifying the terms at play in the case of explicit knowledge and tacit knowledge. Explicit knowledge, which can be represented in formal documents which are easily communicated and shared in the form of hard data, scientific formulae and coded procedures, is only the tip of the iceberg. Tacit knowledge, on the other hand, is personal and difficult to formalise and share: it includes visions, intuition, impressions "rooted in the experience and action of individual, as in their ideals, values and feelings" (Nonaka and Takeuchi, 1995, p.8). Tacit knowledge, in turn, includes two dimensions: technical, i.e. know-how, incorporating skills and abilities which may be deep but cannot be expressed (as in the case of the master craftsman who has the solution to problems at the tip of his fingers but does not know the technical and scientific principles), and cognitive, "being the convergence of beliefs, perceptions, schemes and thought models which are so deeply rooted they are taken for granted and which reflect our image of reality and our view of the future" (Nonaka and Takeuchi, 1995, p. 8).

The problem for organisations is therefore to make tacit knowledge explicit and, vice versa, internalise the knowledge explicit in the thought models and operating practices of the actors. It is a question of reciprocally and systematically converting the two types of knowledge within a spiral, in which, if the interactions between tacit and explicit are well managed, they can gradually increase in scale; a spiral set in motion on the two axes of internalisation/externalisation and socialisation/combination of knowledge. From this point of view, creating organisational knowledge is the subtlest and most complete way of interpreting organisational learning (which, as such, is only the 'internalisation' component of the spiral, the passage from explicit knowledge to tacit knowledge). In Nonaka's approach, the conversion processes can be fostered by continuous managerial action which is consistent with the characteristics and conditions of the 'spiral' and is centred around middle management. The basic objective of middle managers should be to mediate between the visions of the senior managers and the creative abilities spread throughout the organisation, that is, between top-down and bottom-up lines of innovation, in a 'middle-up-down' approach. Alongside this managerial aspect, Nonaka also emphasises the need, when developing the spiral of knowledge, to take account of the characteristics of the expanding 'communities of interaction' which overstep the borders of sections, areas and divisions within the organisation or even its external borders. Developing knowledge is therefore something which involves, at one and the same time, the organisation's processes of management and its processes of communication.

At this level, it is not difficult to observe the close resemblance between this approach and the theories of knowledge management as a "process of gathering the collective expertise of an enterprise wherever it is to be found and distributing it wherever it can foster the generation of returns". "Knowledge management is getting the right knowledge to the right people at the right time" (Malhotra, 1998). This process requires specific management skills and information technologies can play a crucial role by providing the tools to accommodate the bases of knowledge as they are processed by individuals and groups. From this point of view, knowledge management incorporates organisational processes which allow the capacity of technologies to process data and information to be combined synergistically with the innovative capacities of human beings (Malhotra, 1997).

This viewpoint emphasises the interdependence of individuals and organisations with respect to the resources of knowledge at a time when technologies and economic processes tend to overstep the boundaries of specific contexts and move "into the networks of global knowing and of trusted sharing of that collective intelligence which Fordism situated in each enterprise" (Rullani, 1997). In the general economic process, as the dynamics of demand for goods and services and the conditions of production become more complex, the traditional functions of enterprise control become less viable: the greatest competitive advantages can be achieved through a variety of processes (outsourcing and various forms of decentralisation and co-operation) which break down rigid forms of production and split up the centres of control. The value chain becomes external, the new division of labour between enterprises tends to distribute it among a number of points linked by often invisible flows of information, goods and services; co-ordination can take place through meshes of interaction relationships whereby individually autonomous enterprises communicate and co-operate using knowing and powers which continue to be distributed not centralised (Rullani, 1997). This is the process which genetically brings together network-enterprises and enterprise networks in a new morphology of production organisation and of the model of economy and society which characterises the present phase of development and which is represented, at the peak of its achievement, by such models as the 'spider web organisation'. This features a light but complete sphere of operation, without or with only minimum hierarchies or formal authorities having the power to 'give orders' (Quinn, 1992) or the 'virtual enterprise' ("a temporary network of independent companies linked by information technology to share skills, costs and access to respective markets") depicted in relational terms only, widespread in terms of space but limited as to time (Valikangas and Hoffman, 1997) or the 'virtual teams' capable of working "across space, time and organisational boundaries through links which are strengthened by networks of communication technologies" (Lipnack and Stamps, 1997).

The tendency of the post-modern organisation is towards recombined and 'bricolage' organisational solutions:

> "the environment is too complex and multiform for enterprises to be able to identify an optimum structure and have the time to perfect it once and for all. Instead, organisations tend to work by trial and error. Organisational structures become platforms which uninterruptedly produce ad hoc, ephemeral, disposable forms ... The platform is a base which may take different forms ... and on this base temporary forms develop: hierarchies, matrices, hybrid forms, but above all project teams"(Ciborra, 1995).

In terms of the learning organisation, it is clear that in all these contexts the problem of learning is not only that of making thought models compatible and sharing knowledge within the same environment, but also extends to the confrontation-dialogue between different communities and the triggering of knowledge spirals which do not stem from the same matrix of culture and traditions. The phenomena of inter-organisational co-operation and the parallel ones of decentralisation and outsourcing tend to create interesting homologies of structures and relationships between 'inside' and 'outside', between network-enterprises and enterprise networks. The fulcrum of the production processes is the circulation and the appropriate use of knowledge: large and small organisations are articulated into networks serving the processes of knowledge distribution and where organisational aggregations must occur. The space in which the activity of these aggregations takes place and in which their skills are performed is to some extent removed from the rigid control of the organisation.

From this trend stems another important factor in the transformation of the dominant concept of 'learning organisation'. As the role of hierarchies declines and structures become increasingly informal, we are forced to recognise the crucial importance of informal aggregations of knowing and skills around the 'practices' of day-to-day action. The concept of community of practice (which was initially developed within the budding discipline of organisational ethnography and in some respects is a competitor to the learning organisation) in effect relates to aggregations where people, united by a common undertaking, develop and share ways of doing things, ways of speaking, beliefs, values - briefly, practices - as a function of their involvement in the joint activity (IRL, 1993). This way communities of practice can be identified not only by their members, but also by the shared way of doing things. In communities of practice, relationships are created around activities and the activities take shape through the social relations and experiences of those performing them, so that knowledge and skills become part of individual identity and have a location in the community (Gherardi et al., 1997).

At this level, too, the crucial importance of knowledge is evident. It is mainly the traditional aspects which emerge, and the link with people and contexts (embeddedness and situatedness), which seem to be an intrinsic condition of organisational knowledge: the community of practice is the physical and social place where learning, production of knowledge and work take place. The knowledge of the community does not reside in the heads of its members but in the structure and social functioning of the community and hence they are intrinsically situated (Suchman, 1987). In other words, the community is the arena where the processes of transmission of tacit knowledge and of knowledge-in-action takes place (Nicolini et. al.,1996). From this point of view, working, learning and innovating are all activities based on the transformation of knowledge, in the sense of continuous circulation and use of the knowledge possessed by the organisation and creation of new knowledge in response to the need for innovation. Explicit knowledge and tacit knowledge create a synergy with each other in the job context in order to achieve a dynamic balance between know-what (the theoretical level) and know-how (the practical level) without either the one or the other becoming dominant: given their close interdependence a "co-production" of theoretical and practical knowledge occurs (Seely Brown et al., 1989).

Work activities in the community of practice can therefore be regarded as the product of the continuous combination of three essential factors (Orr, 1993): narration (which allows the creation and exchange of the stories which help to maintain and increase the value of the stock of experience acquired by informal practice), collaboration (which helps people participate in the collective flows of situated knowledge), social building (which builds individual and collective professional identities). A typical event in communities is organisational sense-making, which allows events to be situated within appropriate frameworks, to understand intuitively, to build meanings, to interact in the search for reciprocal understanding (Weick, 1995). These are the activities which make the most cohesive and efficient communities operate as 'collective minds', based on continuous heedful interrelating among the actors (Weick and Roberts, 1993).

The development of knowledge within social and cultural communities is also approached in terms of 'communities of knowing', a notion which may be better than 'communities of practice' at expressing complex realities based on technical and scientific knowledge, such as that of large hi-tech enterprises with multiple communities of specialised knowledge workers, each dealing with part of a more complex organisational problem and interacting to create forms of sense-making and behaviour which will be adopted by other communities and by the macro-organisation where they are accommodated (Boland and Tenkasi, 1995).

Brief mention should be made of two aspects which are transversal to the phenomena considered here (crucial nature of knowledge, networking of processes and organisations, communities of practice). The first concerns their intrinsic coherence with the growth of technologies (Internet, groupware, Intranets, etc.), which have passed firmly from the objective of information to many additional objectives, uses and meanings, such as technologies of knowledge, of communication, of co-operation:

> "Hypermedia networks create a sort of plural communication (pluricasting) in which interpersonal communication is no longer separate from mass communication or functional communication from theoretical communication, preferring analogue communication where it can be used, and hence also the tacit and diffuse knowledge which constitutes the enterprise's capital which is hardest to access for formalised and explicit procedures" (Mandelli, 1998).

The second transversal aspect is that the phenomena typical of the world of enterprises also have significant correlation in the world of public administrations, although at a different pace and with different conditions of departure, driven to change by the needs of an increasingly complex society and by the re-shaping of relations between centre and periphery.

The most dynamic task for local administration is not mere decentralisation but the implementation of the principle of subsidiarity (whereby services are provided by the administrations closest to the citizen-users and therefore capable of meeting their needs) and of federalism conceived as a 'network of interdependencies' in which no component (even the state) may dominate the others, but where each needs the others to acquire and share the necessary resources (Handy, 1996). The new centre-periphery dynamics can therefore be interpreted by reconsidering the exploration/exploitation contrast (March and Olsen, 1992), in which the centre traditionally explores new routes and defines new objectives of action, to which the periphery must then adapt by exploiting the resources available. The emerging conditions instead reveal an opposite possibility: the best part of the periphery - under pressure from users - explores new solutions, i.e. maximises knowledge developed through practice and on the basis of its own resources. The centre, on the other hand, is responsible for designing, generalising, disseminating and consolidating the solutions identified, filling the gaps between the various autonomies (Tomassini and Lo Schiavo, 1996). Obviously, the various peripheral components only need to strengthen the networking of their relationships if they wish to avoid a return to the old forms of centralised control.

2.1 Perspective-making/perspective-taking

How does the organisational learning model produced by the classical approach work in the case of the phenomena described briefly here? It should be recalled that the model is mainly based on activating processes of dialogue-confrontation between the actors. Argyris and Schön define them in terms of inquiry, the activity which occurs when the actors try to give shape to their system of relations and to co-ordinate their view with that of others by continuously testing the hypotheses on which each bases his/her reconstruction of the 'theory of action' which are typical of the organisation and conditions his/her interactions and participation in the collective objectives (Argyris and Schön, 1996). Senge echoes this model with the ideas of recognising thought models ("images, assumptions, stories which we carry in our minds, about ourselves, other people, institutions and every other aspect of the world") and of sharing the visions "related to the profound sense of the purpose of an organisation". In both cases the main problem is the defence mechanisms against change rooted in the very routines which make the organisation function and the 'skilled incompetence' underlying individual and group abilities, even at higher levels.

Assuming these models to be generally valid, there is no reason why they cannot help interpretation or intervention in organisations even when there are phenomena at play to transform their internal nature and systems of inter-relation. Some aspects of the transformation, however, require an updating of classical learning organisation models.

In many contexts, and especially where change is greatest, the risks of a breakdown are highest and the processes for sharply reducing complexity are most burdensome (for instance, involving drastic restructuring decisions); learning often has to proceed by uneven leaps and bounds rather than by restoring equilibrium. Frequently, instead of 'unravelling the tangles' which form between partial solutions and between unilateral views of the actors (linked to situational or fragmented forms of learning) it may, paradoxically, be better to increase the tangle and cause an almost natural leap into organisational learning (Rebuffo, 1997). In other words, it may be better to use the autopoietic potential of the context and maximise the properties of situated knowledge, which are not always transparent, rather than rely on reflective opportunities in order to move over to double-loop learning. For instance, praising best practices by creating awareness of tacit forms of collective problem-solving and making them 'speakable' could prove more useful than activating complex methods of overcoming resistance.

As interdependence becomes more complex, both within network enterprises and within distinct forms and different architectures of co-operation between organisations - the need to learn among different contexts grows out of proportion. Often the greatest problems do not lie within specific organisational units but regard activating the 'spiral of knowledge' between communities, each of which has specific practices and knowing. 'Dialogue', as a confrontation between thought models and visions, continues to be a crucial terrain for the development of the diffuse organisation, but the logos on which it is hinged is not a univocal discourse, not a single 'logos' but the site of dissimilar 'logoi', like in an 'archipelago' of different islands, each of which can know itself and co-exist only if it is not "a simple individual unit, a resolved, complete, satisfied unit, to be placed at the centre of a hierarchically oriented space" but a unit in search "of the variable and unexpected shapes which form the harmony of the archipelago" (Cacciari, 1995).

The problem therefore mainly concerns the ways different communities of practice and knowing represent and express themselves. Learning thus appears to imply, at one and the same time, the awareness of one's own abilities to generate knowledge by maximising the intrinsic properties of the contexts and communication between different worlds of thought and repositories of interpretation and sense-making of reality. The problem of achieving consensus on a 'theory of organisation' which is adequately shared is combined, on the one hand, with that of focusing on the best internal practices and innovation mechanisms typical of a context and, on the other, with that of reciprocal understanding between different communities, each of which uses its own 'language games' which are often difficult to translate.

This shows how crucial it is to have a 'representational' dimension of organisation action, which can be traced partly to the tradition of social representations as conventionalisation (of objects, people, events that must be allocated to stable and shared categories and types) and prescriptions (so that, as stated by Farr and Moscovici, 1984, "they impose themselves on us with an irresistible force, this force being the combination of a structure which exists even before we begin to think"). Probably the most appropriate representational dimension for the actual characteristics of organisations derives from attempts at interpreting the organisation in Wittgenstein's terms, where attention is focused on practices in the sense of forms of life of organisational contexts, inextricably related to the use of language. Organising is the place where language is used and developed; conversations and activities in their relationship are language games which create the meanings and conditions for new ways of speech and of acting to evolve continuously in the communities.

In this perspective, the production of knowledge takes place on the two sides of internal communication and communication between various communities of practice, language and knowing. A recent, and fundamental contribution (Boland and Tenkasi, 1995), distinguishes from this point of view "communication which strengthens the community's specific knowledge" (perspective-making) from "communication which improves the community's ability to take account of the knowledge of other communities" (perspective-taking). This, as already mentioned, is a concept developed by studying communities of knowing in large hi-tech enterprises, but in many respects it seems adaptable to other contexts, even paradoxically to provide valid interpretations for less developed situations. Today, it is clear in all contexts that actions need to be taken on both sides of the perspective, as the essential moment in the production of knowledge: "knowledge is produced in a community of knowing by refining and clarifying the perspective of the community" through processes based on puzzles which must be tackled and solved and which serve to develop and perfect the vocabulary, tools and theories which make up the perspective.

"Knowledge advances because the perspective becomes stronger. Unexpected events or discoveries can only be recognised within a perspective, without which the community cannot pick out the anomalies from the background noise and the challenges posed by apparently irrelevant aspects" (Tenkasi and Boland, 1995).

From this point of view, perspective-making is the process whereby a community of knowing develops and continuously strengthens its own area of knowledge and its own practices, managing to include all its complexities in a narrative framing of the experience which allows the switch from undifferentiated and global naming to a more precise explanation of the concepts. Several factors converge in this direction: modelling (concerning the ways in which problems are posed and solved), metaphors (which may enclose innovative forms of understanding reality), narration (whereby the actors continuously build and rebuild the meaning of their world by formulating even divergent narrative accounts).

Perspective-taking is a process of exchange, evaluation and integration of the knowledge of a given community with that of other interacting communities. For perspective-taking to occur, the various knowledge possessed by the individuals in the organisation must be represented as unique and made available to others for them in turn to incorporate it in their perspective-taking. The foundation of perspective-taking lies in giving value to the diversity of knowledge by allowing each type of expertise to give specific representations of what it has achieved and in allowing actors with different expertise to recognise and accept better the ways of knowing which are typical of others. It is an essential process in organisations, but one that is complex and in danger of breakdown. For example, a project may fail because the members of a team are incapable of focusing and reconciling the differences in their knowledge and in their cognitive frames of reference. The likelihood of their succeeding in teamwork based on knowledge diminishes when perspective-taking fails and the activity of creating and exchanging representations does not take place as a result.

The problem is therefore one of conceiving systems of communication which support perspective-taking processes among different communities without attempting to achieve shared images and maps of the organisation too soon but trying to maximise differences and from there being the moment of integration.

There are clear links, but also some differences between the logic underlying perspective-making/taking, and that of Argyris-styled inquiry. Both are processes structured around the cognitive nature of the organisation and around the fact of it being "an artefact of individual ways of representing the organisation" (Argyris and Schön, 1996). In both cases, organising is seen in terms of continuous exchanges in which the ability of individuals to make inquiry, to know and to test knowledge is triggered ("organising is reflexive inquiry"). The difference lies mainly in the size of the outlet of the inquiry.

In the classical concept, as the complexity of cognitive interactions grows, an important role is played by an external 'rational' actor (the researcher-consultant helping the inquiry) who speaks a meta-language, able to have all the organisational actors converge and who can unmask the errors embedded in their decisions and behaviours. The emerging concept of perspective-making/taking tends to stress how increasing complexity complicates the problem of understanding and translating representations, not because the actors as a set are in conflict among themselves but because specific clusters of knowing and meaning occur within that set.

Once again, however, it is important to look beyond the similarities and juxtaposition of trends in management thought and to try to reformulate the questions about the ability of the learning-organisation concept to guide policies and interventions for change on a practical level.

3.   THE EMERGENCE OF LEARNING NETWORKS

The notion of learning organisation which can be derived from a view centred on perspective-making/perspective-taking would seem to be a useful development with respect to traditional models: from this point of view, the learning organisation is the one which manages to foster the development and improvement of organisational knowledge within the community (groups, teams and other formal or informal aggregations with specific practices and knowing) as well as in reciprocal relations between communities inside the same organisation or in relations between different organisations.

Models like the perspective-making/perspective-taking can also usefully be applied not only to large hi-tech organisations but also to large traditional enterprises or public administrations. This type of model can be useful wherever intra- and inter-community communication encounters rigid processes and hyper-specialised cognitive models, i.e. when the communication of the community in play encounters difficulties in defining its own 'perspective' and understanding the perspectives of interacting contexts. The least evolved organisational situations are not often made up of well-formed and precise communities; often they are ecologies of practice and knowing which tend to give life to complex processes involving individuals and groups ('quasi-communities') urgently need to find moments of cognitive and social self-recognition and forms of inter-organisational communication.

It is in this enlarged dimension that extensive meanings of learning organisation can be identified, as a concept to which it is possible to correlate organisational-learning development practices not relating to actors and groups but extended to various types of learning network. Recent experience has shown that learning network experiments have great vitality: a case in point is that of a group of trainers interested in exploring new directions for their skills and commitment within the organisation who link up by telematic conference for the purpose of self-training, sharing knowledge and aligning in respect of a problem which is new to them (Nicolini and Tomassini, 1997). Another example is that of a group of entrepreneurs and managers of small- and medium-sized enterprises operating in the same local context who create a learning network to reflect together on how to renew corporate strategies and human resource policies (FAS, 1997). An important example of an intra-company learning network can be found in a branch of a large multinational corporation among the staff in charge of major corporate tasks. Many other examples are being reported in a number of contexts. In all these cases they are not learning organisation experiments in the traditional sense but forms of learning which involve strengthening knowledge within the community and, at the same time, improving interactions between the knowledge possessed by different communities.

The theory and practice of learning organisation should be developed in this direction, taking account of the multitude of possible forms acquired not only by communities of practice and knowing themselves and internally, but also by their inter-relations.

In this connection, the scheme of a recent research study on the development of best examples in the public administration indicates four essential types of community and inter-community relations for two axes of proximity/distance, both social-professional and physical (Tomassini and Lo Schiavo, 1996). The first type, where there is social-professional as well as physical proximity, can be defined in terms of a community of practice in the true sense, based on forms of shared knowledge and on consolidated repositories of action (e.g. offices and departments capable of arriving at organising which is not hegemonised by bureaucratic rules). The second type, which is found in the quadrant of social-professional distance/physical proximity, covers the connections (necessary but difficult) between communities each possessing their own language, culture, interests and ways of interpreting reality e.g. the scientific and the administrative staff of research bodies, medical personnel and administrative staff in hospitals. The third type includes communities, which have physical distance and social-professional proximity, consisting of networks among the subjects performing the same role in different contexts (e.g. medical directors of various hospitals in the same area). The fourth type, in the quadrant of social-professional distance/physical distance, is conceptually a mix of the previous two and relates to spheres of activity whose strategic importance is destined to increase in the public sector where co-operation must be launched between administrations which have not communicated until now but are involved in the same area of action (e.g. civil protection).

In this sort of perspective we clearly need to encourage the growth of various types of learning networks with different aims, but that anyway tends to strengthen the knowledge within each community and improve cognitive interactions between communities. The learning network therefore appears to be an evolved concept of the learning organisation to be placed on the managerial agenda as well as that of consultancy and training. Its development offers a number of options.

Very briefly, the first option would seem to relate to the basic approach of actions to stimulate the growth of these emerging forms of organisational learning. Unlike actions in the classical perspective of the learning organisation, which tend to affect people, their defence routine and blockages in learning processes, the aim is to focus on flows of knowledge. Action should mainly be centred on practices which make organisational knowledge productive rather than on interpersonal components. It is a different conception: what matters are the solutions that each community manages to reach and the views of reality and of problems behind those solutions. We should seek originality, typical characters, circulation of experience; alignment is a subsequent effect not an objective to be achieved immediately.

This is why we will have to concentrate on the tools and methods of operation of learning networks which can reinforce the 'narrative' not just the 'reflexive' dimension needed to bring the perspectives into focus and communication. It is not by chance that within the Society for Organisational Learning (mentioned at the beginning of this article) there is a growing interest in the narrative techniques applied to learning. From this point of view, the purpose is to help the communities tell their story, create their 'learning histories' which will convey the experiences and understanding of reality by groups of people who have succeeded in expanding their skills. 'Stories' may become advanced forms of organisational memory and help to develop awareness within the boundaries of an organisation and communication with the outside (Roth and Kleiner, 1995).

Naturally, we will have to see how learning networks can be supported by appropriate, broad-band communication technologies, adaptable to various interactive uses (the different types of groupware, especially those based on standards of the Intranet and Extranet type). The technological dimension is intrinsic to the development of these networks in their virtual dimension, but analysis should seek not only to identify the technical factors of success, but also to allow the actors to approach using the technologies with a 'taking care' attitude which will effectively ensure that they are a support to the circulation of knowledge (Ciborra, 1996).

Last but not least, research should also concentrate on the epistemological implications of enlarging the field of concepts linked to the learning organisation. The 'proximal' point of view in organisational analysis, as opposed to the 'distal', according to a distinction proposed by post-modern sociology, seems very much in line with the priority given to the situated factors of organisation knowledge at the community level and to the factors of communication-translation between communities characterised by different language games. While distal attention to the organisation shows that structures are measurable and the boundaries between inside and outside are sharp, the proximal perspective emphasises that organisations are really 'effects' created by a series of mediation tools; where distal theory speaks of isolated individuals, groups and organisations, thereby emphasising the distance separating them, proximal theory highlights their permeability and reciprocal interpretation (Cooper and Law, 1995). This view of organisations as "mediation networks, contact circuits and continuous movements, in any case something resembling assemblies of organising processes" offers a number of ideas for evolving the notion of learning organisation and analysing the emerging reality of learning networks.

4.   CONCLUDING REMARKS

These notes have attempted to re-examine some of the issues connected with the concept of learning organisation. The classical concepts continue to hold the stage in this field: at present the dominant idea of learning organisation, the one capable of developing the metanoia among the actors by using "disciplines" based on a continuous comparison of "visions" and "thought models" (Senge, 1990), has a sound background in the well-established notions of "double-loop learning" and "theories of organisation" and "cognitive maps" (Argyris and Schoen, 1996).

Various phenomena, however - the more crucial role of knowledge as a resource endowed with value, the networking of processes and organisations in parallel with the crisis of traditional models, the importance of informal organisational aggregations based on shared practices and knowing - require a comparison with other views of the creation of knowledge in organisations, starting from the fundamental approach which explains the operation of successful organisations in terms of maintaining the "spiral of knowledge" (Nonaka and Takeuchi, 1995).

Faced with these phenomena, the 'archipelago' dimensions of organisational acting need to be maximised: the actors appear less and less against a general backdrop, the organisation as a whole of cognitive-based interpersonal relations through which sense-making takes place; instead, the actors appear more and more against partial backdrops, the communities of practice and/or knowing, each of which has its own sense-making rules and is built around specific language games.

In this logic, a useful development with respect to traditional models can be found in the concept of learning organisation deriving from a view centred on perspective-making/perspective-taking: the communication which reinforces the specific knowledge of a communities and which improves the community's ability to take account of the knowledge of other communities. In this concept, the idea of learning as problem-solving and reflection on the causes of errors in decisions and in interactions among actors is reinforced, but the learning organisation appears as more closely linked to the socio-cultural characteristics of groups, teams and other formal or informal aggregations with specific practices and knowing (the practice and knowing communities). The basic problem from this point of view is one of improving the awareness of every community concerning their own representation processes of the organisational reality and one of creating appropriate forms of representations and interchange between different communities.

This kind of concept can provide theoretical support for new forms of learning and new kinds of intra- and inter-organisational relationships which are emerging in different contexts and which can be recognised as learning networks, having different characteristics related to the ways in which individuals and groups interact on the basis of their physical and socio-professional closeness. The learning network seems to be an evolutionary construct of the learning organisation.

Different research options are implied in this evolution, especially concerning three factors: the recognition of linguistic and 'narrative' dimensions of organisational representations which provide the hidden fabric of the networks, the need for using telematics not in the mere information transmission mode but also integrating the narrative dimensions, the adoption of new epistemological methods coherent with the 'chaotic' nature of learning networks.

REFERENCES

Argyris C. Schoen D. (1996) *Organizational Learning II*, Addison-Wesley, Reading Mass.

Boland R.J., Tenkasi R.V. (1995) *Perspective Making and Perspective taking in Communities of Knowing*, Organization Science, vol. 6, 4

Cacciari M. (1996) *L'arcipelago*, Milano, *Adelphi*

Ciborra C. (1996) *Lavorare assieme. Tecnologie dell'informazione e teamwork nelle grandi organizzazioni,* Milano, Etaslibri

De Leo F. (1995) *Ripensare l'impresa come piattaforma conoscenze,* Economia & Management, 4di

Easterby-Smith M. (1997) Disciplines of Organizational Learning: Contributions and Critiques, Human Relations, vol 50, 9

Farr R.M., Moscovici S. (1984) Social representations, ed. it. *Rappresentazioni sociali* (1989), Bologna, Il Mulino

FAS, Irish National Training Agency (1997)

Gherardi S., Nicolini D., Odella F. (1997) How People Learn in Organisations, in Wilson D., Rosenfeld R. (eds.) *Managing Organizations: Text, Readings and Cases*, London, McGraw Hill

Handy C. (1995) *Gods of Management. The Changing Work of Organisations*, London, Arrow Books

Keidel R.W. (1994) Rethinking Organizational Design, Academy of Management Executive, vol.8, 4

IRL, Institute for Research on Learning (1993), citato in Winslow C. D., Bramer W.L. (1994) *Future Work: Putting Knowledge to Work in the Knowledge Economy*, New York, Free Press

Lipnack J., Stamp J., *Virtual Teams*, Wiley & Sons, USA, 1997

Malhotra Y. (199s8*). World Wide Web Virtual Library on Knowledge Management* [WWW document]. URL http://www.brint.com/km/

Mandelli A. (1998) *Rete e costruzione collaborativa della conoscenza,* Sistemi & Impresa, 2 (marzo)

March J.G. (1991) *Exploration and Exploitation in Organizational Learning,* ...Organization Science, 2(1)

Maturana H.R., Varela F.J. (1980) *Autopoiesis and Cognition: The Realization of the Living*, Dordrecht, Holland, Reidel

Nicolini D., Gherardi S., Odella F. (1996) *Uncovering How People Learn in Organizations: the Notion of Situated Curriculum,* Università di Trento, unpublished paper

Nicolini D., Tomassini M. (1998) *Distributed Learning Networks for Trainers: A Prototypical Experience within a Trade-Union Environment,* The Learner, 6

Nonaka J., Takeuchi H. (1995)*The Knowledge-Creating Company,* New York, Oxford Univ. Press

Orr J. (1990) Sharing Knowledge, Celebrating Identity: War Stories and Community Memory in a Service Culture, it. transl. in Pontecorvo et al.

Pontecorvo C., Ajello A.M., Zucchermaglio C. (1995) *I contesti sociali dellapprendimento. Acquisire conoscenze a scuola, nel lavoro, nella vita quotidiana,* Roma, Led

Quinn J. B. (1992) *Intelligent Enterprise,* New York, The Free Press

Rebuffo F. (1997) *Processi organizzativi, apprendimento e tecnologie,* Sistemi & Impresa, 2 (marzo)

Roth G., Kleiner A. (1995) *Learning Histories: Assessing the Learning Organization,* The Systems Thinker, vol.6, 4

Rullani E. (1994) *Il valore della conoscenza,* Economia e Politica Industriale, 82

Rullani E. (1997) *La rivoluzione post-fordista e il virtuale made in Italy. Dal controllo all'interazione tra unità autonome,* Ingenium (numero monografico su L'azienda virtuale)

Seely Brown J., Collins A., Duguid P. (1989) *Situated cognition and the culture of learning,* Educational Researcher, 32.

Senge P. M. (1990) *The Fifth Discipline. The Art and Practice of Organizational Learning,* New York, Doubleday Courrency

System Thinking in Action (1997) *Proceeding of the Conference 1997: From Learning Organizations to Learning Communities,* Waltham MA, Pegasus Communications

Suchman L.A. (1987) *Plans and Situated Actions. The Problem of Human-Machine Communication,* Cambridge Mass., Cambridge University Press

Tomassini M., Lo Schiavo L. (1996*) Nuovi modelli di intervento per migliorare le pubbliche amministrazioni. Formazione e diffusione di casi esemplari,* Formazione Domani, 23/24

Valikangas L., Hoffman M. (1997) *Organizzazioni virtuali,*Ingenium (numero monografico su L'azienda virtuale)

Weick K.E. (1995) Sensemaking in Organizations, ed. it. *Senso e significato nelle organizzazioni,* Milano, Cortina

Weick K.E., Roberts K.H. (1993) Collective Mind in Organizations: Heedful Interrelating on Flight Decks, Administrative Science Quarterly, 38

Chapter 12

VET systems and criteria for effectiveness

Fons van Wieringen
University of Amsterdam

1. VARIETY AND EFFECTIVENESS

There is a good deal of variety in vocational education systems in the member states of the European Union. Within the framework of the present report, we are primarily interested in differences between the systems of vocational education which are connected with the social determination of vocational education. The idea is that the effectiveness of vocational education should be measured in a number of ways. There is no single standard of effectiveness by which to judge vocational education in the member states of the European Union. The systems differ in terms of function and especially in the way they are designed. This should not be taken to mean that the functions and designs display an infinite variety. The variety is limited (cf. Brandsma et al. 1995). The differences between the systems in terms of design can be broadly classified in terms of four dimensions: steering, funding, suppliers, and the functional exclusiveness of the institution in which vocational education is provided. Let us consider these four variants in a little more detail.

1.1 Steering

The systems of vocational education in the member states differ in terms of the extent to which national government, regional government, employers' organisations, trade unions and associations of educational institutions have a say in the system. We can distinguish a number of main types on the basis of the major political traditions and structures of the countries involved.

From way back there have been two variants of political structures in Western Europe: the liberal unstructured form and the corporatist structured form. Both variants belong to the democratic heritage of Europe. The first form is mainly recognisable in the British-American variant and the second mainly in parts of Continental Europe. In some respects this difference has something in common with the difference between markets and institutions.

The first form is better known than the second, which is why we will examine the second here. In this variant education policy up to a certain level is pursued via "structures for functional representation by monopolistic, hierarchically structured interest groups" (Schmitter and Streeck, p. 263). This kind of policy-making contrasts with the Anglo-Saxon model in which political parties contest with each other in a parliamentary context based on a programme and the support of voters. Policy is based on agreements with interest groups rather than public debates with parliamentary groups.

In the second variant a societal sector like the education sector is a field in which many forms of consultation flourish within an institutional framework, in which interest groups make agreements with the public sector about concrete questions of policy. In the corporatist policy model the government places as much responsibility for policy as possible upon functional interest groups. They are, as it were, absorbed into the public domain and forced to take up a rather less sectoral perspective. Those pursuing policy in a corporatist setting perpetuate a dependency relationship with respect to the interests they have selected. If social support falls away, the government is trapped in an institutional framework that no longer operates properly. Corporatist policy creates both stability and rigidity at the same time.

The administrative relationships between the state and the education sector are being revised. Within both interpretations a change can be observed in the way in which the different tiers and actors relate, or should relate, to one another. Based on the assumption that the different tiers and actors all have responsibilities, attempts are being made to replace the one-sided authoritarian relationship with a relationship based on negotiation, through which the fair interpretation of the two sides can be brought up for discussion. Agreeing on new forms of communication has turned out to be a rather onerous task. Authorities operate in a context in which other bodies also have the means to exercise power and influence. Developing what is known as polycentric steering nevertheless still seems to have a long way to go in all European countries. The classic steering paradigm concerns the relation between the governor and the governed. The governor is the central actor, his objectives are what count, and the governed are the object of governance. The governing body determines the course to be followed and the resources to be deployed. The criterion of success is the extent to which the objective is achieved. Steering can fail as a result of an incorrect view of the relations between means and end, an information deficiency, resistance on the part of the governed to the good intentions of the central actor, and a lack of control over the process of implementation. The remedies are situated in the same areas. Alternative models usually proceed on the basis of more than one actor and a pluriform ensemble of objectives. This alternative steering model assumes a market-like situation in which actors take certain decisions independently and autonomously.

Central government must above all ensure that these processes can proceed without any obstruction. It removes factors which might disturb these processes and gives the actors as many resources as possible, while minimising its own role as central government. The government both does less and acts differently. It tries in particular to activate the social context of vocational education, to involve it in the process of steering vocational education. Activation of the surroundings concern a form of steering in which it is not so much the direct relation between school and ministry that is at stake, but in which an attempt is made to achieve the policy objective by activating the surroundings because of the value of the contribution of those surroundings and in the hope that the surroundings will promote the same goals as national government. The influence of the surroundings is regarded as being at least as effective as the direct influence exerted by the department. Sometimes it is necessary to create new bodies or procedures in this connection. Where higher vocational education is involved, the activation of the surroundings will be expressed primarily in activation of the international context. As far as intermediate and lower vocational education are concerned, it is the influence of the world of national industry and commerce that will be activated. In some sectors we see bodies of agreements being made between vocational education and the world of industry and commerce or the social partners. Several EU member states have a national qualification structure for vocational education which confers considerable steering capacity on the social partners.

The market or institutional orientation differs quite widely between the European VET systems.

1.2   Funding

There are various sources of funds for vocational education: community funds, training resources made available through terms of employment, company resources, and private contributions by the participants themselves. The criteria for the various flows of funds differ: government will only invest in long-term qualifications that are not specific to a company, whilst companies will show more interest in company-orientated qualifications, and will expect employees to bear the expense of qualifications which go beyond the company. One of the ways that government funds education is by funding educational institutions. However, education is funded in another way too. The granting of tax concessions to citizens and companies is one of these different kinds of funding. A direct form of funding aimed at the potential and actual participants can be a more effective and just form of government activity. These two motives may have different implications for the system that is to be set up. In the first case, for example, it may also concern a limitation of training opportunities. The direct types of funding can be worked out in different variants. Government resources can be deployed in different ways: directly to schools, or to participants in the form of vouchers. Government resources are also indirectly deployed in the form of tax facilities for companies and individual participants. Training resources made available through terms of employment represent important flows of funds for the maintenance and upgrading of employees' qualifications in several member states. Company resources are primarily deployed for company training. Finally, private individuals pay for their own training directly by paying the costs of the training course or indirectly by accepting a lower wage during a period of training on the job. There are various ways in which government can influence company training, for example: legislation (e.g. the right to leave to attend training courses), taxation (a compulsory percentage of the salary is spent on training courses), and subsidies (direct subsidy to companies for training activities).

Training courses are not only developed and given within state-funded education. Training courses are also developed and implemented in private settings. Participation in company training courses is on the increase. This growth may benefit both the individual and the company. Depending on clarity as to whom the benefits accrue, individuals and/or companies are prepared to invest in the required enhancement of qualifications. The enhancement of qualifications can be achieved through company training courses, but there are other structures and procedures to achieve the desired goal, such as work experience, internal work consultation, and internal quality procedures. Company training courses appear to yield large benefits, but the differentiation - differentiation by type of company, training courses in sectors with a high or low degree of labour mobility, etc. - has not been properly investigated yet. The benefits for companies require further investigation as well.

A matter that is allied to the introduction of a polycentric principle of governance is the re-evaluation of private elements in the education system. Privatisation means introducing private elements into the education sector or strengthening such elements. This ranges from setting up a substantial sub-sector of private schools to granting parents some opportunities to choose from a number of different public schools. It is really not to be expected that European countries will abolish state education. However, it is one thing to function as a state school in a purely state-dominated context, and it is quite another thing to function as a state school in a context which also contains a relevant, traditional and non-traditional private sector. For the state this means losing its monopoly in the education sector. Something of this situation can be observed in Western countries where the state sector is more or less detached, as in England and Wales. The United Kingdom well illustrates the complex compartmentalising effect of long-term stagnation in the interaction between the state and private sectors. Once the private sector has become closely associated with an elitist education sector, it is not really possible for there to be any fruitful relationships between private and state schools. The compartmentalising effects are also very restrictive in the USA, where only a few private elements are being introduced gradually and cautiously into the public sector.

Can one say that in the field of vocational education private provisions perform better than public ones? In our field a debate is going on about whether private schools are better than public schools. Does that hold also for vocational education? Private schools perform better in some ways; at least that seems to be the provisional finding of several analyses. Chubb and Moe argue very forcefully that this is true for the United States: "We show that private schools are organised more effectively than public schools are and that this is a reflection of their greater autonomy from external (bureaucratic) control" (p. 24). In the public sector schools can only be granted a very limited room for manoeuvre. Public bodies work through bureaucratic regulations. They prescribe, they control, they monitor, they issue detailed personal instructions, they determine admission standards, they set norms for examination procedures, etc. They do so because that is the way public bureaucracies have always worked. Schools in the public domain are granted hardly any autonomy at all. By restricting autonomy, the range of options and of solutions open to school managers is narrowed. School managers in public schools can only make a selection from a small range of specific options. This range is often inadequate for the severe problems faced by public schools. Chubb and Moe contrast this with their ideal image of private schools. Private schools do not show bureaucratic characteristics because they work for certain groups of clients. All they want is to satisfy the needs of these clients. They do not suffer from the power struggles and political instability in public boards. Private schools work for a specific niche in the market. They "tend to possess the autonomy, clarity of mission, strong leadership, teacher vocationalism and team co-operation that public schools want but (except under very fortunate circumstances) are unlikely to have" (ibid. p. 67). In private schools one can see the furtherance of coherent, strongly led, academically ambitious, vocationally grounded, team-like organisations. This is not the place to fully discuss all the strengths and weaknesses of their analysis, as this has been done by several authors elsewhere. For our purpose it is enough to demonstrate that to some degree the institutional context of vocational education can be seen in terms of the public-private dimension.

1.3   Suppliers

By comparison with the suppliers of basic education, the range of suppliers of vocational education is bewilderingly large. One way to organise this range of suppliers is in terms of the public-private dimension. Public institutions are mainly to be found on the side of the regular 'schools', while private suppliers are mainly to be found on the side of the 'companies'. But there are also many mixed forms: vocational associations which offer their members a legally compulsory additional training, companies which sponsor public schools, etc.

Privatisation is a theme that is avoided in basic education in Europe, but private suppliers and privatisation are naturally a very common phenomenon in the world of vocational education and adult education. is supposed to contribute officially to a changed politico-economic infrastructure (for example by putting less pressure on the government budget), to a reinforced social support for vocational education, and to improved functioning in education. Of course, privatisation need not mean that the government no longer intervenes in the education in question. We can at least distinguish between privatisation of funding and privatisation of implementation. Privatisation of implementation simultaneously with public funding is familiar from basic education in various member states. Privatisation of implementation simultaneously with private funding is familiar from private education, but here too there are important elements of public funding in the form of tax subsidies to participants or companies.

Can vocational education be privatised? In what sense, in what combination of privatisation of funding and of implementation? And by means of what forms of privatisation: payment by participants, farming out of educational programmes, private educational institutions? Which combination is effective and just in this situation?

1.4   Functional exclusiveness of the institution

The member states of the EU differ widely from one another when it comes to the question of whether vocational education is provided in institutions whose exclusive responsibility is to perform these activities (such as schools), or in institutions with a wider range of responsibilities (such as industrial companies, temp agencies, organisational consultancies, vocational associations, private courses, 'Yellow Pages' style training opportunities). An important dimension of variation in vocational education in the EU is that of the extent to which the emphasis is on vocational education within schools or on vocational education within other institutions, particularly companies. The predominant system of vocational education in the German-speaking countries is heavily dependent on training within companies. Schools are only important in the second instance: on the one hand, as bodies which provide a parallel programme that is very closely integrated into the training courses provided in the companies, and on the other hand, as an alternative for those cases where a training course in a company is not available or is not a genuine option for the category of young people concerned. A second variant of vocational education can be found in the Scandinavian countries and in the Netherlands, where far more confidence is placed in vocational education implemented in schools. Companies are certainly important in this connection, but they have a supplementary role vis-à-vis vocational education in schools. Neither of these two variants has really got off the ground in England. England is primarily important because a national system of vocational qualifications is used, not only to make clear the civil effect of completing a course, but also to encourage the facilities which lead to it. In southern Europe, including France, there are mixed forms of these three distinct kinds of systems.

Determining the effectiveness of vocational education will always have to be done in the context of the characteristics of the system of vocational education in question. This will be elaborated in more detail in the following sections. However, the emphasis will still be placed on those variants of vocational education that have a genuine and appreciable component inside schools. This report focuses on vocational education organised in schools.

The educational function in all of the EU Member States has been primarily characterised by an ongoing specialisation: generally speaking, the education sector has become more and more exclusively responsible for education. Schools in different countries have become more and more the exclusive representatives of vocational education in the course of history. All the same, other sectors have a reasonably important educational component, either in continuity with the past or as something that has re-emerged. This shows a high level of development in several countries, such as the dual system of vocational education in the German-speaking countries. This phenomenon can also be seen in company training courses in production and service companies, the health service (training courses in hospitals), and the security and surveillance sector (army, police and surveillance training courses). It can also be observed in more informal educational processes in many sectors of society.

The process of sectorial specialisation has at the same time entailed a certain (threat of) marginalisation of education. Education is gradually being expelled from the centre of society to an educational sector on the periphery of society for children and young people, and for marginalised adults. This means that the significance of education is limited in many countries. It has become limited to something that at any rate cannot be called lifelong education.

Education can be limited to the education sector, but it can also be seen as an activity of various social sectors. It is not easy to move boundaries. The limits of systems, according to De Leeuw (1994, pp. 67-68), should preferably not intersect intensive patterns of relations. The relations outside the boundary should be weaker than the relations inside the unit to be demarcated. The boundary must also be drawn in such a way that there are opportunities for change and problem-solving within the demarcated terrain. Demarcation has for policy the important connotation that, in the words of De Leeuw, "there is the necessary correspondence between the limits of the system and a steering mechanism" (1994, p. 68). Changes in the limits of a system thus also imply a shift in the steering mechanism.

It is difficult to introduce new system boundaries. This can be seen most clearly in adult education. Attempts are still being made to outline a broader perspective of lifelong education, whilst its actual implementation is limited to a change within the limits of the current system. The willingness to formulate policy is expressed again and again, but the conversion into practical activities is modest in comparison with the claims of the policy programme in various EU countries, and is primarily confined to an implementation within the present boundaries of the system.

2.   STEPS TOWARDS EXPANSION OF THE SYSTEM

Work is going on in different ways to develop a new conception of an education system. Without being exhaustive, we can indicate a few steps in this direction. Information and communication technology is deliberately not treated as a separate category here. ICT influences the various possibilities and can accelerate various options. We follow the classification used in the preceding section.

2.1   Steering

2.1.1   Schools as Educational Co-ordinators

Schools can also be understood as the co-ordinators of a chain of sites of educational experience. This was the message of a classic recommendation by the German education council in 1974 (Deutscher Bildungsrat, 1974). Does the transformation of the policy structure contribute to the emergence of a larger variety of educational solutions? Diversity of needs calls for diversity of responses, especially at a time when it is unclear what the best response is. Is it possible to realise such a concept of an educational chain? Can the institutionalisation of education be reduced and room created for new educational experiences? The initiatives towards the dualisation of the training courses were steps in this direction, but they had a limited vision.

2.1.2   Funding: training loans, vouchers, education coupons

A solution which has not been implemented but which is hardly ever absent from any debate on the education of the future is to offer people a fixed budget or opportunities to take out credit. They can be taken up at any moment in the life-cycle.

2.1.3   Funding: tax and insurance approach

Education is promoted in various ways at the moment through tax concessions for participants and companies and through the deployment of various kinds of social insurance funds. As yet there is little that is systematic in the deployment of these resources aimed at a new definition of the system of social education. Generic measures such as tax concessions and the deployment of social insurance funds for educational ends demand more than a Minister of Education can provide.

2.1.4   Encouragement of new suppliers

Can new suppliers be encouraged who provide education directly or indirectly as a temporary or permanent subsidiary activity, such as providing education on a commercial or cost-effective basis, non-profit institutions and organisations,   international baccalaureate, and non-profit organisations which can also engage in certain activities in the field of education on behalf of polytechnics? There are various ways of encouraging or discouraging new entries.

2.1.5   Education as a companion and home

Can schools offer a setting in which all kinds of new initiatives can arise, perhaps even including the use of school premises for initiatives from outside the school? Perhaps that is the function of education in the broadest sense: providing the function of companion and home to individuals and groups that want to develop initiatives (who want to refine their learning capacity and transform it into activities), and to individuals and groups that require protection (in other words, recognition and development of their potential in an environmentally based trust). We can see steps in this direction in 'classic' adult education such as community-based education, but also in courses aimed at starting up one's own business that are provided by the Chambers of Commerce.

2.2   Functional exclusiveness of the institution

There are various steps towards a different conceptualisation of the education system, such as the 'traditional' idea of not confining educational efforts entirely to childhood, but spreading them over the whole life-cycle. Recurrent education has been an attractive principle of educational design for more than two centuries (OECD 1973; Kallen 1974). It is difficult to work in practice, particularly because it transcends the field of activity of a single department, and, in fact, that of the government as a whole.

2.2.1   Organisational strengthening of the educational component in other sectors

Many sectors do something in the way of education and training. This educational intensity of companies, institutions, the army, hospitals, etc. can be encouraged. This is where steps towards the intensification of knowledge and the intensification of education approach one another.

All of these approaches differ in terms of scope, point of entry and content. They also differ in terms of the primary category that they target: suppliers of education, clients, or vocational students. The supply side comes particularly to the fore in the attempts to strengthen the educational component in other sectors, tax and social insurance facilities, schools as educational co-ordination centres, and the encouragement of new suppliers. The clients come particularly to the fore in the training loans, vouchers, in the tax and social insurance facilities, and in the function of education as companion and home.

3.   MEASURES OF EFFECTIVENESS

There are different approaches to investigate the effectiveness of vocational education systems.

We will not attempt an ultimate classification, but we think it is useful to distinguish four approaches to effectiveness.
1. The first one is an approach coming from the accountancy-world. A handy method is the so-called balanced score card of Kaplan and Norton. This card maps a determination of performance from four perspectives: how do the customers see us, in which field should we improve our performance, what image do the shareholders and other financiers have

of us, and how can we continue to improve and grow (cf. Kerklaan et al., 1996)?

2. The second approach looks at the qualification targets which vocational education is expected to meet in the light of the relevant national legislation or regulations that derive from it.

3. The determination of result by attempts to operationalise the functions of vocational education is the third approach. These are economic functions (e.g. unemployed school leavers, transfer of knowledge to small and medium-sized companies, further training by school leavers), social functions (e.g. social reception, integration of newcomers, crime prevention, social cohesion), and cultural functions (e.g. contributions to the formation of local/regional communities, adaptation of youth culture).

4. The fourth approach determines results by attempting to arrive at the operationalisation of effectiveness. This approach elaborates four kinds of concepts of effectiveness: mastery (e.g. stability), innovation (e.g. didactic innovations), productivity (e.g. productivity per class), and involvement (e.g. teacher commitment). The elaboration of the Quinn and Rohrbaugh model is particularly important in this perspective.

The first approach, the Kaplan & Norton balance score card, works with four perspectives:

-   the financial perspective;
-   the customer perspective;
-   the internal organisation perspective;
-   the innovation, learning perspective.

The fourth of these perspectives, learning capacity, relates to innovation and quality improvement, training, intellectual assets, implicit knowledge, etc.

Each perspective is concerned with different kinds of search fields, within which norms and indicators can be drawn up. We follow the four perspectives:

-   Customer perspective: retention of customers, customers' wishes, customer satisfaction. Which aspects are genuinely of importance to the customers?
-   Internal organisation perspective: which organisational processes have the greatest effect on customer satisfaction? What style of work leads to an improvement of the result? This concerns not only the mastery of current operational processes, but also design processes aimed at the long-term development of programmes and services. Aftercare processes are important in addition to operational and innovative processes. The pre- and post-trajectory of the provision of education is equally important.

–   Financial perspective: solvency, productivity and liquidity are the criteria that have already been mentioned. Profit, growth and share prices are important to companies. The score card also shows that the determination of the financial result in terms of solvency, productivity and liquidity only covers part of the financial side. Companies are concerned with the yield on invested capital and added economic value. However, it is not so much a question of obtaining an accurate picture of performance in the past, but of whether the criteria also say something about functioning in the future.

–   Innovation/internal learning perspective: adaptation to new circumstances, new service demands, are new programmes required to meet new needs? The learning capacity of an organisation can be operationalised in a variety of ways. An important distinction concerns what knowledge and experience individuals take with them and what they leave behind. If members of staff leave vocational education, they inevitably take certain things that they have learnt with them in the form of personal property. Still, something is left behind in the organisation, along with other accumulated insights, developed patterns of approaching problems, procedures, routines, contribution to discussions, databases, address lists, quality manuals, etc. In a certain sense a kind of exchange or conflict model is applicable here: it is in the interests of a company to incorporate the knowledge accumulated by an employee as far as possible in internal work and expert systems, while for the individual such an extraction and incorporation in systems independent of him or her is naturally not always the most attractive option.

It is not necessary to base the score card on these four perspectives: there may be more or fewer perspectives. We here apply them to vocational education as an entity. It is also possible to apply them to sectors, divisions, basic units and to the system of vocational education as a whole.

3.1   Qualification targets

It must in principle be possible to use formulations of targets in national legislation to determine whether the system of vocational education works effectively enough. These objectives can also be used to assess alternative solutions for problems in the implementation of policy. For example, the system of vocational education is aimed at theoretical and practical preparation for the exercise of professions, including general education and personal development, for which education leading to a vocational qualification is required, and for the promotion of personal development for the benefit of the social functioning of adults. These objectives are usually summarised in various countries in the attainment of three qualifications:

- vocational qualifications;
- career/development qualifications;
- social qualifications.

The objectives must be formulated in a reasonably specific way, they must be internally consistent (individually and jointly attainable), flexible (ability to adjust to changed circumstances), and of course feasible (feasibility as guiding principle).

The specificity of the objectives is particularly expressed in:
- content (concrete, operational, elaborated in terms of groups);
- standard (unit of measurement, e.g. productivity per full time position, etc.);
- level (how much productivity is required);
- time perspective (period in which the objectives are to be attained).

In different countries there are different solutions in practice for this qualification domain. The UK has developed a NVQ (National Vocational Qualifications) system while in other countries a more general system functions with less emphasis on operational objectives.

4.   SOCIAL FUNCTIONS

Vocational education functions on behalf of certain social sectors and on behalf of society as a whole. For which social sub-systems does vocational education satisfy certain demands?

Let us begin with those social sectors to which vocational education is expected to make a contribution:
a) Socio-economic: vocational education contributes to the security of the pupils in their future working life in terms of work and income.
b) Economic: vocational education contributes to the preparation for a profession and participation in the labour market. It contributes to the knowledge infrastructure.
c) Social: contributing to social and cultural training in preparation for future citizenship in a democratic society, and to the integration of newcomers.
d) Cultural: contributing to character training as part of upbringing and training.

4.1   Socio-economic

Is vocational education socio-economically acceptable to influential groups, internally acceptable, does it yield reasonable performance, and is it flexible? The main problems here lie in the importance of vocational education for increasing labour participation. As far as the relation between income and work is concerned, the system of vocational education can probably perform better. The performance of the system of vocational education appears to be particularly inadequate at the lowest labour level. Newer combinations of training, remuneration and work must be generated from the system of vocational education.

4.2   Economic

Is vocational education economically acceptable to influential groups, internally acceptable, does it yield reasonable performance, and is it flexible? The main problems for the system of vocational education here are different from those in the first category. They concern a perspective of national survival in an internally coherent economic EU block.

4.3   Social

Is vocational education socially acceptable to influential groups, internally acceptable, does it yield reasonable performance, and is it flexible? The main problems here concern the contributions of vocational education to social integration and development. The social perspective of different groups can be improved by practically-orientated vocational education and a consistent and practical integration policy aimed at housing, work, education, culture and administration. In the big cities this concerns a contribution from vocational education to promoting the coherence of decentralised policy sectors such as care for the elderly, housing, education, safety policy, and care for addicts.

4.4   Cultural

Is vocational education culturally acceptable to influential groups, internally acceptable, does it yield reasonable performance, and is it flexible? In cultural terms, the education system has traditionally proved able to make a contribution of its own to the further development and preservation of culture. Vocational education can perform better in this respect. In the first place, it can become better attuned to the modern information technology side of culture; in the second place the vocational education sector can react better to the popular (music) culture; and in the third place vocational education also has an important task to transfer cohesive values in a tolerant form that is suitable for a multicultural context.

5.   ORGANISATIONAL EFFECTIVENESS

Quinn and Rohrbaugh have developed a comprehensive approach through an ensemble of measures of effectiveness. This work is directly applicable to vocational and adult education. They develop a four-theory model for the effectiveness of organisations. They do so by, in the first instance, arranging 17 criteria of effectiveness along three dimensions. These 17 are adjustment, reactive capacity, growth, recruitment of resources, external evaluation, planning, volume of production, efficiency, stability, control, information content, cohesion, development of human potential, ethics, quality, balance of knowledge and profit.

The first dimension concerns the internal (e.g. cohesion, stability) or external (e.g. growth, productivity) orientation of the criteria. The second dimension concerns the structuring of the organisation, and concerns criteria aimed at governance and control (e.g. planning, efficiency) or flexibility and change (e.g. adjustment). The third dimension concerns the relation between means and ends. Is effectiveness a question of recruiting resources or achieving results?

In combining the dimensions, they distinguish four theories. The first is a theory of internal bureaucracy in which an important aspect is that matters are fixed, reasonably predictable, well documented, and offer teachers security and safety. The second is a theory that sees a school as an open system that responds flexibly to internal and external changes. The school organisation develops, is able to recruit support from outside, and adjusts to new circumstances. The third theory, the model of the rational ends, emphasises the key activities. What is the *raison d'être* of vocational education? At any rate to teach pupils, students and student-workers something. That is thus where the emphasis lies in this theory. Target-orientation and task-orientation are important aspects. The fourth theory, that of human relations, concerns above all the internal cohesion and commitment of the teachers and pupils/students within the organisation. Teachers work together, and the exchange of information and participation in decision-making are very important.

The quality criteria in these four theories are different. In the first model, that of the internal bureaucracy, the criteria are stability, control, written procedures, and good information management. In the second theory, the open system model, the criteria lie in innovation, growth and the degree of adaptability that the organisation can muster, as well as in the extent to which vocational education is able to recruit resources from outside. In the third theory, the model of the rational end, the quality criteria are productivity, examination and test results, success rates, clarity of objectives, and working towards goals. In the fourth theory the quality criteria lie in such fields as group ethics, commitment to one another and to the school, participation, openness and involvement. Educational institutions can be reviewed in terms of these four sets of criteria, without being tied down on a Procrustean bed: some institutions will adhere to certain criteria which other schools avoid.

There are also different orientations for vocational education corresponding to these different quality criteria. According to the internal bureaucracy model, the vocational education institutions are expected in the first place to know what is going on in the institution itself. It is important in this orientation for information to be available and to be analysed. Furthermore, vocational education undertakes an ongoing revue of the structure of the organisation and supervises process accountability. Planning, scheduling and drawing up surveys are important activities.

The open system model is concerned with an orientation towards change. Vocational education is aimed primarily at change and at the development and implementation of new ideas. Contacts with the outside world are important, and so are aspects of power. Vocational education of this kind is concerned with improving the external legitimisation of the school. This vocational education is politically alert, persuasive and influential.

In the model of the rational end, the orientation is towards processes of planning, indicating alternatives, and evaluation of performance and instructions. It is concerned with an orientation towards tasks and work, energy and personal dedication. Vocational education assumes responsibility for the performance to be achieved and spurs teachers on to better and harder work and study.

The human relations model is concerned with an orientation towards joint effort, the relations between teachers, and working on good joint solutions to problems. The institutions of vocational education and/or adult education display an attitude of caring about their staff and pupils/students. Vocational education promotes the development and training of the staff.

5.1   VET systems: Criteria for effectiveness

If we try to combine the main characteristics of the VET systems with the favourite approach to effectiveness we can develop a first preference for a effectiveness approach. Of course the preferences are hypothetical. Furthermore it is possible that more then one approach can be practised at the same moment. What the figure shows in any case is that there is no such thing as one ultimate criterion for the quality of the European VET systems. The systems differ in that they employ or might employ different approaches to effectiveness and quality. The figure also makes clear that the implementation of a new quality approach will not be easy when the main characteristics of the VET system concerned is quite different from a VET system that has a natural tendency towards that specific system.

VET System/ Favourite Effectiveness approach	Balanced Score Card	Qualificatio n Targets	Social Functions	Organizatio nal Effectivene ss
Steering: Market	Preference			
Steering: Institution		Preference		
Funding: public			Preference	
Funding: private		Preference		
Suppliers, implementation: public				Preference
Suppliers, implementation: private		Preference		
School/ firm based: School based			Preference	
School/ firm based: Firm based		Preference		

5.2   External groups and internal processes

Although VET systems do vary and, although they have or might have their favourites in terms of effectiveness-orientation, all of the systems have to find a balance between internal processes and external groups.

In the environment of a school there are groups and regulatory bodies which are or become of more or less importance. This is a conception of the environment that considers in the first instance the bodies that are operative within the environment: important groups of clients, resource providers, regulatory bodies, and competitors. We shall refer to this conception as a pluriform interpretation of the environment. It is primarily about the mixture of influences which affect the school.

A second conception views the school less as the victim of a mixture of influences from the environment. A school is itself also an actor, and it can attempt to model the environment as it chooses, either on its own or (generally) through coalitions with other organisations such as other schools or institutions of a different kind. We shall refer to this conception of the environment as a control-orientated interpretation of the environment.

The pluriform interpretation often includes attempts to classify the environment in terms of stability. In a stable environment the mutual relations within the mixture of influences hardly change, if at all. The relations do change in a dynamic environment, but there is a reasonable degree of predictability in the form of change. A turbulent environment is characterised by very rapid change and it is difficult to indicate patterns of change.

In the control-orientated interpretation of the environment, an educational institution explicitly uses the existing opportunities to control or influence certain bodies in the environment. We can break the control down by the main kinds of bodies - resource suppliers, groups of clients, competitors and regulatory bodies. Control of resource suppliers is concerned with financial and material matters, but also with the access to trainee placements and training resources such as advanced equipment. For some institutes the maintenance of a fixed input of pupils and student-workers also implies a permanent relation with the client group. Control of competitors can take place in a variety of ways: driving competitors out of the market, price agreements, the formations of cartels. It is more difficult for individual schools to influence the regulators, but as associations, vocational education and adult education schools are by no means powerless. The formation of networks can be an attractive way to control the environment.

The quality of vocational education is not a technical given that can simply be read by a simple measuring instrument. This is mainly because vocational education is an institution in which a wide variety of bodies and groups have an interest. All those bodies and groups do not share the same view of what vocational education is supposed to do. From the perspective of vocational education, it is important to know what conceptions of quality are adhered to by the different groups and bodies, and which combination of definitions of quality is applicable in vocational education. The four approaches to quality outlined above leave varying amounts of room for different social groups to contribute to the determination of the main criteria of effectiveness. Different groups have different positions and interests in vocational education, and in addition they have different methods and mechanisms to make them known to vocational education and sometimes even to impose them.

This résumé of possible criteria indicates that vocational education is positioned in a relatively complicated field of bodies, groups, administrative organs, government bodies, companies, etc. who all want something from vocational education. This makes the question of effectiveness less simple than it sometimes seems to be in discussions where a single norm, say productivity, is advocated. There is a plurality of parties involved, and a plurality of standards. Which parties are involved in vocational education?

Support groups can be classified in various ways. We make use of the following classification (Mintzberg, cf. Mitroff):

- resource suppliers (central government, local government, employment services, temp agencies, companies, private parties);
- employees (teachers and management and support staff, organised and independent);
- customers (pupils, students, companies and institutions as customers);
- competitors (other vocational education institutions, private training courses);
- allies (other vocational education institutions, regional support groups, sectoral organisations);
- regulators (ministries of education, social affairs, economic affairs, legal pronouncements);
- supervisors (inspectorate, support groups, qualified authorities).

Each stakeholder will try to make its views of effectiveness known to vocational education and sometimes even to impose them. An organisation like vocational education can be regarded in a certain sense as an organised collection of internal and external stakeholders. In such a multiple constituency perspective, an organisation like vocational education resembles a system that arouses differentiated views of effectiveness and puts them into practice for different constituents. Institutions of vocational education are in a certain sense systems which are in fact intersections of the paths of influence of constituents. In spatial terms, an organisation shifts in line with the shifting of the intersections.

Within this perspective effectiveness is plural because constituents also present themselves in the plural. Effectiveness reflects the different evaluation concerns of the different constituents or support groups. Support groups are not independent of one another. Individual stakeholders are influenced by other stakeholders, support groups, and the totality of stakeholders. The properties of a particular stakeholder are a function of those of other stakeholders and of the system of stakeholders in its entirety.

Not every constituent has to be serviced to the same extent at the same time. What counts is that coalitions arise between support groups and that the dominant coalition is important for the question of effectiveness. Effective is what the dominant coalition considers effective.

Stakeholders and support groups contribute to the capacity of an organisation to change its objectives and to create new targets, its capacity to recruit appropriate resources, its capacity to allocate resources to the appropriate parts of the organisation, and its capacity to avoid conflicts between stakeholders or to keep them alive (Mitroff). By incorporating all kinds of claims from different groups in a single system, problems of internal co-ordination arise resulting from a sharp increase in micro politics and internal decision-making. The institutions can express this problem in their internal structure, for example by creating a separate unit for each environmental component. This means that different programmes or groups are given an environment of their own. Depending on the internal organisational structure that is adopted, training courses (sectors, units, departments, target group units, etc.) can maintain relations with relevant parties in the environment with a fairly high level of autonomy. Depending on the internal organisational structure that is chosen, programmes (sectors, units, departments, target group units, etc.) can maintain independent relations with relevant parties in the environment to a certain extent. The tightness of the system must not exclude or seriously obstruct intervention by the environment. The organisational structure must enable adaptation to and interaction with the environment. Various programmes have their own environment. Not every change in the environment is relevant to the same extent and in the same way for each part. Very tightly integrated organisations are not able to direct particular environmental influences towards specific parts of the organisation and to confine them to that. All the same, minimal co-ordination will remain necessary. In this sense, vocational education will probably not be able to be an integrated, tight system. This is unnecessary and undesirable because the quality standards are formulated by various support groups, stakeholders and parties and are too diverse to be able to be realised in a homogenous structure.

Internal processes in provision for vocational education are in many ways important for the outcomes. Two components are emphasised here: the qualifications of teachers, and the way knowledge is managed within the organisation.

Institutions of vocational education and/or adult education can be seen as a compromise between autonomy and co-ordination. This is a difficult compromise because we want more from both parties - autonomy and co-ordination: more room for the vocational judgement of teachers, and more room for responsibility and accountability to the management (Shedd and Bacharach, p5). Nowadays more claims are made by teachers for increasing their autonomy, while at the same time higher demands are imposed on responsibility and co-ordination. The more objectives an institution of vocational education and/or adult education tries to achieve and the more diverse and heterogeneous the pupil population is, the more pressure is put on increasing both teacher autonomy and co-ordination within the school at the same time. Very different groups impose very different demands on schools. All these groups vary in the interest that the school has as regards pupil enrolment, the provision of resources, support, etc. In other words, vocational education never serves a single purpose, but always a number of purposes. Increases of scale usually mean that a more diverse totality of expectations has to be satisfied. More objectives mean more complexity in the work, less objectives mean greater clarity in the work.

In drawing up their plans, vocational education institutions pay attention to the development of qualifications of their staff members. Qualification development is achieved by means of more or less formalised schemes of teacher training, but it is also achieved - and probably more thoroughly - by means of the models and styles of work that are followed. Learning and working can also be better related to one another within the school: by working in a certain way, teachers can learn to do their work better. Teachers can learn from one another. This process can be promoted by co-ordination and also by team spirit and coaching. It is important whether a connection can be made between training and further training of organisational members, teachers, directors and auxiliary personnel, on the one hand, and training and further training of the organisational components and of the organisation as a whole, on the other hand. Learning processes can have a strongly individual orientation (keeping up to date in one's subject), but they can also have a team orientation (learning from colleagues). Such learning processes can be more or less strongly linked to this development. Individual study to keep up in one's subject is the individual responsibility of every vocational professional. Consulting colleagues about problems and regular joint discussions of new insights and practices is a related step. Personnel assessment, personnel training and personal development are a few of the instruments to enhance this capacity further. There are enough opportunities in this respect for the development of indicators.

Organisational learning is a field that is orientated towards the future. It goes beyond the professionalisation of teachers and other members of staff because other organisational aspects are at stake. It is a promising field, but at the same time it is underdeveloped and suffers from a lot of vagueness and idle talk.

An organisation can pay attention to its own organisational learning process. Organisational learning and change can take place successively or simultaneously. An organisational change can lead to a learning process to promote the introduction of change. The processes can also take place in the reverse order: the organisational change is then the result of the learning process. The two kinds of process can also take place simultaneously. Improving the qualifications of the teaching personnel through training and further training can be given shape in a training or further training plan. A plan of this kind could be a part of a wider process of collective learning.

Organisational learning refers to the knowledge of individuals, the knowledge of the totality of individuals, and the knowledge of the organisation.

Organisational learning, according to Levitt and March, 1995, and Cohen, 1995, concerns firstly the acquisition of knowledge (acquired learning, learning from experience, substitute learning, learning by transfer from groups and individuals, and learning from research). The acquisition of knowledge can take place through the contribution of the founders, through learning from experience (trying out, experimentation, individual study, self-evaluation), through second-hand learning (spying, imitation), through transfer (transfer from individuals and groups), and through research (scanning, orientated research, performance monitoring). Secondly it is concerned with the distribution of knowledge (information from various sources is shared and thereby leads to new information or insight); thirdly with the interpretation of knowledge (distributed information is interpreted through shared understanding), and finally with organisational memory (storage and retrieval).

A distinction is usually made in the management of knowledge between a stock and a flow approach. If we view an educational institution from a stock approach, the question is whether knowledge is managed actively. Is there an active insight into where and from whom knowledge is available? Are internal electronic forums for discussions within a particular subject encouraged? Is there a system in which every member of staff's experiences with groups, parts of the curriculum or practical institutions are shared in an acceptable way with others?

When viewed from a flow approach, the level of knowledge is more connected with the individual members of staff, and the organisation builds on the dedication to the personal development of the employees. This can be given form, for example, by indicating each year what the current level of knowledge is in certain areas and what the target level of knowledge is for those same areas. This is a way of indicating whether someone wants to go into a new area: the present level of knowledge is low, the target level of knowledge is high. A flow approach of this kind can be applied at the institutional level.

An organisation learns from and teaches its members. This is a matter of improving the interaction between individual and organisational learning. The question is how vocational education can retain the breadth of individual experiences. How can selections from them be incorporated in the organisation while retaining the breadth and variation of experience (Sitkin 1995)? The more varied the internal capacities of vocational education are in terms of systems, routines and staffing, the better the organisation will be at adapting to unexpected difficulties. Intelligent choices require the effective production of options from which the choices can be made (Sitkin 1995).

How does a VET system build up these options, and how is this variety maintained, with what effects for the preferred set of criteria for effectiveness?

REFERENCES

Brandsma, J., Kessler, F. and Münch, J. (1995), *Continuing vocational training in Europe: State of the art and perspectives*. Utrecht, Lemma.

Bowman, C. and Asch D.(1987), *Strategic Management*, Macmillan, London.

Deutscher Bildungsrat (1974), *Zur Neuordnung der Sekundarstufe II*, Klett Verlag, Stuttgart.

Clegg, S., Hardy, C. and Nord, W. (1996), *Handbook of Organisation Studies*, Sage, London.

European Commission (1995), *Structures of the education and initial training systems in the European Union*, Office for Official Publications of the European Communities, Luxembourg.

Kallen, D. (1974), *Recurrent education: utopia or blueprint?* Paper presented at the Conference of the Comparative and International Education Society. Washington.

Haselhoff, F. and Piëst E. (1992), Strategisch management. in J. Bilderbeek et al. (ed.). *Polybedrijfskundig Zakboekje*, PBNA, Arnhem.

Leeuw, A. de (1994), *Besturing van veranderingsprocessen*, van Gorcum, Assen.

Kaplan, R. and Norton, D. (1996), *The balanced scorecard*, Harvard Business School Press, Boston.

Levitt, B. and March, J. (1995), Organisational Learning, in Cohen M and Sproull L (eds), *Organisational learning*, Sage Publications, Thousand Oaks, pp. 516-540.

Meyer, J. and Scott, W. (1983), *Organisational environments: ritual and rationality*, Sage Publications, Beverly Hills.

Mintzberg, H. (1983), *Power in and around organisations*, Prentice-Hall, Englewood Cliffs.

Mitroff, I. (1983), *Stakeholders of the organisational mind*, Jossey-Bass.

Quinn, R. and Rohrbaugh, J. (1983), *A spatial model of effectiveness criteria. Towards a competing values approach to organisational analysis*, Management Science, 29 pp. 363-377.

Shedd J. and Bacharach, S. (1991), *Tangled Hierarchies*, Jossey–Bass, San Francisco.

Sitkin, S. (1995), Learning through failure, in Cohen, M. and Sproull, L. (eds), *Organisational learning, Sage Publications*, Thousand Oaks, pp. 541- 577.

Chapter 13

Searching For Educational Quality
A Stakeholder Approach

Jan Ax
University of Amsterdam

1.   NEW MEASURES IN SECONDARY VOCATIONAL EDUCATION

Over the past few years the government has instigated measures aimed at a better match between secondary vocational education and the demands posed by society. This is the perception of quality adopted here. The basic policy ideas can be outlined as follows.

A process of institutional reorganisation has resulted in a system comprising a relatively few but large institutions which, in principle, are able to offer a comprehensive range of training courses. This sector used to comprise of a loose collection of small schools offering training for a variety of specific occupations. Comprehensive means all types of training varying in content, level and duration, which are required to satisfy the demand from students and clients in the vicinity. These new institutions are called Regional Training Centres (Regionale Opleidingen Centra, ROCs). The institutional integration of training courses is aimed at a closer integration of the training offered (internal adaptation and co-ordination), optimal planning of training courses, increased transparency for the benefit of external parties, increased capacity for policy decisions at institutional level and the introduction of innovation in education.

In addition, the institutions have been given more room for policy making and at the same time more opportunities have been created for external actors to influence policy. The Regional Competent Authorities for Employment Provision (Regionale Besturen van de Arbeidsvoorzieningen, RBAs) are, for example, involved in establishing training needs, in terms of both content and the number of training places, which they also fund. National Bodies for Vocational Education (Landelijke Organen voor het Beroepsonderwijs, LOBs) set nation-wide educational targets which the courses must achieve. Employers, employees and the education sector are all represented in these LOBs.

The question now arises as to what extent these structural and administrative changes bring about sufficient change in the way the institutions function to meet prior expectation.

The subject of this contribution is the relation between ROCs and other external institutional actors, forged in order to achieve the above-mentioned objectives. This report is an explorative, descriptive inventory in the form of a field study of the external relations of ROCs as perceived by a number of key figures. For the purposes of this study these represent national government policy, institutional policy and the point of view of the `expert'.

They include four policy makers, civil servants from the Ministries of Education, Culture and Science, Social Affairs and Employment, and representatives from the Department of Trade and Industry (2 persons); two Chairmen of ROC Competent Authority Committees (Colleges van Bestuur) and two professors in Organisation Studies with extensive advisory and consultancy experience relating to strategic policy implementation. They differ in the extent to which they are familiar with the education scene.

The study is based on open interviews in which those involved were asked for their views on the external relations which a standard ROC should maintain and what the objectives should be.

The reported findings are preceded by a discussion of the stakeholder approach which focuses on external relations. This formed the basis for the list of topics raised in the interviews.

2.   STAKEHOLDER APPROACH

The multiple constituency (or stakeholder) approach (Connolly et al, 1980; Mitroff, 1983) focuses on strategic external relations. Connolly et al disagrees in particular with the notion that a single statement suffices when assessing organisations for efficacy (for example success in respect of survival). Organisations may be open systems in principle, but the efficacy of the organisation is determined by a great number of external interested parties. As a rule, rather than exceptionally, these interests are dissimilar. Whether an organisation is successful or not depends therefore on the evaluation of the respective interested parties, from which certain evaluation criteria may be derived. Success or efficacy is therefore not a feature of the organisation in question, but an evaluation by interested parties. One should therefore not remain within the walls of the college for an idea of how successfully a ROC functions. It is important to know how interested parties evaluate the school. Although such a composite picture may not lead to an unambiguous final mark, it does lead us, as it were, nearer to the truth.

Mitroff (1983,p.36) puts forward the following presuppositions in respect of stakeholders.

1. An organisation comprises internal and external stakeholders. Being organised means that they maintain relations amongst each other or are at least associated in some way.
2. Each stakeholder has at least one main feature in respect of at least one of the following categories:

- objectives and motives;

- beliefs;

- control over resources;

- special knowledge and views;

- commitment (legal or otherwise);

- relations with other stakeholders in the system.

3. There is a network of stakeholders who mutually maintain relations, sometimes to the advantage and sometimes to the disadvantage of the organisation.
4. Changes in the organisation lead to changes in the network.
5. Changes in the relationship with stakeholders can come about through:

- changes in the stakeholder;

- combating the stakeholder;

- incorporation;

- forming coalitions;

- ignoring;

- giving in;

- capitulation;

- forging emotional ties;

- merger, imitation.

6. The availability of these opportunities should be seen as a feature of stakeholders.

7. The existing situation of an organisation can be considered as the outcome of relationships historically forged with stakeholders. This history is, as it were, the culture of the organisation.
8. The strategy of an organisation *must* be based on *assumptions* relating to behaviour and characteristics of stakeholders and the network, and the power of the organisation to influence relevant relationships.

We can therefore say that ultimately the efficacy of an organisation is determined by the sum of the stakeholders. This means that the organisation is fundamentally dependent on stakeholders. It does not mean, however, that the organisation cannot pursue their own policies. In our opinion the opposite is true. An organisation which does not operate on the basis of their own position and perceived responsibilities is by definition at the mercy of external powers. The result is an ad hoc strategy without any coherence.

ROCs intent on pursuing an education policy which is demand-led must have a proper understanding of the configuration of stakeholders and their interests. Such an understanding is often lacking, according to Mitroff (1983, p.25).

2.1 Identification of stakeholders

Mitroff (1983) distinguishes between a traditional and an extended stakeholder approach. A company has two groups of stakeholders, according to the traditional approach. The shareholders who provide the working capital in return for dividend and customers who receive goods or services and who provide the income of the company. This is a linear input process - output model. The extended view includes more than these two groups, the concept is attributed to all parties who are affected by the actions of the organisation and/or influence these actions. Stakeholders are part of the organisation and they also exist outside the organisation. De Leeuw (1994, p.12) describes an organisation as "the sum of the relations which are observed in the real world from a certain functional perspective, and which is selected from this real world". An organisation is therefore not an obvious constant but a variable in this view. The essence of an organisation is determined by the observer. De Leeuw defines stakeholders as all those who have an interest in the functioning of the organisation. (ibid. p.122). The actors who are part of the perceived functional pattern of relations are then the internal stakeholders. Interested parties who have no part in this are the external stakeholders. The designation external or internal depends therefore on the determination of what is considered to be part of the organisation. Below we apply a number of restrictions to the identification of stakeholders.

Firstly, we are concerned with external stakeholders only. Any actors who are part of the institution through employment contracts concluded with the competent authorities, including the competent authorities themselves, are considered to be internal stakeholders.

Secondly, only institutional actors are considered: organisations and institutions who represent the interests of third parties. Individual stakeholders are not considered here.

We also focus on stakeholders with interests that are closely linked with the educational function of the school. This is, of course, the main basis for the policy. Unions who defend the interests of the staff, suppliers of goods and services relating to maintenance, domestic matters etc. are not considered here.

By educational function we mean all activities aimed at educating and training students. Stakeholders who have direct interests in these activities, or direct interests in respect of maintaining and adapting these, are included in the selected collection of stakeholders. This delineation is obviously an arbitrary one.

We briefly indicated before which are the interests involved which gave rise to the changes outlined in the sector overall. The diagram below shows these in the first column. The right-hand column shows a number of stakeholders who are part of the education establishment. In other words, these stakeholders are important to all ROCs and they represent the bureaucratic control mode.

INTERESTS	STAKEHOLDERS
Match between education and training and the job market	National Bodies for Vocational Education and Training Regional Competent Authorities for Employment Provision
Development of human resources	Project Transito Cognito InnovatieCentra BVEnet
Participation in education and training by the target groups	Local Authorities Regional Competent Authorities for Employment Provision
Individual needs	National Government as Higher Competent Authority

Figure 1. Interests of Stakeholders

The interests of the industrial sectors are looked after by the National Bodies for Vocational Education and Training. Employers, employees and the education sector are all represented in the Competent Authorities of these statutory bodies. The LOBs formulate the targets at different qualification levels and they must agree the number of vocational training places.

The Regional Competent Authorities for the Employment Provisions set out a policy plan which states the regional demand for training and they fund training places for those concerned.

A number of national projects exist whose task it is to stimulate the process of updating knowledge and the introduction of telematics applications in education. InnovatieCentra, independent institutes funded by Ministry of Trade and Industry, may serve as a source of knowledge.

Local Authorities and RBAs pursue policies which lead specific target groups into training.

The provision of tailor-made measures for the individual is explicitly included in the law. The Inspectorate oversees this.

This general outline of stakeholders is, of course, far from complete. Each institution will have to compile a list which applies to their own situation. The question arises as to how such a list can be drawn up. Mitroff (ibid.) distinguishes seven methods which, according to him, are together sufficiently heuristic to identify stakeholders.

1. The imperative method: the determination of the powers which the organisation must take into consideration. The sources of these powers are viewed as potential stakeholders. Mitroff includes unions on the basis of the power of employment unrest.
2. The position method: tracing who has a formal say in the determination of policy.
3. The reputation method: asking key figures which stakeholders they consider important.
4. The social participation method: the identification of actors who participate in the process of policy-making. A weakness in this method is that potential stakeholders are overlooked.
5. The opinion leadership method is based on actors who influence other stakeholders.
6. The demographic method identifies stakeholders on the basis of characteristics such as sex, age, occupation, religion etc. The disadvantage of this method is that it assumes group homogeneity.
7. The focal organisation method investigates which persons or organisations maintain significant relations with the organisation. Significant contacts include suppliers, employees, customers or clients, associates, competitors, regulators or inspectors. The employers as stakeholders are not included here, as mentioned. Mitroff's list cannot be applied directly to educational institutions. We therefore adapt his list of interest categories somewhat.

a) Supply of students and other participants (for example secondary schools (vo), Local Authorities, Regional Competent Authorities for Employment Provision (RBA)).
b) Clients for school leavers such as Higher Vocational Education (HBO), employers.
c) Institutions with a similar task or parallel role, which may mean an association and/or competition.
d) Providers of resources, e.g. of educational tools and machines by local companies.
e) Information providers in the field of the technology of the organisation.
f) Providers of access to local/regional networks.
g) Representatives of target groups.
h) Representatives of social and cultural interests.

Mitroff thinks in terms of power in respect of the imperative method. Not only thinking in terms of power but also a professional imperative is significant as far as external powers are concerned, in the context of policy-making in ROCs. Which powers should legitimately influence the education function. An eighth item should therefore be added to Mitroff's list.

8. The normative orientation method: distinguishing different orientations required for developing the education and training programme. These include:
a) Cultural social orientation. Which knowledge, experiences and attitudes included in the category 'adult citizenship' should the school instil. This concerns training and education objectives which do not directly fall under the heading vocational training. Stakeholders in this context may include: the Centre for Alcohol and Drugs (C.A.D.); Local Health Authority (G.G.D.); organisations involved in public security and crime prevention; cultural and not for profit organisations; local authorities.
b) Orientation relating to the occupational sector. e.g. professional and trade associations.
c) Orientation relating to industry. Local employers and their associations or representatives, agencies, local authorities.
d) Orientation relating to the technology, e.g. training institutions, technology centres.

2.2 Meaning of the stakeholder approach

So what does a stakeholder approach mean when describing and analysing the establishment of a social system? It looks at first sight like an elaboration of the network model. Mitroff indicated that an organisation may be considered as a network of stakeholders. The stakeholder approach as defined above is, in fact, neutral in regard of the various models of social systems (networks). This means that it can be applied widely.

The stakeholder approach aims to map out the actors and the interests which play a role in their relationships. The stakeholder approach is aimed at determining the policy relevance of stakeholders, the identification of stakeholders and the interests which are at stake. This approach is:
- policy-process oriented;
- aimed at determining the components of the social order - the actors and the interests - and at assessing their significance for the organisation;
- suited to developing future scenarios and evaluating the extent to which the organisation satisfies external requirements;
- useful for acquiring knowledge as well as for managing organisations;
- functioning as model representations of reality;
- primarily focusing on a single particular organisation as a study object.

As indicated above, stakeholder requirements will not always be mutually compatible. The actor approach is limited as it assumes a fixed and unambiguous relation between a stakeholder and an interest. In addition, it is assumed that the sum total of the interests corresponds to the total interest which education represents. The latter assumption is disputed by Bull (1988). He speaks of education in this context as a 'self-defeating freedom'. This is a category of freedom in society which defeats itself if everyone fully claims this freedom for themselves. It is necessary to limit freedom in certain cases, precisely to ensure freedom. The most marked example of this is the necessity of laws. Total individual freedom to act leads to lawlessness and such a situation precludes freedom for everyone. The freedom to enjoy education with the exclusive aim of maximising personal development needs ultimately leads to an education situation which has no place for optimal personal development, according to Bull. Any education aimed at completely satisfying an individual's demand risks giving short measure. Personal development requires that people are taught about matters which are outside their direct interests, the value of which they may not at all be aware of. A similar mechanism operates in relation to social development in an economic sense. Education which is aimed solely at realising economic objectives as perceived by the respective actors at any given moment leads to an education system which does not contribute optimally to the economic development of the society. The 'invisible hand' sometimes misses.

According to Bull, the essence is that the demands and interests of actors must be 'well understood'. This requires a form of direction which may go against the wishes of actors. This direction is, of course, determined by government to a certain extent. In this context Bull points out the significance of institutions which have been invested with authority and power by the government. The most well-known example of this is, of course, the law. As far as education is concerned, he can see a place for professionals who are competent for the institute. These cannot operate on the basis of power derived from legislation etc. but must exercise their influence based on authority and trust. The school does not supply the highest quality by simply meeting the direct demand of the actors, according to this way of thinking. This demand must be 'well-understood', i.e. translated into educational measures. This translation process must take into consideration the phenomenon pointed out by Bull. In addition, attention should be paid to interests which are (still) without identifiable stakeholders. Mitroff (1983) calls those hidden stakeholders "snaildarters". This is a species of fish which was championed by the environmental movement and which delayed the building of a hydro-electric power plant in California for years. Snaildarters themselves are not able to defend interests and are therefore dependent on others to act as stakeholders. Does the responsibility of education not include acting as representative of these types of interested parties?

In this way a school is seen not as an institution which offers client-oriented services, but as a social institution which fulfils individual and social education needs, in such a way that we can speak of an optimal development of both, where no groups are systematically overlooked.

A suitable definition of the stakeholder approach in our opinion is seeing it as a decision making oriented evaluation procedure to obtain information relevant to policy. If, for example, we look at the Context-Input Process-Product evaluation model of Stufflebeam and the Responsive Evaluation model of Stake (Guba and Lincoln, 1988) in this context, then the methods and categories described above may be included as systematised strategies for the collection of information.

The CIPP model focuses on four kinds of decision-making:
- The formulation of objectives for which planning decisions must be made. This assumes a continuous process of context evaluation in order to obtain information.
- Structure decisions, the determination of the education processes and procedures. These decisions require input evaluation.
- Input decisions made on the basis of a process evaluation.
- Continuation decisions, the adjustment or otherwise of education. This is done on the basis of the output evaluation.

The stakeholder approach is particularly useful for context and output evaluation.

Stake's responsive evaluation model concentrates on investigating the concerns and issues of the stakeholders in order to collect information on the situational value (context bound) of the education. Stake lists a number of strategies for conducting such research into the concerns and issues of the stakeholders. These strategies are, in fact, a systematic elaboration of the stakeholder approach in education.

It is essential therefore that the stakeholder approach from an evaluation perspective does not assume a direct link between stakeholder demands or interests and the realisation and content of the training. Education and training are not a direct and true-to-life reflection of voiced demands and interests. The stakeholder approach does, however, offer a number of possibilities for the systematic collection of policy-relevant information so as to assess the demands and expectations which education and training should meet, and which ones it actually does meet. This does not mean that the outcomes of the planning, structure, implementation and continuation decisions are thus determined.

3.   FINDINGS

The purpose of the study is to obtain insight into the preferred situation in respect of the relations between ROCs and stakeholders and the problems which (may) arise in this context, through questioning key figures. As mentioned, key figures have been selected who are able to consider the issue from different professional perspectives and formal positions.

This is a first orientation in respect of a preferred situation, and we have therefore chosen an open approach. The interviews with respondents each lasted approximately 90 minutes. The objective was to obtain an insight into the preferred situation. Naturally this can only be done by questioning all stakeholders. Each stakeholder has their own perception of the preferred situation. This study must therefore be considered an exploration. The members of the CvBs were expected to provide an insight into the forging of preferred relations, based on their experiences in practice and their vision of a well-functioning ROC. The policy staff were expected to provide a translation of the policy objectives of government in terms of the ROCs' external relations. The experts might be able to respond from a more objective and reflexive (and not directly involved) perspective.

We would expect the resulting picture to be a reasonably reliable and valid picture of an optimaly functioning ROC. The picture is, of course, a general one. This general picture could be filled in during a subsequent research stage, through case studies. We should add that the interviews mainly dealt with vocational education. Adult education, i.e. the courses run by ROCs which were part of this type of education and training before the reorganisation, was not raised explicitly.

The following diagram indicates the components which we distinguished in the relationships between the ROCs and their stakeholders. Firstly the stakeholder position based on the focal organisation method. Secondly the interests involved. The normative orientation method was used to describe these. We also considered the interests which the ROC ought to honour as well as interests which exist but whose realisation is considered less desirable. This is followed by, respectively, the external characteristics, the ROC internal organisation characteristics and the patterns of relations between the ROC and the stakeholders.

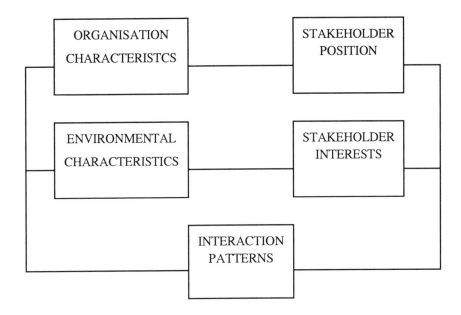

Figure 2. Relations diagram

3.1 Stakeholder identification

Overall, the following picture can be drawn of the stakeholders to which the standard ROC relates. We have used the focal organisation method here, with the addition of the stakeholders who have a formal say in the policy determination of the ROCs.

3.1.1 Administrative bodies and bodies responsible for student provision

The administrative education bodies include the Ministry of Education, Culture and Science, the inspectorate, national bodies for Vocational Education and Training. Bodies responsible for provision for students and other participants RBAs, local authorities, Higher Secondary Education schools. The manner of provision is regulated through government measures, with the exception of the contact with higher secondary education. The provision for students and other participants in respect of initial training is not managed by a clearly defined body of stakeholders, yet a clear stakeholder position has been created (RBA) in relation to the specific training needs for eliminating deficiencies in the job market. We suspect that the ROCs lean heavily on this stakeholder and do not take others into account.

The body of stakeholders related to post-initial and contract education and training, where the potentially successful students do not undergo any form of official employment mediation upon leaving, is not regulated and less transparent. In this context the desirability of viewing alumni as stakeholders has been pointed out. They would be able to provide information on the relevance (or not) of the education experienced and provide a viewpoint of the former student as tomorrow's client. We suspect that this party will have seldom achieved or been assigned a stakeholder position.

It also becomes increasingly important to view other parties in the vicinity as (potential) providers of students. There was mention of temporary employment agencies that have a growing need for training capacity. Industry is expected to demand increasingly more training capacity. This is partially supplied by professional and trade organisations, and another part will be resolved at local level. We can expect significant changes in respect of the provision for students and the ROCs will be well advised to be alert to potential stakeholders.

3.1.2   Customers in respect of school leavers

Higher Vocational Education (HBO) is an important customer, i.e. many students in HBO have an intermediate vocational qualification (MBO). At a national level contacts exist so as to optimise the move. It goes without saying that all kinds of agreements may be made at a local level. These consultations will become increasingly important in future, not least in view of the existing trend in national policy to establish efficient learning routes.

The most important customers are industry, the service providers and the care sector. The respective professional and trade organisations usually occupy the stakeholder position in respect of smaller institutions and small and medium enterprises (SMEs). The systematic maintenance of individual contacts is physically impossible. The other party is often little motivated as these employers are only occasional customers, with widely varying requirements regarding the qualifications of school leavers. Large companies do, however, maintain regular contacts.

The term local industry is to a large extent an abstraction. This may be evaluated in different ways. We will return to this later.

3.1.3 Institutions with similar responsibilities or a parallel function

These include primarily other ROCs in the immediate vicinity. There is an impression that the institutions themselves primarily aim at concluding mutual market agreements and that the competition model is not relevant. The structure has become more transparent as a result of the mergers.

There are also the Centres for Occupational and Vocational Training which will, in the future, no longer be managed by the RBAs.

The company training schemes are less important than they used to be. The extent to which companies train their own employees may vary between regions. One of the CvB chairmen certainly considers them to be a potential competitor in his region.

New providers are also emerging. These include all kinds of private institutions who offer a wide range of courses. Relative newcomers are the temporary employment agencies. These have the advantage that they can combine training and employment brokering.

National professional and trade organisations were also mentioned. These have available substantial sums for training activities and may form close ties with many potential students via regional training centres. This was seen as unfair competition.

3.1.4 Providers of resources

The policy makers emphasise the importance of good relations with companies so as to keep the equipment in schools up to date and 'true to life'. Successful examples of this can be seen at the institution level. This proves to be mainly dependent on the initiative of individual teachers. The question arises to what extent the institutions systematically investigate opportunities to obtain educational aids and machines from local companies through e.g. reciprocal services. It was emphasised that schools and colleges must not come to rely on this.

3.1.5 Information providers in respect of the technology of the organisation

Government emphasises the importance of the availability of new technology for the institutions. This concerns the introduction of advanced technology as a learning objective for the training, as well as the didactic use of technology. Government is an important stakeholder in this respect. It tries to promote the introduction of new technology in schools through special projects such as the Transito Project. Technology centres and leading edge companies in the region were also mentioned. There is an impression that schools do not have easy access to information providers in the area of technology. The impression exists that this is the case to an even greater extent in relation to their own work technology than in respect of technology in the customer field.

3.1.6   Access providers to local and regional networks (positional resources):

One of the experts pointed out that schools must show a clear presence in regional networks. They themselves have a main responsibility in developing stakeholdership, according to him, particularly when it is suspected that there are groups who cannot access the school via their own representation. Clear networks exist in the SME sectors, such as trade organisations and employer organisations. Schools have easy access to such networks. In most cases they probably are their most regular contacts. Networks other than industry networks are hardly ever mentioned.

3.1.7   Target group representatives

Target groups are mentioned little. Their degree of organisation is scant. Target group representatives are important stakeholders in so far as this task is taken care of by 'official' authorities such as the RBA and the local authorities. In cases where such bodies do not represent a certain group, or not adequately, the group's voice is not heard. In certain situations the school probably acts as stakeholder on the basis of its professional responsibility. One of the CvB members indicated that this is the case on an ad hoc basis.

3.1.8   Representatives of social-cultural interests

Hardly any of the interviewees mentioned this category of stakeholders. Such stakeholders only play a role in special cases.

3.2   Interest orientation

The following picture emerges if we view the comments made in the light of the normative orientation method, distinguishing between different orientations required for the development of the education and training programme.

3.2.1   Cultural-social orientation.

Those interviewed are, without exception, of the opinion that this type of orientation does not deserve special and systematic attention. It would seem that the distinction between general education and vocational training (Bildung versus Ausbildung) has strong roots. It was even underlined in one case that the orientation in question can distract from that what education should offer.

The representatives of the institutions indicated that the cultural social orientation only plays a role on an ad hoc basis. The initiative for this often comes from the stakeholders involved.

3.2.2   Orientation towards occupations.

This takes place via the occupational qualifications which have been established by the national bodies. Trade Associations were not mentioned. In addition to the employee organisations (unions) there are virtually no occupational associations in the fields in question. The formal structure regulates this orientation at a national level. This is a threat, according to a number of respondents. It is not clear how the qualifications are arrived at and there may well be a large gap between the actual occupation as carried out by the customers for qualifying students and those who formulate the qualifications. Committees who carry out this work often consist of desk-bound staff who frequently are not in touch with the shop floor. In other words, questions are asked about the validity and representativeness of the qualifications. There are also objections to the level of details in the qualifications. This either leads to frequent changes in the qualification to meet new occupational needs or results in the qualification system remaining structurally behind the present developments. The representatives of the institutions would like more scope for local adaptation. The policy makers have fewer problems with the existing systems. They point to the need for national comparability.

3.2.3   Orientation in respect of industry

This is more a local matter. Orientation is partly via RBAs, partly via representative bodies such as sector organisations and partly involves direct contacts with employers. Two main aspects must be distinguished - the quantitative demand for trained employees and the qualifications which they should have.

The need for the orientation to take place at different levels is underlined. This means that at the level of the CvB contacts are maintained with industry at director level and in industry with local networks.

Contacts should be maintained at the level of the training by teachers with the corresponding level in the companies. The interviewees seem to find the distinction between general policy determination and the implementation via contacts at a corresponding organisation level very important.

Orientation in respect of industry is at best, therefore. formal as well as informal, indirect via representative organisations as well as direct, organised at a strategic level as well as at executive level.

One of the interviewees emphasised the necessity for making choices. A ROC cannot satisfy everybody. Firstly, the demands are by no means always similar. A CvB chairman points out that SMEs like to see function-oriented targets and that the larger companies often prefer more general qualifications. Secondly, a ROC cannot satisfy all demands as this is not feasible in view of the limited means and manpower available. An educational institution must also dare to develop its own profile. Thirdly, one should be aware of the fact that the present demand may not be an unambiguous valid and representative reflection of a desirable future situation. In this context the importance of technology as momentum of the added value which the economy should realise was pointed out. We will return to this later.

In addition, the distinction between targets of the education and training on the one hand and the qualifications demanded on the other was pointed out. In other words, there is no obvious reason why the formulated demand for qualifications must be congruent with the educational objectives. Schools should be experts in translating the requirements into realistic objectives which are within the educational possibilities and the mental development of the students. Industry is said to have a habit of being blind to the personal development perspective and to concentrate too much on qualifications demanded of experienced people who are able to function fully in their post or occupation. This point of view justifies the addition of an orientation framework not mentioned so far - the development perspective of those just starting out in a trade. Education should therefore not exclusively be guided by the demand from the customer organisations but on the contrary concentrate on the qualifications required for further development of the career or the career planning of their successful students. In this context the danger of the demand by the government for the establishment of efficient learning routes was pointed out. This efficiency objective could easily be pursued at the cost of the creation of learning routes which organically match the developmental requirements of the students.

3.2.4   Orientation towards technology

The concept of technology is used here in a broad sense. It includes the 'process technology' of the school as well as the technology used in the customer companies. Government policy sees an important task for intermediate vocational education in updating knowledge in the companies (technology renewal). The ROCs should begin to function as a broker between knowledge developers and users. The interviews with the college chairmen proved that there is not really any question of such a function in their situation. There are no structural contacts with technology centres. Neither is this the case in respect of educational technology. According to one of the experts, the orientation towards technology is crucial and this even imposes the requirement for ROCs to be guided by a wider environment than the immediate vicinity. It is important not just to note the need for technology, but rather to supply a labour force with technical skills and knowledge. Education must make a contribution to an economy in which the provision of services becomes less important and the realisation of added value based on technology increases in importance. To match the policy to the existing training demand from students and the existing demand for qualifications from the direct job market is not good enough, seen from a macro-economic development perspective. Institutions are frequently suspected of not maintaining structural contacts with stakeholders who have access to knowledge relating to the potential demand for technology. Special programmes initiated by government such as the programmes established via Senter fulfil an important function. This means, in fact, that the government acts as a stakeholder in representing the 'technology interest'. It is thought that the institutions have not (yet) made technology orientation into an explicit issue. One of the CvB chairmen interviewed was of the opinion that the ROCs should not really have any responsibility in implementing new technologies in companies and other institutions. It would be interesting to see to what extent that attitude depends on the use of a curriculum which is based on learning subject matter. Competency-based curricula might be able to change this. There might also be some link with the National Qualification Structure (Landelijke Kwalificatiestructuur). This strengthens the relation between the education objectives and content with the practical demand on the one hand, and on the other hand it absolves the individual school from the duty to involve itself to any great extent in this.

3.3 Protection of interests against stakeholders and stakeholders' interests

The representative of the Ministry for Social Affairs emphasised the linking of the initial training to the national qualification framework. This should not be influenced by demands from individual customers. No more than a form of fine-tuning is required as far as matching the content to regional demand. It is preferable for the professional and trade organisations, rather than the individual companies, to act as stakeholder. A ROC should not concentrate overmuch on regional demand.

The experts interviewed question the large role played by stakeholders who act on the basis of representation. One suggests that this leads to an average which never fits in with actual situations. The other is of the opinion that the non-transparent character of the decision making in such committees is problematic. In addition, there is the danger of rigidity or of uncontrollable changes. Both differ in respect of the solution. The first would like to see more direct access by customers. The second expert indicates that the direct demand by employees should be translated by the schools into educational objectives and that criteria other than direct employability should play a role in this translation process. Nor should the government requirement relating to efficient learning routes be an absolute norm. Institutions should make the educative orientation their first priority. The schools themselves must act as stakeholder in respect of this interest.

One of the college chairmen indicated that the interests of the job market are best served when the influence of the national qualification framework and the direct influence of the customers are balanced. He spoke of a fundamental tension between those two, which is essential.

3.4   External characteristics

The field in which the ROCs operate is particularly complex. It contains a plurality of actors. The relevant part of the education system, however, seems quite transparent at present, and the establishment of the ROCs has contributed to this. In addition, there are the local authorities, the RBAs and the National Bodies with whom statutory contacts are maintained. This field is also transparent in principle. One of the ministries has indicated that a reduction in individual regulations and provision, which would all be integrated (breaking down fences), would be desirable - thus enabling increased shared use of government resources.

The customer field is less transparent, usually characterised by fragmentation (a plurality of stakeholders) and organisational associations of representative authorities or those charged with looking after the interests of others. Sometimes a number of large customers are involved. This means that clarity cannot always be obtained.

The field in respect of new providers could be called dynamic. Presently there are many developments in the field of private employment brokering and 'on the job training'. One college chairman made an interesting comment in pleading for co-operation with temporary employment agencies. In addition large sums of money are available through national agreements relating to training and 'employability', and it is not yet clear to what use these will be put or where these will be spent.

There are also considerable differences between the field of initial vocational training and training which can be subsumed under the heading of contract activities. Yet these areas are not really separate when we consider the learning and training routes of people during their entire occupational life, including initial preparation.

3.5 Organisation features

There were not many concrete remarks about the internal ROC organisation. Internal and external information provision and communication would seem important for management purposes.

As far as the internal organisation is concerned, the need not to let the level of ambition and the operations diverge too much, and to aim in particular at vertical consistency in this respect were underlined. The responsibility to defend stakeholder interests cannot be assigned to a particular level of the organisation. There were warnings in respect of too much centralisation, particularly when the school is large.

The importance of dynamic enterprise management was also pointed out. Schools no longer operate in a transparent bureaucratic environment. This means that the school must make choices. As far as the education establishment is concerned, they should be aware of the existence of more than one appropriate solution. The possibility to differ from each other should be there for ROCs. Schools should not remain passive, but should be actively involved in articulating education issues. They will themselves have to balance claims which are contradictory and they will have to distinguish between the demanded education output and that which can be realised in view of the possibilities and perspectives of the students. In other words, dynamic enterprise management must adapt itself to the typical nature of the type of work and the social responsibility associated with it.

The danger that schools risk attaching too much value to procedural rationality and not enough to target rationality within the framework of the internal quality assurance was also pointed out.

The desirability to maintain contacts at various levels in respect of information provision and communication was underlined.

It is suspected that institutions do not handle information provision and communication in a systematic fashion. Knowledge and information is fragmented and is carried by individuals. Some good examples of individual initiatives were given.

The college chairmen were of the opinion that the recent mergers put the institutions in a clearer and stronger position in respect of the outside world.

3.6   Relations

Different models of social order can be found in practice: the market with competition and price mechanisms, the bureaucracy with relations controlled by regulations, the clan with spontaneous co-operation based on traditions and the association or the network which functions on the basis of mutual and complementary interests.

The bureaucratic relations and the existence of a clan are least problematic for schools in the sense that they are not a source of uncertainty. Clans are formed within schools in a region. We suspect two strategies exist for dealing with schools which operate in the same market: merger or mutual agreements which more or less continue the existing situation. At national level there are also many instances where institutions co-operate and it is advantageous to maintain relations and keep them amicable. Direct competition probably only occurs to a very small extent. This applies in particular to initial training.

There is competition in respect of contract activities, particularly in relationships with private providers, which could increase considerably in future, especially in view of the increase of available resources and the dynamic nature of the labour market. It is quite possible that associations will be formed in this area. The task of employment brokers, social partners, companies, expertise centres and education institutions is fundamentally complementary. It is therefore expected that the environmental dynamics and the creation of new relations will take place in this area in particular. Stakeholder relations are, as Mitroff says, not a given but partly the result of one's own actions.

The general picture indicates that there are differences of emphasis in respect of the relative weight to be accorded to the four structure models, but there is no doubt in respect of the basic accuracy of the combination as such. A well-functioning sector cannot manage without bureaucratic rules, market competition, peer co-operation on the basis of trust and regular co-operation aimed at mutually complementary interests. This leads to the complex nature of the field in which schools operate.

The difference between initial training and contract activities plays an important role. Initial training is the subject of many more statutory regulations. A dual regime is involved: a bureaucratic-clan dominated regime for initial training and a market-network dominated regime for the non-initial part. As far as the latter is concerned, there is also a distinction between non-initial training for which the government is responsible via the RBAs and the local authorities, and the genuine private sector. It is obvious that the former type of training is to a lesser extent subject to the free market regime.

REFERENCES

Ax, J., Venne, L.H.J. and Van Wieringen, A.M.L. (1996), "De posities van besturen in bve-instellingen" in Ax, J. and Van Wieringen, A.M.L. (Eds.), *Modernisering van besturen van bve instellingen*, Max Goote, Amsterdam.

Bull, B. L.(1988) "The Limits of Teacher Professionalization", AERA paper 1998, New Orleans.

Connolly, T., Conlon, E.J. and Deutsch, S.J. (1980), "Organizational Effectiveness: A Multi-Constituency Approach" in *Academy of Management Review*.

Delft, T.J.M. van and Van der Krogt, F.J. (1986), *Externe contacten van scholen. Een literatuurstudie en empirische verkenning naar het contactprofiel en de grensorganisatie van scholen in het MTO*, Universiteit Twente, Enschede.

Leeuw, A.C.J. de. (1994), *Besturen van Veanderingsprocessen*, Van Gorcum, Assen.

Ministerie van Economische Zaken, Ministerie van Onderwijs, Cultuur en Wetenschappen en Ministerie van Landbouw, Natuurbeheer en Visserij (1995), *Kennis in beweging. Over kennis en kunde in de Nederlandse economie*.

Mitroff, I,.I.(1983), *Stakeholders of the Organizational Mind*, Jossey-Bass Publishers, London.

Stokking, K.M., Young, R. and Leenders, F.J.(1996). *Kennisnetwerken rond het beroepsonderwijs in beweging. Eerste uitkomsten van een onderzoek*, Isor Onderwijsresearch, Utrecht.

PROGRAMMES AND SECTORS IN
VOCATIONAL AND ADULT EDUCATION

Chapter 14

Introduction to Section 3
Programmes and Sectors in Vocational and Adult Education

Graham Attwell
University of Bremen

This section focuses on different sectoral programmes in vocational and adult education. This embraces both strategies for reform through the introduction of new programmes for particular target groups, especially those disadvantaged on the labour market, and programmes aiming at reform of particular sectors. Whilst the examples are drawn from different countries in Europe and in the USA, taken together they illustrate the varied strategic approaches to reforming and developing vocational and adult education.

The first contribution from Joel Rogers and Laura Dresser is entitled 'sectoral strategies of labour market reform: emerging evidence from the US. Whilst noting the success of the US in creating new employment they point to mounting evidence of the high social costs of a system that lets every worker sink or swim on his or her own in terms of social inequality. If Europeans envy US job creation, they say, many in the US envy Europe's training infrastructure. However attempts at reform are characterised by modest federal leadership, and a hodgepodge of initiatives and reforms, with most of the interesting action occurring on state and local level. These include the development of 'one stop shops' for training and jobs, new roles for technical and community colleges, the School to Work Opportunities Act and the development of national skill standards.

The second section of the study examines the barriers to reform. One major cause is lack of money. Education and training reform in the US is a paradigmatic case of a broader political problem: improving living standards will require substantial public investment, but the public has little confidence in government or the willingness to make that investment in the absence of very clear pay-offs. Further barriers include distributional problems and the weakness in the structure and capacity of government. Finally the biggest problem is that industry is disorganised, or organised in the wrong way.

Rates of investment in new technology are low and only a minority of firms is making the broad changes in work organisation that drive increased skill demand.

Rogers and Dresser discuss various possible remedies for this situation. They point to a number of new experiments, almost always initiated by actors outside the public system, to advance or defend the interests of particular worker constituencies, which, they say, show some promise of remedying the key deficiencies in the US training system. These include programmes to improve dead-end jobs, to improve temporary work through 'hiring halls' and basic skills credentialling, to provide an upward path in mid-level jobs and to bring clarity to labour market access and advancement.

The background to Asa Sohlman's contribution on 'Evaluation and Decision Making in Swedish Adult Education' is the special programme of adult education launched by the Swedish Parliament in 1996. The target group for the programme is the unemployed and those employees lacking upper secondary education. The programme is designed to respond to the new challenges of lifelong learning, the switch from short term policies to long term strategies to combat unemployment and decentralisation and management by objectives. The first section of the paper analyses the goals and underpinning ideas of the programme. As the Swedish government wants to achieve both high growth and social equality, Sweden has to devote more resources to education and training than do countries that do not have such broad goals. This in turn requires the reform of the organisation and methods of adult education.

The following section analyses the implementation of the programme. Some 100,000 full time study places a year are being financed by the national government. The programme is being administered by the municipalities who themselves use different types of educational providers.

In analysing the impact of the initiative Sohlman says that at the political level in the municipalities the programme has generally been enthusiastically accepted. Its strengths include the links to the labour market and to labour market planning, and the new information, recruitment, outreach and validation activities. A more scientific evaluation exercise has attempted to assess the effectiveness of the new provision. This has resulted in some adjustments to the organisation of the programme. More worrying were problems with the pedagogical follow up to training and concerns that the programmes may become isolated from the education sector as a whole. Sohlman concludes with the need for the government to take the lead in developing a systematic approach towards research monitoring and evaluation of the programme.

The third chapter by Lindsy Bagley looks at 'the Role of Distance Learning in Achieving Lifelong Learning. She points to the increased interest in distance learning, given the context of the concept of lifelong learning. Her paper presents the findings of a four year empirical study into the appropriateness of distance learning as a means of updating knowledge and improving practice through participation in lifelong learning. It examines the extent to which the continuing needs of community pharmacists in England can be met through distance learning and considers the wider implications for other professional groups.

The paper first examines the changing role of pharmacists in the UK and the changing nature of their initial education and training. Whilst pharmacy practice has gained academic respectability through the establishment of a degree programme for education the real nature of the community pharmacist's role is becoming less scientific and more people-oriented. In order to carry out this extended role there is the need for continuing training. This has led to an interest in distance learning in order to overcome limitation in funding and resources. However there are questions as to how suitable distance learning is for the needs for lifelong learners, Given that the definition by lifelong learners is by definition a life-long one, it is essential that any system of development, delivery and support is able to maintain their interest and enable them to get involved in the process.

The following section describes the Centre for Pharmacy Postgraduate Education who were commissioned to undertake two separate evaluation studies of the distance learning programme for pharmacists, and provides a description of the methods used for the two studies. In analysing the outcomes of the study Bagley confirms that distance learning is an appropriate way of providing community pharmacists with the means of testing and expanding their knowledge base and subsequently improving practice. Moreover distance learning is able to make a significant contribution to achieving lifelong learning by encouraging community pharmacists to take responsibility for their own continuing education. However for providers of community education distance learning as a model for lifelong learning is only a feasible option if the issue of motivation has been considered and addressed. Only with the support and commitment of the distance learners themselves can lifelong learning succeed.

Kenneth Abrahamsson's contribution called 'Bridging the Gap between Education and Work' looks at the balance between core curriculum and vocationalism in Swedish recurrent education. Whilst the paper focuses on Sweden as an example the dilemmas or problems posed are often of an international nature. The paper deals with various organisational or curricular forms to bridge the gap between education and work including policies of recurrent education, core curriculum, the use of prior work experience as a credit for admission to higher education, on-the-job training and different forms of training for the unemployed.

The paper begins by explaining the context for education in Sweden, based on an extensive public sector and central agreement and consensus between social partners. It looks at current rends in terms of a strong market orientation and the decentralisation of services and provision.

The aim of bridging the gap between education and work is seen as a policy challenge. Policy makers are experimenting with new combinations of the traditional apprenticeship model and the dual system and at the same tome the development of more integrated models. The paper explores the different implications of the various models in the context of a move from direct to extended school to work transition patterns. The new interface between school and work can be seen, says Abrahamsson, as an "accordion phenomenon" with a longer period of socialisation with variations in the opportunities for absorbing a work ethos and values, and with a weaker work connection for many youngsters. These results in the need to articulate a new interface between education policies, labour market policies and social policies.

The paper goes on to examine traditional programmes and policies for school to work transition before examining in more detail a number of current experiments. In particular it concentrates on the introduction of common core subjects in vocational upper secondary school and looks at the increasing vocational function of general adult education. It discusses the efficiency, efficacy and impact of new programmes to provide generic skills in employment training. Abrahamsson concludes by listing the future challenges regarding the societal context of vocationalism and general education.

In the final contribution to this section Nikitas Patiniotis and Dimitris Stravroulakis discuss the case of Greek auto mechanics in a paper entitled 'Forming an Education Policy that meets Practical Needs'. They start by describing the social context of Greek society. Greek business life is comprised of a vast public sector, coexisting with numerous small family enterprises. Whilst the state has traditionally played a leading economic role, and comprises the largest economic sector, the public sector does not seem capable of effectively regulating the economic environment, in terms of setting institutional frameworks or imposing tax law. Despite such weakness many social groups expect the state to provide solutions for sectoral and social problems. Indeed Greek society lacks the exchange mechanisms long ago established in the industrialised countries of Western Europe. Many groups pursue 'guild interest' through violent and disruptive actions, which undermine social cohesion. In this context the case of Greek auto mechanics is unique in following orthodox strategies in order to improve their situation. Auto mechanics have developed a 'European consciousness', by responding to crisis with training.

In the second section of their paper Patiniotis and Stravroulakis analyse the opportunities and prospects for auto mechanics in Greece. They point to a series of problems, based on the structural peculiarities of the Greek environment. These include employment patterns and auto-repair personnel, the recession in the automobile industry, new European legislation and the impact of technical innovation.

Innovation in automobile technology has entailed significant change in the skills of auto repair technicians. New skills are based more on diagnosis than on repair. This has caused sever problems for Greek auto-technicians, for whom the import of modern diagnostic equipment is very expensive and who lack the training to use such equipment. However despite this the Association of Small Auto Repairing Shop Proprietors (SISEMA) have successfully established an educational foundation and, with European funding, have set up a successful programme of continuing training.

The paper concludes that there are two factors behind the success of this venture – technology and the market structure.

Chapter 15

Sectoral Strategies of Labour Market Reform
Emerging Evidence from the United States

Laura Dresser, and Joel Rogers
University of Wisconsin-Madison

1. U.S. LABOUR MARKET REGULATION IN PERSPECTIVE

For good or ill, the sheer economic and political weight of the U.S. make its solutions to employment and training problems important to European policy-makers. Before considering some of the ways it might be changing, we characterise the 'American model' of labour market regulation, and ask how it is performing.

More than any other advanced capitalist economy, the United States relies on competitive labour markets to determine pay, employment, and other aspects of worker welfare.[1] Outside the public sector, only about 10 percent of workers belong to unions. Their collective bargaining agreements generally cover individual firms or establishments, rather than entire industries or regions, and are not extended to non-union employers. Public regulation of labour markets is also minimal. The minimum wage applies to a relatively small number of workers, has no obvious spill-over on the overall level of wages, and recently fell to its lowest level in 40 years before triggering a marginal raise by Congress. Unemployment insurance is more time-limited than in other countries. Outside a cluster of 'means tested' programmes directed to the very poor, the welfare state is largely limited to old-age pensions and health insurance. Exclusive of occupational health and safety regulation and equal employment opportunity laws protecting groups

---

[1] This section draws on joint work with Richard Freeman. See Freeman and Rogers (1996).

from discrimination, the state has few national policies safeguarding workers. Job security, training, even provision of medical insurance are determined at the workplace - through collective negotiations for a small number and through employer policy and individual negotiations for the vast majority. The bottom line is that for most Americans, how one fares in the economy depends overwhelmingly on how one fares in the labour market and thus upon the employer.

For more than two decades now, this market-driven system has led the developed world in job creation. Since 1983, the U.S. unemployment rate has consistently been 3-4 percentage points lower than Europe's. From 1974 to the present the U.S. employment/population ratio has grown from 65 to 71 percent, while Europe's has fallen from 65 to 60 percent. Compared to Europeans, U.S. workers also put in about 200 more hours at their jobs annually - a difference that itself widened during the period - further underscoring relative U.S. success in generating work.

For some Europeans, indeed, U.S. success in job generation, the expense of maintaining a generous welfare state under conditions of high-unemployment, and fears that social protection stifles risk-taking and entrepreneurship together recommend moving toward U.S.-style labour market 'flexibility'. The thought is that if Europe only removed labour market regulations, eliminated job protection laws, reduced unemployment benefits, weakened unions, and decentralised wage-setting, it would enjoy its own jobs miracle. Unemployment would be sufficiently reduced to be fiscally sustainable - especially under diminished expectations of welfare-state support - and what would be lost in security would be more than made up in increased employment and economic dynamism.

There is, however, little evidence for this view, and mounting evidence in the U.S. of the very high social costs to a system that lets every worker sink or swim on his or her own.

Given a rapid secular shift in labour demand toward more-skilled workers, compared to the supply of those workers, flexibility in wage determination assures rising inequality. In the U.S. the college/high-school wage differential nearly doubled in the 1980s, rising from a 34 percent advantage for college graduates in 1979 to a 57 percent in 1993; over the same period, the white-collar/blue-collar premium grew by more than 50 percent and the pay of Chief Executive Officers (CEOs) skyrocketed relative to that of other employees. But inequality has also increased within educational and occupational strata - suggesting the increased importance of sheer luck in labour market outcomes. Over the same 1979-93 period, for example, the ratio of earnings of male high school graduates in the 90th/10th percentiles increased 25 percent; at the same time, similar changes are found within detailed occupations. Here flexibility benefited the lucky few and harmed the unlucky many.

As inequality has risen, moreover, wages have stagnated or declined for much of the U.S. working population. For example, the real hourly wages of men with less than 12 years of schooling dropped 27 percent over 1979-93; wages of high school graduates fell 20 percent; even male college graduates suffered absolute wage declines. Income erosion was especially severe among the young, with the wages of male high school graduates with 1-5 years of work experience, for example, falling 30 percent over the period. And fewer workers experienced life-cycle wage improvement - earning more as they aged and advanced in their careers, gained skills, and attained seniority. In the 1970s the ratio of such life-cycle winners to losers was 4-1. In the 1980s it was halved to 2-1, meaning that one-third of workers actually lost ground as their job experience increased. The contrast with the experience of German workers is like 'night and day': the vast majority of Germans, like the vast majority of Americans in the 1970s, enjoy real wage gains as they accumulate work experience.

With real wage drops concentrated on young workers - those most likely to be starting families - poverty has increased, especially among children. For historical reasons, 'poverty' in the U.S. is defined as an income below three times the cost of a minimal diet 'fit only for temporary or emergency use'. Over the 1979-93 period, the share of the population living below this level rose 29 percent; among children, it rose 38 percent. At present, as many as one-in-four America children are growing up in such poverty.

A comparison of the earnings of the bottom decile of U.S. workers to their European counterparts may help put these trends in perspective. Within respective systems, the bottom decile of U.S. workers earn 38 percent of the U.S. median wage, while the bottom decile of European workers earn 68 percent of the European median. On a cross-system basis, using a purchasing power parity measure - contrasting the cost of a comparable basket of commodities across countries - bottom decile U.S. workers earn just 69 percent of what bottom decile European workers. Compared to their colleagues in a rich country like Germany, they earn just 45 percent.

Wretched earnings at the bottom of the wage distribution, and the difficulty of making even normal gains in income over the life-cycle, contribute to the growth of an 'underclass' in the U.S. - concentrated in our cities, often violently criminal. Lacking any social or economic policies to prevent or remedy this problem, U.S. policy increasingly deals with the underclass through physical incarceration. The U.S. prison population, already a higher share of the general population than any other nation, has been growing since the early 1980s at 7 percent annually. As of 1993, the population directly supervised by the criminal justice system - either in prison, or on supervised probation or parole - equalled 7 percent of the total workforce. At present rates of incarceration, by 2000, 3 percent of male Americans of working age will be in prison - roughly comparable to long-term joblessness among the same population in Europe.

Nor, importantly, does U.S. experience show downward wage flexibility contributing to employment: the massive drop in the real wages of less skilled American men did not improve their employment prospects absolutely, or relative to high-skill workers. Comparing male high school and college graduates in 1980 and 1993, for example, shows lower employment rates for both groups over time, but a sharper drop among the less-skilled. Annual weeks of joblessness in the bottom decile of male workers increased by 8.5 weeks over the late 1960s to late 1980s while remaining unchanged among those in the top four deciles. In the 1990s, for those in the bottom decile, the fall in hours continues, while for those in the top decile hours increased. Studies of the declining real value of the mandatory minimum wage also show no positive employment effect among classes of workers earning it. Thus, U.S. experience provides no support for the proposition that downward wage flexibility *per se* helps cure employment problems.

2.   RECENT EFFORTS TO REFORM THE U.S. TRAINING SYSTEM

If Europeans envy U.S. job generation, many in the U.S. envy Europe's training infrastructure. Indeed, stagnating wages and productivity in the U.S. have widely led mainstream policy-makers to focus on increased training as a principal cure for U.S. productivity and labour market woes,[2] and then in ways often explicitly modelled on European experience. In the early 1980s, the U.S. learned that its K-12 system of primary and secondary school instruction performed more poorly than the basic school systems of leading economic rivals. More recently it has learned that its system of post-secondary vocational training, directed to incumbent workers and the 'forgotten half' of youth who do not attend or finish college, does even worse. In comparative terms, the American system of college and university

---

[2]   While the importance of human capital, like any other input, can be overstated, there is fairly widespread consensus in the U.S. that substantial increases in productivity growth and product quality are unlikely without substantial changes in the organisation of work, including a significant devolution of responsibility to the 'frontline' workforce of production and non-supervisory workers. Effecting this transformation, however, will *inter alia* require significantly improving the skills of that workforce.

education remains unrivalled. But U.S. performance in facilitating the school-to-work transition for the non-college-graduate, in training entry-level workers, in upgrading the skills of incumbent workers, and in retraining displaced and dislocated workers is generally conceded to be poor, and in any case substantially exceeded by the training systems of such commercial rivals as Germany and Japan. Reforming the U.S. training system - here understood as the post-secondary, non-baccalaureate system of vocational instruction and job training - is a major focus of current political energies.

Motivated by such concerns, the Clinton administration has made the reform of the U.S. training system a centrepiece of its economic and social programme. Even as the administration has accepted severe fiscal constraints on federal training programs, and backed off campaign pledges to levy a 'play or pay' training tax on private employers, the administration has moved to support 'school to work' initiatives in youth apprenticeship, national skills standards, and significant consolidation and streamlining of scattered federal training efforts. At the same time that the relative prominence of education and training in national economic policy has increased, however, actual responsibility for economic development and social policy has continued to shift toward the states. As with the recent withdrawal of federal commitments to welfare, so in other areas: devolution is the order of the day. The relevant context, then, is one of modest federal leadership, and a hodgepodge of initiatives and reforms, with most of the interesting action occurring at the state and local levels.

Many states have moved to integrate the delivery of labour market services, offering prospective 'customers' income support, job search assistance, and job training assistance at *'one stop' job centres*. In some of the most developed cases, including Wisconsin, these centres are linked to provide an integrated state system of labour market service access, with a common menu of services for employers and job seekers, and effective integration of policy and service delivery. Responding to the long-standing problem of fragmented labour market services, the one-stop job centres are getting an additional boost from federal welfare reform. The latter has underscored the need to integrate social services with more specific training and other labour market supports, especially for the millions of disadvantaged workers who will soon be forced into the labour market. Federal funds to operate these social and training supports will soon be 'block granted' to the states, meaning that each state will determine the best local distribution of those funds without federal mandate on types or quality of service.

Partly as a result of integration of social supports with training and job services, and partly because resource constraints have required reorganisation, the *role of technical and community colleges* has been changing rapidly as well. Major community colleges have pledged themselves to a more integral role in the community and are working to strengthen their connections both to potential students and firms. In order to be more responsive to community residents and incumbent workers, they are generally offering shorter courses, more computer-based and self-paced learning packages, and more convenient hours and locations for courses. In order to be more responsive to the needs of firms, they are also developing more flexible training for high growth, high-wage industries; working on customised, short-term courses to improve training in specific workplaces; designing basic skills courses which emphasise 'soft skills' such as teamwork and communication and developing improved evaluation procedures to monitor their successes and prepare for future needs. In an education and training system geared most heavily toward the 4-year college-bound, such reform of the 2-year community/technical college system probably offers the best hope for a significantly improved public sector presence in more vocational training.

Long talked about, programmes in youth apprenticeship, or *'school to work'*, are now just beginning to arrive. The U.S. School-to-Work Opportunities Act was passed in 1994, and is currently funded at about a $300 million annual basis, with the money earmarked for providing career education and development in the public schools and for creating work-based learning components. The broad goal of the programme is to link schools to the workplace much more tightly and to make school work more relevant to the world of employment. The Act emphasized local partnerships between schools, employers, labour, community organisations and parents. Access to career information and counseling should lead students to select a 'career major' no later than the eleventh grade. Workplace mentoring is required, as is instruction in competencies required in the workplace. The goal is to provide students with two 'portable and validated' credentials - a high school diploma and a skills certificate - recognised by area employers.

The issue of portable and validated credentials for the incumbent workforce has been recently revived through a programme to create *national skill standards*. The development of skill standards is proceeding on a sectoral basis, although some basic standards, such as literacy and numeracy, may hold across sectors. In banking, for example, the California Business Roundtable and the California Department of Education developed skill standards for positions throughout the California banking industry. These standards are divided into foundation standards (for all positions) and standards for data and item processing, loan processing and sales and services. Generally, the standards are geared towards employees with flexibility and good basic skills, as well as skills that are specific to one of the three occupational areas listed above. Many of these skills are specific to the work process in banking, and clearly would be most efficiently acquired on the job.[3]

2.1   BARRIERS TO REFORM

When all is said and done, however, these reform efforts, while certainly welcome, are floundering. The one-stop job centres capture only a tiny portion of the actual employment flow in most labour markets, and welfare reform threatens to marginalize them as places of interest only to the truly needy. School-to-work initiatives are not reaching their forecast scale, since they generally lack serious employer commitment to taking and training their young participants. Community/technical college interest in getting 'close to their customer' has most commonly taken the form of tailoring programmes to the needs of particular individual firms - without providing workers with broader and more portable occupational skills. And the national skills standards programme, while successfully piloted in a few industries, is generally a failure. In most major sectors, particularly among the larger firms, there simply is no interest in buying into job or occupational standards not set by themselves.

What is the problem here, and how might it be solved?

In part the problem is lack of money. Education and training reform in the U.S. is a paradigmatic case of a broader political problem: improving living standards will require substantial public investment, but the public has little confidence in government or willingness to make that investment in the absence of very clear payoffs, which frequently cannot be demonstrated in advance of scaled investment itself. And with incomes falling, tax resistance solidifies.

Even if some substantial effort were agreed to, moreover, there are lurking distributional conflicts. National policy discussion in the U.S. is framed by the implicit presumption that all Americans should have

---

[3]   The US Departments of Education and Labour developed a set of principles for the design of skill standards in fields not requiring a bachelor's degree. The standards should be: 1) adaptable to rapidly changing organisational structures, technologies, and markets (they should be flexible); 2) based on 'world-class' industry performance; 3) free of discriminatory elements; 4) easy to understand; 5) tied to measurable outcomes; 6) developed jointly by all 'stakeholders' 7) developed independently from 'any single training provider' but should be widely applicable; 8) useful for credentialling both entry-level employees and those moving up in the organisation; 9) inclusive of skills of literacy and critical thinking. The Departments also designed a set of phases for the development of skill standards. The Clinton administration has appointed a National Skill Standards Board, to spread this type of skill certification across the country, and to develop skill standards that are saleble at many employers.

substantially equal access to training, and that the baseline level of training generally provided should be substantially increased. But if this presumption were taken seriously, the sums involved and redistribution entailed would be substantial. The U.S. currently provides approximately $14,000 in government support to each graduate of college. To provide equivalent support to the 75 percent of each high school cohort that does not graduate would cost $29 billion annually. Of the $30 billion U.S. employers currently spend annually on formal training, the overwhelming percentage (96 percent in the case of young workers) is provided to college graduates; were non-college graduates provided with comparable support, the bill to employers would be about $100 billion. German apprentices each cost employers about $4,500 a year, in what are typically four-year programmes of 'dual' workplace-school instruction. Were a German apprenticeship system extended to the U.S., with the 65 percent rate of coverage for the total high school cohort claimed in Germany, it would cost U.S. employers about $32 billion annually. It is most unlikely that anything approaching this effort will be made in the U.S. on behalf of frontline workers anytime soon.

The structure and capacity of government also pose important barriers. At the Federal level, despite some success in consolidation, national training efforts remain littered across more than a hundred different programmes, administered by 14 different federal departments and agencies - many with identical target populations and purposes, but all with different mandates. This sprawling effort becomes slightly less intelligible at the state level, where principal responsibility for federal programme administration and control over a welter of additional programmes resides, and almost unnavigable at the local level, where much effective authority over post-secondary training institutions (including most community colleges), as well as local school districts, is exerted. The maze of programs and decentralised administration has grown into being over more than a century of political conflict over the appropriate role of government in human capital formation, and its structure reflects the best and worst aspects of federalism - from the room it provides for efficient local servicing and experiment to the inequalities it breeds in the byzantine complexities of state and local tax codes. Each programme has a constituency, and systemic reform is not aided by the reserved (and now growing) powers of state and local governments.

Even more fundamental, however, are the institutional incapacities of government as an agent of change - the fact that government is and always has been 'all thumbs and no fingers', and inept at capturing the impacted information and local knowledge key to economic decision-making, particularly inside the firm. Along with budget pressures, this commonly turns reform to caricature, with local governments or educational institutions stumbling after what they it take to be the latest industry 'trend' without the resources to drive it, and usually finding that by the time new programming arrives, the underlying economic conditions have changed.

The biggest problem, however, is that industry itself is disorganised, or organised in the wrong way

On the demand side of the training equation, while U.S. labour markets have shown, since the late 1970s, a strong secular increase in relative demand for skilled as against unskilled labour, overall employer demand for skilled labour remains relatively weak. As measured by occupational trends, business demand for more educated workers is actually projected to *slow* over the next decade, not increase (Mishel and Teixeira, 1990). Such occupational measures are limited by their inattention to within-occupation changes in desired skill, but more nuanced investigations of such changes - themselves driven by changes in work organisation and technology use - are not particularly comforting. Particularly among 'foundation' firms employing fewer than 250 workers, rates of investment in new technology are flat. And only a minority of firms - on no estimate accounting for more than 20 percent of overall employment - are making the broad changes in work organisation that drive increased skill demand.

Much of the present U.S. labour market, instead, appears to approximate to a 'low-wage, low-skill' equilibrium. Given a low skill environment, and little rigidity in wages, even firms operating under increased competitive pressure have continued with low-skill forms of work organisation that require little more than obedience and a good work attitude from direct production or service workers. Having chosen such a strategy, however, the skill demands of these firms are low. While they may wish to remedy deficiencies in very basic worker skills, or provide training to a few in the application of expensive new technology, they generally do not demand or promote broad and continuous skill upgrading among their frontline workforce. Such low-skill, low-wage strategies of course lower overall living standards, but that makes them no less profitable or attractive to firms, and their adoption weakens the political thrust for a stronger training effort.

On the supply side of training provision, meanwhile, most efforts suffer from a series of collective action problems. These include simple co-ordination problems - for example, in matching public training efforts to private firm needs - to mixed motive problems - for example, in getting agreement on industry-wide standards on skill credentialling. Most famously, however, they include a deep co-operation problem in private firm investment in training. Even firms anxious to improve the skills of their workforce face the threat of competitors free-riding on their training efforts. Unless the training they provide is so narrow that it is only useful in their own firm, it will be marketable by the workers who receive it to other firms who do not pay for its provision; one firm's trainee may thus become another firm's asset, with the second firm advantaged by the benefits of training but not burdened by its costs. This threat of free-riders leads firms not to train at all, or to train very narrowly, in ways that are not useful for workers on the external labour market, and that may not be useful for the dynamic efficiency of the firms themselves. In classic 'prisoner dilemma' fashion, individually rational action does not aggregate to socially rational choice. While the economy as a whole would benefit from a better and broadly trained workforce, no firm may have the incentive to start providing it.

One 'solution' to this last problem is design around it - i.e., to design a system in which firm-provided training is accepted as exiguous, or extremely narrow, and in which all broad training is provided through the public system. This, indeed, remains the general 'solution' in the U.S. education and training system. But there are reasons to believe that this sort of 'solution' is no solution at all. Efficient training systems require a substantial firm-based, and indeed workplace-based, training effort. So, the co-operation problem in private firm training remains important.

Comparative experience shows only two solutions to this problem. One - let's call it the 'Japanese' solution - is to limit worker movement between firms, and thus assure management that it will indeed reap the rewards of investments in its workforce. Given the present (and rising) degree of inter-firm mobility in the U.S., and the constraints on management, along with workers, that such a system requires, this seems of little relevance as a general solution in the United States. More relevant is what might be called the 'European' solution to the co-operation problem. This effectively accepts inter-firm mobility, but then forces, either through state or private associative action, a sufficiently large share of firms to train that each becomes more indifferent to that mobility.

How the first variant works is straightforward enough. The state imposes a requirement on firms that they train, or pay the state for doing so, betting that firms will prefer to 'play' than 'pay'. The French system is an example. For the second variant - associative action - Germany remains the best example. The German system features a complex set of institutions - powerful Chambers of Trade and Industry, well-organised trade and employers associations, strong unions and works councils and the national government itself - that organise employers to the point of solving their free-rider problems. By encouraging employers to train and protecting them against defection from the general training regime, these institutions provide for a high level of workplace-based training without eliminating either the worker's option to quit or the employer's option not to train.

The great problem in the U.S. is that we generally lack the relevant sorts of labour market institutions and practices on either the demand or supply side of the training equation.

On the demand side, what is chiefly lacking are mechanisms to drive up the price of labour and compress wage dispersion. Unions are extremely weak, and direct regulation of labour prices is minimal. The result is that, in general, business lacks appropriate incentives to increase the productivity of labour - through, among other things, training - and that the low-wage, sweating response to competition is not effectively foreclosed. That it is not, moreover, tends to erode support for appropriate sorts of upgrading even among firms plausibly positioned to lead the way in such. Large, older, higher-wage firms in manufacturing, for example, find it more cost-effective to spin off parts of their operations to low-wage sub-contractors, and to pressure their existing higher-wage suppliers to take the same route, than to make or pressure the investments up and down the production chain needed to diffuse upgrading. The story of restructuring among the 'Big 3' auto companies and their suppliers is but the best known instance of this.

On the supply side, in our highly liberal political economy, what are lacking are mechanisms of association among firms and worker organisations, or working relations between the private and public sectors, that could address the various collective action problems just noted. U.S. governance tends still to be exhausted by 'live free or die' choices between command and control regulation and market exchange. Secondary associations performing economic functions are generally weak, and in any case rarely explicitly integrated into public governance. As a consequence, virtually all regulation of the kind implicated in the training case - i.e., involving the achievement of goals within diverse, dispersed, and numerous sites of economic activity - suffers from severe monitoring and enforcement problems, the expectation of which renders initial goal specification itself more difficult.[4] In the U.S., we are very very far from the sorts of dense associations that drive the German training system, and that permit, for example, skills standard setting and training enforcement essentially to be almost purely private processes.

---

[4] Regulation of occupational safety and health — involving the monitoring of several million heterogeneous worksites, provides a classic example of this problem in practice. While most European countries mandate some form of employee safety committees to give the state additional eyes and ears, in the U.S. enforcement still resides exclusively in government inspectorates.

3.   REGIONAL SECTORAL EXPERIMENTS AS A POSSIBLE WAY FORWARD

All of the above should inspire considerable caution in looking to the U.S. as a model for training practices. The labour market outcomes being generated by the present system are quite bad for much of the population; the pace of reform efforts is slow; the institutional and political underpinnings for leveraging out of low-road (low-wage, low-skill, low-investment, etc.) equilibria generally not available. In the absence of some fundamental altering of the political landscape, the likely path for the U.S. is growing inequality and stratification, with higher education increasingly starved for funds, and dominated by business undisciplined by any sense of public purpose.

This fairly grim assessment, however, is qualified in at least some labour markets by new experiments in workforce training and job access and advancement. Almost always initiated by actors outside the public system - most commonly, unions or community groups - to advance or defend the interests of particular worker constituencies, they show some promise of remedying the key deficiencies in the U.S. training system. The key strength of these projects is their ability to bring about changes in employer behaviour needed to solve the demand and supply problems in training just highlighted. Some programmes aim to improve the quality of the 'dead-end' jobs that have proliferated in recent years. Others seek to improve incumbent worker training systems, typically by re-establishing some version of a skill-based job ladder, and agreement among several firms in a given industry to common standards and benchmarks on their private training effort. Still others seek to develop better information on labour markets and use that information to improve the access of disadvantaged workers to specific sectors.[5]

3.1   Improving Dead-End Jobs

There are two ways to overcome the problem of dead-end jobs. The first is to professionalise the job. The second is to provide a pathway into decent work out of a dead-end job. A handful of projects have been undertaken in the past few years to move workers into good jobs or to improve the status and prospects of the jobs workers already hold. Most of these projects are

---

[5]   These programme overviews rely on overview documents, interviews, informal discussions, and, in many cases, some of the projects' own documents. The Ford/Mott commissioned studies, Jobs and the Urban Poor, (Seigel and Kwass,1995 and Clark and Dawson, 1995) provide a good overview of a number of the projects.

sectoral in nature. These programmes identify a pool of potential jobs on an occupational basis and prepare workers for employment in those jobs. For programmes that seek to professionalise dead-end work, the key is often improved training which results in increased quality of service, even at the low-wage end of the labour market. For programmes that seek to provide a pathway out of work, the key element is the identification of a series of jobs, where employment at the one job will contribute to quality of work at the next job.

3.2   Temp Work, Hiring Halls and Basic Skills Credentialling

One common trait of dead-end jobs is their 'spotty' demand. In labour pools, temp services, personal services, and hospitality, demand shifts quite dramatically from day to day. The costs of that fluctuation is generally born by the individual worker who is simply not called in, or sent home and does not receive wages. Some projects attempt to steady demand by spreading the pool from which demand is drawn. Hiring halls in the hospitality industry, for example, service banquet and set-up requests from multiple firms. By co-ordinating with more than a single firm, these hiring halls can turn some transient work into a steady job. The development of worker owned temp agencies will also focus on increasing the hours that worker are guaranteed. Again, as the hours are made more reliable, workforce and job quality rise together. Rather than transient workers, firms get employees that are connected to the industry. Rather than transient jobs, workers get steady work and reliable income.

Basic skills credentialling could also help to improve dead-end jobs, by providing a pathway into better work. The basic idea here - now subject to informal experimentation in Michigan in the fast-food sector - is to certify workers with demonstrated work ethic (reliability, punctuality, motivation, etc.) in the secondary labour market, thus making them more attractive to better-paying employers in the primary market. The gain to the primary market employers is reduced search costs on reliable employees; the gain to the secondary employers is a more stable workforce, intent at least on achieving the certification; the gain to the workers getting certified is a way out.

3.3   Providing an Upward Path in Mid-Level Jobs

Even in slightly better paying sectors, ability to advance has been restricted by work reorganisation and economic change. The non-professional tracks in insurance, financial services and business services have extremely short ladders - in many instances the only step up is to shift supervisor. To move up from clerical usually requires a college degree, not the kind of training that is easy to get on the job or on the side. The health care sector often looks the same way; many hospitals discourage movement from food service to patient care to technical work. In manufacturing, competitive pressures have pushed many firms to cut back on training, just when training investments are most needed. In these manufacturing firms, workers are expected to produce more with the same skills, or firms shift inexorably toward lower-end product market strategies. In a few cases, however, industry organisation has found a way around these problems. The Cape Cod Hospital Career Ladder Program is a joint union-management training program, 'premised on a comprehensive system of internal promotion in which vacant job positions are filled by upgrading existing workers.' The programme is designed to 'simultaneously maximise human resource potential and meet the personnel needs of the hospital' while 'enabling workers to continue their employment as they advance their education, skills, and job position.' Key steps have been to define the career ladders themselves, to provide training, to link training to career progression, and thus to wages, and to formalise access to training opportunities.

In a further venture the Wisconsin Regional Training Partnership, based in the metalworking industry, with a membership of more than 40 firms collectively employing approximately 40,000 workers in Southeastern Wisconsin has grown to be the largest sectoral training consortium in the country, and the most advanced in overall programme goals. Member firms benchmark a growing percentage of payroll to training front-line workers train according to standards set on a supra-firm basis; gear their hiring and internal labour market promotions to worker achievement on those standards; and administer the enhanced training budgets (resulting from their benchmarked contributions) through joint labour-management committees.

3.4   Bringing Clarity to Labour Market Access and Advancement

Understanding the rules in the labour market, making those rules explicit, and providing the support for people that they need to make their way through the labour market can significantly improve the opportunities for disadvantaged workers. Clarity of this sort in the labour market can help overcome the barrier of informal access to work by establishing a clear system of rules on access and advancement. Moreover, the information would help students, the workforce and employers plan for the future. One firm representative summarised it this way: 'As these students leave high school, it would be nice if there was something to say: this is what the need is in your community. There's this number of jobs that are becoming available in the community in this area, and these are the skills that you're going to need to fill one of those positions.... But that's not being done now.' If it were done, a labour market map would also allow adults opportunities to change careers, and aid the process of finding new employment after job loss.

Projects rarely take 'labour market transparency' as their key goal. However, two projects seek to improve labour market information and use that information to improve workers' mobility.

San Antonio's Project QUEST was developed in direct response to community perceptions that there were increasing inequalities in the San Antonio job market. Local community organisations COPS and Metro Alliance met with business and political leaders, and secured commitments from firms to provide access to skilled jobs with a potential for advancement. They also negotiated with state and local authorities for funding to run the program. QUEST targeted particular sectors with a potential for providing good jobs (which were defined as paying $7 to $8 an hour, with potential for advancement). These sectors were health care, electronics, environmental services, maintenance and repair, and business systems. QUEST got employers to commit, collectively, to hire graduates in each of these areas.

As a model of a successful jobs programme, QUEST offers the following important lessons: jobs programmes must be tied to the community, and involve commitment from business, community organisations, and the state. All participants need to be held accountable. Businesses need to commit to particular required skill sets and wage norms, training institutions need to commit to providing these skill sets, and trainees need to commit to doing the preparatory work needed for available jobs. Finally, there needs to be a coordinating organisation which is competent and puts all of these pieces together.

QUEST, of course, like many other jobs programmes, has relatively little emphasis on moving employees through career ladders or other mechanisms for advancement, except in that it places employees in jobs which have the potential for advancement. However, the QUEST approach could be extended to filling slots higher up on a career ladder, using incumbent employees instead of entry level workers. The basic approach - identifying nascent, unfilled demand in the labour market, and then moving decisively to fill it - would still bear fruit. Since incumbent workers are employed, they are less likely to need ancillary support services; the firms that would benefit from filling these jobs could contribute to the provision of these services.

The Dane County 'Jobs With a Future' Project is developing a community career ladder project to make 'jobs with a future' available to all Dane County residents.

In three sectors - manufacturing, health care, and insurance & finance - extensive interviews with human resource and training personnel at leading firms to identify the skill and workforce needs that are shared by the firms in each industry, have led to employer/union decisions to establish sectoral consortia.

Together, all three partnerships will be working with the Dane County Job Center (the local 'one stop') to reach out to workers in the county who are presently trapped in poverty-wage jobs. It is clear that in Dane County, information on wages and opportunities does not reach into communities that need the information the most. The collaborative work of the partnerships and the Job Center will allow for new means of recruitment and orientation to be developed and new connections to be made.

4.   THE PROMISE OF REGIONAL HIGH-ROAD PARTNERSHIPS

While still in their infancy, we believe these sorts of 'high road regional partnerships' show considerable promise as the foundation for a new sort of 'American model' in training. In effect, they provide at the regional level what is not provided nationally - a genuine infrastructure of industry and union collaboration that both drives industries toward more demanding skill demands and provides the flow of information, and assurances against free-riding, needed to meet it. Given pressures for devolution, moreover, there is no reason why such efforts could not be more effectively integrated into public labour market administration.

More particularly, such sectoral projects - typically focusing on a collection of firms with shared production methods and/or labour forces - display three obvious efficiencies not widely captured elsewhere in the U.S. system. First, there are considerable economies of scale to be realised when working with a cross-section of firms with shared labour force needs. Unlike workforce development or job connection initiatives that have adopted a narrowly customised firm-by-firm approach, the sectoral approach does away with the need for constantly renewing personal relationships and inspiring management good-will or civic mindedness. By organising a sector, solutions to recurrent problems can be improved and programmes refined. Second, a sectoral initiative can leverage economies of scope as well. A sectoral intermediary which understands and is responding to the shared needs of a number of firms can develop diverse programmes which will weather economic shifts and the problems of single firms. Just as the scale of the project can be used to continuously improve common elements of the curriculum and training routines, the scope of the project protects it from being captured by a single firm and uniquely beholden to that firm's needs and fortunes. Finally, sectoral initiatives are associated with positive network externalities. The positive network externalities will be generated as firms come together and find ways to solve common problems. If programmes are helping multiple firms in a sector, then the region's sector at large can become more vibrant and competitive. Firms, by sharing information and solutions, also become more tied into the local community. So, as a valued sectoral intermediary is developed in a region, the sector itself becomes revitalised and more rooted.

Nor is it much of a step from there to the more functional integration of regional labour market services, with representatives of regional sectoral consortia providing the natural ballast and direction for programme administration. Whatever the many confusions of U.S. training reform at present, it is fairly clear that block-grants are coming, and that the most natural structure for their administration will be some descendant of the 'Private Industry Councils' first mandated under the Job Training Partnership Act (JTPA) - the most important federal training programme. Various states, Wisconsin included, have already established 'Workforce Development Boards' along these lines, with an essentially private governance (with a majority of seats assigned to business) broadly mimicking that of the original PICs. Were sectoral consortia more widely developed, representatives of those consortia would provide a natural source of such business (and union and community) presence, with the effect of tying the public system much more closely to the real local economy. Consolidation of labour market services, moreover, might be naturally extended to include elements of the fledgling manufacturing modernisation infrastructure the Clinton administration has been at pains to preserve and develop. This federally supported, but essentially state-based, system of support for small and medium sized manufacturers is now capable of reaching tens of thousands of firms annually with assistance on upgrading. Operating at some $300 million annually, it is the most significant U.S. programme acting directly on the demand side of the training equation.

The result would be, in effect, a series of regional labour market boards, with financial resources to apply to both the supply and demand sides of that equation, and considerable leverage within a more organised private sector.

How movement to such a system might be incented is also straightforward enough. Without mandating such industry organisation, participation in it could reasonably be offered as a condition for discounts on public training assistance - the rationale being that public dollars are best spent where private leverage and representativeness is demonstrated - with reciprocal premia applied to supports for non-participating firms. Such boards could be charged as well with local implementation of the national skills standards, providing some baseline coordination of their activities. And the process of organising regional industry and labour - based on our experience, perhaps surprisingly, not a desperately hard thing to do - could be supported through demonstration grants and a minimal national technical assistance infrastructure.

Of course, whether this really happens, or happens fast enough to capture the energies now unleashed by reform-mindedness and devolution, is not something we can confidently predict. But it is certainly a development worth watching, and for Europeans the fact that it is already happening unselfconsciously, without almost any explicit public support, may carry some interesting lessons. Based on the experience in the most liberal of polities, with the greatest hostility to government, with the weakest associational structures in business and the most decimated labour movement, it appears that there is at least a plausible way to functional, flexible, and politically-supported labour market administration - at the regional level. That level of administration appears to capture the operative efficiencies of associational action, while being sufficiently tutored by local experience, and allowing a speed and flexibility in government response, to satisfy firm demands for such attention to their new competitive realities.

REFERENCES

Bernhardt, A.D. and Bailey, T.R. (1998), *Making Careers out of Jobs: Policies to Address the New Employment Relationship*, Institute on Education and the Economy, Columbia University, New York.

Carnevale, A.P. (1991), *America and the New Economy*, American Society for Training and Development, Washington.

Chubb, J.E. and Moe, T.M. (1990), *Politics, Markets, and America's Schools*, Brookings Institution, Washington.

Clark, P. and Dawson, S. (1995), *Jobs and the Urban Poor: Privately Initiated Sectoral Strategies*, The Aspen Institute. Washington.

CSAW (Commission on the Skills of the American Workforce) (1990), *America's Choice: High Skills or Low Wages!*, National Center on Education and the Economy, Rochester.

CWFC (William T. Grant Foundation Commission on Work, Family and Citizenship) (1988), *The Forgotten Half: Pathways to Success for America's Youth and Young Families*, William T. Grant Foundation, Washington.

DOL (Department of Labor) (1989), *Investing in People: A Strategy to Address America's Workforce Crisis*, Department of Labor, Washington.

Freeman, R. B. and Rogers, J. (1996) "Die Quintessenz der Inneramerikanischen Debatte", *Mitbestimmung*, July-August1996, pp12-17.

Mishel, L. and Teixeira, R. (1990), *The Myth of the Coming Labor Shortage: Jobs, Skills and Incomes of America's Workforce 2000*, Economic Policy Institute, Washington.

Osterman, P. (1993), "How Common is Workplace Transformation and How Can we Explain Who Adopts it? Results from a National Survey", paper presented at the meetings of the Allied Social Science Association, Anaheim, California, January 1993.

Seigel, B. and Kwass, P. (1995) *Jobs and the Urban Poor: Publicly Initiated Sectoral Strategies*, Mt. Auburn Associates, Somerville MA.

Chapter 16

Evaluation and Decision Making in Swedish Adult Education

Åsa Sohlman
Commision for the promotion of Adult Education and Training, KLK, Stockholm

1. BACKGROUND

The Swedish Parliament decided in 1966 that a special programme of adult education should be carried out for five years, beginning in July 1997. The target group is, in the first place, the unemployed and those employees who lack or who have only partial upper secondary school education.

The municipalities are responsible for carrying out most of the programme. They are to make up plans for training provision and apply for the special state grants that are awarded to the municipalities for this programme by the Government. There are also special study grants for the individuals participating in the programme.

The municipalities are to choose the course organisers that meet the requirements of the target group and local conditions in the most efficient way and they are to consult with the social partners when drawing up their applications for state grants. An individual study and action plan has to be established for each individual participating in the programme.

The programme is designed both to respond to various new challenges and to serve as a basis for further decisions as to:
- lifelong learning and government involvement in lifelong learning, education and training;
- a shift from short-term policies towards long term policies to combat unemployment;

– decentralisation, management by objectives and the continuous
  monitoring and evaluation of public education and training at both local
  and national level to promote efficiency and distributional goals.

Below, in section 2, the goals and programme theories of the Swedish
Government as found in the steering documents for the Adult Education
Initiative are analysed. Then, the implementation of the Adult Education
Initiative and its impacts so far are described in sections 3 and 4. Finally, in
section 5 the possibilities to improve the knowledge base and the decision
making processes through monitoring and evaluation are discussed.

2.   THE ADULT EDUCATION INITIATIVE - GOALS AND PROGRAMME THEORIES

The Government's general hypothesis is that educational policy is
important for economic growth, for increasing employment, reducing social
inequalities and securing economic welfare. As the Swedish Government
wants to achieve *both* high economic growth *and* social equality, Sweden
has to devote more resources to education and training then countries that do
not have goals that are as broadly defined. However, to meet the educational
needs of adults in a knowledge society, the organisation and teaching
methods of adult education have to change. The Adult Education Initiative is
therefore intended to set in motion an educational reform process and at the
same time to produce evidence as to further needs for improvements in adult
education and training.

Moreover, as laid out in the Government Bill Prop 1995/96:222, the
Adult Education Initiative is also an important part of the government's
package of measures to halve open unemployment by the year 2000 (to four
per cent from currently around eight per cent).

The programme is thus to promote goals within the sphere of labour-
market policy, economic policy and education policy. The main criteria
according to which the results of the programme are to be judged by the
government can be summarised as follows:
– the improvement of skills and knowledge of adults lacking upper
  secondary education;
– the reduction in unemployment;
– the increase in employment and economic growth;
– the reform of adult education.

Several factors explain why education and training are judged to be so
important by the Swedish Government. They relate to the current changes in
production methods and work organisation and to the increasing flow of

information and knowledge events that expand the demand for highly qualified labour. An ageing population is another factor that adds to the need for adaptational skills in the existing labour force.

Formal basic education is one method by which individuals can prepare for further education and training and for adaptations to structural and other changes in working life. Adults with low levels of formal education risk losing their jobs and become marginalised. On this point the Government Bill refers to the report by the Commission for the Promotion of Adult Education and Training, (SOU 1996:27), where it is argued that the minimum level of formal education for all individuals ought to be upper secondary education (in Sweden 12 years of schooling). A high level of education in the population is important not only for economic reasons but also for the democratic development of the community and the personal development of individuals.

It has been estimated that 1,7 - 2,4 million Swedes aged 20-54 lack knowledge corresponding to upper secondary education in basic subjects such as Swedish, English, mathematics and social sciences (SOU 1996:27). Although the OECD (1995) International Adult Literacy Study, IALS and its sequels (OECD, 1997a; OECD 1997b), have shown that the Swedish literacy results are the best among the participating countries, still, around 1 million Swedes were below literacy level 3 in 1994. This figure has to be substantially reduced by the turn of the century for both economic and social reasons according to the Swedish Government.

The IALS studies show that literacy and unemployment are negatively correlated.

In Sweden individuals with low formal education also
- have a higher level of unemployment than other educational groups (SCB, 1996a):
- dominate among the long-term unemployed (NUTEK, 1996);
- have over time remained at low formal educational levels (SCB, 1996a) ;
- are mainly found in the private sector. The private sector also has relatively few employees with higher education and does not provide much further education and training.

The rate of unemployment has increased especially for groups with low formal education. According to Swedish forecasts the demand for individuals with higher education will continue to grow while the demand for individuals with low education will be further reduced. There is a risk that there will be an under-supply of individuals with higher education and an over-supply of individuals with low education (SCB, 1996b; NUTEK, 1996). According to the government, if the demand for people with higher education cannot be met the growth of GDP and employment is endangered as well as the reduction of unemployment.

Another inefficiency on the labour market that is noted by the government is segregation by gender. Women are under-represented at high positions in working life in spite of the fact that women normally have a better formal education than men do.

What is needed for young people is a high quality education preparing for working life as well as:
- primary school without losers;
- secondary school for all;
- more students in higher education and post graduate education.
  For adults what is needed is:
- more formal education for those lacking upper secondary education;
- better links between learning at work and recurrent education.

However, the budget of the municipalities does not permit them to increase their outlays on education. Therefore, if educational investments are to expand *now,* and in an equitable way all over the country, the government has to pay for them.

3.   IMPLEMENTATION OF THE ADULT EDUCATION INITIATIVE

The Adult Education Initiative consists of some 100,000 full time study places per year that will be paid for by the Government for five years and mainly handled by municipalities. Other parts of the programme, that will not be further analysed in this paper, consist of state grants for special study places at the Folk High Schools and for pilot projects of advanced vocational training for adults at post secondary level.

The study places are to be provided by the municipalities on top of their regular provision of such study places. The level of this "basic" provision has been established by the National Agency for Education as the average of the number of (full time, whole-year) study places provided by the municipalities over the last three years. If there is a reduction in the municipal supply of study places their state grants for the programme will be reduced.

The municipalities already have a legal obligation to provide primary and lower secondary education (9 years in Sweden) to all individuals who demand it. Therefore the government did not at the outset intend to pay for such study places. However, adults who study at primary and lower secondary levels qualify for the new special study grants on the same conditions as adults studying at upper secondary level.

The special study grants correspond to the unemployment benefits. They could initially be obtained for 12 months studies and are available for unemployed individuals aged 25-55 qualifying for unemployment benefits and for employees on the same conditions, given that they have five years work experience and the employer replaces the individual by an unemployed person. Normal study grants for adults are available for studies lasting more than one year and they are also available for other adults participating in the programme but they are only available on less generous terms.

The reasons for choosing the municipalities as main executors of the programme are the following:
- their knowledge of local conditions is seen as a guarantee for efficiency and creativity;
- they are already responsible for basic adult education;
- they have a well functioning organisation;
- they have the right to provide school leavers with official school marks and certificates.

To promote the reform of adult education the municipalities are requested:
- to analyse the local labour market and to consult with the social partners and the public employment services when drawing up their applications for state grants;
- to make an inventory of the education and training needs of individuals.

An individual study and action plan has to be established for each individual participating in the programme:
- to choose the course organisers that meet the requirements of the target group and local conditions in the most efficient way;
- to develop new forms of information and outreach activities as well as new counselling methods and new techniques for validation of prior learning;
- to develop new teaching methods including, for example, distant learning and different combinations of theoretical studies and practical applications;
- to engage in local monitoring and evaluation.

These rules and requirements are supposed to increase the efficiency of the programme. For instance, labour market needs are to influence the implementation of the programme in the municipalities in a substantial way. The municipalities are to consult with the social partners and the public employment services and involve them in the planning of the programme. A basic grant corresponding to fifty percent of the amount available will normally be distributed to the municipalities according to their share of the unemployed and on average ninety per cent of the participants are expected to be unemployed and only ten per cent employees. Moreover, each employee that participates is to be replaced by an unemployed person.

On the other hand, individual needs are also central to the programme. To be able to motivate individuals with low formal education it is necessary that the education corresponds to their needs both as to subject areas and as to teaching methods. Therefore individual study plans are required and new teaching methods desirable. Competition and co-operation between many different types of educational providers are also important in this respect. The municipalities are not only supposed to automatically involve only Municipal Adult Education units as educational providers but also study associations, Folk High Schools and private providers.

As an example it can be mentioned that during the period 1970 to 1990 among the 268,000 men and 286,000 women aged 25-34 in 1970 with only 9 years or less of formal education, only 46,000 men and 86,000 women completed lower or upper secondary education (SCB, 1996a).

In an earlier, similar programme out of 23,000 study places paid for one year by the government the net effect was only 10,000 study places. The reason for the low level of the net increase was in this case a reduction in the study places provided for by the municipalities (Skolverket, 1996b).

While fifty per cent of the amount available is expected to be distributed to the municipalities according to unemployment, other aspects considered are:

- the level of similar state grants received earlier for courses for the unemployed. It is to be avoided that municipalities receive less money than earlier;
- the course mix provided - vocational training, general training and introductory courses.

Quality aspects include:

- inputs for increased gender equality;
- recruitment of groups under represented in adult education;
- measures to develop and upgrade adult education and training in response to changes on the labour market and in society.

4.   IMPACTS OF THE ADULT EDUCATION INITIATIVE

At the political level in the municipalities the programme has generally been enthusiastically accepted. And one thing is clear, the *local governments* are much more involved in *planning* their participation in this programme than they have been in planning their normal educational activities. Since the decentralisation of responsibility for primary, secondary and adult education to the municipalities in 1991 the local government should be engaged in educational planning and evaluation but that involvement has been difficult to establish. It took some time until the majority of municipalities had a school plan and even in 1995 only around ten per cent had evaluated it in its entirety (Skolverket, 1995, 1996a, 1997). The importance attached to the programme by the local politicians has been important for the general awareness of the importance of adult education and the status of adult education.

One of the new aspects of this adult education programme is its direct link to the labour market. The municipalities have already for some time expressed an interest in taking over more of the labour market policy from national bodies. Municipalities often have some general economic development plan and the adult education programme is rather linked to that plan than to the school plan for the municipality and used as an *instrument for development.*

Other aspects of the programme that seem to have been well received are *information, counselling, recruitment, outreach and validation activities.* As part of their normal educational activities the municipalities have for sometime earlier been expected to engage in such activities but judging from their initiatives to reorganise, co-ordinate and develop these activities their efforts in these fields must have been rather rudimentary, or the challenges bigger or taken more seriously with the new programme. These plans for reorganisation are often linked to pre-existing bodies that under different labels - Infotechs, Infocentres, Knowledge centres, Educational centres etc. - have started to develop information, counselling and open house learning activities, to serve as a basis for distant learning and to provide introductory courses for the programme. They will often also make investigations as to the educational needs and interests of individuals and work out the required individual study plans. During preparatory courses the individual will have time to orient himself or herself not only as to why and what to study and how to finance the studies but also as to study techniques and working methods. After the introductory course the centre may also be responsible for directing the individual to the 'right' educational provider and for following up the study plan of the individual. In smaller municipalities the public employment services may function as a co-ordinating centre.

The municipalities use different types of educational providers. The *'external' educational organisers* are expected to bring new impetus to the traditional municipal units. Fields mentioned in this respect are organisation of education, introductory and vocational courses and teaching methods.

However, in many cases the public providers will be spared competition in their core activities (theoretical upper secondary courses) and generally they remain the biggest providers of Municipal Adult Education.

This new setting is a challenge to the study associations and Folk High Schools of *popular education*. On the one hand there are those who argue that the competition for this type of credit oriented education cannot be combined with the educational ideals of popular education. Others contend that if the government wants the Folk High Schools and study associations to participate in the Adult Education Initiative it should allocate more resources directly to the National Council of Adult Education which is the body that normally redistributes state grants to the different units within popular education. Still others argue that partnerships can be established with the municipalities within present framework. But this feeling of being side-stepped does not only characterise organisers of popular education but also to some extent the organisers of traditional Municipal Adult Education.

Distance learning is developing in many municipalities. Some municipalities have created local study centres with modern ICT equipment in different places within the municipality. They might be used as a basis for studies at different educational levels - primary, secondary and higher education and are often designed for flexible use. Some individuals may come and work daily at the local study centres and need at lot of counselling while others may use them very rarely (SOU 1998:57; SOU 1998:84).

It is, of course, too early to have any precise ideas about how the AEI is developing. A few figures from the initial phase can, however, also be added:

- participation in adult education at *upper secondary level* seems to have increased by some 60,000 individuals comparing November 1997 and November 1996. One age cohort consists of approximately 100,000 individuals in Sweden;
- during the six last months of 1997 the volume of full time study places financed by the state was approximately 80,000 and the amount financed by the municipalities 35,000;
- participation in adult education at *lower educational levels* has remained unchanged comparing November 1997 and November 1996. The total amount of full time study places at this level during the six last months of 1997 was around 30,000;
- during the same period external educational providers stood for thirteen per cent of the volume of courses at upper secondary level (of which popular education is four per cent and other educational providers nine per cent). That figure may seem low but it still represents a big change bearing in mind that earlier external providers were hardly used at all in Municipal Adult Education;

– the supply of vocational training has increased both in comparison with the estimates of the municipalities in their applications for AEI-state grants and earlier years when it was practically non-existent. In the Adult Education Initiative vocational training accounted for thirty-nine per cent of the course volume during the last six months of 1997 (Skolverket, 1998; SOU 1998:51).

5.   EVALUATION STRATEGIES AND DECISION MAKING

A programme such as the Adult Education Initiative can never be fully motivated by scientific evidence. Even though it might be reasonable to assume that adult education of the kind envisaged in the programme will reduce unemployment and increase employment and economic growth it can never be definitely proved in advance. Why start with 100,000 study places? Why not 50,000 or 150,000? Why so much more basic adult education instead of more post secondary vocational training or more higher education?

Over time the knowledge base increases but with rapid changes in the external environment scientific evidence can not always be awaited before making decisions. One approach to this dilemma in Sweden has been to start new investment projects on a preliminary basis and set up monitoring, reporting and evaluation procedures. For the AEI where the municipalities are to report to the National Agency of Education and the latter to the Government. The Commission for the Promotion of Adult Education and Training is also to report to the Government both in 1998 and in 1999 before it presents its general proposals for long term reforms of adult education, training and lifelong learning in the year 2000.

The Commission for the Promotion of Adult Education and Training has also been given the task of co-ordinating evaluations undertaken at national level as well as organising independent national evaluations. A number of national bodies have, according to their normal responsibilities, to follow and evaluate the AEI as far it concerns them - the National Agency for Education (for Municipal Adult Education), the National Board of Adult Education (for the Folk High Schools) and the National Board of Labour Administration (for the interaction between adult education and labour market training).

The process of engaging experts to carry out the independent national evaluations has resulted in a database at Statistics Sweden and different projects located at Swedish universities (Commission for the Promotion of Adult Education and Training, 1998).

Already the monitoring process has produced some changes in the programme. The government has, for instance, increased the number of study places available to the programme by forty per cent. The number of study places will increase by 10,000 study places each year from 1997 to 2000 so that it in the year 2000 some 140,000 study places will be available. Evidence from the municipalities shows that they have a capacity to provide more study places and have more unemployed persons willing to participate in training than earlier expected. If the programme is not extended there is a risk that all interested unemployed individuals will not be offered training. The government expects that a large number of these additional study places will be used by long term unemployed persons older than 25 years (Prop 1996/97:150).

The government has even, to some extent, revised the principal of no special government funds for primary and lower secondary education. On the condition that the municipalities not only keep up the regular supply of adult education at primary and lower secondary level but also increase it by ten per cent, additional study places could be financed by state grants.

More possibilities for employed people to participate in the programme have also been opened up and the special study grants for individuals are, on certain conditions, to be extended beyond the 12 months' limit.

Moreover, in the first round of evaluation one study concerned with the costs of the different types of courses, found that while the average level of the state compensation for the courses seemed to be about right, the introductory courses were more expensive than expected. This will lead to some changes in the calculations of the state grants for 1999 (Statskontoret, 1998).

Of great interest in the implementation and monitoring processes are, of course, the initiatives taken by local actors. Continuous adaptations and improvements at local level are of vital importance for improvement of programme performance. A planning process, including self-evaluations, implemented by municipalities and schools, is necessary.

In the municipalities monitoring and evaluation will normally be directed by the AEI project manager. The educational providers are supposed to make their own follow up studies and evaluations. The public schools are already obliged to do so and the 'external' educational providers will, to the extent they are used, be required to do so. These pedagogically oriented follow ups are necessary for the municipalities to be able to judge and compare different educational providers, in order to be able to change the supply mix of courses and to adapt the content of courses to the demand of individuals.

The feed back from these more pedagogically oriented follow ups to over all municipal evaluation and planning seems to be more problematic. General strategies for the complete planning process including goals and targets, follow up studies and evaluations as well as the revision of goals and targets seem to be lacking in most cases.

There is also a concern that at local level the AEI project as well as its planning and evaluation processes may become isolated from those applied to the rest of the local educational system. In that case the AEI would not provide the inspiration and revitalisation of the educational sector aimed at by the government.

To the extent researchers and evaluation specialists are involved by the municipalities they seem to be used mostly to handle student surveys.

Much remains to be worked out both at local and national level. There is also the question of how these two levels should be related to each other both as far as research and evaluations are concerned. Both bottom-up and top-down evaluations are clearly necessary and links between them and research can promote the process of continuous improvements.

The matrix below shows a number of areas that need to be covered by monitoring, reporting, evaluation and research for these types of programmes. At the centre are the results of the programme in terms of knowledge effects. To the left are the inputs, the factors influencing the knowledge results - the costs and the organisation of education and the teaching and learning processes. To the right are found the further effects of the knowledge results in terms of employment, economic growth, social change etc. As indicated in the figure these factors and effects can be studied from an individual, local, national or even international perspective (Husén and Tuijnman, 1994; Hasan and Tuijnman, 1997a).

The intention here is mainly to use the figure to discuss how to plan for improvements in the knowledge base and decision making rather than substantive aspects. It should, however, be pointed out that 'knowledge' in this case is to be interpreted in a broad sense. It includes the foundations for further learning: life skills such as capacity to communicate, adapt and learn new things social competence including capacity to co-operate, self confidence and creativity, basic skills such as reading, writing and mathematics and a common frame of facts and references.

The municipalities may be expected to follow and evaluate the development of the educational organisation and teaching methods and the effects on individual knowledge and employment. The results from such individual and local studies can be enhanced if compared with results from similar studies in other municipalities and at national level. The responsibility for the latter type of studies has been conferred to national experts by the Commission. These national projects are also to produce more detailed and penetrating case studies at municipal level to provide a deeper understanding of the processes and outcomes. As such the independent national evaluations can also serve as objects of reference for the municipalities.

In the present situation with so much local variation, cost effectiveness studies must also be referred to case studies at the municipal level. Such studies are both of a national and a local interest. Therefore, the Commission has taken an initiative in this field and engaged about 50 municipalities (out of the 288 Swedish municipalities) in an on going-pilot study.

Figure 1. *Areas for monitoring, reporting, evaluation and research*
                                        Organization Results
                                        Processes   Knowledge
Labour Growth Society
     Individual
     Local
     National
     International

Professional expertise is also required for the more far reaching effects, e.g. individual employment effects, and their relations to input factors and knowledge results where the use of relevant statistical methods is of great importance.

Knowledge effects at the local level may also be more complicated to analyse when both secondary leakage and leverage effects are to be included. The AEI programme may on the one hand raise the awareness in municipalities at the political level, among employers, employees and others about the profitability of investments in education and training and thus lead to increased educational investments. On the other hand, the state-funded programme may displace investments in education and training that might otherwise have been undertaken - by the municipalities, the public employment services, restructuring enterprises etc. Substitution effects may also occur.

Another reason for external expertise is that the programme combines education, labour and economic policy actions which may call for new approaches. Traditionally, educational planning and school planning, nationally and locally, to the extent it existed in the municipalities, has been rather restricted and not so much related to the outside world and working life. However, it is important to stimulate the municipalities to work on the evaluation of the more aggregate effects at local level.

International comparisons may also be necessary to discover the effects of different types of adult education and educational policies - for instance the expansion of adult education versus the expansion of higher education or youth education. However, these type of studies may be more related to research than evaluation proper. Other areas more suited for research than evaluation may be the long-term effects of the present changes on education and learning and the concepts and measurements of education, learning, knowledge, skills and competencies.

At present in the Swedish context, all the monitoring and evaluation activities are also carried out more or less on an experimental basis. In the long run a new institutional framework may be needed, an institutional framework that does not include only monitoring and evaluation but also research and not only evaluation and research related to this special programme but to the whole area of lifelong learning. Lifelong learning has become such an important fact of life that it probably needs its own institutions.

Further tasks for such a research and evaluation institution would be to increase the efficiency of national monitoring, linking the national and local evaluation closer to policy making as well as creating links between research and policy implementation. Both national and local experiences should enrich the knowledge base as fully and as rapidly as possible.

Summing up, one might say that what is needed to develop a system of lifelong learning is:

– continuous monitoring, reporting and evaluation processes;
– combinations of top down and bottom up approaches, i.e. external evaluations and self-evaluations;
– studies focusing both processes and outcomes;
– research to develop methods, basic concepts and a more fundamental understanding of long-term development tendencies;
– an institutional framework to secure monitoring and growth of the knowledge base so that policies at both national and local level can continuously remain in line with the emerging features of the knowledge society.

To implement a systematic approach towards research, monitoring and evaluation governments must take the lead (Belanger and Tuijnman, 1997; Hasan and Tuijnman, 1997a, 1997b).

REFERENCES

Belanger, P. and Tuijnman, A. (1997) "The 'Silent Explosion' of Adult Learning", in Belanger, P. and Tuijnman, A. (Eds.), *New Patterns in Adult Learning: A Six-Country Comparative Study*, Pergamon and UNESCO, New York.

Commission for the Promotion of Adult Education and Training (1998), *The Commission for Adult Education and Training and Evaluations of the Adult Education Initiative.*

Hasan, A. and Tuijnman, A. (1997a), "Adult Education: A Policy Review", in Belanger, P. and Tuijnman, A. (Eds.), *New Patterns in Adult Learning: A Six-Country Comparative Study*, Pergamon and UNESCO, New York.

Hasan, A. and Tuijnman, A. (1997b), "Methodologies for Monitoring Adult Education Participation", in Belanger, P. and Valdivielso (Eds.), *The Emergence of Learning Societies: Who Participates in Adult Education?*, Pergamon and UNESCO, New York.

Husén, T. and Tuijnman, A. (1994), "Monitoring Standards in Education. Why and How It Came About", in Tuijnman, A. and Postlethwaite (Eds.), *Monitoring the Standards in Education*, Pergamon Press, Oxford.

NUTEK (1996), "Ett puzzelförsök - matching mellan utbud och efterfrågan av olika utbildningskategorier år 2010. Bilaga till Arbetsmarknadspolitiska kommitténs betänkande", *Aktiv arbetsmarknadspolitik*, SOU 34, Stockholm.

OECD (1995), *Literacy, Economy and Society*, Paris.

OECD (1997a), *Education Policy Analysis 1997*, Paris.

OECD (1997b), *Literacy Skills for the Knowledge Society*, Paris.

Prop (1995/96), *Vissa åtgärder för att halvera arbetslösheten till år 2000, ändrade anslag för budgetåret 1995/96, finansiering m.m.*, p.222.

Prop (1996/97), *1997 års ekonomiska vårproposition*, p.150.

SCB (1996a), *Efter 20 år på arbetsmarknaden.* Information om utbildning och arbetsmarknad 1996:2, SCB-Tryck, Örebro.

SCB (1996b), "Framtida tillgång och efterfrågan på utbildade - konsekvensberäkningar för år 2010. Bilaga till Arbetsmarknadspolitiska kommitténs betänkande", *Aktiv arbetsmarknadspolitik*, SOU 34, Stockholm.

Skolverket (1995), *Beskrivande data om skolverksamheten,.* Skolverkets rapport nr 75, Stockholm, Norstedts Tryckeri.

Skolverket (1996ª), *Beskrivande data om skolverksamheten,.* Skolverkets rapport nr 107, Stockholm, Norstedts Tryckeri.

Skolverket (1996b), *Efterfrågan och tillgång på gymnasial vuxenutbildning*, Stencil.

Skolverket (1997), *Beskrivande data om skolverksamheten*, Skolverkets rapport nr 135, Stockholm.

Skolverket (1998), *Kunskapslyftet och den kommunala vuxenutbildningen*, Stockholm.

SOU 27 (1995), *En strategi för kunskapslyft och livslångt lärande*, Stockholm.

SOU 51 (1998), *Vuxenutbildning och livslångt lärande - situationen inför och under första året med Kunskapslyftet*, Stockholm.

SOU 57 (1998), *Utvärdering av distansutbildningsprojekt med IT-stöd*, Stockholm.

SOU 84 (1998), *Flexibel utbildning på distans*, Stockholm.

Statskontoret (1998), *Kommunernas kostnader för Kunskapslyftet*, Stockholm.

Chapter 17

The Role of Distance Learning in Achieving Lifelong Learning for Community Pharmacists

Lindsey Bagley
University of Manchester

1. LIFELONG LEARNING AND COMMUNITY PHARMACISTS

The concept of lifelong learning and its increasing importance is one of the prevailing educational themes of the `90s. The need to reskill and extend the knowledge base of the professional workforce has escalated in response to economic and social developments throughout the EU. *"Today, continuing professional education is considered essential, not only because of increasing legislative mandates, but because of the rapidly expanding bases of knowledge in most, if not all, areas of professional endeavour"* (Schuttenberg *et al.* 1986). The growing urgency for education and training is not always met with the necessary funding and resources. Lifelong learning is frequently called upon as a means of encouraging professional groups to take responsibility for their own continuing education, partly as a means of relieving the pressure on those educational institutions, government agencies or professional bodies previously charged with the task. From the provider's point of view, it is essential that the model of lifelong learning is sustainable as a cost-effective and efficient means of keeping the professional workforce up-to-date.

With this aim in mind, distance learning has relatively recently enjoyed a period of increased interest and attention from the education and training community. This paper presents the findings of a four year study into the appropriateness of distance learning as a means of updating knowledge and improving practice through participation in lifelong learning. It examines the extent to which the continuing education needs of community pharmacists in England can be met through distance learning and considers the wider implications for other professional groups.

Over recent years as a consequence of the restructuring of the National Health Service in the UK the role of the community pharmacist has changed with a significant shift in emphasis in pharmacy practice. Community pharmacists have increasingly adopted a health promotion role in areas as diverse as smoking cessation, footcare, oral hygiene and asthma. Some pharmacists have gone further in offering a health screening service to complement their advice, on nutrition or diabetes for example. Indeed, this implementation of the concept of 'primary care' with community pharmacists acting as part of the health care team has meant that they are increasingly required to have a high degree of public contact, counselling patients, carrying out diagnosis and making referrals. To achieve these tasks community pharmacists need to be able to offer sometimes complex advice, based on their awareness of recent developments and an up-to-date knowledge base. According to Morrow & Hargie (1986) the heightened 'patient' rather than 'product' emphasis in pharmacy practice and the growing requirement to interact with other health care professionals increases the need for appropriate postgraduate training.

More recently community pharmacists have come under pressure from consumers to deliver consistent, appropriate and reliable advice; various independent studies, often involving covert observation techniques, have suggested that pharmacists are not fulfilling their extended role to a satisfactory standard (Consumers' Association, 1991). The need for a *"systematic continuing education programme"* (SCOPE, 1994) to enable community pharmacists to cope with the changes to their professional role is even more important given that the emphasis in their initial pharmacy education and training is on clinical, scientific areas.

The undergraduate course for pharmacists in the UK comprises a three year degree (from October 1997 it will be four years) followed by a separate pre-registration year spent in practice and an accompanying examination. This academic focus on a clinical and theoretical grounding has only relatively recently been implemented, the emphasis initially having been placed on learning through practice. Although pharmacy practice has gained academic respectability as a result of this change in emphasis *"...by converting preparation for the profession into training in an applied science"* (Barnet *et al.* 1987), the 'real' nature of the community pharmacist's role is clearly becoming less scientific and more people-oriented.

The pharmacists' professional body, the Royal Pharmaceutical Society of Great Britain (RPSGB), acknowledges the need for its members to participate in continuing education in order for them to carry out their extended role. It recommends as a condition of annual registration that they undertake 30 hours of continuing education each year. This is however neither monitored nor enforced.

In 1991 the uptake of continuing education in England was 5 to 20% depending on the region involved. For pharmacists the motivation to engage in continuing education comes from "internal" rather than "external" factors; there is no direct financial remuneration or reward. The most cited obstacle to participation as far as pharmacists are concerned is that of time, particularly now that the business environment of community pharmacy is itself undergoing reorganisation, placing greater commercial pressure on the independent community pharmacist.

The providers of continuing education for community pharmacists have received criticism from independent evaluation studies; according to Dunn and Hamilton (1985) *"...the courses lack relevance to immediate needs, the approach is too theoretical, the audience are talked at rather than communicated with, the times and places of meetings are frequently unsuitable, and there seems little attempt to cover topics in a systematic fashion"*. They go on to recommend that distance learning be considered as an option for provision.

Faced with inadequate funding and insufficient resources generally, those responsible for training are increasingly turning to distance learning as a potential solution to their problems. In the UK this is also the case in many institutions of higher and further education where educationalists and administrators are coming to regard this form of instruction and learning as an inexpensive way of remaining competitive whilst increasing student numbers. Without doubt, for the providers of continuing education, distance learning does enable some of the potential problems associated with an unpredictable demand for courses, wide geographical spread and particularly low or high student numbers to be overcome. However, the implications for lifelong learning are not straightforward. How suitable is distance learning to the needs of lifelong learners?

Given that the commitment by learners to lifelong continuing education is by definition a *life-long* one, it is essential that any system of development, delivery and support is able to maintain their interest and enable them to get involved in the process. According to Schuttenberg *et al.* (1986) adult learners need to feel part of (and able to) influence their learning programmes this is particularly true at higher levels of education. Distance learning is cited in the literature as one form of learning that allows, moreover encourages, learners to participate in, and ultimately take control of, their own learning experience. They make the critical decisions regarding the environment, the pace, timing, frequency and sometimes the content of their study and benefit from the flexibility and convenience that this brings.

However, learner motivation is the key to distance learning. Crophy and Kahl (1983) compared distance learning and face-to-face instruction in terms of the psychological dimensions and concluded that internal motivation is a prerequisite of the former and a desirable in the latter. Learners in a face-to-face situation, even unwilling ones, are encouraged to engage in learning activities. Distance learners, however, are isolated from conventional learning situations and are often faced with tasks demanding behaviour different from that required of the learning task. The apparent absence of motivating factors is strengthened further by the lack of social competition in the form of tutor or peer group pressure. Distance learners must rely on their own motivational resources. Indeed, Rebel (1987) goes further in stressing the importance of a learning arrangement free of coercion.

But how realistic is it to expect such a high level of commitment from an audience of busy professionals undergoing a period of reorganisation and increased competition at work and with little free time at home?

2. THE CENTRE FOR PHARMACY POSTGRADUATE EDUCATION

The Centre for Pharmacy Postgraduate Education (CPPE) was established by the UK Government's Department of Health in 1992 with the responsibility for the provision of continuing education for the 18,500 community pharmacists in England. CPPE's central model of provision offers a distance learning programme and workshops. A network of 80 part time tutors deliver the workshops and support the distance learning programme at a local level. The distance learning is offered in a variety of formats: print-based workbooks, audio-visual packages and computer-assisted learning programmes. This flexibility enables participants to select the medium or combination of media that is most appropriate to their learning needs and lifestyle. Study groups are encouraged and facilitated by tutors.

The annual budget for CPPE is currently £2.2 million. All forms of continuing education offered by the Centre are provided free of charge to community pharmacists working in the community or intending to return to practice within six months. Although the distance learning system and all the packs available are advertised in a direct mailshot only twice a year, community pharmacists can request the packs from the catalogue at any time throughout the year.

Validation and evaluation form a significant part of CPPE's programme. The Centre reports back regularly to the Department of Health with information regarding the efficiency and cost-effectiveness of its programme.

Validation data relating to each distance learning package are provided by those who choose to study that particular topic and then to complete the validation form and computer-marked assessment that accompanies it. The data this process generates, whilst valuable in informing subsequent decisions about the way in which the topic is approached, are not necessarily representative of the experiences and perceptions of the general target audience because the process relies on a skewed sample of participants being both assessment- and topic-influenced. The validation data also do not provide any indication as to the impact of the pack in terms of learning outcomes.

In order to gain more accurate information relating to the appropriateness of the whole distance learning system and the impact of the packs on practice, two separate, independent evaluation studies were commissioned by CPPE in 1995.

3. RESEARCH METHODOLOGY

The overall aim of the main evaluation (Study A) was to examine the extent to which distance learning could meet the continuing education needs of community pharmacists in England and encourage them to engage in lifelong learning. This project was put out to competitive tender (as part of CPPE's contractual agreement with the Department of Health and the University of Manchester) and was awarded to a joint bid submitted by the Scottish Council for Research in Education, Edinburgh, and the Centre for Medical Education at the University of Dundee.

The data collection techniques involved quantitative and qualitative methods and were designed to access, gather and explore the views and experiences of users and non-users of CPPE's distance learning programme from its potential target audience of the 18,500 community pharmacists in England. The data collection took place in two stages.

4.   RESULTS

4.1   Study A

Firstly, a postal survey of 1100 community pharmacists, comprising of a random sample of 1000 from the RPSGB database and a stratified sample of 100 'high' users from CPPE's distance learning database, was carried out. High users were defined as those who had already requested, completed and returned the computer-marked assessment for at least two of the four specified packs. The four packs were selected to include a range of topics, approaches and formats. Two of the packs led to certification (required by the Health Authorities in order to receive payment for providing these services in the community).

Secondly, having examined the findings of the postal survey, six separate focus groups of six or seven community pharmacists with varying degrees of experience of CPPE's distance learning system were conducted to explore the emergent issues. The focus groups gave non-users the opportunity to examine, handle and work through the packs. The advantage of this two stage method was that it enabled the researchers to develop and test action strategies as the evaluation procedure developed. For Study A the response rate to the postal survey was fifty-two per cent.

Sixty-six per cent of respondents worked full time in community pharmacy, the remainder worked part time. Thirty-seven per cent worked for an independent pharmacy, thirty-five per cent for a multiple group, sixteen per cent for a small chain and twelve per cent in a variety of premises as a locum. The majority of respondents worked in a town or suburb (sixty-six), nine per cent worked in a rural location, nine per cent in an inner city location and the remainder in various locations. The largest group of respondents (thirty-three per cent) was aged over 51 years. Twenty-six per cent were aged between 31 and 40 years, twenty-two per cent between 41 and 50 years and nineteen per cent were aged less than 31 years. Slightly more females (fifty-two per cent) responded than males.

When respondents were asked whether they had undertaken any continuing education during the previous year eighty-seven per cent of all respondents indicated they had studied CPPE distance learning materials (removing the skewed sample of high users reduced this to seventy-three per cent).

The main reasons for participation were: *"to update original training"* (ninety-three per cent*): "to develop professional expertise"* (eighty-one per cent) and *"to be kept informed of professional developments and new practices"* (seventy-five per cent). In the sample of users, eighty-six per cent cited *"personal training needs"* as the main reason compared to sixty-six per cent of the random sample. The least frequently cited reasons overall were: *"my employer requires participation"* (five per cent) and *"to help implement Department of Health priorities"* (nine per cent).

The views of respondents were sought using an attitudinal scale. The overall response to the CPPE distance learning programme was *"overwhelmingly positive";* users regarded the method as *"worthwhile, convenient and interesting"* (Wilson *et al.* 1996). Nonetheless sixty-four per cent of respondents agreed that distance learning was time consuming. When comparing the responses of users and non-users significant differences were found with non-users expressing less favourable views on distance learning.

In terms of how the materials were studied, seventy per cent reported that they studied at home during the week and fifty per cent said they studied at home over the weekend. The finding that the packs were used mainly outside of working hours in the home environment was reinforced in the focus groups.

The computer-marked assessment was most likely to be completed for the two CPPE distance learning packs that lead to certification. The return rate for these packs was thirty-five per cent whereas for the two other packs there was an average return rate of twenty per cent.

Attendance of a study group was variable and sixty per cent of respondents reported that they would like more study groups to be held in their area. This was challenged by the focus groups who considered it to be more a question of increasing the awareness of community pharmacists regarding study groups rather than increasing provision.

The perceived relevance of the packs was reported as vital for community pharmacists. How much a pack was liked was clearly linked to its usefulness. Regular users of distance learning were pragmatic in their preferences, emphasising course content over pack design. This applied irrespective of whether completion led to remuneration. The most frequently expressed reason for non-participation by non-users was lack of time (sixty-five per cent). Overall a significant majority of respondents believed that incentives, such as accreditation and financial reward, would increase pack completion rates. However, this was not the finding of the focus groups; the most cited factor to help increase completion rates recognised by the focus groups was the provision of relevant topics.

Overall eighty-four per cent of respondents were satisfied with the distance learning offered by CPPE (thirty-seven per cent of those were very satisfied). This sentiment was reinforced by the ninety-six per cent who felt that the distance learning programme should continue in its current form (fifty-seven per cent) or with minor changes (thirty-nine per cent). The topic range was the most frequently applauded factor of the system; ninety seven per cent considered it to be satisfactory. Similarly, the academic value of the content was reported with a high degree of satisfaction by the focus groups.

In reference to content layout, a strong preference for a personal, direct style of writing, incorporating clear text with frequent breaks, summaries, in-text exercises and case studies was expressed. The inclusion of an index and contents page was commonly regarded as useful and reinforced the value of the materials as subsequent sources of reference. Reactions to the employment of humour and cartoons were mixed. Generally, relevant photographs were valued although colour was requested only when educationally justified, to illustrate skin conditions for example.

The administration and support elements of the system were regarded as satisfactory and efficient, although fourteen per cent of respondents requested a greater degree of contact with CPPE and their local tutor. There were also requests for a formal logging system of continuing education hours to be introduced along with more certification and accreditation.

4.2 Study B

A smaller scale, topic-specific evaluation (Study B) was also carried out to examine the influence of the distance learning programme on the practice and knowledge levels of community pharmacists using the CPPE pack entitled *Health Promotion and Health Screening*. This print-based distance learning pack was presented in an A4, workbook format and included self-assessment devices, in-text exercises and case studies. It was written by a team, comprising of community pharmacists, an educationalist, an expert practitioner, a patient representative and a tutor, in accordance with the house standards developed by CPPE.

The data collection process involved a postal survey of 1000 recipients of the pack and a telephone survey of a control group of 220 community pharmacist who had not requested the pack. Both were conducted six months after the pack was mailed out to those 5000 community pharmacists who had requested it. For Study B the overall response rate was thirty one per cent

In terms of the attitude of the community pharmacists to health promotion and health screening there were no differences in the perceived importance of the topic between those who had requested the pack and those who had not. There was also no significant differences in the perceived future importance of health promotion as an issue for community pharmacists.

However, those who had requested the pack had a higher self-reported awareness of health promotion and health screening than the control group. This was determined by their own rating of their knowledge of health promotion and health screening and their confidence in dealing with patients on these issues.

Moreover, when their practice was examined there clearly was a difference in behaviour between the two groups of community pharmacists. Six months after receiving the pack, the majority (ninety-six per cent) of the experimental group was carrying out more health promotion activity than prior to receiving the pack, compared to twenty-three per cent of the control group. Forty-six per cent of the experimental group also reported that they intended to improve the quality of the service they provided even further in the future.

4.3 Analysis

During the period of this study, from 1992 to 1996, the uptake of continuing education in England rose considerably from five to twenty per cent in 1991 to seventy-three per cent in 1995. Prior to the introduction of CPPE, each region negotiated and was responsible for its own budget from the Department of Health. Not only was the uptake of continuing education extremely variable, in some regions good and in others very poor, but the standard of provision and its relevance to practice was also very mixed. As a result of the central model represented by CPPE, all community pharmacists in England wishing to engage in the Centre's continuing education programme receive a consistent standard, irrespective of where they live and the medium for delivery they select. To ensure a high level of relevance to individual community pharmacists a local focus can be provided at workshops and in the distance learning study groups.

Although it is important to bear in mind that CPPE operates as a provider of all forms of continuing education, including workshops, it cannot be refuted that a huge increase in the uptake of continuing education occurred during the period of the study. This is particularly striking when one considers that no external motivators, such as remuneration or compulsory continuing professional development, were introduced between 1992 and 1996. The model of voluntary continuing education offered free-of-charge would appear to be 'successful' if uptake is a reliable indicator. This becomes even more significant when the satisfaction of participants with the system is examined; ninety-seven per cent of participants were satisfied with CPPE's existing system.

The majority of respondents using distance learning for continuing education purposes believed that it was important for personal ('internal') rather than 'external' reasons; eighty-one per cent undertook distance learning to develop their professional expertise. This supports the notion that distance learning relies on internal motivators and points to its suitability as a vehicle for lifelong learning.

It is significant that non-users believed external factors, such as remuneration, to be more important than those respondents in the user sample. The distinction between the groups becomes even more apparent as their involvement in the distance learning programme increases, with higher users feeling much more positive about their learning experience and more motivated generally to engage in continuing education. This reinforces Marland (1989) who indicated that distinct groups with different needs and expectations emerge as the system develops.

If a participation rate of greater than seventy-three per cent is required, external motivators, for example accreditation and mandatory continuing professional development, might be introduced by CPPE to attract new users. It would appear that the perceived quality and relevance of the CPPE materials themselves would ensure that any new users were motivated and satisfied enough to continue with the programme. Ninety-eight per cent of those using CPPE's materials reported that they would go on to study other CPPE distance learning packages.

The distance learning system offered by CPPE adheres largely to the CRISIS criteria developed by Harden & Laidlaw (1992) from the recommendations of Dunn & Hamilton (1985). CRISIS refers to the considerations of any effective distance learning programme, namely Convenience, Relevance, Individualisation, Self-assessment, Interest, Specialisation and systematic. The convenience of CPPE's distance learning suits voluntary participation and therefore lifelong learning which depends on the long term motivation and commitment of learners. However, the convenience of the materials could by enhanced further by standardising the design and presentation of the packs. The results of this study indicate that a portable, storable and easy to use format is preferred by community pharmacists who, like most professionals, have very little time to commit to continuing education and therefore need to have access to clear, concise and flexible distance learning materials.

The relevance of the topic and the contents of the pack were stressed as important features in determining how well the learning experience was perceived by users. Ninety-seven per cent of the respondents who had used the packs found the relevance to be satisfactory. As the duration of the distance learning provision increases and new topics are added each year (CPPE offers approximately four new packs each year and updates packs at least every two years) community pharmacists have greater scope to prioritise their choice of topics to meet their own continuing education needs.

The wide selection of topics contributes to the individual nature of the continuing education offered by CPPE. Community pharmacists are also able to decide when to receive the pack, how to approach it, which media to use and whether to complete the computer-marked assessment to return to CPPE. In addition, self-assessment devices incorporated in the text enable learners to test their understanding as they progress through the materials and to apply any newly acquired knowledge to real life case studies. The option of peer group interaction is also available in the form of study groups if community pharmacists wish to support their learning experience or extend their understanding further. Study groups also serve to stimulate their interest in an informal and non-competitive study environment.

The speculation and systematic criteria of the CRISIS model are particularly difficult to meet when designing a continuing education model for community pharmacists whose previous education and training has focused on reaching scientific, clear cut decisions at the expense of the controversial, ambiguous or 'grey' areas. This is increasingly true as the role of the community pharmacy becomes even more patient-oriented and diagnostic. The use of professional judgement is becoming increasingly important. The distance learning packs go some way in achieving this by including in-depth case studies. These present issues and discuss the decisions reached and actions recommended by the 'expert' authors and a panel of community pharmacists. This approach enables community pharmacists to see how their understanding and application differs from that of some of the acknowledged experts in the field and, perhaps more importantly, their peer group with similar work pressures and experiences.

The results from the comparative study (Study B) examining the behaviour and attitude of community pharmacists indicate that those in the experimental group had changed their practice over the six months following their request and receipt of the distance learning pack. In addition, their self-reported awareness levels were higher than those in the control group. This would suggest that the distance learning pack had been instrumental in improving their perceived knowledge levels and more importantly their practice. Moreover, forty-six per cent of the respondents in the experimental group expressed an intention to continue to raise the quality of the advice they offered patients.

Whilst recognising the limitations of self-reporting techniques, these results indicate that distance learning has a role to play in equipping community pharmacists with the necessary tools to keep up-to-date.

5.   CONCLUSION

In conclusion, this paper confirms that distance learning is an appropriate way of providing community pharmacists with the means of testing and expanding their knowledge base and subsequently improving their practice. Moreover, distance learning is able to make a significant contribution to achieving lifelong learning by encouraging community pharmacists to take responsibility for their own continuing education.

The real advantage of distance learning lies in its focus on the learner, initially as part of an homogenous group of community pharmacists whose professional role is changing and extending but also as part of a heterogeneous group of individuals with different work experiences and domestic circumstances. A system of provision that is relevant to current practice motivates community pharmacists in the short term as they benefit from increased confidence and improved job satisfaction. A system that also offers flexibility and convenience on an individual level goes further in encouraging them to become involved on a long term basis. Lifelong learning requiring the minimum amount of personal investment in time and effort then becomes a feasible option from the learner's point of view.

For the providers of continuing education, however, distance learning as a model for lifelong learning is only a feasible option if the issue of motivation has been considered and addressed. The model of distance learning offered by CPPE relies on voluntary uptake by busy professionals. Because it is voluntary, it can be assumed that participants in the system have already reached a level of commitment to continuing education and have recognised the professional and personal value of keeping up-to-date. This commitment should be maintained by allowing the learners maximum control over their own learning experience so they make the critical decisions regarding what, when, where and how they study.

If the requirement of the RPSGB were to change so that continuing education became compulsory as a condition of registration each year, uptake might increase. The reasons cited by pharmacists participating in lifelong learning if it was mandatory, however, might be different from those reported in these studies with an increasing emphasis on external motivators. Significantly, it is internal motivators that are most conducive to successful distance learning and this should be borne in mind by providers of mandatory continuing education. The different needs and expectations of those committed to lifelong learning and those engaging in continuing education because it is enforced must be accommodated by the providers of the system.

The potential obstacle of poor motivation to continuing education generally is being tackled by CPPE at the undergraduate level. Since 1995 pharmacy students in England receive four CPPE distance learning packs at the beginning of their pre-registration year. By introducing the notion of continuing professional development and the role of distance learning during the initial training of community pharmacists, CPPE has taken measures to encourage support amongst its future target audience. Although the decision to supply undergraduates was largely in response to demand from the students themselves through the British Pharmaceutical Student Association, it will enable CPPE in the future to evaluate whether it has had a positive impact on the attitude of students to distance learning and their commitment to lifelong learning once they qualify as community pharmacists.

The findings of the studies reported in this paper are relevant to all those involved in continuing education and lifelong learning, particularly those concerned with lifelong learning in the professional workforce. Distance learning has undoubtedly a role to play in meeting the economic and social demands made on the education and training community today. It should not, however, be regarded as an easy option. The needs, expectations and life circumstances of its target audience must be considered and accommodated. This ongoing investment in time and effort is vital, without it the system will ultimately fail. Only with the support and commitment of the distance learners themselves can lifelong learning be achieved.

REFERENCES

Barnet, R., Becher, R. and Cork, N. (1987), "Models of professional preparation: pharmacy, nursing and teacher education", *Studies of Higher Education*, Vol.12 No.1, pp.51-63.

Consumers' Association Report (1991), *Which? Way to Health*, London.

Crophy, A.J. and Kahl, T.N. (1983), "Distance education and distance learning: some considerations", *Distance Education*, Vol.4 No.1, pp.27-41.

Dunn, W. and Hamilton, D. (1985), "Competence-based education and distance learning: a tandem for professional continuing education?" *Studies in Higher Education*, Vol. 10, No. 3., pp. 277-287.

Harden, R and Laidlaw, J. (1992), "Effective continuing education: the crisis criteria", *Medical Education* 26, pp.408-422.

Morrow, N. and Hargie, O. (1986), "Communication as a focus in the continuing education of pharmacists", *Studies in Higher Education*, Vol.11 No.3, pp.279-288.

Rebel, K. (1987), "The role of group learning in multi-media distance learning", *Open Learning*, Feb. 1987, pp.19-24.

Rekkedal, T. (1983), "The written assignment in correspondence education: effects on reducing turn-around time. An experimental study", *Distance Education*, Vol.4 No.2, pp.231-252.

Schuttenberg, E., Gallagher, J. and Poppenhagen, B. (1986), "Learner preferences in continuing professional education", *British Journal of In-Service Education* 13, pp.15-19.

SCOPE (1984), *A continuing education strategy for NHS pharmacists in England*, HMSO.

Wilson, V., McFall, E., Harden, R. and Laidlaw, J. (1996), *Learning at a distance*, Scottish Council for Research in Education internal evaluation report for CPPE, HMSO.

Chapter 18

Bridging the gap between education and work
The balance between core curriculum and vocationalism in Swedish recurrent education

Kenneth Abrahamsson
Swedish Council for Work Life Research

1.   EDUCATION AND WORK

"Building and reinforcing bridges between schools and businesses can do nothing but good, for both sides, and helps to underpin equal employment opportunities. With respect to the world of learning in its widest sense, stretching from primary to higher education, training courses provided must be better matched to employment opportunities......

Therefore, bringing schools and the business sector closer together is a priority in which the social partners must play their role and which involves three conditions:

First, education must be opened to the world of work. Without reducing the point of education solely to the purpose of employment, an understanding of the world of work, a knowledge of enterprises and an insight into the changes which mark production processes are some of the basics which schooling must take into account.

Second, companies must be involved in the training drive, not only as regards workers but also young people and adults. Training cannot be seen purely as a way of supplying skilled labour to firms; they themselves bear a responsibility, i.e. that of giving a chance - often in the form of a job - to those who were failed by the traditional education systems. Companies need to grasp this more clearly. Some have made substantial efforts to reskill their staff, thus enabling them to cope with the technological innovation, while others have not, throwing onto the streets workers who clearly could be retrained.

Third, co-operation must be developed between schools and firms. Reinforcing links between schools and the business sector must be based primarily on apprenticeship/trainee schemes. This training approach is suitable for all qualification levels, and is catching on in higher education, following initiatives by engineering or business schools.

Apprenticeship/trainee schemes are able to provide young people with both the required knowledge plus experience of life and work within companies. By providing them with their first contact with the world of production, it places them at a considerable advantage for entering the job market. Promotion of apprenticeship/trainee schemes at European level will provide added value for both young people and companies."

(From "White Paper on Education and Training")

1.1   Models of Practice

Given the educational mission reflected in the White Paper on Education and Training, the purpose of this paper is to discuss the interface between education and work with reference to recurrent education policies in Sweden. Special interest is paid to the balance between vocationalism and core curriculum models in post-compulsory education in Sweden.

The paper focuses on Sweden as an example, but the dilemmas or problems discussed are often of an international character. More specifically, the paper deals with various organisational and curricular forms to bridge the gap between education and work. The models discussed include policies of recurrent education, the core curriculum idea at upper secondary level, the use of prior work experience as an admission merit, on the job training and the effort to 'educationalise' unemployment experience through various forms of employment development programmes. In a general sense, these education and work interface models are built on ideas of integration and/or alternation of theory and practice. It is typical for Swedish educational policy to aim for a comprehensive and integrated model of education. In organisational terms this means a postponed differentiation in compulsory schooling and an effort to avoid a dual or binary model at the upper secondary level.

2.   SWEDISH EDUCATION AT THE CROSS-ROADS

The Swedish model of renewing society has attracted significant international attention over the last three or four decades. The high level of interest does not, however, correspond to a common understanding of the main features of the Swedish model. At the risk of oversimplification, some of the main features will be mentioned below. In comparison with most other industrialised countries, Sweden has an extensive public sector. It is a fact that has a major impact on the economy, on the structure of the labour market as well as on the organisational solutions chosen to manage certain societal problems and challenges, the field of education and competence development being no exception.

Another cornerstone is the tradition of central agreement and consensus between the social partners on the labour market, a tradition that is losing its strength and importance especially in a period of retrenchment, of economic crises and no increase in productivity. The typical Swedish principle of solidarity over wage policies is more a part of trade union history than its future.

Furthermore, the Swedish model is built on the principle of general welfare policy by the provision of a variety of public services. Another feature of the Swedish system of societal building has been the strong focus on distributive or re-distributive objectives. Access and equity are central policy values in many political fields such as social policy, health and welfare, education at all levels, media and culture.

The last decade has seen a fundamental shift in the Swedish model over societal building and social problem solving with a transition that is both vertical and horizontal. The Swedish system of public administration is nowadays much more decentralised than it was ten years ago. The two step model of change and reform through the use of regional boards has been abolished in most fields of public service. A new pattern of direct and dynamic communication between the government and the needs and interests of cities and municipalities is replacing the traditional hierarchical model.

There is also a strong market orientation in society. This new market orientation not only implies various methods of privatisation, but also, and probably to a greater extent, it implies new incentives within the public sector. The contractor-provider model has been used in various sectors of the public service. The system of education provides several examples of this new market oriented context.

Independent schools have started or are opting out from the compulsory school system and from upper secondary education. In volume this shift only represents a few percent of the total population of pupils in youth education. The changes are more evident in adult and higher education. The national provider of employment training in Sweden, the Employment Training Group, (AMU-gruppen) has been transformed into a state owned private enterprise competing with other agencies on the competence market.

Commissioned adult education is now quite common both in municipal adult education and popular adult education, especially folk high schools. The former government was successful in stimulating one university of advanced technology and one regional university college to become private foundations.

The current transformation of the Swedish system of education is a combination of public policies and changing societal context. The need for decentralisation has been promoted by most parties in the Parliament. Another joint political mission is to expand the educational system and increase the transition rates from upper secondary to higher education. One of the ideas dividing Parliament is privatisation and increasing competition between public and private provision, where the current government has a more restrictive policy. The great adult education reform (kunskapslyftet) giving all adults the right to core curriculum subject knowledge at upper secondary level, symbolises the current Swedish policy of increasing access and limiting social bias in education.

3.   BRIDGING THE GAP BETWEEN EDUCATION AND WORK – A POLICY CHALLENGE

The gap between education and work can be described in an epistemological dimension. One major aspect concerns the world of concepts, theories and ideas in education and work. A simplified or superficial approach is to connect school-knowledge with theory and work with practical skills and specific context-bound knowledge. Another way of understanding the gap is to talk about different knowledge settings characterised by various concepts, intellectual tools, assumptions and practical solutions. A more traditional comprehension is that school knowledge is organised around and in school subjects and that work is an organised setting for the application of school knowledge, occupational skills and practical intelligence. It is the presumption of this author that the gap between education and work cannot be resolved only by making school knowledge more similar to everyday experience. The challenge lies in a dynamic interface between school-knowledge, experience based knowledge and practical applications at work.

Educational policy makers are trying to solve or resolve this dilemma by finding new combinations of the traditional apprenticeship model and the dual system on the one hand, and the use of a more integrated model on the other. The disadvantages of a more traditional apprenticeship model is, of course, that it can be a preparation for a vocation that is decreasing in numbers or being totally redefined. Furthermore, it has some restrictions and limitations with respect to further education and equality of opportunity. The integrated or general model, on the other hand, might loosen the connection with work, and be excessively future oriented and fail to take account of the fact that most occupations do not disappear overnight.

Thus, the context for bridging the gap between education and work is shifting over time, between and within countries. In the pre-industrial society with its guild system, there was a close connection between the apprentice and the master depending on the specific cultural, economic and social context as well as the fact that the trainee was prepared for a specific lifetime occupation. In an industrialised context this preparation has increasingly been taken over by vocational schools or by internal learning platforms within larger corporations. Still the distributive model was built on the premise that pupils were allocated to occupations by social determinants and vocational heritage in combination with personal interest and talent.

When the structural transformation of the labour market intensified, a growing number of employees had to be retrained to meet the needs of the new and expanding sectors of the labour market. The epoch of a single occupation for life for all education experience had seen its last days. Employment training and retraining schemes became an important tool of modern labour market policies. In Sweden, this model was almost perfected in a period of low unemployment, increasing labour market participation among women, and the development of new sectors of working life, in particular in the public sector for education, health and care of elderly people.

The fundamental transformation of modern Sweden has among other things, substantially raised employment and work orientation in the population at large. Thus, the move to a period of high levels of unemployment and increasing competition for jobs between various groups, has created a quite different context for the "bridging dilemma". The mainstream policy solution seems to be to invest increasing amounts in education and provide vocational experience to develop the social competence and flexibility necessary to get a job.

It is quite obvious that the "bridging-dilemma" illuminates a number of policy issues and has major repercussions for the role of continuing vocational training in a lifelong learning society. Educational architects and construction workers have invested substantial interest and time in building new bridges to work. Nowadays, they are receiving significant assistance from the other side of the river, from labour market policy people designing new forms of work-study links. Some of the questions to be discussed in this context are:

- How school-to-work programmes in general and vocational platforms in particular affect mobility within the formal education system?
- How school-to-work programmes affect career mobility for employed youth and adults?
- The extent to which school-to-work programmes combine vocational and general education?
- In what ways and to what extent is work-based learning used?
- How is the completion of a school-to-work programme scheme certified?

The Swedish system of education has recently been subject to significant change at the upper secondary level. The number of study programmes have been reduced and the curriculum structure of the vocational programmes broadened in order to provide more scope for lifelong learning and continuing vocational or general education. The high level of unemployment, especially youth unemployment, has, however, dramatically changed the context for traditional school-to-work programmes.

3.1   From direct to extended school to work transition patterns

Completing an education or a work-study programme does not in itself guarantee employment. Thus, individual learning routes take the form of various combinations of formal education (FE), school-to-work-programmes (SWP), unemployment (UE), temporary employment (TE), real employment (RE) and other life activities, such as family setting (FS) or globe trotting (GT). There is, however, no typical individual pattern, on the contrary a more flexible and uncertain learning context is emerging. The traditional FE-SWP-RE pattern is increasingly being replaced by a FE-SWP-UE-TE pattern, sometimes followed by exit points in the form of globe trotting (GT), family setting for young women (FS) or a new "roundabout" in state financed work-study schemes.

Furthermore, the structural transformation of the Swedish labour market and the high level of unemployment have resulted in a new and inverted learning pattern, namely work-to-school programmes (WSP), which reflect the need for down-sizing, outsourcing or outplacement of redundant employees. Labour market education at corporate level for employees at risk (LMEC), is another educational tool operating in between the SWPs and the WPSs.

This new interface between school and work can, for the younger generation, be labelled as an "accordion phenomenon" with a longer period of socialisation with variations in the opportunities available for absorbing a work ethos and values, and with a weaker work connection for many youngsters. Another impact of this situation is the need to illuminate and articulate a new interface between education policies, labour market policies and social policies.

Thus, overall development in Sweden as far as school-to-work transition is concerned has to be analysed with respect to:

-   the extension of youth education within the 0+9+3+x? formula with its decreasing scope for work experience or work oriented periods at different transitional stages in the education system, (almost no work experience prior to upper secondary education and the limited value of work experience as an admission merit to higher education).
-   a more open definition and less time allocated to working life orientation in the compulsory school, structural changes on the labour market with reference to the unemployment crises, the growth of new jobs, the development of an information society and the rapid growth of a new service sector present a new setting for school-to-work transition. It will be more difficult for individual pupils or students to perceive, understand and make their own choices when choosing vocational careers.
-   finally, the period of living together with parents is extended for many young persons, especially boys. If you do not have your own apartment and are also unemployed, the solution is to move back home to your parents. School-to-work transition is thus also a question of independence from parents, as well as access to good jobs.

3.2   Recurrent education revisited?

The aim of promoting recurrent education has been a central value in modern Swedish educational reforms. The expression 'lifelong education' or as it is sometimes referred to 'lifelong learning' has not only been used to characterise adult education, but rather to spell out the lifelong learning potential of youth education. The reforms in upper secondary education designed in the late 80s and implemented during the 90s have been supported by the idea of lifelong learning.

More common, however, is the concept of recurrent education, which over the years has been used in a number of more or less elastic conceptual contexts. When it was launched in the late 60s, it had the flavour of a broader and more coherent educational strategy, described here by the OECD (CERI, 1973, p. 16):

> "Recurrent education is a comprehensive educational strategy for all post-compulsory or post-basic education, the essential characteristic of which is the distribution of education over the total life-span of the individual in a recurring way, i.e. in alternation with other activities, principally with work, but also with leisure and retirement."

Rubenson (1992) has illustrated the conceptual transformation of recurrent education with its early focus on equity and access in the light of second-chance policies to a much stronger economic perspective in the last few years.

The early 90s can be characterised by a significant shift in education values and ideas. The role of working life orientation and preparation is redefined in the new national curriculum for compulsory school and for upper secondary school and municipal adult education. More attention is paid to quality of subject content and academic preparation at the expense of working life orientation.

Nowadays the model of recurrent education has been more or less abolished in preference to the broader concept of lifelong learning. In practice, however, the major shift in the educational landscape comprises an extension of the educational career by expanding the educational route both at the starting point (adapting to the European early school start), and also postponing or delaying the point of educational departure. This development is in sharp contrast to models based on recurrent education where learning is distributed over the life-span of an individual.

Traditionally, transition from school to work was valid in a labour market context where pupils completing compulsory school still could get a job on the open labour market. The next step represents the situation in Sweden during the 1970s, when work experience prior to higher studies was recommended in many policy quarters. The third and fourth cases cover the situation in the 1990s, with its significant extension of the years of formal schooling. Unemployment and the competition for study work programmes have also resulted in a shortage of relevant work experience options.

Thus, some students of the 1990s might live in educational quarantine for almost twenty years until the age of 25 with the accompanying problems of finding a job. The general policy view in Sweden tends to focus educational upgrading as a means of preparing for a future labour market with a number of job-shifts and growing uncertainty. This search for more generic knowledge and skills - in Sweden reflected through the system of core subjects in upper secondary education - also has its price if the connection with work does not function in practice.

4. IN SEARCH FOR NEW BRIDGES BETWEEN EDUCATION AND WORK IN SWEDEN

Bridging the gap between education and work is today a much more complicated endeavour. It is not only a question of supply and demand on the labour market seen in a broader demographic context. Nor is it the challenge of linking the experience of education and work together in a functioning chain for the individual. The dynamic interaction between vocationalism and "generalism" in education reflects the character and social structures of our modern societies.

The Swedish school-to-work transition model is no longer as simple as it used to be two or three decades ago. At that time, young people with "practical talents" left school after the compulsory years, or dropped out before completing their studies and entering a vocation in a sector of the labour market. Theoretically gifted students continued to upper secondary level in order to collect marks and merits for further university studies.

Gifted children with practical skills could advance in a learning-at-work environment, while theoretically oriented students received glimpses of working life realities through summer jobs or practical experience as part of their educational programmes. It was not a dual system, rather a social and educational mechanism monitoring early selection of pupils or students within the organisational framework of the education system.

The extension of youth education with the objective of creating a single integrated upper secondary education system was implemented without really changing the former pattern of two cultures, one driven by an occupational focus and the other by a stronger academic ethos. Despite the organisational renewal of the system of upper secondary education, the transition to higher education has constantly been low in a majority of vocational programmes in comparison with theoretical alternatives.

The value of work and the stress on working life orientation received strong policy priority during the 1970s and also part of the 1980s in Sweden. This priority was principally expressed not only in various aspects of the school-to-work transition, but also by the objective of reflecting work, working life and work environment issues in the teaching and learning content of Swedish schools. Work experience and different forms of experiential or experience-based learning
were introduced.

More generally, this development was reinforced by the idea that different types of knowledge in society, scientific, academic or experience-based, had equal value. At the risk of oversimplification, it could be said that the early 1990s are characterised by stronger subject-orientation and a culture of academic discipline at the expense of a weaker working life learning orientation.

The last few years have dramatically changed the conditions for implementing full employment policies in Sweden. The rejection of young individuals without sufficient education and the exclusion of older blue as well as white collar workers have strong repercussions on the need for the future education and training of the work force.

The threat of social exclusion of minorities may not be as evident in Sweden in comparison with other countries with a strong ethnic and multi-cultural mix. It is, however, a problem that cannot be neglected. Immigration during the last decade has mainly comprised refugees from third world countries and former Yugoslavia. Many refugees have very short if any formal schooling from their home countries.

"The main policy themes of Swedish vocational training have thus been the growth of school based provisions on a large scale, administrative and institutional unification of general and vocational education, and faith in what schools can achieve by the way of socialisation to work and citizenship. The system is expensive, however, and the match between training specialities and later work is poor. In spite of renewed interest in training based at the workplace, efforts to promote this as a direct extension of school-based vocational education have fallen short of expectations; and the main thrust of policies is to develop the school further by adding time, broadening specialities, allowing for more individual choice of curriculum components, and adding more general education.

All along, policy has assumed that the demand by youth for training must be accommodated to the industry's demand for skilled labour. The main device for coping with a short-term mismatch between these demands has been a broad vocational education whose boundaries with general education have become increasingly blurred. There are nagging doubts that this schooling may be "too slack" and too remote from real production to give adequate socialisation for the demands of the workplace, and for Swedish industry to be competitive with, for example, Germany and Japan."

J. Lauglo 1994 in The International Encyclopaedia of Education, 2nd ed., Volume 11

4.1 Towards common core subjects in vocational upper secondary education

In the autumn of 1992, the new three year upper secondary school was introduced in around 70 of Sweden's 280 municipalities. From 1996/97 the reform will be implemented all over the country. In total 16 national programmes replaced the previous 30 'lines' and numerous specialised courses. All national programmes confer general eligibility for further studies at post-secondary level.

At least 15% of the teaching hours in the new vocational programmes should be provided as workplace training and other forms of learning taking place at work. The goal of the vocational programmes is not to provide a complete set of skills and combination of subject knowledge needed in a specific vocation. Rather it aims at a more general or generic platform with good learning opportunities both at work and in further studies.

A recent follow up study by the National Agency for Education (1996) shows that almost 90% of pupils are satisfied with the new form of work-connected learning with respect to the utilisation of subject knowledge from the school. An even higher percentage is satisfied with the options of learning at the workplace. The problems in recruiting and administering options for workplace learning have, however, been more substantial due to local patterns of co-operation between school and business. Pupils are also very positive to the new options for choosing subjects and alternatives and also influencing their teaching and learning conditions.

Another field of policy interest is the motivational aspect concerning the extension of the vocational programmes as well as the increasing scope of general core curriculum subjects. There is some evidence, mostly of an anecdotal nature, indicating a drop-out trend for male students not feeling at home in a core-curriculum culture that is too strong. Thus, the creation of new teaching and learning methods in vocational programmes forms a crucial development field for the future.

Curriculum reform has been combined with the introduction of a new system of grades, built on the knowledge structure and hierarchical order of the subject in question. The new system of upper secondary education is to a large extent based on an individual choice of course models. In practice, these courses are spread out over a certain period that is not necessarily a term. This means that feedback from grades will occur when the course has been finalised. Also in this field, there is no evidence so far of the learning impact of this system.

To sum up the new three year vocational programmes with their broad focus on knowledge, will hopefully play a central role in the development of good continuing vocational training standards in Sweden. This is not a final step but the first or possibly the second step in a lifelong learning career, which is needed much more than before.

The new educational and societal context for upper secondary education leads to new qualification requirements for teachers in vocational programmes. A recent task force initiated by the former government has analysed the impact on teacher training in vocational upper secondary education of the reforms and trends and policies mentioned above.

Their survey comprises an overview of current teacher training in this field, international experiences and models and the expectations of tomorrow's upper secondary school in Sweden. After teacher training and a few years of teaching experience, the vocational teacher will receive a special certificate. Attention has also been paid to the didactics of vocational programmes as well as the learning impact of various work place connected educational initiatives.

4.2   Increasing vocational function of general adult education

Adult education in Sweden is widely distributed at regional and local levels. There are great regional variations as regards different types of adult education, study circles, municipal basic adult education and municipal upper secondary adult education. These are all available more or less in practically every municipality, whereas folk high schools, employment training and higher education courses involve travelling within the county.

Distance teaching is another educational alternative now being developed in Sweden. In addition to national distance teaching at upper secondary level, there are joint arrangements by universities and folk high schools, as well as Educational Broadcasting courses.

The new decentralised and market oriented context for Swedish adult education raises problems in defining the role of vocational orientation and/or function within adult education. Certain institutions in adult education are definitely providing vocational training in more traditional forms. Others are entering the field as a consequence of the unexpectedly high level of unemployment.

Municipal adult education and short courses at folk high schools have been reduced in volume since the end of the 1970s. Adult basic education, labour market education or employment training have been subject to a significant increase. Other forms of adult education have been rather stable. In-service training, paid and sometimes organised by the employer has declined due to the high level of unemployment.

In total, however, there was a new adult education boom during the fiscal year 1992/93. Labour market education and folk high schools show a strong increase, while in-service training is declining due to a higher level of unemployment. In 1995, however, the rate of in-service training participation rose to higher levels than before; in total 42% of the labour force participated in in-service training organised and paid for by the employer. With the exception of shorter folk high school courses, there are signs of a small expansion in all other fields.

Municipal adult education is one of the most important providers within general adult education. Komvux has existed since 1968. It offers adults education leading to formal qualifications in individual subjects or to the equivalent of a complete compulsory school or upper secondary school leaving certificate. Komvux thus includes vocational education, corresponding to the vocational programmes of upper secondary school, and in addition it includes certain vocational courses which are not available in the youth sector. Komvux is available in practically every municipality in Sweden, but the smaller municipalities offer only a very limited selection of courses.

Komvux confers knowledge and skills equivalent to those conferred by youth education. The volume of teaching can thus be reduced compared with youth education.

The subject-course system makes for great flexibility and gives students an extensive choice of subjects and subject combinations. Studies can be pursued on a full-time, part-time or leisure-time basis, students can take one or more subjects and they can pursue intensive studies in one subject or parallel studies of some. One impact of these teaching and learning conditions is that we can find a mixture of young students and adults in the same class or teaching group. This age mix has both risks and options.

The komvux studies lead to credential leaving certificates. To some extent there are no special admission requirements; students are admitted providing there are places available but must be considered as fulfilling the requirement needed for keeping up with the course.

Komvux forms one of the most important access channels for adults in Sweden. It has had a strong impact on the increasing participation of women in the work force during its two decades of operation. SCB, Statistics Sweden, has made an evaluation of the access role of komvux during a period of twelve years from the autumn of 1979 to the spring of 1991. This evaluation resulted in the following access pattern:

- More than a million Swedes, roughly one adult citizen out of five, had a komvux experience during this period.
- Vocationally oriented courses attracted many participants, almost half of the total group. The same interest was shown in courses at upper secondary level. Only 16% of the participants had enrolled at the level of the upper stage of the compulsory school. Over a longer period of time, however, there has been a substantial decrease in supplementary vocational education in the komvux system.

- More and more adults study on day-time courses, between 45-50%.
- Women have been in the majority for the whole period covering around 60% of the student places. The average age level is falling from somewhat above 30 years of age to 25, especially in the upper secondary theoretical programmes. Participants at compulsory education level or vocational programmes are somewhat older, just below 35 years of age on average.
- 150,000 participants (of a total of 1,147,000) or 13% continued to higher education after the komvux experience. Every third new applicant to higher education has received a komvux experience prior to higher studies. Two thirds enrolled on undergraduate degree programmes, while the rest applied for shorter courses or municipal higher education.

It is also obvious that komvux plays an important follow-up function for young students temporarily dropping out from upper secondary studies.

4.3   Generic skills in employment training?

The purpose of employment training is, by means of rapid and flexible educational influence, to adapt the qualifications of job seekers to actual labour demand. This training provides a form of support for persons at a disadvantage in the labour market, while at the same time making it easier for employment offices to fill vacancies. Employment training often takes the form of 'bottle-neck' training, i.e. training programmes for key areas where there is a shortage of skilled labour.

Some employment training takes the form of support given to employers for the training of employees. This also gives the Employment Service the opportunity of referring replacements for the person who is being retrained or in some other way obtaining a quid pro quo from the individual company for the training grant paid.

Specially organised employment training at AMU centres has been reorganised twice during the last decade. During 1986 to 1991 a special authority, the National Employment Training Board, was set up to take charge of this. AMLT was conducted on a commercial basis; training is purchased and sold, mainly to the labour market authorities. The new Board comprised a central directorate and 24 county employment training commissions, which in turn are responsible for around 100 local training centres.

The next development step was taken July 1 1993, when AMU became a state-owned enterprise on the competence market, thereby providing an interesting example of the ongoing market orientation of Swedish adult education.

The overall aim is to make it easier for unemployed persons to get back to work, to assist adults in acquiring new professions and also to generate the skills required by the employer. Major target groups are:
– Immigrants
– Returnees to the labour market after some years of absence (forced or voluntary)
– Jobless people due to closure of workplace or reduction of employees
– People forced to change occupations due to illness or injury

The dramatic changes in the Swedish economy call for increased attention to the choice between competence strategies in different time perspectives. One of the current problems is that there is a growing mixture between short-term, not very acute or emergency oriented strategies on the one hand and very long-term strategies on the other hand.

The policy context involves two different developments or trends. The first problem concerns the dramatic shift on the labour market and growing unemployment levels. The more urgent challenge is who should get access to employment training and labour market education.

Unemployment has risen to 8.4% of the work force which is placing the employment training institutions and the competence market as such under extreme pressure. In spite of steadily increasing resources through the labour market policy budget, the relative chance for each new unemployed adult of getting retraining or employment courses is decreasing.

A new focus on traditional labour market education (AMU) is due to the need for more theoretical upgrading and less vocationally specific knowledge and skills. Providers apart from 'AMU centres' have taken almost 60% of the 'AMU market', a few years ago customised training sold by the formal adult education system tended to be a successful competitor to the Employment Training Group/AMU-gruppen, but today other private providers in the form of independent training enterprises have significantly increased their market share.

Youth employment programmes today account for a major part of the resources used for educational initiatives by the National Labour Market Board. Traditional labour market education is now in second place.

Also the so-called 'employment development programmes' - a kind of work-study programme for unemployed adults and used as a preparatory step towards employment later on - are increasing.

The training or retraining for a 'job-waiting' situation or a temporary non-job situation is more a dilemma than a new educational challenge ('working life development programmes'). Such programmes vary from introductory courses in large enterprises such as Volvo to new priorities directed towards the need to get, displace, or outplace big groups of employees. Paradoxically, some enterprises invest more money in competence upgrading for 'leavers' than for 'stayers'.

Finally, the increasing use of customised adult education and the growing market for different providers has resulted in a quite new mixture of employment training. The share of labour market education provided by the AMU Team has decreased significantly and is now less than half of what it used to be when AMU was part of the Swedish National Board of Education.

Thus, the increasing market-orientation of employment training has also led to a structural transformation and a rationalisation of the AMU centres and their provision of vocational programmes and courses. In addition, it should be mentioned that there is an ongoing shift in priorities for access to labour market education or employment training. Employment training is now provided for the better educated part of the labour market, while the undereducated person will have access to fewer learning options.

4.4   New vocationalism in higher education

It is a question of definition whether the system of higher education should be included in models of vocationalism. Generally, academic degrees are necessary requirements for the certification of certain professions. Further education options for academics in various working life sectors might be labelled continuing professional education or continuing higher education.

If we exclude degree programmes at undergraduate level and research training components in the system of higher education, examples of vocational profiles could be picked from the wide provision of shorter courses used for occupational upgrading. Other examples are shorter vocational programmes for technicians (YTH, yrkesteknisk högskoleutbildning).

The former government decided to initiate a task force with the goal of developing a new system of advanced vocational education at higher education level. The background to this initiative was also in comparative terms the low level of transition to higher education from upper secondary level. The policy to be implemented was to expand the annual level of higher education transition from 30,000 students per year to 50,000 per year, an extraordinarily high political ambition, so far only manifested through small experimental schemes for vocational schools at higher education level.

The launching of the 25:5 scheme or later on 25:4 scheme in the early 1970's is another interesting example of the bridging the gap between education and work metaphor (Abrahamsson,1986). The Swedish model for recognition of prior work experience as an admission merit to higher education was one of many tools used to broaden the social recruitment to higher education. It was also an effort to up-grade the value of prior experience from work or life in general. The label of relevant work experience was not used in this context. Rather it was seen as a special asset for higher studies to accumulate life and work experience prior to the higher education experience. Today, the role of prior work experience has lost much of its value and more attention is given to a general study aptitude test (Högskoleprovet).

4.5   Corporate classrooms and in-service training

Statistics Sweden has assessed the provision of in-service training since 1986 and there has been an almost permanent increase in the average number of the workforce taking part in in-service training from 23% in 1986 to 42% in 1995. This trend was interrupted, falling in 1993 to only 23% due to unemployment and more defensive competence strategies among employers.

In-service training or personnel training is unevenly distributed. Senior executives received twice as much education and training as manual workers. These differences are greater if the duration of educational training is also taken into account.

The number of persons taking part in personnel training is greater in the public sector than in the private sector. Personnel training is more widespread in service enterprises and authorities than in industry. Policies from the national labour market board to expand corporate education or employment training within enterprises have not been successful.

In fact, the national labour market board could not spend the SEK 2.5 billion it got from the former government for 'in-house' employment training in the private sector. Especially within small and medium-size enterprises, the difficulties of creating a new learning climate have met a number of obstacles. The funds were then partly used to support employment in municipalities and county councils.

4.6   New competence contracts on the Swedish training market

Sweden has a large number of education enterprises. A number of these offer not only education but also consultancy and information technology services. There are also educational institutes providing education for manual workers. Education companies too are very much concerned with the training of senior executives.

Education companies, however, account for a relatively small share of the total volume of educational activities. Various surveys have indicated that only 15-20 per cent of this volume is provided by outside educational organisations.

A survey initiated by the commission for the privatisation of the National Employment Training Agency estimated that around 80% of corporate training or in-service programmes were organised by external education enterprises. AMU and komvux each had about 0.7% of this market, while study associations and institutions of higher education had more than 2% each of the same market. The total annual cost for employers was estimated at SEK 100 billion, if costs of 'lost production' and replacement needs were also included on top of the educational costs.

The AMU commission had also made an effort to describe different development trends or stages in corporate training. The first stage comprises a situation with a centrally located staff-development unit separated from the strategic development of the corporate business idea. The participants are mainly white-collar workers and management staff at higher levels. Employees are 'sent to courses' and the education budget is seen more as a corporate expenditure than a strategic investment for the future.

The second stage is a more decentralised model of in-service training giving the main responsibilities to local executives or to foremen working in close co-operation with the employees on the 'floor'. This model increases the utilisation of in-service training as a measure for increasing productivity but lacks the strategic frontiers.

Finally, the third model divides central and strategic responsibility on the one hand and local, production oriented training on the other. Education and corporate development are integrated and the aim is to mix management staff with white and blue-collar workers in order to support the corporate business idea. Most corporations are operating at the first or second stage and regard the adult training budget more as a cost than an investment. Increasingly, they are moving towards the third stage.

The corporate culture and the model used to organise in-service training are major access determinants. A centrally located education unit tends to favour the top level in the corporation as well as staff in service and management positions, leaving few learning opportunities to workers on the floor. Swedish experience in this field tells us, however, that the trade unions can be very efficient in recruiting members to new learning options as well as taking part in surveys of learning needs at the workplace.

4.7 Learning organisations and on the job training

There have been a number of public task forces in Sweden indicating the need for a renewal of the learning climate at work (e.g. commission on productivity and commission on competence development). It is more and more obvious that "the efficiency and effectiveness of organisations are dependent on the skills, initiative and commitment of the work force and their continual development".

This quote originates from the report 'Learning at work', from the Swedish Work Environment Fund, SWEF, abolished in July 1995, which gives a theoretical review of the concept of learning organisations as well as numerous examples of practical applications of new learning ideas in various corporations both in the public and private sector.

There are many definitions of learning organisations. According to one of the dominant contributors in this field (Senge, 1990) learning organisations have a process that can be described in the following way (SWEF 1994; page 8):

"The learning organisation is one that is continually expanding its capacity to create its own future to create the results they truly desire, where new and expansive patterns of thinking are nurtured, where collective aspiration is set free, and where people are continually learning how to learn together."

The SWEF's programme on learning organisations has focused on five different learning issues:
- core competencies;
- practical knowledge;
- continuous business development;
- functional and cultural integration;
- managing and motivating learning and competence development.

The processes and methods used vary from company to company. The programme mentioned comprises around 35 case studies from industry, commerce and the public sector in operation from 1989 to 1995.

One of the most well known examples in Sweden is the ABB T-50 project, which aims at a total reorganisation of the production system in order to reduce production time by 50%. The success of this project is to a large extent dependent on a new perspective on the work organisation, and multi-skill requirements of employees within the context of lower production.

It has to be remembered, however, that many Swedish frontier projects relating to learning organisations result from the structural transformation of the enterprise with a great reduction in the number of employees, especially older groups with low education and a non-Swedish background. Thus, it is not infrequently the case that there is a social price - or a social deficit - for organisational transformation aiming at increasing efficiency and effectiveness.

"This White Paper contends that it is by building up the learning society of Europe as quickly as possible, that this objective can be attained. This move entails radical change. All too often education and training systems map out career paths on a once-and-for-all basis. There is too much inflexibility, too much compartmentalisation of education and training systems and not enough bridges, or enough possibilities to let in new patterns of lifelong learning.

The aim is much more modest, namely to help, in conjunction with education and training policies of the Member States, to put Europe on the road to the learning society. They are also intended to pave the debate for a broader debate in the years ahead. Lastly, they can help to show that the future of Europe and its place in the world depends on its ability to give as much room for personal fulfilment of its citizens, men and women alike, as it has up to now given to economic and monetary issues. It is in this way that Europe will prove that it is not simply a free trade area, but organised political entity, and a way of coming successfully to terms with, rather than being subject to, internationalisation."

4.8   Vocationalism and the hidden contracts of the learning society

The overview of policy developments in Sweden illuminates the difficulties of defining the future internal and external context of vocationalism. There is a strong need to clarify the role of continuing vocational training in a more diversified provision of post-compulsory learning options in Sweden. The traditional borders between general adult education and vocational training or between youth education and adult education are no longer useful.

It becomes increasingly difficult to design a continuing learning project aimed at a certain vocation. Increasingly policy makers underline the importance of general education and generic competencies. In practice, this leads to more policy attention to broad programmes instead of early specialisation e.g. an apprenticeship model adapted to a certain vocation.

Customised education and training has stimulated different actors and providers to collaborate in a way that was not possible four or five years ago. In order to analyse the role of continuing vocational training in Sweden it is also necessary to consider the impact of the policies of independent schools and school-voucher models. New independent schools are not only starting at compulsory level, but also in the field of upper secondary education.

There is a risk that some of the new privatised vocational schools based on just one or two programmes may not be competitive with respect to quality, professional development and efficient resource allocation. Thus a stronger vocational or occupational profile may support vocational training for a specific occupation, but might have a negative impact on the continuing learning process needed in a pattern of recurrent education or lifelong learning.

In addition to the important task of producing relevant and critical overviews of the system of vocationalism in various countries, there is growing importance for a policy discussion and analysis of the objectives, values, functions and organisational patterns of vocational training in a learning society. There is also a need to illuminate and clarify the hidden contracts in this part of the education system. One part of this contract is the agreement between public interest and the market on who is paying for various learning experiences that are provided in a system of vocational education and training. This is of particular interest with regard to the need for upgrading the competence of the present work force, but also for various aspects of school-to-work transition patterns for youth.

Educational leave of absence and various forms of study assistance are crucial support systems for those who need external vocational education. A learning oriented work environment is one of the cornerstones on which to build efficient patterns of vocational education in a lifelong perspective. Last but not least, there is the responsibility and the commitment of the individual employee to keep his or her learning tools and study motivation in good shape.

The quality of initial education or compensatory programmes for adults with a lack of education are the best guarantee of the individual's commitment to lifelong learning. Thus, the learning interest and study motivation needed for such a task could also be provided outside the system of vocational education, in Sweden the Folk High school is a good example. The mixed pattern of learning goals and provision of good educational programmes signifies a learning society.

4.9 Voucher models and the need for continuous competence development

The creation of new incentives for lifelong learning has, in fact, been a significant political issue widely debated through the initiatives of the former government and its strategic project Agenda 2000 with its strong focus on the educational standing of Sweden in a comparative sense. The expansion paradigm launched by the former government comprised the following priorities:

– more investments in degree programmes at undergraduate level at the expense of shorter courses
– the creation of a new type of post-secondary education with a theoretical and vocational profile
– the implementation of a new right for all adults to study core subjects at upper secondary level

- significant expansion of post-graduate training and research capacity
- new forms of continuous competence development

One of the major ideas proposed, was that a system of continuous competence development implies a fundamental shift in the system of public administration as well as the structure of labour laws and regulations, tax regulations and income policies. The agenda project pointed out the need for a new attention to the link between learning and earning. The major obstacle to competence development was not, in its view, social barriers but the weak incentive system and low aggregate individual rate of return for any kind of longer adult study project.

Thus, one of the most controversial aspects of the agenda concept tended to be its focus on the risk of an overprotecting society not stimulating the individual's own learning spirit. Another hot political issue in the agenda project was the emphasis on increasing income differences between various vocational and professional groups with respect to their own investment in education, or 'life income/life education years'.

This perspective was to a large extent perceived as an attack on the Swedish model of social security and welfare by the then active social democratic opposition, which stressed the need for social and economic support in order to reduce social barriers and increase the educational transition from one level to the next. This constitutes an alternative view of the former government, which received strong empirical support from a governmental task force on social barriers to higher education. From a post-conflict perspective, it seems that both perspectives are important and useful.

The social and economic benefits of any adult learning project, especially if it involves individual economic investments as a prerequisite, is a major motivational factor. No adult student voluntarily embarks on a highly demanding learning project if it would imply a permanent reduction in earnings and standards of living in comparison with people who are either working or unemployed.

On the other hand, it seems likely that a drastic and total abolition of all social and financial support systems would at best, however, be beneficial to the 20 or 30% of the most advanced and affluent adult learners, while the great majority, especially workers with short formal education would not take the chance - or risk - of an uncertain learning project. In conclusion, it is necessary to discuss various individual or collective arrangements in order to create long-term financial support for continuous vocational training and competence development.

5.   CHALLENGES AND FUTURE ROUTES OF EUROPE AS A LEARNING COMMUNITY

Swedish membership of the European Community is a bridge to a mutual understanding and exchange of experience in the field of education. Sweden has long experience of both educational policies as well as labour market policies with respect to the concept of full employment. The White Papers on 'Growth, Competitiveness Employment. The Challenges and ways forward into the 21st century' and 'Teaching and learning: Towards the learning society' underline the crucial role of the education system and the need for recurrent vocational training and lifelong education. Education and training are, as has been mentioned previously, dimensions that colour a number of EU initiatives including the following:

– paragraph 126 and 127 in the Maastricht Treaty with their focus on schools and universities on the one hand and vocational education and training on the other;
– the SOCRATES and LEONARDO programmes as educational responses to the above mentioned paragraphs;
– the educational and training component of the structural funds and in particular the Social Fund and its Objective 3 stressing the need for education and training for long-term unemployed, especially youth, immigrants and adults with functional impairments and Objective 4 underlining the need to give educational protection and competence development for risk groups at the workplace;
– the EMPLOYMENT and ADAPT programmes created to support the implementation of Objective 3 and 4 in the Social Fund;
– the focus on education and training and social exclusion in the targeted socio-economic research sub-programme within the Fourth Framework Programme launched by the European Commission.

The synergetic impact of these investments in the European learning society creates a new challenge to the educational landscape of Sweden. Continuing vocational training (CVT) plays a frontier role in this respect and also as a system for recurrent and lifelong learning.

The 'educational business idea' of the White Papers seems to have been stimulated by the German dual system of promoting direct access to vocational experience, apprenticeship and workplace learning. The Swedish response to the rapid and fundamental structural transformation of the labour market has taken another route by promoting general education and core curriculum models to avoid too narrow a definition of the vocational knowledge and skills needed.

A new balance between vocational education and general education is needed. One of the lessons of employment training in Sweden the last few years is that the needs-structure is increasingly oriented towards general educational upgrading in the core subjects of Swedish, English, mathematics and civics as well as computer literacy. In a long-term perspective, and also with the objective of combating social exclusion, it might be necessary to give all young individuals not only formal access to a general upper secondary curriculum but also corresponding knowledge and skills.

Independent of what alternatives are preferred - a further development of the dual system or a general educational elevation of the whole young generation - it is quite evident that the quality and content of initial education has major repercussions for both continuing vocational training as well as a system of recurrent or lifelong education. In the long run, a dysfunctional system of initial education cannot be the major production system for adult and continuing vocational training for new priority groups.

The educational impact of an individual embarking on new learning is, of course, directly dependent on the quality and retention of prior learning, life and work experience not excluded. International competition and growing skill requirements at the workplace as well as the need to combat unemployment, call for joint actions and new deals between the public educational system, employer sponsored programmes and education investments as well as the individual's own commitment to learning and change.

6.   FUTURE CHALLENGES

The conclusions of this paper are that there a number of future challenges regarding the societal context of vocationalism and general education and also its objectives, institutional patterns and working forms in the context of lifelong learning :
-   How can we strengthen the school-work connection in order to better combat unemployment, in particular long-term unemployment?
-   What is the role of vocationalism in adapting to and anticipating the transformation of technology at the workplace (ADAPT challenge)?
-   How should the supply of vocational education be adjusted to demographic trends & new demands?
-   How can new incentives for learning and development at corporate level be created, especially in SME's?
-   What role will vocational upgrading play in the renewal of work organisation and production systems focusing on quality and output

indicators? And what are the options of a lean organisation in accommodating trainees and creating links between school and work?
- How can synergetic interfaces between various actions of learning be strengthened in a lifelong perspective?
- Which systems should be developed for financing systems of vocational training and lifelong education as well as systems and rights to leave of absence?
- How can we create learning incentives that not only promote "stay-where-you are patterns" but support increasing mobility on internal, external and international labour markets
- And finally, will this lead to a new balance between vocationalism and generalism in a lifelong learning society?

REFERENCES

Abrahamsson, K. (1996), *Time Policies for Lifelong Learning. International Encyclopedia of Adult Education and Training*, Pergamon Press.

Abrahamsson, K. and Henriksson, K. (1991), "The European Skill Gap, Introductory comments" in *New challenges in education and training of the European work force. Final report: Reports 91:2*, Swedish National Board of Education.

Achtenhagen, F., Nihoj,W. and Raffe, D. (1995), *Feasibility study: Research scope for vocational education in the framework of COST social sciences*, European Commission, Directorate-General Science, Research and Development, Brussels.

Lauglo, J. (1994), "Vocational Training Modes: Sweden, Germany, and Japan", in *The International Encyclopedia of Education*, Second Edition, Volume 11, pp. 6690-6699.

OECD (1973), *Recurrent education: A strategy for lifelong learning*, OECD - CERI.

OECD (1995), *Education at a glance*, Paris.

OECD (1995), *Literacy, Economy and Society*, Paris.

Rubenson, K. (1992), *25 years of Recurrent Adult education Policy in Sweden*, Swedish Ministry of Education and science.

Skilbeck, M., Connell, H., Lowe, N. and Tait, K. (1994), *The vocational Quest. New Directions in Education and Training*, Routledge, London and New York.

Statistics Sweden (1995), *Utbildningsstatistisk årsbok 1995. Annual Statistical Yearbook 1995*, Stockholm.

Statistics Sweden (1995), *Personalutbildning 1994 och 1995. In-service training 1994 and 1995*, Stockholm.

SÖU (1996), *Aktiv marknadspolitik. Active Labour Market Policies*, Stockholm.

Swedish National Board for Industrial and Technical Development (1996), *Towards Flexible Organisations*, Stockholm.

Swedish Ministry of Education and Science (1992), *The Swedish Way Towards a Learning Society*, Stockholm.

Swedish Work Environment Fund (1994), *Learning at work*, Stockholm.

White Paper on Growth, Competitiveness, Employment Challenges and Ways forward into the 21st Century, Brussels.

White Paper on Education and Training. Teaching and Learning: Towards the Learning Society, Brussels

Chapter 19

Forming an Educational Policy that meets Practical Needs
The Case of Greek Auto Mechanics

Nikitas Patiniotis, and Dimitris Stavroulakis
University of Patras, Greece

1. SOCIAL CONTEXT

Greek business is comprised of a vast public sector, co-existing with numerous small family enterprises (Patiniotis, 1993; 1996). Traditionally, the state has been oriented towards exercising a most influential role, by intervening into collective bargaining between employers' associations and union federations, as well as by becoming engaged in business activities normally undertaken by the private sector, through the acquisition of hotel chains, textile industries, shipyards etc. Nevertheless, despite its enormous size, the public sector does not seem capable of effectively regulating the economic environment, neither in terms of setting forth appropriate institutional frameworks, nor of imposing the law concerning tax evasion. Therefore, in spite of its tenacious presence in all aspects of economic life, the state is characterised by 'weak management'. Among other repercussions, the compliance of the Greek public administration to pressures seems to incite the submission of numerous economic and institutional claims on the part of the various social groups. The latter have come to believe that it is solely the state's obligation to provide solutions for sectoral and social problems, they themselves not feeling bound at all to make their own contribution.

On the other hand, Greek society seems to lack the exchange mechanisms established long ago in the consolidated industrialised countries of western Europe (Gesellschaften). In this respect, it still functions as if comprised of small communities (Gemeinschaften), individuals and groups often approaching their problems through emotional outbursts and ceremonial exhortations instead of rational planning and goal-setting. Following this trend, many groups representing local and sectoral interests have lost all sense of proportion, tending to adopt irresponsible tactics, such as road blocking, for the promotion of their narrow, *guild interests*[1]. In this sense they are inclined to uncritically harm other groups' interests as well, a fact resulting in an intense conflict between the affected social strata (teachers on strike against pupils' parents, sailors on strike against farmers, farmers on strike against truck-drivers etc), most likely to undermine societal cohesion. The disproportion between the relative unimportance of a claim and the severity of the selected means for its satisfaction is remarkable; for example, clerks of a ministry claiming a petty allowance may block a central avenue for hours, causing paralysis to the already congested traffic of Athens. Juridical decisions designating such excessive protests as harmful to the citizens' interests are almost never implemented, because the government seems reluctant to shoulder the political cost (Tzannetakos, 1984).

Such practices are usually encountered in the public sector, where employees have secured permanent employment, therefore they are not in danger of losing their job in case of retaliation on the part of their employers. Nevertheless, certain private employees and free professionals also have occasionally become particularly vigorous in pressing the state for the satisfaction of their institutional and financial claims; among others, taxi-drivers have sought to bar the entrance of prospective newcomers to their profession, farmers have demanded additional subsidies for their crops, construction workers have demanded the expulsion of their foreign colleagues.

In this context, the case of Greek auto mechanics is unique in following orthodox strategies in order to improve their situation. As will be demonstrated in the following section, auto mechanics have developed a 'European consciousness', by responding to the crisis with training, instead of resorting to the more or less futile protests of other suffering

---

[1]   The term "guild interests", or "guildism", was first introduced within the Greek context at the beginning of the 1980s, denoting the acquisition of excessive privileges by the employees of the public utility monopolies (banks, telecommunications, air transports etc). These privileges consisted of a very slack work pace, as well as in financial rewards much higher than those granted to other public employees with similar qualifications. In order to achieve their goals, the respective powerful unions exploited the strategic importance of their corporations for the national economy and the social welfare, by proceeding to lengthy, and particularly violent strikes, often involving the threat of sabotages. Later on, the concept of "guildism" expanded to the private sector, indicating wildcat strikes and citizens' action involving analogous violent means as negotiation weapons.

professionals. An important aspect of this process concerns their quest for help directly from EU through their participation in training programmes, instead of addressing their demands to the responsible local institutions. This toilsome task was conceived and developed by the Association of Small Auto-Repairing Shop Proprietors (SISEMA), with the collaboration of a small private consulting agency, but without any support from the responsible public authorities.

2.   AUTO MECHANICS IN GREECE: PERSPECTIVES AT THE SECTORAL LEVEL

Within the Greek context, a car serves fundamental practical needs, as it is the most commonly used means of transport; its practical importance is enhanced by the poor public transport networks in the big cities. On the other hand, as elsewhere, a car is also a major status symbol, reflecting income differences between social strata. The fact that Greece is not an automobile producing country, however, has rendered cars very expensive for the average citizen, because of the heavy taxation combined with the low incomes (compared to EU standards). Consequently, owners in general are reluctant to replace their cars, and tend to use them longer than the average European (Patiniotis *et al,* 1996). A massive car renewal program involving subsidised withdrawal had been carried out during 1991-1992, but cars in Greece are still likely to be older than in West European countries.

Under these circumstances, the occupation of auto-repairers seemingly might appear a profitable vocational outlet for Greek youths. Nevertheless, the concurrence of various factors seems to negate this first impression; actually, auto mechanics are confronted with cumbersome problems, as will be demonstrated in the following section. Specifically, these problems have to do with the structural particularities of the Greek environment, such as employment patterns and auto-repair personnel, as well as with the trends at European level, such as new legislation, the prospects of the automobile industry, and, last but not least, the impact of technical innovation. This last aspect constitutes the focus of our research, therefore it deserves to be examined in more detail.

2.1   Employment Patterns

The auto-repair market is extremely segmented, the predominant form of business being the small maintenance shop; about 2,100 garages employing less than five persons are estimated to operate in the Athens area. Working conditions are generally of poor quality, salaries may be very low, and work time is determined by the workload. Employers are usually of low educational level, having started their career as apprentices. The market is characterised by constant restructuring because of the continuing entrance of fully equipped authorised repair agencies over recent years. Nevertheless, these are considered very expensive for the average consumer, therefore they have not managed to acquire so far the market share they really deserve.

2.2   Auto-Repair Personnel.

In the past years auto maintenance had been considered as a most promising vocational outlet by the responsible authorities, a fact resulting in the creation of numerous schools all over Greece. As in other occupations (the most striking example being tourism), however, this endeavour was not accompanied by market research. Consequently, hosts of young auto mechanics keep on entering the market, despite the gloomy trends. Auto-repair studies are formally provided at higher second-level education, at post-secondary education, as well as at tertiary, non-university technical education. Although graduates tend to have a satisfactory education background, they possess mainly general knowledge, therefore being considered rather useless by the small employers, desperately searching for experienced employees, specialised in the latest cars and models.

2.3   Legal Implications

The EU-subsidised car renewal programme completed in 1992 resulted in a significant drop in work for auto-repairers. Another major threat to them concerns the EU guideline about the impending replacement of super petrol by unleaded. According to rough estimates, about half the employment in the Greek auto-maintenance sector will be eliminated because of the forthcoming massive wave of car renewals.

2.4   Prospects of the Automobile Industry

Data indicates that the volume of automobile production is past its zenith. Although sales in Europe did increase in 1996 compared to 1995, profit margins dropped significantly due to the intense competition leading to price-cuts. Forecasts for 1997 suggest stabilisation of the market in terms of sales, the most gloomy overview concerning French companies, expecting a 9.5 percent squeeze in sales (Financial Times, Quarterly Review of the

Automotive Industry, 6.3.1997). This has been underlined by the recent dramatic closure of the Renault factory in Belgium. The insecurity prevailing in the automobile sector is likely to affect all specialisations depending on it directly or indirectly, including auto mechanics. Following this trend, youths are often admonished to refrain from entering the auto-repair sector (Sellin, 1995).

3. VOCATIONAL EDUCATION AS A RESPONSE TO TECHNICAL INNOVATION

Innovations in automobile technology have entailed significant changes in the skills of auto repairers. By the term "skill" we mean both the physical and mental competences necessary for the conception and the execution of a task, being measured along the dimensions of substantive complexity (level, scope, and mode of integration of manual and mental sub-tasks within the job), and autonomy-control (Spenner, 1990). The temporary character of skills is emphasised, since they seem to depend both upon work features and the social environment (Attwell, 1996). Following this trend, the skills of auto mechanics have been substantially altered over time. Originally a long apprenticeship allowed the acquisition of skills through experience and practice. However, new technology has reduced their importance, emphasising more the operation of modern electronic equipment. New skills based more on diagnosis than repair have resulted from changes in technology (Smith, 1991). Along with other craftsmen, auto mechanics have become detached from the object of their job, this distance being both physical and mental. Concerning the physical distance, normally there is little need any more for repairers to dirty their hands, because eventually their job requires the replacement instead of repair of defective integrated parts. Concerning the mental distance, auto mechanics pay attention to the readings of electronic devices, instead of inspecting the car in terms of hearing and sensing.

Changes in repair skills have caused intense anguish among Greek small employers, feeling incapable of following these rapid developments. Modern diagnostic equipment (being imported) is very expensive, and furthermore presupposes continuous support in terms of maintenance service facilities, and most of all, training. Despite these difficulties, being aggravated by the low educational level and technophobia of many garage owners, SISEMA decided to develop a concrete training strategy, thus getting to the root of the problem.

SISEMA have established an educational foundation in order to promote its training activities. A building was bought with the contributions of members, and laboratories have been developed. Training expenses are mostly covered by EU programmes (LEONARDO and FORCE), but trainees often have to pay a contribution. Proposals to the EU administration have been formulated with the help of a private consulting company (Athenians Business Consultants). A strong interest in attending training programmes is evident among professionals of all ages and educational levels, in-class participation being very active. No permanent syllabus has been established yet, the programme being molded according to learners' needs. Although learners many times insist on being taught purely practical courses, the foundation's policy emphasizes the theoretical fundamentals, especially for older and the less educated participants. On the other hand, practical aspects are also covered in detail, concerning the particularities of the latest car makes and models.

The programme is considered successful, since a lot of learners have regained their self-confidence and have acquired considerable knowledge, permitting them to stand up to the competition. Possibly the biggest problem of this endeavour, however, concerns the difficulty in obtaining updated information and training material. Once again, the fact that Greece is not a car producer constitutes a major drawback for the renewal of training programmes. The foundations' officials are occasionally obliged to go to Germany and to Italy in order to fetch the latest technical information. They are dependent on the goodwill of car manufacturers since local authorised repair agencies with the relevant data are not very helpful due to competition.

4.   CONCLUDING DISCUSSION

Although the fatalistic Greek culture tends to dissuade professionals from solving their problems through orthodox voluntary action, auto mechanics have followed this path quite successfully. We identified two main reasons for the shift of auto mechanics in this direction.

The first is technology. Auto maintenance is a technology intensive vocation, necessitating constant contact with the latest developments. This is an one-way process, since the companies that lag behind in this race run the risk of eventually losing their customers. On the other hand, although from the outset there was marked resistance to training, especially from the older repairers, this resistance proved to be surmountable. In this respect, auto mechanics have been somehow fortunate in terms of being trained in their own specialisation. Indeed, practice has shown that professionals compelled by circumstances to be retrained to a new specialisation are likely to suffer from anxiety, fear of the future, as well as from adaptation problems.

The second is the market structure. The interests of auto-repair employers vary due to their differences in size, equipment, experience, and know-how. Therefore, it is impossible for them to initiate together a common campaign. The auto maintenance market is a highly competitive one, where ultimately the fittest will survive. In this sense, high-technology based and large authorised firms would rejoice at the eventuality of a strike of the small shops, resulting in the immediate loss of the latters' regular customers, a fact well understood by all organized interests. Consequently, small garage owners were compelled to overcome their hesitations pertaining to culture and to embrace training as the unique remedy to their case.

Another important feature of the training policy of auto mechanics is that the outset they applied for subsidies from the EU, without addressing the responsible authorities in Greece (Ministry of Education, Ministry of Labour). The reasons for this most unusual approach (according to the Greek customary practice) seem to be associated with lack of trust in the competence of the state authorities. Firstly, the bureaucratic state procedures would delay significantly the implementation of this urgent training plan, according to SISEMA officials. Secondly, auto mechanics insisted on selecting their trainers themselves, through their own criteria. The results in terms of effectiveness of their training policy seem to justify auto mechanics' choices so far.

REFERENCES

Attwell, G. (1996), "Occupational Competence for Vocational Education and Training Professionals. Profiles, Taxonomies, Content", paper presented at Leonardo Project Workshop, Hydra, Greece, April 25-27.

Financial Times Quarterly Review of the Automotive Industry, 6.3.1997.

Patiniotis, N., (1993), *Dependence and Immigration: The Case of Greece*, EKKE Publications, Athens (in Greek).

Patiniotis, N. (1996), "Education and Labour Market in Greece", Paper presented at the Leonardo Project Workshop, Bremen, January 28-30.

Patiniotis, N., Stavroulakis, D. and Spiliopoulou, K., (1996), "VET Instructors and Trainers in Greece", Paper presented at the Leonardo Project Workshop, Evora, Portugal, 16-18 October, 1996.

Sellin, B., (1995), *Situations and Trends: Supply and Demand for Skilled Workers*, CEDEFOP, Berlin.

Smith, A. E. (1991), "New Technology and the Non-Manual Labour Process in Britain", *Relations Industrielles,* Vol. 46 No. 2, pp. 306-328.

Spenner, K.I, (1990), "Skill: Meanings, Methods, and Measures", *Work and Occupations*, Vol. 17 No. 4, pp. 399-421.

Tzannetakos, V. (1984), "Strikes and 'Guild Elitism'", Vima, Weekly, 18.3.1984 (in Greek).

RETURNS AND OUTCOMES OF VOCATIONAL AND ADULT EDUCATION

Chapter 20

Introduction to Section 4
Returns and outcomes of vocational and adult education

Fons van Wieringen
University of Amsterdam

Both the educational scientist and the economist are interested in the outcomes of the vocational and adult education system. Education theory centres on school effectiveness and seeks the factors which explain the effectiveness of schools. Effectiveness can be measured in terms of learning outcomes but also in terms of employment and earning capacity. This is where the economist comes into the picture: he or she is also interested in effects as seen in terms of returns from investment in education. Access to training is not the same for everyone. Some workers are offered more opportunities for investment in training than others. As investment in human capital (e.g. training) creates inequality between workers, these differences in training participation increase social inequality (wage inequality, employment opportunities, etc.). It seems that on-the-job training is becoming an increasingly more important source of human capital investment.

Human capital theory makes a distinction between *general* and *specific* human capital. General human capital comprises skills which can be made productive in all firms; specific human capital relates to training which can only be made productive at one specific firm.

The increased attention to training by firms, unions and policy makers has been associated with an increase in workers' participation in training.

Groot surveys the results of some recent studies on training. Does participation in training differ between groups of workers? Is participation in training determined by individual characteristics or job characteristics - or both? What are the returns from training for firms and for individual workers?

The value of the training investment is usually mainly observable to the participant him or herself - to the worker and his or her current employer -

and not to any other employer. The National Vocational Qualifications (NVQ) in the United Kingdom serve to certify and standardise training investment. This form of certification may decrease uncertainty among employers about the value of the training. It may, on the other hand, increase poaching, as information about the quality of training the worker has taken becomes more widely available.

What factors are associated with participation in continuing training? Which activities influence an employed adult's decision to participate in these activities? Evaluating, characterising and understanding active adults' behaviour in relation to continuing training activities will make an important contribution to the design and setting up of adequate, effective and efficient continuing qualification programmes. Continuing qualification of the human resources constitutes a *sine qua non* condition for increasing business effectiveness - which is essential for economic progress.

Participation in continuing vocational education and training activities constitutes the most effective strategy to both increase and maintain workers' employability (employment/self-employment) and keep human resources permanently qualified in order to respond to external changes. Over the last two decades, given the introduction of new technologies and increased business competition, rapid changes have been occurring in the organisation of production and the structure of employment and unemployment.

Analysing and understanding, as Figuira does, the nature of the factors and the relationships associated with active adults' participation in training activities constitutes an important basis for formulating adequate and effective policies and strategies for the different socio-professional groups. Knowledge and understanding of the participation phenomenon in training activities allows the stronger and more adequate setting up and implementation of strategies aimed at sensitising the active population in general and the socio-professional groups in particular to the importance of their continuing and systematic participation in learning activities. Participation results from the interaction between external context, social background, personality, attitudinal dispositions, retained information and situational aspects.

Participation in educational programmes or in learning on the job can have several effects. Many factors influence the training and its consequences. The question is, which of the impacts - and to what extent - are really due to the training. The effectiveness of training or education may have a narrow or a broad definition. From a narrow point of view, the operationalisation of the effectiveness is based only on some quantitative measures, e.g. labour market training has only employment or income effects. From a broader viewpoint, there are many short-term and long-term goals and functions of many stakeholders in or parties to the training that one has to take into consideration and whose realisation one has to evaluate. These goals may from the participant's point of view be for example occupational development or the reorganisation of their lives in general. Participants may also have some special, individual goals when they start labour market training. Mikkonen tries to look at the effectiveness of labour market training from the participant's point of view as broadly as possible within the empirical data. He defines effectiveness on the basis of how training has promoted on an individual level the attainment of both individual and administrative goals set for it.

Occupation, occupational commitment or flexibility and occupational transitions are also of great interest from the viewpoint of this study. Calls for flexibility, changes towards multi-skilling in the working life and demands for new, non-vocational qualifications have created the need for a new kind of occupational orientation. A strict commitment to only one occupation is no longer necessarily desirable, and adult education may offer a way to broaden an individual's occupational orientation.

In the Finnish case, labour market training has, on average, increased employment by some 5 percent and correspondingly reduced unemployment by some 6 percent. According to the findings of the present study, there are no grounds for excluding the ageing and the aged from labour market training, because compared to control group members of the same age group, the labour market status of participants aged 45 and above has developed in a more positive direction. The results concerning the long-term unemployed are similarly encouraging: those who have taken part in labour market training are less likely to remain unemployed than those who did not participate.Many people entering vocational basic training and retraining aim to broaden their field of occupational competence, which may substantially improve their opportunities on the labour market.

Human capital theory distinguishes not only between general and specific education but also between formal education and (informal) job experience, in order to explain income differentials on the labour market. The respective measures contain little or no information on the actual qualifications related to the respective educational programmes. The international adult literacy survey (IALS) provides a complement to the measures. Proficiency measures should go together with attained individual income.

Can individuals profit from specific training? Are the returns from investments in education only associated with general, highly transferable skills? Literacy as defined in IALS can, as Peek and Lehmann state, be considered as transferable in this sense. The typical arrangement for vocational education in Germany - the so-called dual system of part-time schooling and in-firm apprenticeship training - introduces a strong element of job-related learning, the transferability of which is limited to certain occupational areas. By providing vocational education situated at the very intersection of the education and the economic subsystems of society, each programme in the dual system will deliver a wide array of competencies, of which literacy is only one. This means that specific, practical competencies may function - at least to some degree - as an equivalent for the cognitive ones measured in IALS. The survey was also undertaken in Belgium by Vandamme et al. A more important finding is that young people who are only performing at the lowest level by the end of their compulsory schooling do not manage to achieve higher levels of skills later. In other words, if you do not learn the basic skills during your compulsory school years, you will not manage to do this later on. This is not to say that the learning process stops after secondary school as far as functional literacy and numeracy skills are concerned. Although many young people reach the highest level in higher education, others do so through confronting real language and numeracy tasks in their daily life. This shows that pupils at secondary school do not get much experience of the kind of complex literacy and numeracy tasks which present themselves in everyday life. The IALS study in Flanders shows that, at the other end of the scale, students leaving education without minimal literacy skills will be at risk in their social life and on the labour market for the rest of their life.

Chapter 21

Enterprise Related Training: A Survey

Wim Groot
University of Amsterdam

Participation in Training

In most European countries, the socio-economic policy debate is dominated by the belief that the labour market should become more flexible. Labour market flexibility is supposed to increase economic competitiveness of countries and is seen as a means to increase welfare. It is this belief that has, for example, motivated the following statement by the European Council: 'Every worker of the EC must be able to have access to vocational training and to benefit from throughout his working life'[1]. It is widely believed that continuous training is a prerequisite for enhancing economic performance.

The recent OECD Job Study contains a number of policy recommendations made in order to make labour markets more flexible. One of these recommendations is to increase the quality of the labour force by education and training (OECD 1994). Special attention is paid to training of employed workers within firms. The assumption underlying this recommendation is that enterprise-related training increases the productivity and employability of workers and that this will increase the competitiveness of firms.

Trade unions have also become increasingly interested in enterprise-related training. In many European countries unions have made training for workers part of their contractual arrangements in collective wage agreements with firms. The main aim for unions is to have firms provide training for all

---

[1]   Article 15 of The Charter of Fundamental Social Rights for Workers adopted by the European Council in Strasbourg (9 December, 1989).

workers. The underlying idea is that training makes skilled workers more scarce and that this will enable unions to negotiate higher wages for them.

In many European countries the training of workers is seen as the shared responsibility of workers and firms, whereas in the United States it appears that training is taken to be the sole responsibility of the worker. European countries have taken various approaches to the provision of new or updated skills to the workforce. In some countries there are central regulations for training, while in other countries enterprise-related training is left to market forces. One important aspect of centralisation of training is regulations concerning a mandatory amount of money for training. The most far reaching of these central agreements is in France where a mandatory 1.5% of the wage bill has to be spent on enterprise-related training. In other countries the amount is lower: 0.7% in Spain, 0.25% in Belgium, and 0.2% in Greece. In Sweden workers have a legal entitlement to educational leave.

At the other extreme there are countries where the government completely refrains from imposing regulation. In Germany training is regarded as a market good which should remain as free as possible from government regulation. A self-regulating system also operates in the Netherlands. Here the role of the government is of a subsidiary nature: inform, signal, stimulate, formulate rights and impose obligations. In Italy government intervention in training is also of a limited nature. In these countries enterprise-related training is mainly the responsibility of the enterprise or the industry.

The increasing attention paid to training by firms, unions and policy makers has been associated with an increase in the participation in training by workers. For example, figures for the Netherlands from the Central Bureau of Statistics (CBS) show that between 1986 and 1990 the participation rate in enterprise-related training increased by 36%. In the year 1990 24% of all workers participated in training (CBS 1990). With the increase in training, the scientific interest in the topic has also grown. Over the past years this has resulted in a number of studies on the determinants of participation in enterprise-related training and on the returns to training for workers and firms.

In this paper we will survey the results of some recent studies on training. Two topics in particular will be discussed. The first concerns access to training: does participation in training differ between groups of workers? Is participation in training determined by individual characteristics, job characteristics, or both? The second topic concerns the returns to training: what are the returns to training for firms and for individual workers. And what explains the differences in returns found in different studies and how do returns differ between workers and firms? Before that, we will first briefly discuss the theoretical framework underlying most of the empirical studies.

Human capital theory

One of the most useful insights offered by human capital theory is the distinction between *general* and *specific* human capital. General human capital are skills which can be made productive in all jobs; specific human capital relates to training which can only be made productive at one specific firm. General and specific human capital are relative terms. Most training is neither completely general nor fully specific. However, some training is more specific than other. Formal education, for example, is usually more general than enterprise-related training.

Human capital theory predicts that the benefits of investments in general training will completely accrue to the worker. The worker will also pay for the cost of investment in general human capital. The costs and revenues of specific training will be shared between the worker and the firm. If the firm retains part of the gains to the worker of the investment in general human capital, the worker will leave for another job in which his/her skills are more fully rewarded. If the firm on the other hand pays for the investment in general human capital it faces the risk that the worker will leave the firm after completing the training. In that case the firm loses its investment. For similar reasons the firm will not be willing to pay all the costs of investment in firm specific training. Because of the possibility of lay-off, the worker will not be willing to pay all the cost of human capital investment which can only be made productive at the current firm.. By sharing both the costs and the revenues of investment in specific human capital, the tie between worker and firm will be strengthened and sharing both the costs and the revenues of investment in specific human capital will reduce the probability of external mobility.

Although the distinction between general and specific human capital is appealing, it has several drawbacks. First, as pointed out by Stevens (1994), training that is useful only in the providing firm and in a small number of other firms is neither general, nor specific, nor a combination of general and specific. The market in which the worker has to sell his/her skills in order to capture its returns is neither competitive (as is the case with general training) nor monopsonistic (as is the case with specific training). Instead the worker faces a oligoponistic market. With such a market form it is possible for the providing firm to capture some of the returns, hence the firm is prepared to share the costs. Second, Becker's model of general training assumes symmetric information for current and potential employers. Potential employers are assumed to possess the same level and type of information about the contents of training as the firm that provided the training. Katz and

Ziderman (1991) show that to the extent that information is a-symmetric the value of general training to other employers decreases. Therefore the worker is unable to capture the full returns of the training elsewhere and for that reason the current employer is capable of extracting part of the returns and is, hence, prepared to pay a part of the costs of general training.

In addition to these two theoretical remarks, the distinction between specific and general training is not operational at a direct empirical level. As Stern and Benson (1991) note, the main empirical support for the existence of firm-specific training is the difference between rates of return to working experience in general and tenure. Other explanations for this finding, however, cannot be rejected. The pessimistic, but realistic, conclusion that Stern and Benson draw is that "given the difficulty of directly measuring the degree of specificity in training, we may never know which of the theories account for the observed greater pay-off to continued experience with the same employer" (p.139).

Little is known about the distribution of costs and benefits of investments in specific human capital between the worker and the firm. The findings from Oosterbeek, Groot and Hartog (1994) show that a sizeable percentage of the workers that invest in training share in the benefits of the investment, although they do not contribute to the cost of it (neither in the direct financial costs, nor by sacrificing leisure). Other workers that participate in training contribute to the cost of it, but do not share in its benefits. Both findings are contrary to the predictions of the human capital theory. It may be that there is a 'hold-up' problem. Hold-up problems may occur with investments in specific human capital. Hold-up problems occur because it is not possible prior to the investment to make legally binding contracts for all future contingencies. Arrangements about investment in specific human capital are an *incomplete contract*. After the employer and the worker have made the cost of the investment in specific human capital, the employer may decide not to let the worker share in the benefits of the investment (although this may be at the expense of the employer's reputation).

Access to enterprise-related training

Access to job related training is not equal for all workers. Some workers are more likely to receive on-the-job training than other workers Following a study of 22 cases of the determinants of participation in training the following conclusions can be drawn:

The likelihood of participation in on-the-job training increases with the level of education: higher educated workers receive more on-the-job training than lower educated workers;

Men receive more on-the-job training than women. Women with young children have an especially low probability of participating in training;

Full-time workers receive more training than part-time workers;

Participation in training decreases with age, experience and tenure;

Workers from ethnic minorities receive less training;

The probability of receiving training is to a large extent determined by occupational and industrial characteristics. Workers in higher level positions participate in training more frequently.

Public sector workers participate in training more frequently than private sector workers.

Workers in large firms receive more training than workers in small firms;

Participation in training decreases when the unemployment rate rises;

Union members receive more training than workers who are not a member of a trade union;

The characteristics that determine participation in on-the-job training differ from those that determine participation in off-the-job training.

We will discuss each of these findings, separately. The overall impression from the summary of the findings is one of labour market segmentation. Access to training is associated with the characteristics, such as gender, ethnicity, hours of work, union membership, occupation and firm size, that make it more likely that the worker has a job in the primary job market.

A survey on the participation in training by education level for some OECD member countries revealed that between 30% and 40% of workers had participated in training in the past year (OCED, 1991). The participation rate among highly educated workers is three to five times higher than among lowly educated workers. Among low educated workers between 10% and 20% of the workers has participated in training, while in all countries surveyed this is over 40% among high educated workers.

In Thurow's job competition model it is argued that employers use observable characteristics of individuals, such as education, as selection device for hiring new workers (Thurow 1975). Education is seen as a proxy for the amount of on-the-job training and company-related schooling which the employer needs to invest in the worker. Highly educated workers need less company-related schooling. For this reason employers hire the best educated worker, irrespective of the requirements of the job. If firms hire the best educated worker who applies for the job, it is possible that the skills of workers are under-utilised and workers are over-educated. In short, the job competition model predicts a positive return to over-education and a negative relation between over-education and the participation in company-related schooling. The job competition model further predicts a negative return to under-education and a positive relation between under-education and participation in company-related schooling.

If formal education and enterprise-related schooling are substitutes, over-educated workers will invest less in company-related schooling than workers who are correctly educated. By extension, under-educated workers will invest relatively more in company-related schooling. If over-educated workers have to invest less in company-related schooling the social wastage of over-education will be less, as the lower investment costs in enterprise-related schooling (partly) compensates for higher investment costs in formal education. The capacity for substituting between (over-) education and enterprise-related schooling could also explain the persistence of over-education, in particular if education is subsidised by the government.

Some studies find evidence to suggest that there is a trade-off between (over-) education and investments in other components of human capital, and that over-educated workers receive lower amounts of on-the-job training than workers with the required level of schooling (Sicherman 1991). The alternative hypothesis is that over-education and enterprise-related schooling are complementary. If education has an allocative effect and general human capital enhances the ability and reduces the costs to acquire specific human capital, over-education and company-related schooling may be complementary. The results from empirical research summarised in the first conclusion above suggests that education and training are complementary rather than substitutes. OECD (1991) also concluded that higher educated workers are more likely to receive on-the-job training and that education and post-school training seem to be complementary' (OECD 1991, p. 152).

If over-education and enterprise-related schooling are substitutes the social costs of over-education are less. One study finds that correctly allocated workers have the highest probability of participation in enterprise-related schooling, while undereducated workers have the lowest probability of participation (Groot 1993). There is no evidence of *over*-education and enterprise-related schooling being either substitutes or complementary.

If education and training are complementary, any training increases social inequality between individuals. Increased wage inequality increases the risks of social exclusion of some groups of workers who do not have access to training provision. This poses a challenge for policy makers

The second conclusion - men receive more training than women - points at a *vicious circle* between men and women. Women still have a weaker labour market position than men. Women have lower labour force participation rates than men. Women's average hours of work are lower as well. The main reason for the weaker labour force position is that women leave the labour market for a while after child birth and, after they have re-entered the labour market, women work fewer hours than before. As a result women, on average, have higher quit rates and lower job tenures than men. Because of this weaker labour market position women have less incentive to invest in on-the-job training than men. For employers, the expected profitability of investments in on-the-job training for women is lower than the expected profitability of training for men. The pay-back period of the training investment is shorter for women than for men. This reduces the returns to female on-the-job training. Lower returns for women lower the investments in on-the-job training.

If women invest less in on-the-job training, their earnings growth is lower than the male earnings growth. This increases the male-female wage gap. With a rising labour supply schedule, women will supply less labour on the labour market than men. Further, if it comes to the division of household work and paid labour between men and women, men have an absolute advantage in doing paid work because they are able to earn higher wage rates. The male-female wage differential will result in women being oriented towards household work and care for children and men specialising in paid labour. And if men specialise in paid employment and women in household work, women's labour force position will be lower than men's labour market attachment. This completes a circle of weaker labour market position - less on-the job training - lower wage growth - lower wages - and weaker labour market position for women relative to men.

Differences in the pay-back period of the investment explain why full-time workers receive more training than part-time workers. As it is less profitable to invest in training for part-time workers, these workers participate in training less frequently.

Two explanations can be given for the finding that participation in training decreases with age, experience and tenure. The first is a matching argument: training may be necessary to adjust skills of workers to the requirements of the job. Young and inexperienced workers frequently need training in order to be employable at all at their job. Before a new employee can be made productive, some form of induction training is required.

The second explanation focusses on the returns to training. The expected pay-back period of the training investment returns is longer for young workers and recent employees, than for workers with longer elapsed tenure. The longer the pay-back period of the investment, the higher the returns to the investment, and the higher the returns, the more profitable it is to invest in training.

The fourth conclusion further indicates that demographic trends may have serious implications for training investments. What are the effects of the 'greying' of the labour force on the need for continuous training? If productivity decreases with age (e.g. as a result of depreciation of human capital and loss of physical strength), this might be compensated by training. Empirical evidence shows, however, that the incidence of training decreases with age. With the exception of Sweden, participation in training among older workers is lower than among younger workers. The participation rate among workers aged 45-64 is only a quarter to two third of the participation rate among workers aged between 25 and 34.

It is difficult to find an economic explanation as to why ethnic minority workers participate less frequently in training. Possibly racial discrimination by employers has something to do with it.

Firm and job characteristics are important in explaining participation in training. It can be argued that training is related to jobs rather than workers. The decision to train is frequently a joint decision of the employer and the worker. In most cases the employer offers training to the worker, and the decision of the worker to participate is conditional on training being offered. In other cases the worker takes the initiative, but the employer has to approve it.

Differences in training intensity are also related to differences in economic development and technological change between industries. In firms and industries with rapid technological change the need to train workers will be larger.

The industrial structure may be important as well. In industries with a high concentration rate, where firms have some degree of market power in product markets - for example monopolistic or oligopolistic markets - the profitability of firms will be larger. Firms may share these excess profits with their workers by offering higher training intensities. Monopoly power of firms also may reduce the chance that workers who are trained for jobs that are specific for the industry leave the firm for better paying competitors. For example, a train driver can only make his/her firm specific skills productive at the railroad company. In most countries railroads are a monopoly industry, which means that the railroad company does not have to fear that trained train drivers are poached by competitors.

The relation between training and industrial structure not only concerns market power, but also the threat of take-over. If a firm wants to prevent a (hostile) take-over it will have to pay high dividends and it has to have large cash reserves. This capital cannot be spent on training to increase the productivity of workers. Firms that are relatively sheltered from take-over (for example by legal protection) are therefore probably more inclined to invest in training.

The relation between the industrial structure and training of workers may first of all explain why workers in large firms invest more in training than workers in small firms. It also explains why public sector workers - i.e. workers who are employed at the monopolist public services and fully protected against take-over - participate more in training than workers in the private sector.

The nature of the training may also be important. The probability that trained workers leave the firm for a better paying one will be higher, if skills learned through training can also be made productive at other firms or industries. In that case firms will be less willing to invest in training for their workers. This is what Stevens (1994) refers to as the 'transferability' of training.

Two explanations can be given for the finding that workers at higher job levels participate in training more frequently than workers at lower job levels. Firstly, training is sometimes a pre-requisite for promotion to a higher job level. Training for each job takes place by workers at the previous level, and prepares workers for advancement within the firm. Training not only provides workers with the skills necessary for promotion, training may also be used by employers as a selection device to screen workers for promotion. Both the skill preparation and the selection argument suggest a positive relation between training and promotion. In Groot (1996) empirical evidence is found to confirm this. Data from the British Household Panel Survey show that on-the-job training and job promotion are positively correlated. Workers who participated in on-the-job training are promoted to other jobs in the firm during the year after the training had taken place significantly more frequently than untrained workers. This may also explain the positive effect of firm size on training. Large firms usually have more hierarchical levels and offer more opportunities for advancement within the firm. On-the-job training may prepare workers in large firms for promotion to a higher job level.

Secondly, training may be a reward or compensation for achievement. With progressive taxation, high paid workers at higher job levels may have a relative preference to receive part of their compensation in the form of an untaxed investment in training.

We have already given two explanations for the positive relation between firm size and training intensities: the greater opportunities for promotion within the firm and the larger degree of market power in product markets which large firms may have. An alternative explanation is that the fear that trained workers are poached away by better paying competitors is a greater deterrent to train workers for employers in small firms than for employers in large firms. If small firms are more risk averse than large firms, small firms may be less willing to invest in training for their workers.

Small firms may be faced by tighter liquidity constraints as well. It may also be possible that the (opportunity) costs of training weigh more heavily on small firms than on large firms. Workers at small firms may be more difficult to replace during the time they are in training. It may be easier for large firms to arrange for workers to be trained. Further, large firms have more opportunities to organise courses themselves and this enables large firms to develop courses which cater to the specific training needs of the firm. Small firms more frequently have to rely on ready-made training courses outside the firm. Training outside the firm through standard courses offered by training institutes supply workers with skills which are more likely to be of use at other firms as well, than courses which are specifically developed for the firm itself. If small firms can only supply general training at external training institutions, the risk that the trained worker may be poached away by other firms may be higher. This will lead to lower training investments by small firms, especially if small firms are more risk averse than large firms.

The negative relation between unemployment and training may reflect the effect of the business cycle on training. During recessions, when unemployment is high, firms may be forced to cut production costs. One of the activities which will be amongst the first to cut back are training investments. It may also be that during recessions the supply of skilled workers is higher, which reduces the need for firms to invest in training.

Two explanations can be given for the finding that union members participate in training more frequently than non-members. First, the bargaining power of unionised workers is stronger. If workers and unions value training, it will be easier to negotiate training for workers if one has a stronger bargaining position. Secondly, unions sometimes negotiate special arrangements for training for union members. The special training arrangements result in union members participating in training more frequently than non-members.

Finally, Greenhalgh and Mavrotas (1994) in a recent paper inquire into the implications of the distinction between on- and off-the-job training. In particular they stress the importance of career aspirations and financial constraints. According to Greenhalgh and Mavrotas off-the-job training is an option for workers who have high aspirations but are not offered on-the-job training opportunities by their employer.

The returns for training for workers

The returns for workers are usually measured by wage effect of training. The productivity effect of training is the main return for the employer. During the past years a number of studies have appeared that estimate the returns to training. Most of these studies are concerned with the wage effects of training. Only a few studies deal with the productivity effects (exceptions are Barron, Black and Loewenstein (1989), Bishop (1994) and Groot (1994a,

1994b)).[2] The reason why the returns for workers have received more attention than the returns for the firm, is that data on individual workers are more widely available than data on firms.

Within the literature on the returns of training for workers, two methods can be distinguished to determine the effects of training. The first is based on a comparison of wages for workers who have participated in training with wages of workers who were not trained. In the second method wages before and after training are compared.

A summary of 26 studies on the returns of training for workers leads to two conclusions. The first is that the returns to training are high. Studies using data for the United States find that the wage effect of training is between 4% and 16%. For the Netherlands and Great-Britain wage effects of over 20% are found. The second is that there is a large variation in results. We deal with the second conclusion first.

Five explanations can be given for the large variation in results. First, there are differences in the statistical and econometric techniques by which the results are obtained. This concerns the treatment of self-selection and simultaneity problems. Self-selection refers to the fact that participants in training are not a random sample of all workers, but rather a (self-)selected group of workers for whom the returns to the investment are higher than average. The wage effects of training are higher for workers who have invested in training, than they would have been for workers who have not participated (had they participated in training). Simultaneity refers to the fact on the one hand training increases wages, while on the other decisions about training investments are based on (expected) returns to the investment. Empirical studies show that: firstly correction for self-selection is important to establish the true effects of training and secondly the wage effects of training are higher for workers who have participated in training, than they would have been for workers who have not participated in training (if they had participated).

A second explanation for the large variation in results can be found in the definition of the training variable and in differences between surveys. Sample differences relate to the age group studied (cohorts of young or older workers or cross-sections of the entire population), the year in which the data are collected, etc. Regarding the definition of training, it should be kept in mind that on-the-job training is a broad concept that ranges from informal learning-by-doing to courses that are almost equivalent to formal education. The nature and intensity of the training may also differ between studies. It

---

[2] In Groot (1994a,c) it is found that the average productivity effect of training is 16%. This study further shows that workers receive less than a quarter of the total returns to training. (i.e. the average wage growth of training is 4%).

further matters whether one looks at all on-the-job training received, training obtained at the current firm, or training received during the past twelve months. Finally, the period over which the returns are measured may be important.

A third explanation is that the differences between results are caused by institutional differences between countries. An important - but not well documented - determinant of the returns to training is the rate of mobility of production factors. This concerns the mobility of labour (change of jobs) as well as the mobility of capital (technological change). High labour mobility may result in low returns and low investment in on-the-job training. Labour mobility in the United States in general is much higher than in Europe (see OECD 1997). This corresponds to the finding that the wage effects of training in European countries appear to be higher than those in the United States.

Fourthly, there are differences in returns by type of training. In Groot (1995) it is found that the wage effects of technical training is much lower than the wage effects of other types of training. This may be caused by differences in the rate of technological change between industries and occupations. If the rate of depreciation of technical skills is higher and technical skills become obsolete faster than other types of training, the returns to investment in technical skills will be lower. It may also be that technical training is more firm specific; human capital and that part of the returns to investments in technical training accrue to the employer. This lowers the wage effects for the worker.

Finally, the high wage effects of training found in some studies may be a result of a productivity increase resulting from a change of production methods (for example, automation of production methods, the change to process industry). A change in production methods is frequently accompanied by training for workers. Training then is necessary to re-skill workers for the new production methods. If the change in production methods implies an increase in productivity, this may be reflected in higher productivity and wages for trained workers.

If training precedes promotion to a higher job level, the wage effect of training may further partly reflect the wage effect of promotion to another hierarchical level.

What explains the high wage effects of training? In Groot and Oosterbeek (1995) four possible explanations are given for the high wage effects of training. Firstly, part of this high return may be a risk premium for greater uncertainty about the return to investments in firm related human capital. Sources for uncertainty about returns are: Finally there is uncertainty about the remaining workers at the firm (i.e. the length of the pay-back period); and uncertainty about the true productivity effects of the training (it is sometimes not clear whether worker's performance will improve because of the training) and uncertainty about the rate of depreciation of the newly acquired skills (as the future rate of technical change is unknown).

Secondly, as was already mentioned above, there may be a relation between market power in product market and training. Monopolistic power in product markets increases the returns to labour and capital, and the returns to training as well. Firms which exercise market power may also have a greater need to train their workers: some of the skills necessary for production are not learned at school because they can only be made productive in a few firms (e.g. manufacturing work in the automobile industry).

Thirdly, part of the return may be an effort inducing, wage premium or efficiency wage. Trained workers need less supervising in production. Generally, the tasks of a supervisor are twofold: to assist employees in production and to monitor the amount of effort they put in their jobs. Trained workers need less assistance. Training workers may therefore make supervision less efficient. If trained workers are no longer supervised, firms will look for incentives to increase effort. One way of doing this is by paying efficiency wages. As a result, training of workers and paying them incentive pay may be positively associated.

Fourthly, most training is not fully firm specific. Skills learned in training can be made productive at other firms as well. Fear of poaching by other firms may result in under-investment in training on the part of the employer. Workers may be unable or unwilling to contribute in the costs of training, because of liquidity constraints and risk aversion (see Stern and Ritzen, 1991). If the investment level in training is less than efficient, the rate of return will be above equilibrium level.

In Bishop (1985) some other possible reasons are given why employers under-invest in general on-the-job training:

Other employers receive part of the benefits of general on-the-job training if the worker quits and moves to another firm;

If other employers have imperfect information about the quality of general on-the-job training of the worker, the investment in training will not be fully compensated at the old firm;

If the internal rate of return for the worker is above the market interest rate for capital with the same amount of risk, due to constraints, workers cannot borrow money at a reasonable rate of interest for their investment in general on-the-job training;

The marginal tax rate on the benefits of the investment in on-the-job training for the worker is higher than the marginal tax rate of the investment costs.

Ritzen (1989) also presents some theoretical considerations to explain possible under-investment in on-the-job training:

A legally binding minimum wage may make it impossible for workers to contribute to the costs of training by lowering their wage rate below the minimum wage. This may be a particular concern for young workers, lowly educated workers, and workers who have been unemployed;

If general and specific human capital are complementary, high labour mobility will result in a decline in the returns to general human capital and less investment in general human capital;

The costs for the worker of transacting information about general human capital investments to other employers. If individual productivity differences are not observable or only observable at high cost for other potential employers, these productivity differences will not be reflected in wage differences;

Unemployment benefits, income transfers and wage costs subsidies for unemployed workers that encourage the displacement of older workers by young workers.

Conclusions and policy issues

In this paper we have surveyed the literature on participation in, and returns to investment in training. Two general conclusions emerge from this. First, access to training is not the same for everyone. Some workers are offered more opportunities for investment in training than others. As investments in human capital such as training create inequality between workers, these differences in training participation increase social inequality (wage inequality, employment opportunities, etc.). It seems that on-the-job training becomes an increasing important source of human capital investment. If training opportunities are not the same for all workers, the increase in investments in on-the-job training will result in an increase in social inequality.

The second conclusion that can be drawn is that the wage effects of investments in training are high, both if wages are compared to wages of workers who have not invested in training and if wages are compared before and after the training.

The high wage effects of training may reflect a risk-premium, rent sharing, liquidity constraint on the part of the worker and may indicate that training is not completely firm specific human capital. All this may result in training levels which are less than efficient. Market failure in training may call for government intervention.

The risk-premium might be reduced, and the participation increased, if the government would step in, with schools and subsidies. The rent-sharing could only be attacked with general competitive policies. With partly specific training and liquidity constraints, collective action by the industry may solve the problem of under-provision of training.

Training may be provided by firms themselves (by a training department within the firm), industry associations, private training institutions or the government. The initiative to train workers may come from the employee or from the firm. It may be available for all employees of a firm, or it may be organised as a programme for new employees only. Financial arrangements may also differ. Depending on the type of training, it may be financed by the worker, the firm, or the government. The government may restrict itself to providing free or cheap training, it may pay the opportunity cost (i.e. lost wages), or it may give tax deductions to employees. Costs of training (instructors, fees to training institutions) are considered as labour costs, which can be fully deducted in the year in which they are incurred before profit taxes are levied. Hence, the cost of investment in human capital has a preferential tax treatment relative to investment in physical capital. Opportunity cost (production lost) is deductible if the employer carries the burden (as wages paid for non-productive time), but is not deductible if the employee bears the burden in terms of reduced wages while in training. Opportunity costs may easily outrun the direct cost. But they are not easily verified. Hence, for purposes of stimulation through tax facilities one may apply a multiplier on direct training expenditures as a deductible for profit taxes. Increasing the multiplier in a recession may be a method to counteract employers' cutbacks on training.

The value of the training investment is usually mainly observable to the participants themselves - i.e. the worker and his/her current employer - and not to any other employer. The National Vocational Qualifications (NVQs) in the United Kingdom serve as a certification and standardisation of training investment. This form of certification may decrease uncertainty among employers about the value of the training. It may, on the other hand, increase poaching, as information about the quality of training the worker has taken becomes more widely available.

REFERENCES

Alba-Ramirez, A. (1994), "Formal training, temporary contracts, productivity and wages in Spain", *Oxford Bulletin of Economics and Statistics* 56, pp.151-170.

Altonji, J. and Spletzer, J. (1991), "Worker characteristics, job characteristics, and the receipt of on-the-job training", *Industrial and Labour Relations Review* 45, pp.58-79.

Arulampalam, W., Booth, A. and Elias, P. (1996), "Modelling work-related training and training effects using count data techniques", University of Warwick Economic Research Paper No. 448

Barron, J., Bishop, J. and Dunkelberg, W. (1985), "Employer search: the interviewing and hiring of new employees", *The Review of Economics and Statistics*, pp.43-52.

Barron, J.,Black, D. and Loewenstein, M. (1989), "Job matching and on-the-job training", *Journal of Labour Economics* 7, pp.1-19.

Bartel, A. (1995), "Training, wage growth, and job performance: evidence from a company database", *Journal of Labour Economics* 13, pp.401-425.

Bartel, A. and Sicherman, N. (1995), "Technological change and the skill acquisition of young workers", NBER Working Paper 5107.

Bishop, J. (1985), *Preparing youth for employment*, The National Center for Research in Vocational Education, The Ohio State University.

Bishop, J. (1994), "The impact of previous training on productivity and wages", in Lynch, L. (Ed.), *Training and the Private Sector: International Comparisons*, University of Chicago Press, Chicago, pp.161-200.

Blanchflower, D. and Lynch, L. (1994), "Training at work: a comparison of US and British youths", in Lynch, L. (Ed.), *Training and the Private Sector: International Comparisons*, University of Chicago Press, Chicago, pp.233-260.

Blundell, R., Dearden, L. and Meghir, C. (1994), *The determinants and effects of work related training in Britain*, University College, London.

Bishop, J. (1994), "The impact of previous training on productivity and wages", in Lynch, L. (Ed.), *Training and the Private Sector: International Comparisons*, University of Chicago Press, Chicago, pp.161-199.

Booth, A. (1991), "Job-related formal training: who receives it and what is it worth?", *Oxford Bulletin of Economics and Statistics*, pp.281-294.

Brown, J. (1989), "Why do wages increase with tenure? On-the-job training and life-cycle wage growth observed within firms", *American Economic Review* 79, pp.971-991.

Dolton, P., Makepeace, G. and Treble, J. (1994), "Public- and private sector training of young people in Britain", in Lynch, L. (Ed.), *Training and the Private Sector: International Comparisons*, University of Chicago Press, Chicago, pp.261-282.

Duncan G. and Hoffman, S. (1978), "Training and earnings", in Duncan, G. and Morgan, J. (Ed.), *Five thousand American families - Patterns of Economics Progress*, Annn Arbor, Institute for Social Research, Michigan, pp.105-150.

Duncan, G. and Hoffman, S. (1979), "On-the-job training and earnings differences by race and sex", *Review of Economics and Statistics* 61, pp.594-603.

Elias, P., Hernaes, E. and Baker, M. (1994), "Vocational education and training in Britain and Norway", in Lynch, L. (Ed.), *Training and the Private Sector: International Comparisons*, University of Chicago Press, Chicago, pp.283-289.

Greenhalgh, C. and Mavrotas, G. (1994), "The role of career aspirations and financial constraints in individual access to vocational training", *Oxford Economic Papers* 46, pp.579-604.

Groot, W. (1994a), *Het rendement op bedrijfsopleidingen*, Uitgeverij VUGA, Ministerie van Sociale Zaken en Werkgelegenheid, 's-Gravenhage.

Groot, W. (1994b), "Bedrijfsopleidingen: goed voor produktiviteit en loon", *Economisch Statistische Berichten 3988*, pp.1108-1111.

Groot, W. (1995), "Type specific returns to enterprise-related training", *Economics of Education Review* 14, pp.323-333.

Groot, W., Hartog, J. and Oosterbeek, H. (1994), "Returns to within-company schooling of employees: the case of the Netherlands", in Lynch, L. (Ed.), *Training and the Private Sector: International Comparisons*, University of Chicago Press, Chicago, pp.299-307.

Groot, W. and Oosterbeek, H. (1995), "Determinants and wage effects of participation in on- and off-the-job training", Tinbergen Institute Research Memorandum TI , pp.95-122.

Groot, W. and Maassen van den Brink, H. (1997), *Scholing en arbeidsmarktflexibiliteit van oudere werknemers*, Uitgeverij Delwel, Den Haag.

Holzer, H. (1990), "The determinants of employee productivity and earnings", *Industrial Relations*, pp.403-422.

Kennedy, S., Drago, R., Sloan, J. and Wooden, M. (1994), "The effect of trade unions on the provision of training: Australian evidence", *British Journal of Industrial Relations* 32, pp.565-580.

Laulhé, P. (1990), "La formation continue: un advantage pour les promotions at an accés privilégié pour les jeunes et les techniciens", *Economie et Statistique*, pp.3-8.

Lynch, L. (1992), "Private sector training and the earnings of young workers", *American Economic Review*.

Maassen van den Brink, H. and Groot, W. (1994), *Obstakels: vrouwen tussen arbeidsmarkt en gezin*, Amsterdam University Press, Amsterdam.

Mincer, J. (1989), "Human capital and the Labour market: a review of current research", *Educational Researcher* 18, pp.27-34.

Mincer, J. (1991), "Education and Unemployment", Working Paper 3838, National bureau of Economic Research, Cambridge, Massachusetts.

NEI (Koning, J. de, Gelderblom, A., Hammink, A. and Olieman, R.) (1991), *Bedrijfsopleidingen: omvang, aard, verdeling en effecten*, RVE Beleidsstudies 1, Ministerie van Onderwijs en Wetenschappen.

OECD (1991), "Enterprise-related training", in *Employment Outlook 1991*, Organisation for Economic Development and Co-operation, Paris, pp.135-176.

OECD (1993), "Enterprise tenure, labour turnover and skill training", *Employment Outlook 1993*, pp.119-155, OECD, Paris.

OECD (1994), *Jobs Study*, Organisation for Economic Development and Co-operation, Paris.

OECD (1997), "Job insecurity", in *Employment Outlook 1997*, Organisation for Economic Development and Co-operation, Paris.

Oi, W.Y. (1962), "Labour as a quasi-fixed factor", *Journal of Political Economy* 70, pp.538-555.

Oosterbeek, H. (1996), "A decomposition of training probabilities", *Applied Economics*.

Oosterbeek, H., Groot, W. and Hartog, J. (1994), "La participacion en los costos y benificios de la formacion de empresas", *Revista de Treball* 22, pp.97-113.

Stevens, M. (1994), "An investment model for the supply of training by employers", *Economic Journal* 104, pp.556-570.

Teulings, C. and Budil-Nadvornikova, H. (1989), *De betekenis van bedrijfsopleidingen in Nederland*, Stichting voor Economisch Onderzoek, Amsterdam.

Theodossiou, I. and Williams, H. (1995), *Employer-provided training and tenure effects on earnings*, University of Aberdeen, Aberdeen.

Wooden, M. (1992), "Training in the Australian labour market: evidence from the ,How workers get their training" survey"', *Australian Bulletin of Labour* 18, pp.25-45.

Wooden, M. (1996), "Firm size and the provision of employee training: an analysis of the 1993 survey of training and education", *Australian and New Zealand Journal of Vocational Education Research*.

Chapter 22

Participation of SMEs' employees in Continuing Training in the Alentejo Region

Eduardo Figueira
University of Evora

1. INTRODUCTION

In the context of this research, *Continuing Training for Active Adults* is non formal training essentially oriented to acquisition of professional competencies and abilities and centred on the strategy of *learning how to learn continuously*. In this perspective, continuing training for active adults is seen as a process aiming at developing an individual's autonomy on his/her own learning process. For this reason, the trainer should essentially play a *facilitator* role in the individual's learning activities.

The success of the development process in any region depends essentially on the qualification level of the existing human resources and the capacity of increasing, developing and keeping them continuously qualified in order to respond to change resulting from the development process. In fact, it has been found that adult continuing education provision are directly related to economic development since they improve quality of the work force (Carnevale, 1983). Continuing education programmes can provide training for new or expanding business, can prepare workers to go into new professional activities, or can help the existing workforce to remain professionally up to date (Moore, 1990).

This condition assumes more relevance for the relatively less developed European regions in which the business tissue is very weak and the majority of the people have a low level of qualification. However, it also plays a crucial role in the development process of the more developed European regions. In fact, the sustainable development of the European Union as a whole can only be reached through developing the human resources needed to promote and implement modernisation and technological progress of Europe's less and more developed regions. It is, then, essential and urgent, that efforts be made to promote adequate policies and strategies for continuing vocational education and training for active adults. Adequate and effective continuing education and training policies have to be developed and implemented if the emerging needs of European society and citizens are to be met. Participation in continuing vocational education and training activities constitutes the most effective strategy to both increase and maintain European workers' employability (employment/self-employment) and keep human resources permanently qualified in order to respond for changes resulting from the development process. This is very important to both promoting business and regional competitiveness and combating social exclusion, mainly unemployment. In addition, developing adequate and effective continuing education and training policies and strategies requires a scientific and prospective analysis of the labour market and organisations' needs and workers' participation in continuing training activities. It also requires a scientific understanding of workers' adaptation to change in the workplace as a resource to use for improving a sustainable development of human occupation.

Over the last two decades, given the introduction of new technologies and increased business competition, rapid changes have been occurring in the organisation of production and the structure of employment and unemployment in the European Member States and other industrial nations. For this reason, increasing training for workers has been identified as an essential strategy for a nation, a region, or an organisation to remain competitive in a rapidly changing environment (Hodson, Hooks, Rieble, 1994). In terms of human capital theory, skilled workers are far better able to manage people and manipulate data and objects, mainly in environments characterised by new technologies and new production techniques (Spenner, 1990).

The level of business productivity depends essentially on effective and efficient use of new technologies, which is only possible with (qualified) human resources. For this reason, if a firm is to be the competitive, continuing qualification of human resources ought to be a component of its business strategy. However, implementing continuing training programmes for workers requires firm investment, high level training skills and managers prepared to delegate greater decision-making responsibility to workers. Although most firms were interested in having employees with high level of human capital, fewer of them are prepared to give more responsibility and autonomy to their workers (Hodson, Hooks, Rieble, 1994).

The acquisition of skills and knowledge by workers through continuing training programmes constitutes a new management philosophy for which few managers are prepared. This management philosophy assumes that firstly labour training is an effective business strategy to face the changes and the increased competition of the market, secondly employees' responsibility and autonomy over their workplaces should continuously and systematically increase and thirdly better relationships between the firm and its employees should be promoted (Hodson, Hooks, Rieble, 1994).

Individuals' participation in learning activities has been thoroughly researched. However, studies of participation of active adults in continuing training activities are sparse. Adult educators, in general, and continuing education administrators, in particular, seldom have the time to systematically study characteristics and learning behaviours of the current and potential adult participants in their training programmes. In addition, in Portugal there are not studies that allow knowledge and understanding the mechanisms that regulate adults' attitude to the continuing learning process. Factors influencing adults' attitude of passivity, reluctance or even resistance to training are also unknown. This makes difficult to design, plan and implement effective continuing training programmes.

The knowledge of the Portuguese adults' participation in continuing education has to be improved if adequate and effective continuing training policies are to be developed. Increasing adults' participation in continuing qualification activities constitutes one of the more relevant strategies to prevent social and economic exclusion. Promoting participation and access for continuing training activities of those who are out of the labour market, namely those who are less qualified, is an important contribution to combating the exclusion of the less favoured. In addition, the continuing qualification of the human resources constitutes a "sine qua non" condition for increasing business effectiveness, which plays an essential role for economic progress and social development of any region. Business effectiveness depends on the level of productivity and this depends essentially on effective and efficient use of new technologies, which is only possible with continuously qualified human resources.

The present research aimed to identify, analyse, and understand the factors associated with active adults' participation in continuing training activities in the Alentejo Region. Evaluating and characterising workers' attitudes in relation to participation in continuing training programmes will be an important contribution to designing and setting up adequate strategies that allow an increase in the effectiveness and efficiency of continuing training programmes. In addition, it is intended to evaluate and characterise workers' attitude towards participation in training activities. As a is result, the study intended to contribute to establishing policies and strategies that promote and increase the level of workers' participation in their own professional qualification. In this way, the study will make an important contribution promoting equal access to continuing vocational training to all workers (and those are out of the labour market) throughout their working life.

More specifically, this study had the following objectives:

- To identify and analyse the factors associated with active adults' participation in continuing education activities and to understand how they influence workers' decision to participate in these activities.

- To assess and characterise active adults' attitude towards participation in continuing education programmes.

- To contribute to designing and implementing continuing education policies and strategies for promoting and increasing participation of workers in continuing training programmes.

- To evaluate a model of adult participation in continuing education to enable policy makers and practitioners to understand and implement the best approaches to encourage workers, managers and employers to embark in continuing education.

2. THE PROBLEM

Analysing and understanding the nature of the factors and the relationships associated with active adults' participation in training activities an constitute important basis for formulating adequate and effective development policies and strategies for the different socio-professional groups. In addition, this understanding is fundamental for creating measures and tools to improve the quality of the human resources, and to define policies and strategies for structuring and organising the continuing training systems aiming to adapt the nature of training provision to training demand. On the other hand, knowledge and understanding of the participation phenomenon in training activities allows, the establishment of and implementation of strategies aiming to sensitise the active population, in general, and the socio-professional groups, in particular, to the importance of their continuing and systematic participation in learning activities. In addition, understanding participation, namely the factors that may influence that participation, facilitates the definition of adequate training programmes for adults' needs and sensibilities.

Individuals' participation in learning activities has been one of the most researched areas in the adult and continuing education field (Yang, Blunt, & Butler, 1994). Adult educators have been very much interested in questions concerning the factors that influence active adults' participation in training activities and how this participation can be predicted (Yang, Blunt, & Butler, 1994). However, in spite of the substantial research in this domain, few conceptual models have demonstrated utility in predicting adults' participation in training activities (Yang, Blunt, & Butler, 1994). Many researchers followed Fishbein and Ajzen's (1975) behavioural intention model and other models exploring the relationship between motivation and participation (Yang, Blunt, & Butler, 1994). However, there are other conceptual models that propose to explain adults' participation in training activities from a broader theoretical basis than that emphasising those relationships between attitude or motivation and participation. In addition, factors influencing adults' attitude of passivity, reluctance or even resistance to training are not well known. This makes it difficult to design, plan and implement effective continuing training policies and strategies.

How could we, then, study active adults' participation in continuing education activities? Is there any kind of participation model, which could explain a significant portion of the variance in adults' participation in continuing education activities? Could a test of a conceptual model be utilised to identify relevant predictors of active adults' participation in continuing education? Would it be possible to identify and test significant relationships among the identified predictors of adult education participation?

3. THEORETICAL FRAMEWORK

Research on adults' participation in continuing training has been guided by two assumptions. The first is that the adult learning is essentially a voluntary activity. The second assumption states that adults' characteristics and their reasons to participate in training are very variable (Houtkoop and Kamp, 1992).

Mechanisms that regulate and/or are associated with active adults' attitude towards continuing and systematic learning processes are not yet well known. In addition, factors associated to adults' passivity, reluctance, and even resistance to participation in training are also not yet well known. This problem means, in practical terms, it is difficult to design and implement training programmes to satisfy the needs and interests of individuals, organisations and the socio-economic development process in general. This is very important because learning skills are required to promote and enhance both individual fulfilment and community development (Delors, 1993).

The factors that appear to be associated with active adults' participation in learning activities are of diverse nature. Participation in training is influenced by factors of personal and psychological order, normally related to individual's experience in social and educational processes. Factors of social and context nature related to the characteristics of environment and training and conditions it is offered are also associated with participation in teaching-learning activities.

According to studies made in other countries, the active adults participating in educational activities were, mainly, individuals with technical professions, people with high socio-economic status and/or with higher levels of education, and young adults (Brunner, Wilder, Kircher and Newberry, 1959). According to the same study, individuals' level of formal education appeared to be the more determinant factor in adults' participation in training. Although carried out in the 1950s, that study achieved results that appear to be very close to the situation of the less favoured European regions.

Motivation specialists have tried to link adult motivation and/or attitude with participation of adults in training activities (Houle, 1961; Boschier, 1971; Bourgess, 1971; Morstain and Smart, 1974; Grotelueschen and Caulley, 1977). Others have based their participation research on social psychology theory (Boshier, 1973; Cross, 1981; Darkenwald and Merriam, 1982). However, studies carried out more recently open different perspectives of research and post new problems. For instance, active adults' decision to undertake training appears to be influenced by factors related to the marketing of training programmes, individuals' social involvement, personal and professional difficulties, and individuals' motivation (van Tilbourg, 1989). On the other hand personal, difficulties , lack of confidence, financing costs, lack of interest in formal educational activities have been used as criteria to establish a typology of non-participantion (Darkenwald and Valentine, 1990).

More systematically, Peter Cookson from the USA has been studying adults' participation in learning activities based on a social participation model known by ISSTAL (*Interdisciplinary, Sequential-Specificity, Time-Allocation, Lifespan*) developed by Smith (Smith & Macaulay, 1980). This model appears to serve as a good theoretical framework for studying the determinants of active adults' participation in learning activities (Cookson, 1986). Furthermore, this model appears to be an adequate research framework for identifying and understanding the core components of the workers' needs, to analyse the influence of their past experience, and to understand their perceived needs for future training.

In fact, the ISSTAL model presents three characteristics of particular importance to theory and researching active adult's participation in continuing training:

(1) A conceptual and interdisciplinary research framework;

(2) Sequential specificity of relationships among independent variables and participation;
(3) The perspective of time distribution along with an individual's life.

The main elements of the theoretical framework for this study were then based on the ISSTAL model of social participation developed by D.H. Smith and already used in USA by Cookson (1986) for studying adult participation in learning activities. The model postulates individual discretionary behaviour resulting from a complex interaction among a set of predictive (independent) variables organised into six classes (Cookson, 1985). These variables are (1) External context, (2) social background, (3) personality, (4) attitudinal dispositions, (5) retained information, and (6) situational aspects (Fig 1).

Fig 1. Model of adult participation in continuing education
Note: Adapted by Cookson (1986) from Smith´s ISSTAL model (1980)

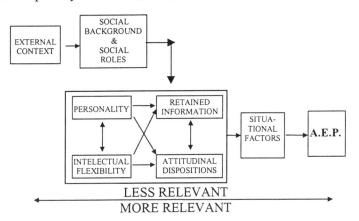

The criterion (dependent) variable (adult participation) is assumed to have both diachronic and synchronic covariation and the model implies causal ordering of the factors (Smith, 1985). The variable classes and the variables adapted from Smith and Cookson for inclusion in the study are indicated in Table 1.

3. METHODOLOGY

The study used a cross-sectoral survey

Table 1 - The ISSTAL model: List of variables

Classes	Variables
Social background & social roles	Ascribed social roles Achieved Social roles Experience & activities Resources & resource access
Personality & intellectual flexibility	Psychological functioning Beliefs & values Intellectual activities
Attitudinal dispositions toward to	Learning & education Profession & job Training entities Training activities
Retained information	Level of participation in training Satisfaction with training Satisfaction with schooling Self-perception as student
Situational factors	Marketing of training Participation barriers Job characteristics
Criterion variable	Participation in continuing training

approach with an instrument specifically developed to collect data from a stratified random sample (Table 2) drawn from a population constituted by all the individuals working in the Alentejo Region for SMEs in the industrial, commercial, tourism, leisure, and personal services sectors.

Table 2 - Sample

Economic Sector	CAE *	Workers	%
Extractive Industry	2	13	3,4
Transforming Industry	3	203	53,8
Commerce & Tourism	6	148	39,3
Leisure activities	94	5	1,3
Personal services	95	8	2,1
Total	---	377	99,9

Note: * CAE - Economic Activity Code

According to the theoretical framework, the predictive factors (independent variables) of the adult participation (criterion variable) were framed by six classes (Cookson, 1986):

> *Class 1 - External context*
> *Class 2 - Social background and social roles*
> *Class 3 - Personality and intellectual flexibility*
> *Class 4 - Attitudinal dispositions*
> *Class 5 - Retained information*
> *Class 6 - Situational factors*

The ***External context*** concerns characteristics of the place where continuing training is taking place. These characteristics are of the diverse nature: social, economic, cultural, organisational, environmental, and even political characteristics. However, this variable was not taken into consideration for the present study. The study was conducted in a region with no relevant internal differences in terms of the external context of the continuing training activities. The ***Social background and social roles*** are related to adults' ascribed and achieved social roles, life and professional experience and activities, and resource availability and access to resources. These factors together influence the specificity and meaning of each one's world (Reddy, 1980). ***Personality and intellectual flexibility*** includes factors of psychological functioning, personality characteristics, and intellectual capacities of individuals. Individuals' personality characteristics are associated with their self-confidence, level of performance and stimulation (Smith, 1980). ***Attitudinal dispositions*** constitute a class of factors concerning individual's values, attitudes, expectations and intentions. These characteristics are closely related to individuals's motivation. ***Retained information*** frames variables related to adults' learning orientation and images, beliefs, and knowledge they have about learning. The ***situational factors*** concern variables that describe temporary situations and aspects that can be associated with the participation of individuals in learning activities.

In the present research, **adult participation in continuing training,** the criterion variable, is defined as the active adults' involvement in purposful and deliberate learning through continuing training programmes.

The instrument for collecting data was developed taking into consideration the ISSTAL model. It was organised into five parts: (1) Social background and social roles was composed of four groups of indicators: a) *Ascribed social roles*, b) *Achieved social roles*, c) *Experience & activities*, and d) *Resources and resource access*; (2) Personality and intellectual flexibility was subdivided into three scales: a) *Psychological functioning*, b) *Beliefs and values*, and c) *Intellectual activities*; (3) Attitudinal dispositions included items collecting four types of attitudes toward: a) *Learning and education*, b) *Profession and job*, c) *Training activities*, and d) *Training entities*; (4) <u>Retained information</u> was organised into four scales: a) *Level of participation in training activities*, b) *Satisfaction in relation to experienced training activities*, c) *Satisfaction in relation to past learning activities in school*, and d) *Self-perception in relation to performance as student* ; and (5) <u>Situational factors</u> comprised three aspects: a) *Marketing of training activities*, b) *Barriers to participation in training activities*, and c) *Job characteristics*. Most of the variables were measured by scales of multi 6-point Likert-type items developed along the domain of each construct. This approach was taken because composite measures provide a broader range of variable variation and minimise a biased measurement of the construct (Babbie, 1973).

The first approach to the research instrument was personally delivered to 35 individuals of the population for pre-testing. These individuals were not a part of the research sample. All of the multi-item scales were examined in terms of reliability and discriminant validity. Scale reliability was assessed by the Cronbach´s alpha coefficient (Table 3). Results suggest that each multi-item measure has a very good reliability. Alpha coefficient for all scales clearly exceeds the 0.70 cut off recommended by Nunnally (1978).

Table 3 - Scale Reliability

Scales	Alpha Pre-test	Alpha Final
Personality and Intellectual Flexibility	0.8279	0,8018
Attitudinal Dispositions	0,7153	0,8838
Retained Information	0,5380	0,7512
Situational factors	0,6069	0,7823

Validity of the multi-item scales was estimated by two ways: (1) Content validity through a panel of judges, and (2) Discriminant validity through Spearman correlation (Table 4). Findings suggest that all of the multi-item measures have discriminant validity.

Table 4 - Discriminant Validity of Multi-item Scales

Scales	Personality	Attitude	R.Information	Situational

Personality	1.0000			
Attitude	0.2986	1.0000		
R.Information	0.2326	0.3131	1.0000	
Situational	-0.0359	0.1313	- 0.0142	1.0000

Data was firstly submitted to (*linear and non-linear*) *principal component factorial analysis* to identify class dimensions of factors influencing individuals's participation in continuing education activities. Relationships between the different predictive factors and the criterion (dependent) variable (participation) were estimated by *multiple regression analysis*. Relationships between the independent variables were also evaluated and analysed. All of the statistical analyses were performed at 0.05 level of significance.

4. RESULTS

Data analysis for this research involved two distinct steps. Firstly, each multi-item scale was submitted to *(non-linear and linear) principal component factorial analysis* to identify the main dimensions influencing workers' participation in continuing training activities. Secondly, assumed predictive factors were regressed on participation in training to assess *predictiveness* of the variables posited in the ISSTAL model as sources of direct and indirect effects on individual's involvement in training activities.

Results from principal component analysis allow the conclusion that class dimensions of the factors influencing individual's participation in continuing training activities in the Alentejo Region are slightly different from the ones initially considered (Table 5).

Results from the multiple regression analyses show that the majority of relationships and factors associated to adult participation in continuing education considered in the ISSTAL model apply to the Alentejo. However, the ISSTAL model as such needs some adjustments in order to be useful for explaining how and why those factors influence the participation of Alentejo SME employees in continuing training activities.

Findings are presented in the sequence in which they are posited in the ISSTAL model.

I - *External Context Factors*

As was stated in the methodology, the external context factors were not taken into consideration in the present study.

Table 5 - Variable Class Dimensions

CLASSES	Dimensions considered	Dimensions resulted
Social background & social roles (SOC)	Ascribed social roles Achieved Social roles Experience & activities Resources & resource access	Family & Life cycle position Education, social class & income Financing dependency Residency & mobility
Personality & intellectual flexibility (CINDV)	Psychological functioning Beliefs & values Intellectual activities	Intellectual activities Human relations & information Superstition Self-confidence Morality and rules Money & autonomy Anxiety Cultural Values
Attitudinal dispositions towards (ATITU)	Learning & education Profession & job Training entities Training activities	Learning & continuing training Trainer & training strategies Quality of training Training facilities Profession & job
Retained information (APREN)	Level of participation in training Satisfaction with training Satisfaction with schooling Self-perception as student	Satisfaction with training Satisfaction with schooling Self-perception as student
Situational factors (SITUA)	Marketing of training Participation barriers Job characteristics	Participation barriers Job conditions Professional valorisation Marketing of training
Criterion variable	Participation in continuing training (PARTI)	Participation in continuing training

II - *Social Background Factors*

The social background factors together are moderate and significantly related to adult participation in continuing training in the Alentejo region (MR=0.51; p=0.000) (Table 6). As a result of non-linear principal component analysis, four dimensions were identified: (1) *Family & life cycle position*, (2) *Education, social class & income*, (3) *Financing dependency*, and (4) *Residency & mobility*. Within this class of variables, the *Education, social class & income* dimension appears to be the more relevant class of factors influencing AEP (Table 7). However, in single terms, results indicated that *level of schooling, personal income, closeness of mother's residence, married descendant, type of employer, interruptions in the school life,* and *financing self-sufficiency of father* were the most influential characteristics in adult participation in training programmes. On the other hand, a set of the social background class variables was found to be not significantly related to participation in continuing training activities.

Table 6 - Multiple Regression Analysis

Var. class dimensions (predictor variables)	Criterion Variables	MR	Explained Variance (%)	Significance
Social background & social roles (SOC)	CINDV	0.5297	28.06	0.0000
	ATITU	0.4425	19.58	0.0002
	APREN	0.4105	16.85	0.0036
	SITUA	0.4263	18.18	0.0025
	PARTI	0.5110	26.20	0.0000
Personality & Intellectual flexibility (CINDV)	ATITU	0.5660	32.04	0.0000
	APREN	0.4493	20.19	0.0102
	SITUA	0.4330	18.75	0.0327
	PARTI	0.4309	18.57	0.0375
Attitudinal dispositions (ATITU)	APREN	0.6142	37.72	0.0000
	SITUA	0.6401	40.97	0.0000
	PARTI	0.6796	46.19	0.0000
Retained information (APREN)	SITUA	0.0805	0.65	0.6581
	PARTI	0.2230	4.97	0.0003
Situational aspects (SITUA)	PARTI	0.7251	52.58	0.0000
CINDV + ATITU + APREN	SITUA	0.7334	53.79	0.0000
	PARTI	0.7980	63.68	0.0000
SOC+CINDV+ATITU+	PARTI	0.8984	80.71	0.0000

APREN +SITUA				

The level of schooling has been frequently identified as the single most influential factor in participation in adult education activities (Lawrence, 1991). Educational background contributes to individual's self-confidence and success during initial education and motivates adults for further learning. In fact, initial educational attainment has been *"consistently observed as the most powerful predictor of participation"* (Houtkoop and Kamp, 1992, p 539). However, influence of the level of schooling may not be as relevant in more homogeneous groups of professionals (Grotelueschen, 1985).

Financing aspects such as personal income also appear to influence AEP. This may be related to the fact that training costs are a participation barrier (Houtkoop and Kamp, 1992).

Characteristics linked to work have also been identified as relevant factors for AEP. In fact, it has been found that the chance of one receiving training is influenced by a cluster of factors related to work (Houtkoop and Kamp, 1992). For instance, *"certain work roles offer a better chance of access to continuing education"* (Houtkoop and Kamp, 1992). In Alentejo, *type of employer* may resume that cluster of work characteristics that influence participation in training.

Age was not found to have a significant relationship to participation. Although some literature has reported that older professionals are less participant than young people are (Cervero, 1988), that finding is consistent with the fact that educational level and occupational status are more influential than age in learning abilities (Houtkoop and Kamp, 1992).

III - *Personality & Intellectual Flexibility*

Factors comprised by the *Personality & Intellectual Flexibility* class are also moderated but significantly related to AEP (MR=0.43; p=0.037) (Table 6). As a result of principal component factorial analysis with orthogonal rotation, eight dimensions were identified: (1) *Intellectual activities,* (2) *Human relations & information*, (3) *Superstition*, (4) *Self-confidence*, (5) *Morality & rules*, (6) *Money & autonomy*, (7) *Anxiety*, and (8) *Cultural values*. However, only two of the eight class dimensions showed to have significant influence on APE (Table 7). In fact, only the *intellectual activities* and the *superstition* factors presented some significant relationship to adult participation. Since this class of variables has presented higher relationship to *Attitudinal Dispositions* (MR=0.57; p=0.000) which its turn has presented in significant relationship to APE (MR=0.58; p=0.000), the influence of the most variables of this class in participation appear to be indirect. However, *self-evaluation, reading* and *writing books and believing in life beyond death* were found to be the relatively most significant single factors.

Table 7 - Multiple Regression Analysis (Criterion variable: AEP)

Variable Class Dimensions	MR	Explained Variance (%)	Significance
Family & Life cycle position	0.28	7.7	0.0141
Education, social class & income	0.36	0	0.0000
Financing dependency	0.26	12.	0.0024
Residency & mobility	0.23	97	0.0305
		6.6	
		7	
		5.2	
		3	
Intellectual activities	0.25	6.22	0.0140
Human relations & information	0.13	1.57	0.6628
Superstition	0.23	5.20	0.0060
Self-confidence	0.11	1.21	0.7172
Morality and rules	0.08	0.61	0.8097
Money & autonomy	0.16	2.69	0.1194
Anxiety	0.13	1.70	0.1722
Cultural Values	0.12	1.46	0.3618
Learning & cont. training	0.57	32.49	0.0001
Trainer & training strategies	0.52	27.04	0.0004
Quality of training	0.54	29.16	0.0001
Training facilities	0.56	31.36	0.0000
Profession & job	0.12	1.33	0.5443
Satisfaction with training	0.22	4.63	0.0000
Satisfaction with schooling	0.05	0.21	0.3776
Self-perception as student	0.06	0.10	0.2446
Participation barriers	0.67	45.16	0.0000
Job conditions	0.22	4.89	0.0094
Professional valorisation	0.20	4.04	0.0039
Marketing of training	0.66	44.08	0.0000

IV - *Attitudinal Dispositions*

Attitudes toward training has been reported as an important cluster of determinants of participation in training activities (Lawrence, 1991). Consistent with those reports, results from the present study showed that *Attitudinal dispositions* toward training of individuals working in Alentejo (Portugal) have a relevant influence on their decision to participate in training activities (Table 6).

As a result of the principal component factorial analysis with orthogonal rotation, five dimensions were identified: (1) Attitudes toward *learning and continuing training*, (2) Attitudes toward *trainer & training strategies*, (3) Attitudes toward q*uality of training*, (4) Attitudes toward *training facilities*, and (5) Attitudes toward *profession and job*. All attitudinal dispositions class dimensions but *Attitudes toward Profession and Job* were found to have a significant relationship with AEP (Table 7). That is, only attitudes directly related to training were found to be significantly related to participation. It appears that perception of the importance of training and value of learning is more relevant for participation in training activities than perception of the profession and job characteristics.

V - *Retained Information*

The class of retained information included three dimensions: (1) *Satisfaction with training,* (2) *Satisfaction with previous schooling, and* (3) *Self-perception as student.* This class of factors is postulated to have greater influence on the criterion variable (AEP). Contrary to research results reported by the literature, this variable showed only a very low significant relationship with participation (Table 6). In fact, only the *Satisfaction with Training* dimension was found to have a significant, but very weak, relationship with participation (Table 7).

VI - *Situational Factors*

Situational factors are those which are assumed to have the greatest influence on participation (Lawrence, 1991). As result of the principal component factorial analysis, four factors were identified: (1) Participation barriers, (2) Job conditions, (3) Professional valorisation, and (4) Marketing of training. All of the dimensions were found to have significant relationship with participation in training activities (Table 7). However, *participation barriers* and *marketing of training* are the most influential set of factors. *Job conditions* and *professional valorisation* showed to have a very weak relationship with participation. These findings are consistent with results obtained in the classes of *Attitudinal dispositions* and *Retained information* factors. In fact, in all of the three last classes of factors, dimensions directly referring training were the relatively most significant characteristics within the class.

5. CONCLUSIONS

The findings point to three major conclusions. Firstly, the ISSTAL model offered a comprehensive and adequate theoretical framework to examine relationships between a multiplicity of factors in participation in training activities of the Alentejo SME employees.

Secondly, it can be said that the ISSTAL model, in general, applies to the Alentejo reality. On one hand, the factors examined were related to classes of independent variables considered by the ISSTAL model. On the other hand, classes of independent variables (predictors) showed to relate to each other along a continuum of relevance concerning influence in participation (criterion).

Thirdly, the nature and number of class dimensions were found to be slightly different from the ones posited in the ISSTAL model (Table 5). In addition, a number of factors (individually considered) were found to have a different relationship to participation from the one assumed in the ISSTAL model. These differences may be a result of the differences between data collection instruments and/or characteristics of the context, the first class of variables considered in the ISSTAL model, which was not measured in the present research.

6. RECOMMENDATIONS

Results from this study suggest that public training institutions, training providers and employers should implement strategies to promote participation of SME employees in training activities. The dimensions, individually considered, having higher relationship to participation were *Attitudes toward learning & training, trainer & training strategies, quality of training and training facilities* and *participation barriers* and *marketing of training* (Table 7).

Public training institutions should implement strategies focusing on the need for quality training. Consistent with this, they also should establish a certification system for trainers and training providers.

Training providers should concentrate their efforts on marketing of training and on evaluation of the quality of their training offerings.

Employers should place emphasis on the strategies of incentives focusing the role and importance of training for job performance. They also should establish recognition for those employees who participate in training activities. In addition, they should make efforts to reduce participation barriers, namely the ones related to work.

Further research should also be recommended. It was recognised that differences of findings to ISSTAL model might have been due to differences in the data collection instruments. In addition, since the present research did not take into consideration the *external context* class of factors, future research should focus on comparative surveys complemented by a set of case studies conducted in a collaborative way in various European regions.

REFERENCES

Brown, A. (1994), Review of the characteristics of effective learning programmes for the development of occupational competence, University of Surrey, Guildford.

Brunner, E., Wilder, P.S., Kierchner, C. and Newberry, J.S. (1959), "An overview of adult education research", Adult Education of USA.

Collins, M. (1991), Adult Education as Vocation, Routledge, London.

Cookson, P.S. (1986), "A framework for theory and research on adult education participation", Adult Education Quarterly, Vol.36 No.3, pp.130-141.

Darkenwald, G.G. and Valentine, T. (1985), "Factor Structure deterrents to public participation in adult education", Adult Education Quarterly, Vol.55 No.4, pp.177-193.

Delors, J. (1993), Growth, Competitiveness and Employment (White Paper), European Commission, Brussels.

Engeström, Y. (1994), Training for change: New approach to instruction and learning in working life, International Labour Office, Geneva.

European Commission. (1995), Teaching and Learning: Towards Knowledge based Society, European Commission, Brussels.

Heidegger, G. and Kuhn, M. (1995), New Forms of Basic and Further Education of Professionals for Vocational Education and Training, unpublished project application, Institut Technik und Bildung, University of Bremen, Bremen.

Hodson, R., Hooks, G. and Rieble, S. (1994), "Training in the workplace: Continuity and Change", Sociological Perspectives, Vol.37 No.1, pp.97-119.

Kovács, I. et al. (1992), Sistemas flexíveis de produção e reorganização do trabalho, CESO I&D-PEDIP, Lisboa.

More, A. (1990), "Participation in Continuing and vocational education as an investment strategy for adults", Adult Literacy and Basic Education, Vol.14 No.2, pp.102-115.

Nieuwenhuis, A.F.M. (1991), „Practical learning situations as a preparation for lifelong job oriented learning", paper presented at the International Workshop on Developing Education for Lifelong Learning, Tampere, Finland.

Pryor, B. (1990), "Predicting and explaining intentions to participate in continuing education: An application of the theory of reasoned action", Adult Education Quarterly, Vol.40 No.3, pp.146-157.

Smith, D.H. (1980), "General activity model", in Smith, D.H., Macaulay, J. et al. (Eds.), Participation in Social and Political Activities, pp.461-530, Jossey Bass, San Francisco.

Van Tilbourg, E. (1989), "Participation and persistence in continuing lifelong learning experiences of the Ohio Cooperative Extension Service: an investigation using expectancy valence", Journal of Agricultural Education, Vol.30 No.4, pp.42-46.

Yang, B., Blunt, A. and Butler, R. (1994), "Prediction of participation in continuing professional education: A test of two behavioral intention models", Adult Education Quarterly, Vol.44 No.2, pp.83-96.

Chapter 23

Returns of Labour Market Training under Conditions of Recession
An individual trainee point of view

Iiris Mikkonen
Labour Institute, Jyväskylä

1.   LABOUR MARKET TRAINING IN FINLAND

The study looks at the effectiveness of labour market training (LMT) in Finland from the point of view of the individual trainee. LMT is offering training opportunities to the disadvantaged in the labour markets, mainly for the unemployed, i.e. for people who in their current life situation are excluded from adult education through vocational institutions and through in-company training. Responsibility for the planning, development and execution of LMT in Finland lies with Labour Administration who purchase services from different training suppliers. The number of people who have started LMT has, in recent years, been some three to four per cent of the Finnish labour force. The duration of LMT courses is on an average three to four months.

Because LMT represents one of the tools of active labour market policy in Finland, it has some obvious labour policy goals. The most important goal is to decrease the level of unemployment, both in the short term and in the long term. At the same time it also represents a form of adult education with its own educational policy goals. However, as a labour and educational policy measure LMT is beset with many problems. Those concerned have high expectations for its effectiveness, particularly its ability to help trainees find employment. However the environment in which LMT operates, above all the general employment situation but also radical changes and uncertainty characterising today's labour market, have essentially weakened its potential efficacy. These changes include the qualification demands in the labour markets, the appreciation of different age groups, different educational levels and different levels of working experience.

1.1   Some conceptual considerations

The effectiveness of training is not easy to measure. There are many factors influencing training and its outcomes. The main question is which impacts, and to what extent, are really a result of the training. The effectiveness of training or education may have a narrow or a broad definition. From a narrow point of view the operationalisation of the effectiveness is based only on some quantitative measures, e.g. LMT has only employment or income effects. From a broader viewpoint there are many short-term and long-term goals. The interests of many stakeholders have to be taken into consideration and these must be evaluated. Those goals may from the participant's point of view be, for example, occupational development or the reorganisation of their life in general. Participants may also have some special individual goals when they start LMT. The study tries to look at the effectiveness of LMT from the participant's point of view as broadly as possible given the empirical data. It defines effectiveness on the basis of how training has promoted the attainment of both individual and administrative goals set for it.

The effectiveness of LMT can be seen in the development of trainees' labour market status. Because of this, the study has adopted the concept of labour market pathway (LMP) that makes it possible to describe changes in an individual's labour market status over time. Instead of a cross-sectional analysis at a given point of time the study deploys a longitudinal description. Attention is paid particularly to whether the pathway changes its direction or undergoes other changes connected with training. LMP refers here to a sum total of the different stages and passages of an individual's labour market history and their serial continuity, describing the relationship or the meeting point of an individual and the labour market. Each stage has its own duration and is determined by a specific labour market status. The separate phases of the pathway can be dominated by employment, entrepreneurship, unemployment, studying or another activity. An essential feature of every phase is the relationship between the individual and the labour market, their contacting surface. The occupational commitment and occupational flexibility an individual displays at various stages may also be seen as an aspect of his or her LMP. Another component used in assessing the effectiveness of LMT is the trainees' perceptions of the effects of their training on various aspects of their life, and their assessment of how important the training was from the point of view of their finding employment and taking up studies. The study also evaluates how far and in what ways various characteristic features linked with an individual and with LMT are related to the effectiveness. The general labour market situation will also be considered as an intervening factor for the effectiveness of LMT.

There has been an extensive transitional period in the labour market of Finland during the last ten years. There is now 'a permanent temporariness': a large proportion, maybe the majority, of jobs are temporary and, at the same time, unemployment is high (nearly 20 per cent of the labour force). This means from an individual's viewpoint that individual LMPs have become sinuous and fragmentary, often including short periods of work, study and unemployment. An unbroken, harmonious working career from entry into the labour market until retirement is quite uncommon. There is often unemployment, studying as adult, changes of occupation, moves into new occupational fields and general insecurity. However, in this study there is a hypothesis that people themselves have a kind of view regarding their LMPs. They have some expectations, a vision of the 'main thread' of the pathway. This vision determines the value and significance of particular labour market phases to them. They try to act intentionally under given social and economical preconditions to carry out the plot of their pathways.

There are many individual and societal factors influencing the beginnings and the later course of the LMP. Bourdieu (1984) speaks of social and cultural capital getting transferred into individual life trajectories, e.g. into choices regarding one's career, through some individual traits. There is also debate as to the extent to which occupational preferences are established during the initial educational period or to what extent they may originate from the social status of the family (Rinne et al. 1991). Poor opportunities for education and poor placement in the labour market tend to have a cumulative effect.

Adult education occupies a place in the integrity of an individual LMP. It usually has some connection with the previous course of the pathway. In-company training and perhaps also other forms of adult education may be connected to career advancement, while LMT is often connected to a regressive or unstable phase of the LMP. It is claimed that adult education does not have any continuity (Cedefop 1985). According to this view, education should be based on the life and working experience and the preceding LMPs of adults. The experiences should be integrated to maintain the adults' motivation for schooling. It is not an easy task, because adults with their different experiential backgrounds form a much more heterogeneous target group than the young. It is also technically more difficult to tailor training to individual requirements than to offer the same package for all.

Occupation, occupational commitment or flexibility and occupational transitions are also of great interest from the viewpoint of this study. Calls for flexibility, changes towards multi-skilling in the working life and demands for new non-vocational qualifications have created the need for a new kind of occupational orientation. A strict commitment to only one occupation is not necessarily desirable any more, and adult education may offer a way to broadening an individual's occupational orientation.

The significance of unemployment as a part of LMP has also increased, the majority of the labour force have been unemployed at some point of their LMPs. Unemployment is partly connected to motivation for education and to general life orientation, too. It is said that long-term unemployment is leading to a fissure in occupational identity and education may help to reconstruct this identity (Lindroos 1993). The general weakening of motivation for education is understandable in a situation like this when not even an academic degree can guarantee a steady career. What is the function of vocational education and especially LMT now? What is the point of training if there are no jobs? Do we have to motivate the unemployed for schooling and how? These are some crucial questions in my study.

However, we have to remember that there are various kinds of unemployment. People deal with unemployment differently, depending on the circumstances of their life, age, gender, their own life orientation and their vision regarding their LMP. Therefore, training has a different relationship with life situations for different categories of the unemployed. Training is not necessarily always a very positive, not to mention right, solution, whereas some other services of Labour Administration or some other activities could be more profitable. According to Manninen (1993), study may, however, represent a survival strategy, by helping people adapt to unemployment, by decreasing anxiety or by offering ways out of the situation.

1.2   Implementation of the study

The investigation is a follow-up panel study using a quasi-experimental research design financed by Finnish Ministry of Labour. The main objects of the follow-up are individuals' labour market phases, their employment, unemployment and studies and their occupational and geographical mobility. The main target group comprises a total of 4,583 persons who started their LMT course in spring 1993. The control group (5,197 persons) consists of those job-seekers at employment offices in spring 1993 who did not take part in LMT. The members of the control group were selected on the basis of a parity principle to serve as pairs to members of the main target group, ensuring that each control pair's place of residence, gender, age, educational background, occupation and labour market status of that time corresponded as closely as possible with those of the pair admitted to training. In addition the study covered a separate group of people who took part, while enjoying LMT benefits, in examination-oriented training provided in vocational schools on what are known as single places. This group of examination-oriented trainees numbered 311 people, and they had begun their two or three year training in autumn 1991.

The most important task of the study is a consideration of LMT as an aspect of an individual's LMP, the stage of the path where LMT is taking place and whether it causes a turn in the pathway's direction or whether the pathway, on the contrary, continues on its old course. The study examines a period totalling 4-5 years, which in temporal terms represents some 10 per cent of the average length of a LMP, and during which time the main group received LMT while the control group was given none. Thus, the questionnaires cover a total of some two years of the target groups' LMPs both before and after training (the starting point). The study attempts, by means of its quasi-experimental research design, to estimate the link between training and the pathways and the turns they take by comparing the LMPs of those who took part in LMT and those who did not participate in training.

The training discussed in the study has been classified, on the basis of the content descriptions of the relevant courses, into six basic types (Figure 1). According to its goals and teaching contents training may firstly be divided in two main groups, vocational and non-vocational training. Vocational LMT comprises vocationally oriented training clearly linked with certain occupations or occupational fields, represented by vocational basic and re-training for those without vocational skills and those in the process of changing their occupation (8% of the total main research group, average length 6.6 months) and vocational further and in-service training (with the aim of maintaining and enhancing vocational skills or upgrading occupational competence in a certain occupational field, 54%, average 3.9 months). Also under the heading of vocational LMT belong vocational training for special skills (e.g. instruction in foreign languages and automatic data processing not targeted for any specific occupational group, 7%, average 2 months) and entrepreneurial training (15%, average 2.7 months). Non-vocational LMT consists of preparatory training (e.g. guidance for young school leavers and career planning courses for university graduates) where the aim is to sort out the participants' living situation and plans and disseminate information about training and job openings (10%, average 2.4 months), and training for immigrants comprising among other things instruction in Finnish language, civics and the basics of working life together with guidance (6%, average 3.3 months).

Figure 1. Classification of labour market training

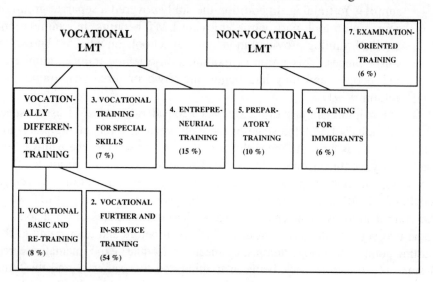

At the individual level the study is based on panel data gathered mainly through postal surveys, carried out in four different stages, and complemented with data from the computerised records of the labour authorities. The computerised records have, apart from personal particulars, yielded comprehensive information on subjects' educational background and work and unemployment history and specific details of the training under study. Postal surveys have been used to gather more detailed information on subjects' activities before training, factors behind their decision to apply for training, their assessments of the training they have received, their activities and labour market history after training and their further plans, orientation and expectations. The first questionnaire was sent to the main research group before they began their training in spring 1993 and the last one two years after they had finished their training. The control group received their questionnaires according to a similar schedule so that the total period of time covered in the follow-up was about two years. The response rates were moderately good. In the main research group the first questionnaire was completed by 70 per cent, the last questionnaire by 62 per cent of the subjects, in the group of examination-oriented trainees by 79 and 70 per cent and in the control group by 58 and 52 per cent respectively.

2.   FINDINGS: THE COURSE OF THE LABOUR MARKET PATHWAY

The respondents were asked to describe their main activities during certain time periods both retrospectively for the preceding two years and separately for each year covered in the follow-up. For the preceding time the periods were six months, for the time covered in the follow-up four months long. The data must be interpreted as implying that the activities described as major for each period cover most of the period in question but that the respondent may also have engaged in other activities. The findings concerning the course of the LMP presented onwards are mainly based on this data describing the main activity of each period.

The average labour market status of members both of the participant group and of the control group has improved fairly steadily during the two years of the follow-up if their situation is described in terms of the proportions of those who have found a job and those without a job. The groups differ, however, in that as compared to the control group, the participant group at first has less (24 and 20 per cent respectively), but at the end of the second year of the follow-up to a statistically significant degree more (41 and 45 per cent respectively), people who had found paid job. During training the trainees are not likely to have been very active job seekers, which in part explains why they are immediately after their training more often without a job. As for entrepreneurs, they are more common in the trainee group during all follow-up periods, as are full-time students. Correspondingly, those who have been unemployed are, during all follow-up periods, less common in the trainee than in the control group, though in both groups the proportion of unemployed people decreases period by period. While during the first four-month period some 64-65 per cent of each group were unemployed, at the end of the second year of the follow-up only 29 per cent of the trainee group but 36 per cent of the control group were still without a job. Most successful in finding a job have been the male participants in entrepreneurship training who have started enterprises of their own (34 % had an enterprise and in addition 25 % had a paid job at the end of the follow-up period). This good result is partly explained by the fact that those who enter entrepreneurship training have more often a stable working career behind them than participants in other types of training. Next most successful in finding employment are those who have completed vocational basic or re-training, vocational further or in-service training and examination-oriented training. Those who had taken part in vocational training for special skills, preparatory training and training for immigrants were most often unemployed.

Figure 2. The main activity of LMT participants and the controls after training in thirds of year

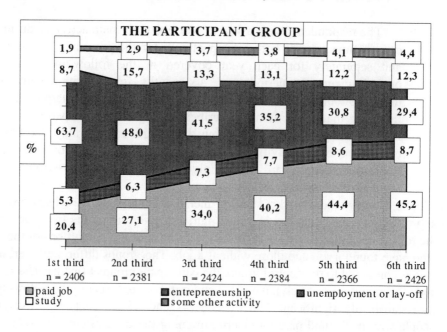

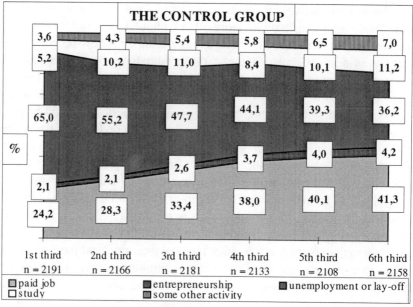

2.1   Proportion of employment and unemployment before and after

One way of describing the LMP preceding and following training (in the case of the control group, preceding and following the starting point) is analysing the respective proportions of employment and unemployment in the period under consideration on an individual level. The analysis involves summing up the total duration of periods chiefly characterised by employment (either a paid job or entrepreneurship) and of periods chiefly characterised by unemployment and proportioning them to the total duration of periods. During the two-year preceding period, the proportion of employment was on average 52 per cent in the trainee group and 55 per cent in the control group, but during the follow-up the proportions went down to 40 per cent in the trainee group and 35 per cent in the control group. The proportion of employment in the LMP has thus decreased fairly clearly in both groups, but in the trainee group the decrease was a little less. Correspondingly, in the preceding period the proportion of periods of unemployment was on an average 29 per cent in the trainee group and 26 per cent in the control group, but during the follow-up it increased in the trainee group to 39 per cent and in the control group to 45 per cent. A description in terms of proportional unemployment thus again indicates that the average labour market status has in both groups deteriorated when comparing the preceding and the follow-up period, but less in the trainee group. As regards different types of training, it is those who have taken part in entrepreneurship training who were most often employed and least often unemployed both during the time preceding training and during the follow-up. Among participants in vocational basic and re-training the employment situation was below average in the period preceding training, but after training their LMP was nearly as positive as that of entrepreneurship trainees.

2.2   Labour market pathway before and after

The two-year preceding period comprised a total of five, and the follow-up period a total of six, separate periods. On the individual level the combinations of data describing the chief activities of each period, action combinations, were used to form seven types of LMP. A stable working career is mainly characterised by a paid job or entrepreneurship. A combination of a stable working career and unemployment consists of a stable career turning to unemployment or vice versa. An unstable working career comprises periods of employment alternating with periods of unemployment. A student career consists mainly of full-time studies or of alternating periods of studies and employment. Long-term unemployment comprises consecutive periods of unemployment and recurrent unemployment or periods of unemployment interspersed with periods of some activity. The category of other activity includes activities other than employment, entrepreneurship, studying or unemployment and those activity combinations that do not clearly fall into any other type of labour market path. A cross-tabulation at the individual level of the type of labour market path characterising the preceding period and the follow-up period makes it possible to examine in the long term whether the pathway has taken a turn for the better or a turn for the worse, or whether the person's labour market path may be said to belong to the same type both before and after training (after the starting point). Both in the trainee and control group LMP has remained unchanged equally often (30%). By contrast, in the trainee group 32 per cent, but in the control group only 23 per cent, have seen a turn for the better in their LMP, while correspondingly in the trainee group 38 per cent, but in the control group as many as 48 per cent, have seen their LMP taking a turn for the worse. We may thus conclude that LMT has checked a tendency for the LMP to take a turn in a direction dominated by unemployment and leading away from a stable working career.

Table 1. Turns of labour market pathway

	participant group		Control group	
	n	%	n	%
a turn for the better	469	32,1	308	22,6
a turn for the worse	551	37,8	650	47,7
good course remains	261	17,9	232	17,0
bad course remains	178	12,2	174	12,8
in all	1459	100,0	1364	100,0

2.3   Perceived effectiveness

Those taking part in LMT were asked to assess the effects their training had had on their own situation and prospects both immediately after finishing the training and one and two years later. According to assessments given immediately after training it corresponded fairly well with the participants' expectations (only 4 per cent felt that the training had completely failed to meet their expectations). Expectations had been best answered in vocational training for special skills and in examination-oriented training, least well in preparatory training and training for immigrants. In assessments given one and two years after training the positive effects of training are quite clearly linked with the participants' occupational skills, self-esteem and life situation. Two years after training a very or fairly positive effect on their occupational skill was perceived by 68 per cent, on their self-esteem by 65 per cent, and on their life situation in general by 52 per cent of the main group (Table 2). Both one and two years after training, the assessments of those who had taken part in examination-oriented training are on average clearly more positive than those of the main group. Among other types of training vocational basic and re-training and training for immigrants have been assessed most positively and preparatory training least positively. However, the effects perceived by participants of different types of training are linked with somewhat different things. The effects on self-esteem and living situation are described in very positive terms in all types of training. In addition, participants in vocationally oriented training feel that their training had very positive effects on their occupational skill, while participants in entrepreneurship training feel similarly about its effects on their starting or continuing with entrepreneurship, and participants in preparatory training or training for immigrants about its influence on their starting or continuing with studies and on their further education prospects.

Table 2. To what extent and in which direction has LMT influenced the following fields

	very positive	quite positive	no influence	quite negative	very negative	in all
			percentages			
my professional skills	13,8	54,7	30,8	0,3	0,4	100,0
self-esteem	15,3	50,0	33,1	1,1	0,4	100,0
my life situation in general	11,4	40,6	46,7	0,8	0,4	100,0
my opportunities to study further	7,1	30,5	60,3	1,0	1,2	100,0
starting or continuing studying	7,7	26,8	63,0	1,5	1,0	100,0
opportunities for getting a job	9,4	25,1	63,3	1,1	1,1	100,0
my career	5,2	27,9	65,0	1,0	0,8	100,0
finding a new profession	7,3	21,2	69,5	0,7	1,2	100,0
my financial status	5,0	19,5	71,2	3,1	1,2	100,0
my family situation	4,5	15,1	78,3	1,3	0,8	100,0
starting or continuing enterprise	4,7	14,4	77,7	1,6	1,6	100,0
keeping my job	4,2	10,6	82,9	0,6	1,6	100,0

In addition, respondents who, two years after training, had a job or an enterprise of their own or who were studying were asked to estimate the effects of LMT on the activity in question. Of those in employment 31 per cent thought that LMT had had a very or fairly significant effect on their finding a job. Three types of training were perceived as clearly more important in finding a paid job than other types: examination-oriented training (76%), vocational basic and re-training (46%) and training for immigrants (45%). Among participants in entrepreneurship training two out in three of those who had started a business estimated that their training had been a very or fairly important factor in their starting an enterprise of their own. As regards taking up studies, LMT was perceived on average as a slightly more important influence than on finding a job. A total of 39 per cent of the main group members who were studying two years after finishing their training felt that LMT had been a very or fairly significant factor. In summary we may conclude that two years after respondents had finished their training, 23 per cent of the whole main group and 46 per cent of the examination-oriented training group feel that their training has had at least some influence on their either finding employment or taking up studies, i.e. their labour market status of that time.

3.   CONCLUSIONS

The study also appraised how the process of application and selection had affected the results of the research. According to the estimate, the factors that may cause selection bias cancel each other out. The final result of comparing the participant and control groups is that over two years, LMT has on an average increased employment by some   5   percentage   units   and   correspondingly   diminished unemployment by some 6 percentage units. According to the findings of the present study there are no grounds for excluding older people from LMT, for compared to control group members of the same age group, the labour market status of participants aged 45 and over has developed in a more positive direction. The results concerning long-term unemployed people are similarly encouraging, for those who have taken part in LMT have remained in long-term unemployment less often than those who did not participate. In implementing LMT attention should be paid to the individual needs of adults, who often have abundant prior living and working experience. The participants should be seen as subjects who are constructing their own learning and development process and their own LMPs, not simply as objects of training.

Both the development of trainees' labour market status and their own estimates and experiences reveal that vocational basic and re-training is more effective than was expected. Indeed, it seems that there is even an increasing need for training of this kind, though in recent years there have been cuts in this type of LMT in Finland. Many people entering vocational basic and re-training aim to broaden their field of occupational competence, which may substantially improve their opportunities on the labour market.

By contrast, the findings regarding the effect on labour market status of vocational further and in-service training are less favourable. In the present data the focus of further and in-service training lies heavily on the training of technical personnel and industrial workers, and attention should be paid to ensuring a more even provision of training that would also serve the needs of other occupational fields. In addition, more women should be admitted to further and in-service training. However, as far as its effectiveness in improving occupational skills are concerned, further and in-service training may be judged fairly successful. After vocational training for special skills trainees' labour market status has on average developed even less favourably than after further and in-service training, actually less favourably than in the control group. On the other hand, the participants do not anticipate that their training will substantially improve their chances of finding a job, with the result that their assessments of the training they have received are fairly positive. Most of those who took part in this type of training are unemployed people with a fairly good education whose attitude to training is rather positive and who are very willing to participate in training. Obviously training of this kind is also needed, for adult people must develop particularly instrumental skills needed in working life, and it is precisely when they are out of work that they should be offered opportunities for doing so.

The most favourable development of their labour market status is discernible among participants in entrepreneurship training, which is, however, partly explained by the circumstance that their initial situation was better than that of other trainees. However, a third of those who were starting their own enterprise feel that entrepreneurship training has little or no effect on their starting an enterprise. The problem of entrepreneurship training may be said to lie in the fact that this type of training targets people whose labour market status is clearly better than that of those served by other kinds of LMT, with the result that we may wonder whether this group would have been able to improve their labour market status even without any training. However, those who become entrepreneurs often give employment opportunities to other people so if the multiplier effect is taken into account, entrepreneurship training may significantly affect the labour market.

The problem of preparatory training may be said to be that its perceived effectiveness is clearly less than that of other training types. In the area of personal development for instance, where preparatory training might be expected to excel, the perceived effectiveness of the training is lowest among all types of training. It is among participants in preparatory training that we also find the greatest number of persons who feel that their training has had no effect on their situation and prospects in any area. There should be careful consideration of the reasons behind this low degree of perceived effectiveness so that the contents of preparatory training can be improved.

As regards training for immigrants there are difficulties about drawing conclusions because the low response rate means the results are not very reliable. The respondents are likely to represent the immigrants most articulate outside their mother tongue and best adjusted to Finnish life. Those who did respond have fairly positive perceptions of the effectiveness of their training, and nearly half of those who had a job two years later, for instance, think that it was at least partly due to the labour market training they had received. However, the immigrant trainees' labour market status has clearly developed less favourably than that of the other labour market trainees, and if we take into account the small number of the respondents, immigrants' labour market status in Finland may be said to be noticeably worse than that of the majority population. However, the trainees' favourable assessments do indicate that it is highly necessary to organise LMT for immigrants.

Examination-oriented training bought for the customers as single student places is very favourably assessed by its participants, and their labour market status has developed more favourably after training than is the case in the main group. More trainees have found a job and the perceived significance of the training is noticeably higher than that of LMT proper. However, the problem of training of this kind may be said to lie in the fact that there are more people asking for a student place than the labour authorities have been able to buy. Accordingly, in recent years the authorities have bought only placements on short courses while giving up examination-oriented training. It is important that public authorities support adults' examination-oriented training, but such support must be implemented in an equitable manner.

The present organisation of the Finnish LMT is to a degree flexible and is able to pay attention to changes in working life and in training needs, but in some ways it is also inflexible because the average price targets set to the training restrict to some extent its qualitative development. Because of the high unemployment rate in Finland there has been set some quantitative targets for labour policy measures and on the basis of these the Ministry of Labour has set target-oriented average prices for LMT per day per trainee. In addition, increasing the volume of training has made it impossible to adequately control its standard. Though some of the training may be of very high quality, on the basis of participants' comments it must be concluded that a part of the training is of low standard, leads to doubtful results and damages the reputation of LMT as a whole. In view of this, improving the standard of LMT and above all maintaining it at a high level must, from the point of view of the future labour and educational policy status and function of LMT, be seen as the most important question.

Another factor diminishing the effectiveness of LMT are its links with the conditions of unemployment benefit. Taking part in LMT, like taking part in adult education in general, should be based on personal interest and motivation. If trainees participate only to secure their economic subsistence, and to ensure that they will receive adequate unemployment benefit in the future, the outcomes are not likely to be very good. Trainees perceive training as an external necessity and have no interest in its content. While giving guidance to potential trainees and selecting the participants, attention should be paid to training motivation and attempts should be made to avoid admitting to training people whose only aim is securing their means of subsistence. In addition, it is of course very important to discuss the general principles of the policy regarding rights of the unemployed to get benefits and their obligations to participate in training or some other activity and above all the relationship between these two things.

REFERENCES

Bourdieu, P. (1984), *Distinction. A social critique of the judgement of taste*, Routledge and Kegan Paul, London.

Lindroos, R. (1993), *Työ, koulutus, elämänhallinta. Elämäkertatutkimus työllisyyskoulutukseen osallistuneiden työorientaatioista. Helsingin yliopiston kasvatustieteen laitos*, Tutkimuksia 136.

Manninen, J. (1993), *Akateemiset työttömät työnhakijat. Elämäntilanne ja työvoimakoulutus. Helsingin yliopisto*, Kasvatustieteen laitoksen tutkimuksia 137.

Mikkonen, I. (1995a), "Labour Market Training: Underlying Motives of Participation", in Juuti, P. Mikkonen, I. and Räisänen, H., *Three Essays on Labour Market Training*, Labour Policy Studies Nr. 108, Ministry of Labour.

Mikkonen, I. (1995b), "Motivation, Expectations and Realization of Individual Experiences", in Mikkonen, I. and Räisänen, H. (Eds.), *Evaluating Labour Market Training - Outcome and Effectiveness. Proceedings from the Seminar in Helsinki, August 1995*, Labour Policy Studies Nr. 122, Ministry of Labour..

Mikkonen, I. (1996), "Labour market training and turns of the labour market pathway. Assessment of the effectiveness based on the first follow-up year", paper presented at 18th Conference on European Employment Systems and the Welfare State 9-14 July 1996.

Rinne, R., Kivinen, O. and Naumanen, P. (1991), *Aikuiskoulutuksen yhteiskunnalliset lähtökohdat. Turun yliopiston täydennyskoulutuskeskus*, Painosalama Oy, Turku.

Chapter 24

Outcomes of Vocational Education/Training versus General Education
Results from the German Contribution to the International Adult Literacy Survey

Rainer H. Lehmann, and Rainer Peek
University of Berlin

1.   QUALIFICATIONS IN GERMANY

The German system of education offers students a great number of options, with multiple tracks leading to the various exit points. Originally, there was a clear-cut distinction between academic education, leading to a general certificate of eligibility for university studies, and the various forms of vocational education, building upon minimal or intermediate general education and leading directly to employment on the labour market. As a consequence of a series of educational reforms during the last decades, this distinction has been lessened to a considerable degree. Now, the system responds with much flexibility to individual needs, allowing young people to move through the system in various career patterns (OECD, 1996). Officially, vocational and academic education at the upper secondary level have been declared 'equivalent', with the consequence that the International Standard Classification of Education (ISCED: UNESCO, 1989) provides only one category for both.

There is great interest in the question whether or not there are differences in terms of the actual qualifications acquired in the various tracks of the system. The data provided by the *International Adult Literacy Survey* (IALS: OECD and Statistics Canada, 1995) render a unique opportunity to investigate this question with reference to the adult population as a whole, for those age groups which constitute - at least in principle - the country's labour force. While the German sample of this survey ($N = 2061$) does not allow for comparisons between all possible career patterns defined in the system, it is at least possible to describe the characteristics of major groups. This implies that the respective group definitions are also applicable to the older cohorts who have received their education and training before the reforms were implemented.

2. THEORETICAL BACKGROUND AND RESEARCH QUESTIONS

Originally, the neo-classical approach to *Human Capital Theory* (Schultz, 1960) did not distinguish between different forms of education, assuming that purely formal indicators, such as 'years of education' were sufficient to explain the differences in productivity which determine the role of education for economic growth. Later refinements of the theory (Becker, 1964; Mincer, 1974) introduced the distinction between *general and specific education* as well as that between *formal education and (informal) job experience* in order to explain income differences on the labour market. However, the respective measures still contained little or no information on the actual qualifications related to the respective programmes. In measuring different components of the qualifications IALS provides an important complement to the measures used in Human Capital Theory. In principle, at least, proficiency measures should prove to be superior predictors of the individual income. It has been reported that this is true, at least in countries where the education system itself lacks the internal differentiation which is typical of Germany, and other countries with similar articulated systems (Kirsch and Murray, 1996).

If such differentiation is present, it is likely that much relevant information is conveyed in the process of channelling individuals through the system and into the labour market. Individual choice and institutional recruitment practices will be related both to background factors (such as parental education or ethnic background) and to the qualifications obtained during the earlier stages of the education process. Whilst, in the absence of longitudinal data, the latter aspect cannot be dealt with here, it is of considerable interest to see which general qualifications are associated with the various exit points of the education system. The rationale behind this interest is that, according to Human Capital Theory, individuals cannot profit from specific training, but harvest returns from investment in education only with respect to general, highly transferable skills. Literacy as defined in IALS can, no doubt, be considered as transferable in this sense.

In the German system of education, vocational education and training and academic education differ in the emphasis placed on the generality of content. The typical arrangement for vocational education - the so-called *Dual System* of part-time schooling and in-firm apprenticeship training - introduces a strong element of job-related learning, the transferability of which is limited to certain occupational areas. Vocational full-time school fulfils a similar role. By contrast, academic education is intended to be general in the sense of enabling the student to enter any field of tertiary study; at the same time, increasing numbers of successful graduates from this track enter some vocational programme, in order to complement their general skills by intermediate-level job-related qualifications. There appears to be a trend in the direction of increased demand for general qualifications even at the stage of entry into vocational education and training (Arbeitsgruppe Bildungsbericht am Max-Planck-Institut für Bildungsforschung, 1994).

The question of the relationship between qualifications (as measured by IALS) and income cannot be dealt with here. Instead, the scope of analysis will be restricted to relationship between selected background variables, types of education and the levels of literacy.

3. DATABASE AND METHODS OF ANALYSIS

The database analysed here refers to the international IALS scores in the domains of prose literacy, document literacy and quantitative literacy (Kirsch, 1995).

The distinction between the various types of education is fundamental. Since, because of the limited number of cases, not all possible career patterns can be interpreted meaningfully, three groups are distinguished here:

- persons who have left the educational system without successful completion of the upper secondary level, be it academic or vocational (*N*=207); this type of education is called 'incomplete';
- persons who have left (or are about to leave) the educational system upon the successful completion of a full-time vocational or part-time vocational (apprenticeship) programme (*N*=1205), this type of education will be referred to as 'vocational';
- persons who have left (or are about to leave) the educational system with a college or university degree or a university admission certificate (*'Abitur'*: *N*=365); here this type of education is labelled 'academic'.

For *N*=284 persons, there is insufficient information for this classification.

Obviously, the division of the sample is inherently related to the structure of the German system of education. Table 1 demonstrates these relationships between types of education as used in this paper and the structure of the system in terms of the sample distribution.

Table 1: Description of the Sample

Definition:	Type of Education		
	incomplete	vocational	academic
still in full-time school (general / intermediate school vs. *Gymnasium*)		60	64
still in technical college *(Fachschule)*		15	
left the educational system without successful completion of the upper secondary level	11	13	
successful completion of **general school** *(Volks-/ Hauptschule)* (and: unsuccessful vs. successful completion of a vocational programme)	152	572	
successful completion of **intermediate school** *(Realschule)* (and: unsuccessful vs. successful completion of a vocational programme)	36	305	
successful completion of East German **polytechnic school** *(POS)* (and: unsuccessful vs. successful completion of a vocational programme)	7	143	
successful completion of **college for applied science**		97	
successful completion of **academic upper secondary programme** *('Abitur')*			121
successful completion of **university course**			181
	207 (11,6 %)	1.205 (67,8 %)	365 (20,6 %)

The following findings are based on a number of group comparisons, performed separately for the three domains of literacy tested. In order to give due consideration to the changes in the education system over the five decades covered by the data set, the various age groups in the sample will be considered separately, before a path-analytic model is presented which is intended to summarise the findings encountered.

4.   FINDINGS

If the average literacy studies by the IALS is plotted simultaneously for the three types of education and the three domains, it is readily seen that - from an international perspective - the German respondents have performed relatively better in the quantitative domain, followed by the document and the prose domains (Figure 1).

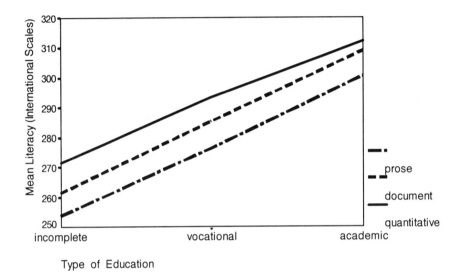

Figure 9. Mean Literacy by Type of Education and Domain

Differences between the three types of education are highly significant ($p < .001$). They are almost uniform across domains, with the only (but interesting) exception that German 'academics' have not achieved the average level of quantitative literacy which the overall pattern might suggest.

Nevertheless, an inspection of the actual distribution of scores demonstrates that in all three domains of literacy, the dominant pattern is that of a heavy overlap between groups, even in the case of respondents with 'incomplete' upper secondary education as opposed to the 'academic' group. Persons who have successfully completed a vocational programme at the upper secondary stage represent the intermediate group - and the typical one, given that they constitute over two thirds of the sample.

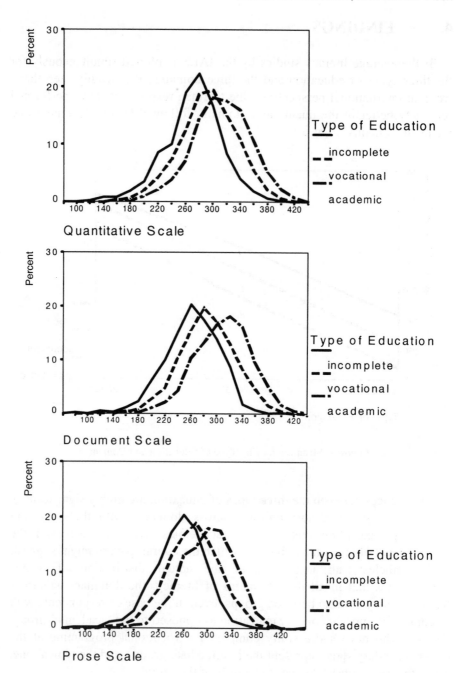

Figure 10. Distribution of Literacy by Type of Education (and Domain)

The latter observation suggests that there may be interesting differences *within* this group of vocationally educated people. The interviewees can be classified into four sub-groups: blue-collar occupations from industry and trade (*N*=505), occupations related to domestic and catering services (*N*=57), commercial occupations (*N*=375), and occupations related to social services (*N*=102).

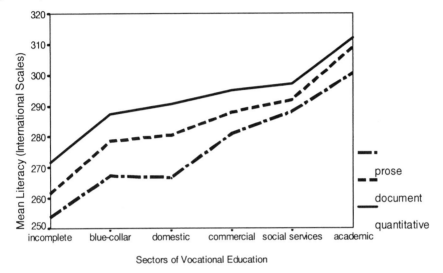

Fig. 3: Mean Literacy by Type / Sector of Education and Domain

The overall tendency is quite clear. Within the stratum of people with their highest education certificate gained from some form of vocational education, there are highly significant sectoral differences (*p*<.01) - the only exception being that between 'blue-collar' and 'domestic' respondents on the prose scale. Apparently, there is a certain 'hierarchy' among these four sectors with respect to literacy performance (and demands?) which is fairly uniform across domains. These differences exist in spite of the fact that formally, all forms of vocational education are considered equivalent.

So far, the presentation of findings has failed to take into account that the broad distribution of age in the sample corresponds to substantial changes in educational demands and aspirations, which are closely related to the economic development of the country. The five decades covered incorporate the period of forced stagnation (or, at best, reconstruction) during and after World War II as well as many years of rapid expansion of the educational system which started in the 1950s. On the basis of the simple ordinal scale used here (with '0' for 'incomplete', '1' for 'vocational' and '2' for 'academic education'), Figure 4 shows how these changes have affected the population.

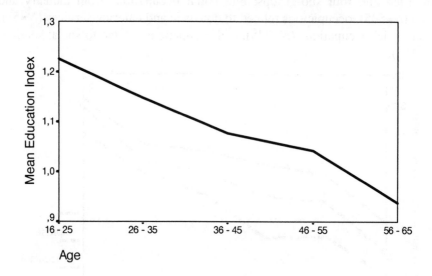

Figure 4. Mean Education Index by Age

Whilst the average member of the age cohort born between 1929 and 1938 - and especially the women - did not even have an opportunity to complete some form of upper-secondary level vocational education, the balance has continuously shifted towards tertiary education.

Obviously, this development is bound to have influenced the distribution of literacy as encountered in the sample. Figure 5 depicts the mean for prose literacy by age group and type/sector of education.

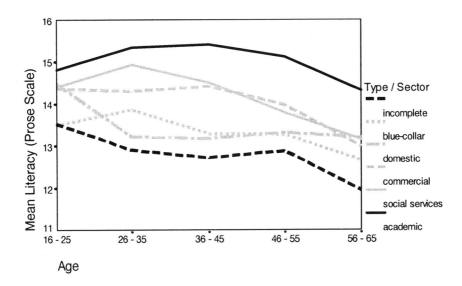

Figure 5. Mean of Prose Literacy by Age and Type / Sector of Education

The diagram presents averages for a total of 30 sub-groups, which implies substantial errors of measurement, especially for certain sectors of vocational education. Nevertheless, the findings appear to be sufficiently consistent to be presented here.

The selection processes involved in the recruitment for academic programmes become visible across the whole age spectrum. The combination of learning beyond school and possibly also of the changes in the intake of academic programmes has resulted in a positive correlation between test performance and age, up until approximately the age of fifty. Only then, certain reductions in performance (the reasons of which cannot be determined on the basis of the present data) become noticeable.

Within the framework of contemporary programmes of vocational education, no literacy differences seem to exist between domestic, commercial and social occupations. However, the respective patterns over the age group are not entirely uniform. It appears that the socially oriented occupations were able to attract a particularly 'literate' group among the birth cohorts 1959 to 1968, while, at the same time, commercial activities had relatively little attractiveness for well-educated young people. Commercial and social occupations appear to be normally followed by persons who are remarkably similar in terms of their literacy. They retain a relatively high level of literacy until their mid-career, with a subsequent gradual decline which follows very much that of the 'academic' respondents. If there is a gap with respect to the latter, it widens only slowly over the span of a lifetime.

The small group of respondents from domestic/food and catering occupations is, in some ways, a special case. Predominantly female, this small group illustrates best the influence of changes in the role of vocational education and training over time. The underlying development seems to be that these occupations have lost much of their appeal for academically inclined women, although once women from the middle classes were attracted to these occupations. Thus, an apparent positive linear trend is produced which offsets the negative tendencies among the older cohorts of all other groups. The only exception from this rule (to be found in the youngest age group) refers to four cases and thus should not be over-interpreted.

Perhaps the best illustration of the positive effects associated with the attendance of a vocational programme can be gained from comparisons between blue-collar occupations and those respondents who have not finished any upper secondary programme at all. These groups are relatively large, so that sampling errors are less serious. It seems that blue-collar trainees and workers, during their formative years, are distinguished from the respective group with 'incomplete' education by clearly superior levels of literacy (26 to 35-year-olds). Beyond that point, both groups display similar trends which appear to result from the combination of changes in the educational system and possible effects of ageing which have already been commented upon.

Given the multiple inter-relationships between the variables considered so far, path analysis can be applied to map these effects - and a few others which must not be omitted, in order to gain a clearer picture . Figure 6 presents the results of such an analysis.

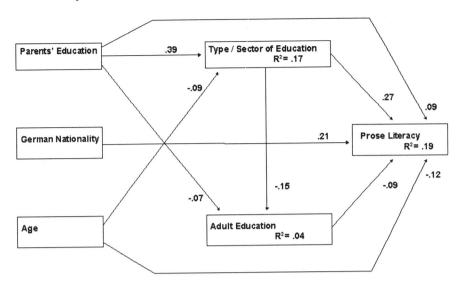

Figure 6. Path Analysis. Selected Determinants of Prose Literacy

As can be seen from the size of the path coefficients, the key element in the model is the type and sector of education. It is strongly related to the antecedent parental education (p=.39), and in turn, is the best available predictor for prose literacy as measured by IALS (p=.27).

Age demonstrates its relationship with the changing structure of educational opportunities through its negative effect on type/sector of education (p=-.09); the residual influence on prose literacy itself (p=-.12) is a weak indication of reduced performance levels among the older cohorts.

As expected, German nationality with all its linguistic connotations has an influence on literacy (p=.21). The fact that it shows no relationship with either type or sector of education or with further education activities appears to be derived from the particularly low response rate among migrants with low levels of education.

Adult education activities, finally, display very clearly their compensatory function. In the sub-sample under consideration, this type of education is prevalent among those from families with a less favourable educational background (p=-.07) and among those who themselves have participated in less secondary and tertiary education (p=-.15). Also, such activities do not seem to add to the competencies measured in IALS (p=-.09). [1]

---

[1] All coefficients reported are statistically significant.

5.   DISCUSSION

The causal model presented is not satisfactory in every respect. While the effects which it demonstrates are plausible and compatible with the earlier uni- and bivariate findings, the explained variances leave much to be desired. Incidentally, this corresponds in a remarkable way to the weak relationship between literacy and income ($.11 < r_{pm} < .15$). The question is how this exceptional situation in Germany can be explained.

In the absence of decisive evidence from the data itself, it seems advisable to begin the search for explanations by considering the overlap in the distribution of literacy between the various types and sectors of education investigated here. Whilst the respective mean differences are substantial ($.06 < Eta^2 < .09$), literacy as measured is far from providing a perfect criterion in the distinction of strata defined by type of education. In fact, *any* classification according to some system-related criterion would render some overlap. What is remarkable here, however, is that the German system of education has never been as 'meritocratic' as is sometimes alleged. There are some indications (e.g., in the case of women in 'domestic' occupations, but also in the 'blue-collar' and 'incomplete' groups) that the older age cohorts in the sample have been affected, early in their lives, by a considerable lack of educational opportunities, given their general ability levels. In the case of the younger cohorts, overlap may well be the result of the increased flexibility between the various programmes in the system. *If* literacy is not just a function of instruction, but also of general ability levels, a high degree of within-group variance is to be expected under such circumstances.

A second explanatory element may be seen in the fact that a highly differentiated array of school leaving diplomas (which corresponds to the complex structure of the German educational system) will increase the 'signalling effect' (Thurow, 1975) of educational certificates: such state of affairs is both a cause for and a symptom of a flourishing 'diploma disease'. Whilst it potentially facilitates the consideration of a wide range of possible selection criteria, it will also tend to reduce the role of easily testable qualifications such as literacy. Under such conditions, literacy is tendentially dissociated both from its institutional antecedents and from its consequences in terms of income.

Thirdly, a certain clue may be the fact that literacy performance in Germany (relative to the international standards) shows an anomalous pattern in the sense that 'academics' do relatively less well in the quantitative domain, as has been observed above. Although the effect is small, it coincides with the traditional stereotype which states that pragmatic skills (such as those related to numbers) are less appreciated in the dominant *bourgeois* culture, whilst they constitute a strength of the lower and middle-level labour force. This, too, would operate against a close association between literacy and the hierarchy of educational programmes on the one hand, and between literacy and income on the other.

Perhaps the most important explanation for the relatively isolated role of literacy in Germany may lie in the very nature of education programmes in this country. By providing vocational education which is situated at the very intersection of the educational and the economic sub-system of society, each programme in the *Dual System* will deliver a wide array of competencies of which literacy is only one. This means that, at least to some degree, specific practical competencies may function as an equivalent for the cognitive ones measured in IALS. Similarly, it has long been recognised that such programmes also function as very effective socialising agencies which convey habits and attitudes much appreciated by potential employers and which are possibly good predictors for the individual economic success. It seems plausible, then, that the recruitment for apprenticeship programmes also follows patterns which are more loosely connected with literacy than one might expect.

Finally, the analysis of bivariate relationships has demonstrated quite clearly that any interpretation of the findings will have to take underlying historical changes in the educational and economic systems into account. Unfortunately, the present sample is too small to render more than a few illustrations of this fundamental principle. It remains to be seen whether the examples given are corroborated or refuted by corresponding findings from parallel samples in IALS.

REFERENCES

Arbeitsgruppe Bildungsbericht am Max-Planck-Institut für Bildungsforschung (1994), *Das Bildungswesen in der Bundesrepublik Deutschland. Strukturen und Entwicklungen im Überblick*, Rowohlt, Reinbek bei Hamburg.

Baethge, M., Hantsche, B., Pelull, W. and Voskamp, U. (1988), *Jugend: Arbeitund Identität. Lebensperspektiven und Interessenorientierungen von Jugendlichen. Eine Studie des Soziologischen Forschungsinstituts Göttingen (SOFI)*, Leske und Budrich, Opladen.

Becker, G.S. (1964), *Human Capital: A Theoretical and Emprical Analysis, with Special Reference to Education*, Columbia University Press, New York.

Kirsch, I.S. (1995), "Literacy performance on three scales: definition and results", in OECD and Statistics Canada (Ed.), *Literacy, Economy and Society. Results of the first International Adult Literacy Survey*, Organization for Economic Co-operation and Development/Statistics Canada, Paris/Ottawa, pp. 27-53.

Kirsch, I.S. and Murray, S. (Eds). (1996), *Adult Literacy in OECD Countries. Technical Report of the First International Adult Literacy*, Statistics Canada/Educational Testing Survey, Ontario/Princeton NJ.

Lehmann, R.H. and Peek, R. (1996), "Wie gut können Deutsche lesen und rechnen?" *UNIVERSITAS. Zeitschrift für interdisziplinäre Wissenschaft*, 51. Jg., pp.975-989.

Mincer, J. (1974), *Schooling, experience and earnings*, National Bureau of Economic Research, New York.

OECD (1996), *Education at a Glance. OECD Indicators*, Organisation for Economic Co-operation and Development, Paris.

OECD and Statistics Canada (Ed.) (1995), *Literacy, Economy and Society. Results of the first International Adult Literacy Survey*, Organisation for Economic Co-operation and Development/Statistics Canada, Paris/Ottawa.

Schultz, T.W. (1960), "Capital Formation by Education", *Journal of Political Economy* 68, pp.571-583.

Thurow, L. (1975), *Generating inequality*, Basic Books, New York.

UNESCO (1989), *International Standard Classification of Education*, UNESCO, Paris.

Chapter 25

Functional Literacy Skills of School Leavers in Flanders

D. Van Damme, L. Van de Poele, and E. Verhasselt
University of Ghent

1. THE DISCOVERY OF MODERN 'ILLITERACY'

The 'discovery' that - despite compulsory education, despite school attendance that is only problematic among marginal population groups, and despite the many resources invested in education - a significant number of people in the industrialised countries can be considered 'functionally illiterate', dates from relatively recently and has been a shocking revelation. Following England and France, the front runners in this field, Belgium and the Netherlands have also been developing initiatives to tackle 'illiteracy' since the late 1970s. It has been the aim of these initiatives to address the question of whether the adult population as a whole has sufficient basic skills, including literacy, at a high enough standard. This implies, on the one hand, that people with a low level of basic skills may be able to manage to function and communicate despite that, and, on the other hand, that people with relatively high skills levels could be faced with serious problems. The participation of Flanders in the International Adult Literacy Survey (IALS) was one of the efforts to gain a more differentiated view on the literacy levels of the population and of pupils completing compulsory education.

2.   LITERACY AND THE INTERNATIONAL ADULT LITERACY SURVEY

The IALS methodology has brought us a long way from the traditional approach to illiteracy, which was geared to find out what percentage of a population was 'illiterate'. We would like to briefly clarify the most important conceptual and methodological developments by IALS. As the whole, the debate around 'functional illiteracy' has demonstrated that literacy is a relative concept that can lead to very diverse experiences in different contexts. The definition of literacy used by IALS is clear on this point: *"Using printed and written information to function in society, to achieve one's goals and to develop one's knowledge and potential."*

This definition does not define literacy or illiteracy in terms of something that people lack, but as a broad range of information-processing skills related to written language, which adults are confronted with in different situations.

Firstly, the negative 'deficit' approach to illiteracy has been abandoned and replaced by a more positive approach to literacy as a basic skill (see also Van der Kamp, et al., 1995). Secondly, and in connection with this, there is a distancing from the dichotomous approach, which uses a continuum to divide the population into those who are 'illiterate' and those who are 'literate'. It is impossible to make such a distinction, and it would be very difficult to gain a social consensus on a specific desirable standard. Instead, IALS distinguishes five (in practice four) levels on each scale, but these do not define degrees of 'illiteracy'. Thirdly, literacy is being studied as a multi-dimensional phenomenon. It is not possible to measure literacy on a single dimension. Thorough preliminary research led to the development of the IALS methodology, which works with three different scales: a *prose* scale, a *document* scale and a *quantitative* scale. The same person can show very different results on each of the three scales.

2.1   School-leavers

A separate sample of 17 year-olds was taken in Flanders, to investigate the functional literacy and numeracy skills of pupils at the end of their compulsory education. Pupils were surveyed individually in school.

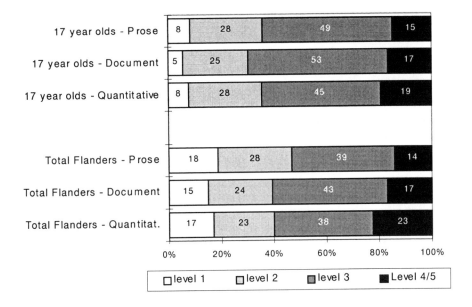

Figure 11. Percentage distribution of the Flemish adult population from 16 to 65 years, and of 17 year-olds at school, over the literacy levels on the prose, document and quantitative scales.

The results of the 17 year-olds are better than those of the overall population (level 3-4/5 as opposed to level 1-2), which was to be expected. Pupils at school are trained on a daily basis in the use of language and in numeracy. This, together with their familiarity with pen and paper tests and the fact that they took their tests at school, place the 17 year-olds at an advantage compared with the other respondents.

This advantage is not visible, however, at the highest level of literacy and numeracy skills. There is no difference between the 17 year-olds and the population as a whole in the proportion at level 4/5 on the prose and document scales. On the quantitative scale, the 17 year-olds perform worse at level 4/5 than the general population.

At the lowest skills level, the proportion of 17 year-olds is 10% lower than that of the total population, with 5% to 8% still leaving school with the lowest level of literacy. The main advance for the 17 year-olds is at level 3, a (relatively) high level of skill which 65% to 70% attain, 10% more than the general population. Given the advantage outlined above, and the underlying idea that every pupil should at least have literacy and numeracy skills measured at levels 3, 4 and 5 on these scales at the end of their period of compulsory education, one has to report that the results do not meet expectations.

Flanders is the only country which studied a separate sample of 17 year-olds, so it is not possible to make international comparisons. However, it is interesting to see how the 17 year-olds' results compare with those of the youngest age group, 16-25 year-olds, in the general sample. This age group includes the 17 year-olds and also, in addition to that group of pupils, comprises young people who are on average only a little older than 17: students (57%), employees (30%) or job seekers (12%).

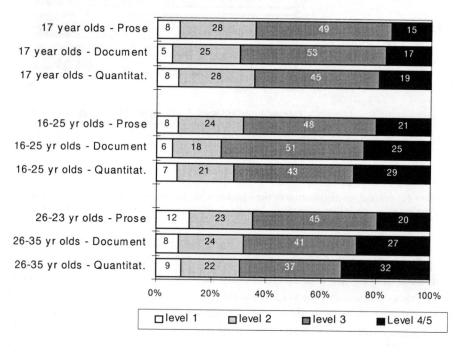

Figure 12. Percentage distribution in the age groups 16-25, 26-35 and 17 year-olds at school over the literacy levels on the prose, document and quantitative scales.

The 16-25 year-olds gain better results overall than the 17 year-olds. This suggests that people continue to learn, in terms of functional literacy and numeracy skills, after the age of compulsory schooling. For some young people over the age of 17, learning will continue in secondary schools, as many pupils do not leave secondary school at age 18. The greatest gains by the 16-25 year-olds compared with the 17 year-olds is found at the highest skills levels. This could be ascribed to higher education, which encourages higher levels of thinking in students. Even the increase between the 16-25 year-old group and the 26-35 group could be related to that.

However, the differences between the scales deserve closer examination. By the time that people reach the older age group (26-35 years), the proportion with the highest literacy level on the prose scale fall, whereas learning continues on the document and quantitative scales. On the one hand, this could be interpreted positively by ascribing learning outcomes to confrontation with real problems in the workplace and at home. On the other hand, it could be argued that schools offer pupils few opportunities to deal with reality-based documents and number problems, to enable them to develop functional literacy and numeracy skills at the highest level.

This gives rise to a question: "Is it the school's job to make pupils numerate and literate with documents?" The proportion with the lowest level of literacy is no different among the 17 year-olds than among the 16-25 year-olds. The theoretical advantage enjoyed by the 17 year-olds due to the type of tests and testing situation does not show itself here. There is no progress to be seen between the 17 year-olds and the 16-25 year-olds when measured in terms of the difference in the proportion at level 1. The learning effect due to experience that was visible at the highest levels is totally absent at the lowest level. In other words, people who do not acquire functional basic skills by the end of their school years do not acquire them later. From then on, over the population as a whole, it is a question of forgetting what has been learned rather than further learning.

3.   CONCLUSIONS

Pupils are actively working with language at school every day. Reading, writing and number skills are acquired in the pupils' daily working environment, that is in the school. They spend a lot of time reading and writing but this is mainly with a view to school activities. Almost 60% of the 17 year-olds regularly go to a library, far more than any other group in the population. However, pupils evidently mainly use libraries to support their studies, because only one in four 17 year-olds reads a book at least once a week. Unprompted use of newspapers and magazines to find information has in no way taken root among Flemish young people. One in three 17 year-olds read a newspaper or magazine every day. This is less than for the total adult population. It does not seem that the younger Flemish generation will be any more active as readers than today's adults. Schools evidently succeed in helping pupils to acquire the technical skills of reading and mathematics, but books, newspapers and magazines are not often picked up outside the school walls. It may be that they are being replaced by other media. We are not being successful enough in helping pupils enjoy reading. Consequently, they tend not to do much involving literacy after they leave school, with the risk that their literacy and numeracy skills will deteriorate.

The tasks given to all the respondents, including the 17 year-olds, were of a degree of difficulty that they all fell within the supposed learning objectives of secondary education. It would be reasonable to expect, therefore, that all pupils should be able to perform the IALS tasks with some success by the time they reach the end of secondary education. A less arbitrary norm may have been expressed at level 3. This means investigating whether at least 80% of the pupils are in levels 3, 4 or 5. A rule of thumb in educational science is that for minimum objectives, 90% of the pupils should be able to master 90% of the objectives, which results in a realisation level of about 80%. The findings of the IALS study show that we are not achieving this target: only 70% of the pupils achieved 'sufficient' functional literacy and numeracy skills at age 17. However, many young people stay at school after their 17th year and continue to learn. A more important finding is that young people who are only performing at level 1 by the end of their compulsory schooling do not manage to achieve higher levels of skills later. In other words, if you do not learn the basic skills during your compulsory school years, you will not manage to do this later. This is not to say that the learning process stops after secondary school, as far as functional literacy and numeracy skills are concerned. Many young people reach the highest level in higher education, and through confrontation with real language and numeracy tasks in daily life. It does show that pupils do not gain much experience of complex literacy and numeracy tasks in secondary school, of the kind which present themselves in everyday life. The IALS study in Flanders shows that, at the other end of the scale, students leaving education without the minimum literacy skills will be at risk on the labour market and in social life for the rest of their lives. Spontaneous learning through confrontation with real life situations does not seem to occur at the lower level of literacy.

[1]. Streeck & Schmitter (1985) did not use the word `governance', but their article can be considered one its the important roots.

[2]. I prefer `networks' to `clans' as the former is most neutral in this respect, while the latter also evokes a community image to some extent, due to its roots in the study of non-western societies in cultural anthropology.

REFERENCES

Organisation for Economic Co-operation and Development - Statistics Canada (1995), *Literacy, Economy and Society. Results of the first International Adult Literacy Survey*, OECD, Paris.

Van Damme, D., Van de Poele, L. and Verhasselt, E. (1997), *Hoe geletterd/gecijferd is Vlaanderen? Functionele taal- en rekenvaardigheden van Vlamingen in internationaal perspectief*, Garant, Leuven.

Van der Kamp, M., Scheeren, J. and Veendrick, L.J. (1995), "Van geletterdheid naar basisvaardigheden", *Comenius*15/2, pp. 159-178.

Index

accreditation 117
administrative education bodies 249
administrative strategies
  controlled consumption of education
    146–47
  free consumption of education 147–48
  promotion of autonomous institutions
    147
adult education
  general
    vocational function of 330
  government policy 115
  in Finland 393, 395, 396, 407
  in Sweden 290, 293, 294, 295, 296,
    297, 300, 301
  market orientation of 330
  municipal 320, 328
  passive/reluctant participation 377,
    379
  popular 320
  voucher system 116, 117, 129
adult education and training
  government intervention in 24
Adult Education Initiative 290, 297
  impacts of 297
  implementation of 294
Adult Education Initiative 290, 292, 294
Adult Education Initiative (Swedish) 296,
  302
adult education participation
  and initial education 388
adult education programmes 289
  in Sweden See . See
adult participation in continuing
  education 381
  attitudinal dispositions 383
  external context 383
  situational factors 383

Adult Vocational Education Council 137
advanced technology
  as a learning objective 251
AMU-gruppen (Employment Training
  Group, in Sweden) 320, 330, 331, 332,
  334
apprenticeship
  dilemmas of 34–35
apprenticeship contracts 117
apprenticeship model
  German 34
apprenticeship schemes 318
apprenticeship system
  German 56, 64, 85, 86
apprenticeship training 411
Association of Small Auto Repairing
  Shop Proprietors (SISEMA) 267
Associations for training (ASFO) 97

business
  expectations 3–4
Business firms
  and vocational training 33

Cedefop 137
Centre for Pharmacy Postgraduate
  Education (CPPE) 306, 307, 308, 309,
  310, 311, 312, 313, 315, 316
Centres for Occupational and Vocational
  Training 251
certification 371
chambers of commerce and industry 23
Chambers of Commerce and Industry
  in France 97
Chambers of Industry and Commerce 2
Chambers of Trade and Industry
  in Germany 278
change

in work 35
 technological 2, 13
collective labour 141
collective learning 184
Commission for the Promotion of Adult
 Education and Training 297, 298, 302
Commission for the Promotion of Adult
 Education and Training, Sweden 291
communication
 and technologies of knowledge 202
communities of practice 168, 194, 201,
 202, 204, 205, 208, 211
company cultures 39
company training 218, 221
 in Germany 221
competence
 development of 177
competence development 335, 337
competencies
 development of 183
competitiveness
 and the German economy 34
 economic 2, 5
 in the business community 43
Conservative Party, British 52
context evaluation 247
continuing education programmes 375
Continuing Professional Development
 (CPD) 167, 168, 170
continuing training
 evaluation 354
 participation of adults 379
 participation of SMEs' (small and
  medium-sized enterprises)
  employees 375–92
continuing training programmes
 effectiveness 378
continuing vocational education 354
continuing vocational education and
 training
 for active adults 376
continuing vocational training 163
corporate culture. 36
corporations
 transnational 33
cost effectiveness studies 300

deregulation
 of markets 52

distance learning 265, 296
 accreditation 309, 310, 312
 and knowledge updating 303
 and motivation 305, 306, 313, 315
 and self-assessment 313
 learning packs 308, 314
 study groups 309
 voluntary participation 313
distance teaching 328
Dutch Department of Economic Affairs
 52, 53, 54

economic development
 and technological change 364
economic intervention 40
economics
 institutional 66, 67, 84
 neo-classical 51, 61, 62, 65, 66, 70,
  72, 83
 transaction cost 66, 67, 68, 71, 72
economy
 advanced 31
education
 academic 411
 accessibility 319
 adult 7
 and core curriculum models 339
 and equality 44
 and the competitive process 31
 and the social security system 140
 and work 319
 basic 143
 continuing 303, 304, 305, 306, 307,
  308, 310, 311, 312, 313, 314, 315,
  316
 demand-oriented 145
 formal 24
 general 2, 35, 36, 37, 38, 43, 45
 incomplete 411, 412, 413, 415, 418,
  420
 initial 5
 integrated 26–27
 post-secondary 337
 post–structured 25
 pre–structured 25
 public sector 144, 145
 recurrent 26
education and training
 adult motivation 380

customised 336
    equity considerations 114
    funding 303
    liquidity constraints 110
    state intervention in 58
    targets of 254
    within labour organisations 5
Education and training
    and economic growth 3
education and training funding
    by firms 22
education and training markets
    the 'poaching problem' 109
education and training policies 376
education and training system
    trends in 135–36
education enterprises
    in Sweden 333
education system
    and social developments 139
    and social expectations 139–40
    mobility within 322
education systems
    worldwide 36
education theory 353
educational centres 295
educational organisations
    efficacy of 240, 242
educational planning 300
educational policy
    and economic growth 290
    and social context 343–45
    Swedish 319
educational strategies 27, 142–45
educational strategy
    in lifelong learning 21
employer organisations 23
employer training
    government subsidies 119
employer-paid training
    cost-benefits 16–17
employers
    in Germany 36
    in Japan 36
employment
    low-skilled 35, 46
    public service 45–47
    skills-based 29–47
    sub-contracting and franchising 39

    subsidised 141
employment agencies 142
employment brokers 258
employment patterns
    in Greece 345
employment training 330
enterprise management 257
entrepreneurship training 399, 401, 403,
    404, 405
equal opportunities 24
EU (European Union) 137
European Commission 162, 163
European Conference on Educational
    Research (ECER) 161
EUROPROF (New Forms of Education
    of Professionals for Vocational
    Education and Training) 155, 161,
    162, 163, 165, 167
evaluation
    of educational programmes 307
    of public education and training 290
    topic-specific 311
evaluation models
    Context-Input Process-Product 247
    Responsive Evaluation 247
evaluation of adult education
    in Sweden 289–302
evaluation of training and development
    credits model 8
evaluation specialists 299
evaluation strategies
    in adult education 301
evaluation studies
    by Centre for Pharmacy Postgraduate
        Education 307–11
experiential learning 325
expertise 168–69
    in the formulation of social scenarios
        136–39

Federation of Professional Training, the
    99
financing of training activities
    in France 101–5
firm-dominated economy
    collective action in 33–41
folk high schools 320, 328
Folk High Schools 292, 294, 296, 297
Fordism 199

Fordist economy 32
French Centre for Research and
    Qualification (Cereq) 87
French Ministry of Education 96
French Ministry of Labour (AFPA) 96
French training system 278
French vocational training system
    development of a supply system 94–
        98
    market relationship 88, 89, 90, 93
    markets and institutions 29–47
    service relationship 89, 90, 106
    supply and demand 29–33
    the association sector 97
    the company sector 97
    the public sector 96–97
French vocational training systems
    the private profit-making sector 98,
        100, 102, 103
From direct to extended school-to-work
    transition patterns 323
functionalism 51, 52, 62, 63, 66, 70
funding
    of education and training 217, 223,
        231
further education and training
    in Sweden 291
further vocational training
    in France 88, 94, 100

general education
    publicly funded 43–45
global competition 37
global economy 33
governance mechanisms 50, 65, 67, 68,
    69, 73, 74, 75, 78, 82
    and collective actors 70, 73, 74
    definitions of 68
    typologies of 69
governance theory 50, 67, 70, 71, 72, 73,
    74, 76, 82, 83
government agencies
    loss of confidence of 6–10
government educational policies 25
government strategies
    skill maximization 40
governments, European
    relationships with education sector
        216–17

group analysis 61
group cultures 183

high level training 103
high school (US) 270, 271, 272, 274, 276,
    283
higher education
    vocationalism in 333
Higher Professional Education Council
    137
higher vocational education 137
Higher Vocational Education (HBO) 245,
    250
Higher Vocational Education Council 137
human capital
    general 353, 359
    specific 353, 359
human capital investment 353
human capital theory 22, 109, 359, 360,
    376, 410
human interaction 51, 62
human resource development (HRD) 180
human resources development (HRD)
    163, 164, 166, 172, 174
Human Resources Development (HRD)
    175, 191
human resources management 101

IALS (International Adult Literacy
    Survey) 355, 356
illiteracy 423
    functional 424
ILO (International Labour Organisation)
    137
independent education/learning 26, 143–
    44
independent schools 320
information technology 31
in-house training
    in French companies 88, 89
InnovatieCentra 243, 244
innovation
    technological 39
innovative corporations 32
institutions of vocational and adult
    education 234
integrated education 145
integration
    western European 33

intermediate vocational qualification
   (MBO) 250
International Adult Literacy Study
   (IALS), Sweden 291
International Adult Literacy Survey
   (IALS) 409, 410, 411, 413, 419, 421,
   423, 424, 428
International Standard Classification of
   Education (ISCED) 409
international trade 31
ISO standards 100, 104
ISSTAL (Interdisciplinary, Sequential-
   Specificity, Time-Allocation,
   Lifespan) 380, 381, 382, 383, 385,
   391, 392

Job creation
   in the USA 32
job placement agencies 42
job rotation 180, 183, 188
Job Training Partnership Act (JTPA), in
   the US 285
jobs
   dead-end 280
   mid-level 281

Kammern 34, 36
knowledge
   academic 166
   and diffuse organisation 197–203
   and employment 29–33
   creation and transfer 13–14
   explicit 196, 198, 199
   generic 324
   school- 320, 321
   situated 204
   tacit 197, 198, 199, 201
knowledge centres 295
knowledge development 166
   and innovation 166–67
knowledge distribution 201
knowledge management 196, 198, 199,
   236
knowledge production 205
komvux (adult education programme in
   Sweden) 329, 330, 334
kunskapslyftet (adult education reform in
   Sweden) 320

labour
   and capital 114
   highly skilled 30
   low-productivity 30
labour market
   future opportunities 36
   transformation of 321, 339
   women's position in 362
labour market access 282
labour market in the US
   'high-road' partnerships within 286
   regional sectoral developments 279–
      84
   strategies of reform 269–87
labour market pathway (LMP) 394, 395,
   396, 397, 399, 401, 402
   and unemployment 396
   before and after training 401–2
labour market regulation
   in the US 269–72
labour market regulations
   in Germany 271
labour market training
   effectiveness of 393, 394, 395, 402,
      405, 406, 407, 408
   trainee's point of view 393, 399, 401,
      402, 407
labour market training (LMT)
   effects 394
   in Finland 393–98
   vocational 397
labour markets
   deregulation of 32
   oligopolistic 364
labour mobility 368, 370
Labour Party, British 30
labour process innovations 190
labour protection regulation 186
labour-market policy 290
learner motivation 306
learning
   at work 175–76
   critical-reflective 179
   employee 180–81
   in work teams 156
   role of managers 187
   situated 171
   theoretical 169
   work-directed 180

learning network
   intra-company 208
learning networks
   and inter-community relations 208
   emergence of 207–10
learning organisation 179, 183, 189
   evolution of 157
learning organisation, the
   definition of 193–97
   dominant approaches 194–97
   epistemological implications 210
   perspective-making/taking model
      203–7
learning organisations
   and on-the-job training 334–36
   definition of 335
learning possibilities
   of jobs 176–89
learning processes 175, 177, 183, 185,
   186, 187
learning situation
   definition of 180
learning society 29, 32, 38, 44, 45
   of Europe 335
learning strategies 181
LEONARDO programme 339
lifelong learning 4, 7, 8, 21, 24, 25, 26,
   107, 108, 109, 116, 123, 144, 162,
   163, 168, 175, 289, 297, 301
   and community pharmacists 316
   and cost-effectiveness 303
   in Swedish society 322, 323, 324, 328,
      336, 337, 339, 340, 341
   instruments for 107–9
   policies 49–83
   policy instruments in 24
   role of distance learning 303–16
Lifelong learning 21
literacy
   and unemployment 291
   definition of 424
   distribution of 414, 416, 420
   functional 424, 426, 427, 428
   in Germany 421
Literacy 427
local authorities 2
low level training 103

Maastricht agreement 172

macro-economic growth 3
male-female wage gap 363
management
   Strategic 11
   top 71
market analysis
   neo-classical approach to 61–65
Market exchange
   and the service relationship 89
market failures
   in education and training 108, 109,
      114, 115, 116, 117, 123, 125, 129
Market Operation, Deregulation and
   Legal Quality (MDW) 52, 53, 54, 55
market transactions 67
markets
   institutionalist approach to 66–75
markets and systems
   of vocational education and training
      49–50
merger policy
   in Dutch schools 60
methodological individualism 51, 61, 63,
   69, 70
minimum wage 112, 113, 117, 129, 370
Ministry of Economic Affairs 147
Ministry of Education, Culture and
   Science 137, 147
model for social scenarios 138
modular programmes 144
modularity 144
monitoring
   educational programmes 298
multi-skilling 177, 181, 185, 188
Municipal Adult Education 294, 296, 297

National Agency for Education, in Sweden
   327
National Bodies for Vocational Education
   (Landelijke Organen voor het
   Beroepsonderwijs, LOBs) 240
National Bodies for Vocational Education
   and Training 243
National Council of Adult Education, in
   Sweden 296
National Employment Training Board 330
National Vocational Qualifications
   (NVQs) 17, 227, 354

national vocational qualifications (NVQs)
   in England 221
neo-classicism 50, 51, 62, 63, 64, 66, 70

OECD (Organisation for Economic
   Cooperation and Development) 107,
   108, 109, 115, 119, 127
on the job learning (OJL) 2
on-the-job learning (OJL) 175, 176, 179,
   187, 188, 189, 191
on-the-job training 156, 360, 361, 362,
   363, 365, 366, 367, 368, 369, 370,
   371, 372
on-the-job training (OJT) 176, 179, 180
On-the-job-Learning (OJL) 12
Organisation for Economic Co-operation
   and Development (OECD) 29, 32, 38,
   42, 44, 46, 47
organisational learning 164, 235, 236,
   237
over-education 361, 362

pension system 139, 141
personnel policies 188
policy
   labour-market 42
policy implications 41–45
policy instruments 24–25
principal-agent theory 115
Private Industry Councils (PICs) 285
privatisation
   within the education system 218
problem solving 178, 183, 184
production methods
   automation of 368
professional and inter-professional
   organisations 23
professional education 135, 137, 139,
   140, 142, 143, 144, 145, 146, 148
public agencies
   and development of high skills 41–43
public authorities
   and training organisations 23
public policy
   on vocational and adult education 21

qualifications
   in Germany 410
QUEST Project, San Antonio 283

recurrent education 144–45
   jin Sweden 317, 318, 323, 324, 337
Regional Competent Authorities for
   Employment Provision 243
Regional Competent Authorities for
   Employment Provision (Regionale
   Besturen van de
   Arbeidsvoorzieningen,RBA) 239, 244,
   250, 251, 253, 256, 258
Regional Training Centres
   Dutch 158
Regional Training Centres (Regionale
   Opleidingen Centra,ROCs) 239, 240,
   242, 243, 245, 248, 249, 250, 251,
   255, 256, 257
   interaction with stakeholders 248

scenarios
   definition of 131
   development of 134
   formulation of 133–51
   learning 133
school
   effectiveness 353
school diplomas
   in Germany 420
School to Work Opportunities Act 263
school to workplace transition 25
schooling
   enterprise-related 362
school-leavers 424
schools
   and external bureaucratic relations 258
   and initial training in the Netherlands
     54, 55, 56, 57, 58, 59, 60, 71, 73,
     74, 76, 78, 79, 80, 82
   and stakeholdership 252
   and the business sector 318
   training in 22
   vocational 321, 332, 336
school-to-work programmes 322
school-to-work transition 55, 57, 58, 85
   in the Netherlands 57
Scottish Council for Research in
   Education 307
secondary vocational education 137
   developments in 240
self-learning 22

service industries 31
SISEMA (Association of Small Auto-
    Repairing Shop Proprietors) 345, 347,
    349
situated knowledge 157
skill
    acquisition 41
skills
    and employment 29–33
    basic 5, 22, 423, 427, 428
    communication 35, 170–71
    diagnostic 347
    general 4
    intermediate 52, 53, 54, 55, 56, 57, 58,
        64, 76, 77, 84, 85
    practical 325
    research 169–70
    social-communicative 183
    temporary 347
    transferable 410
    vocational 397
skills and knowledge
    and social shaping 165–66
small and medium enterprises (SMEs)
    139
small and medium-sized enterprises
    (SMEs) 250, 254
small firms 42
small work groups
    and learning strategies 183–86
    problems and risks 186–89
SMEs (small and medium-sized
    enterprises) employees in continuing
    training 375
SMEs' (small and medium-sized
    enterprises) employees in continuing
    training 382
social environments
    economic and technological 135
    labour system 135
    policy and administration 135
    training and knowledge 135
social renewal in Sweden 319
social scenarios
    in vocational education and training
        132–50
social scenarios in vocational education
    and training
    the aloof society 139

the dual society 139–40
the pick-'n'-mix society 141–42
the secure society 141
Society for Organisational Learning 193,
    209
socio-economic policy 357
stakeholder approach
    evaluation perspectives 245–48
    orientation towards technology 255
stakeholder interests
    protection of 257
stakeholders
    characteristics of 241
    methods of identification 245
state education 219
strategies
    educational 179
strategies for advanced VET 40
strategy
    skills 30, 33
study associations 294, 296
supply/demand relationships 101
Swedish Work Environment Fund
    (SWEF) 335
systems
    becoming markets 51–53
systems of education
    Swedish 320, 322

Thatcherism 52
trade unions 23
    members of 361
Trades Union Council (TUC) 120
trainees
    blue-collar 418
training
    and social inequality 362
    customising 106
    development of 375
    enterprise-related 359, 360–66
    examination-oriented 399, 404
    firm-based 22, 278
    for immigrants 397, 399, 402, 403,
        404, 406
    funding of 358
    general 110
    industrial 2, 7, 9, 12, 16
    initial 4

in-service 328, 329, 333, 334, 397, 399, 405
  of young people 34, 35
  preparatory 397, 399, 402, 403, 406
  returns for workers 366–70
  role of trade unions 357
  specific 22, 109, 110, 111, 112
  trade union members 366
  under-investment in 24–25, 109, 111, 112, 125
Training and Enterprise Councils (TECs) 42
training contracts 122
training models
  government income contingent loans (ICLs) 119, 120
training organisations
  and professional streamlining 106
  in France 87, 89, 90, 93, 94, 99, 100, 105
    specialisation 101–3
  in the association sector 23
  in the private, profit-making sector 23
training programmes
  auto mechanics industry 345
  for the unemployed 113
  in the US 122
  interpretation of 104–6
  personal development 104
  professional insertion 104
training systems 378
  in France 121
Transito Project. 252

upper secondary schools
  in Sweden 328
up-skilling 30, 32, 35, 37

vocational and adult ecucation
  in Europe 1–17
vocational and adult education
  and the labour market 25, 26
  economic benefits of 14–17
  institutional aspect of 10–11
  instructional aspect of 11–14
  learning and organisation in 153–59
  markets and institutions in 21–27
  markets and systems 10–13
  organisational models 229–37

  programmes and sectors 267
  returns and outcomes 351–56
  sectoral characteristics 8–10
  social distribution of 6–10
  social-cultural functions 4–6
  social-economic functions 5
vocational and adult education and training
  systems in Europe 1–3
Vocational and Adult Education Council 137
vocational and adult educaton systems
  performance of 14–16
vocational and educational training
  future environment of 133
vocational and educational training strategies
  in relation to specific scenarios 131–50, **Error! Not a valid bookmark in entry on page** 149
vocational education
  and privatisation 220
  and technical innovation 347–49
  at higher education level 332
  effects of privatisation on 220
  external 337
  human interactions in 50
  in the Scandinavian countries 221
  off-the-job 123
  organisational effectiveness of 229–37
  public sector 25, 26, 143
  school-based 326
  secondary 158
  support groups 233
  the stakeholder approach 240–48
vocational education
  social functions 228
vocational education and adult education 131, 134, 135, 136, 137, 139, 140, 143, 144, 145, 146, 148, 149, 150
vocational education and adult education schools 232
vocational education and training
  and concept of 'Gestaltung' 155
  changing social environment of 131–33
  governance mechanisms 23
  in Germany 410, 411, 418
Vocational Education and Training

in France 29–47
vocational education and training (VET)
professionals
education of 161–74
vocational education and training (VET)
30, 34, 35, 37, 38, 40, 41, 42, 43, 45,
49, 50, 53, 54, 55, 56, 57, 58, 59, 60,
61, 65, 74, 75, 76, 78, 79, 80, 81, 82
and concept of 'Gestaltung' 162
and functional exclusiveness of
institutions 220–22
and inter-sectoral relationships 9
as an industry 8
as personal investment 3–4
company-led 56
decentralisation of 164
Dutch systems 49–83
funding 217–20
in Germany 37
market approaches to 54–60
operation of markets 49–83
professional development of 167–68
professionalisation of 162, 163, 172,
174
suppliers 220
vocational education and training (VET)
market
efficiency of 58
vocational education and training (VET)
markets
English 55
German 55
state intervention in 60
vocational education and training (VET)
professionals
role of 164
vocational education and training (VET)
system
expansion of 222–24
vocational education and training (VET)
systems
external bodies 231–37
steering 217
the corporatist policy model 216
variety and effectiveness 215–22
vocational education and training
strategies
definition of 131
future developments 131–50

vocational education and training system
Dutch 158
vocational education programmes
contemporary 417
vocational education systems
effectiveness of 227
qualification targets 227
vocational eduction and training
and the labour market 3–4
vocational skills 397
vocational training 322, 326, 327, 328,
336, 337, 338, 339, 340, 341
as a supplementary activity 100–101
company-led 37
expenditure 95
for special skills 402
in lycées 100
in Sweden 292, 294, 297
in the company sector 23
in the industrial and market sector 23
policies 94, 95
vocational training organisations
principal characteristics of 23–27
vocational training suppliers
in France 98
Vocational Training/Adult Education
Department 137
vocational upper secondary education
core subjects 327
vocationalism
and the learning society 336
societal context of 340

'wind–tunnelling' 149

Wisconsin Regional Training Partnership
282
work groups 182
work organisation in the US 277
work organisation structures 181
work planning 182
work process knowledge 165
work teams 156, 157
autonomous 181–83
learning and innovation in 175–429
working and learning 13
workplace training 327
work-related knowledge 166
work-related knowledge

    importance of 166–67
works councils 88
workshops 306, 312
work-study programmes 331

youth training 57